A dynamic work of unlearning and relearning, researched and written in conversation with Black and Indigenous artists, scholars, historians, and critics past and present. In retracing the steps of Sophia Burthen, a Black woman born in eighteenth-century New York, enslaved by Kanyen'kehà:ka (Mohawk) leader Joseph Brant and later sold to Englishman Samuel Hatt, Andrew Hunter unsettles the Hamilton/Dundas of his upbringing—"a place of cataracts, where an accurate view of history has been obstructed." Chapter by chapter, with archives and anecdotes, Hunter troubles the whiteness he knows he can neither escape nor outperform. Hunter's journey makes visible the systemic chalk and fog that continue to mask the fact of chattel slavery from Canadian historical narratives.

— CHANTAL GIBSON, author of *with/holding*

It Was Dark There All the Time is an explosive text in that it *explodes* the myths of the benevolent north and the haven of Canadian destination. It names and maps—in the best senses — the land through which the pieced-together narrative of Sophia winds. The book does not strive to *contain* languages of anyone lost-to-history but instead loudly acknowledges the silence that such loss has left. It's as though by asking the ground itself to bear witness, a reader or a critically committed curator might glimpse a bigger truth or series of truths than "history" tells. *It Was Dark There All the Time* journeys literally through our present-day landscape of upstate New York and southern Ontario, a landscape festooned with local museums and roadside historical markers that tell and retell the familiar stories of white conquest and settlement. But the far reach of Hunter's book engages both recorded testimonies of nineteenth-century men and women and the voices of contemporary writers to tell the resonances of a larger story, one that continues to exist.

— C.S. GISCOMBE, American Book Award-winning author of
Into and Out of Dislocation

Provocatively written, this book promises to destabilize and reshape studies of North American history and culture by struggling directly with how little we still know about the enslaved individuals who shaped our past and present. In sharing the story of Sophia Burthen, a woman of African descent who was kidnapped and enslaved in Canada around the turn of the nineteenth century, Hunter simultaneously tells origin stories of social injustices, environmental emergencies, and other issues troubling our world today. *It Was Dark There All the Time* joins publications that dismantle the myth of Canada as a colour-blind utopia at the end of the Underground Railroad to create narratives that typically have been invisible or erased within official archives. Hunter offers both a critique and a new model of writing "history," one that demonstrates the impossibility of authoring a biography about a person who was violently denied connections to her own ancestors and thus her own history.
 —LAYLA BERMEO, Kristen and Roger Servison Associate
 Curator of Paintings, Museum of Fine Arts, Boston

Andrew Hunter has used the so-called blank and in-between spaces of the archive to pen a compelling historic and self-reflexive account of the life of Sophia Burthen, a Canadian enslaved woman. In the midst of a current social amnesia regarding Canada's complicity in both slavery and empire building, Hunter handles Burthen's story with care, using her narrative to navigate the complex intersecting ley-lines of empire and its enduring legacy of trauma and erasure. Hunter puts himself in conversation with Burthen, not to centre himself, but to emphasize why Burthen's story is all OUR history.
 —MARENKA THOMPSON-ODLUM, Curator, Pitt Rivers
 Museum, Oxford

It was dark there all the time

SOPHIA BURTHEN AND THE LEGACY OF SLAVERY IN CANADA

ANDREW HUNTER

GOOSE LANE EDITIONS

Edited by Fazeela Jiwa.
Tracy K. Smith, excerpt from "Declaration" from *Wade in the Water*. Originally from *The New Yorker* (November 6, 2017). Copyright © 2017, 2018 by Tracy K. Smith. Used with the permission of The Permissions Company, LLC on behalf of Graywolf Press, graywolfpress.org.
"Veronica?" from *How She Read* (copyright © 2019 by Chantal Gibson) reprinted with permission of Caitlin Press and the author.
Cover and page design by Julie Scriver.
Cover illustration: "Niagara River and Surrounding Country, Showing the Proposed Ship Canal, Rail Roads, &c, Drawn by the late Captain W.G. Williams, U.S. Topographical Corps," detail from *Traveller's Map of the Middle, Northern, Eastern States and Canada. Showing all the Railroad, Steamboat, Canal and Principal Stage Routes* (New York, 1849).
Background elements: (orange and blue texture) Photo boards on unsplash.com; (pattern) © Yan Koev, dreamstime.com.
Printed in Canada by Marquis.
10 9 8 7 6 5 4 3 2 1

Goose Lane Editions
500 Beaverbrook Court, Suite 330
Fredericton, New Brunswick
CANADA E3B 5X4
gooselane.com

Library and Archives Canada Cataloguing in Publication

Title: It was dark there all the time : Sophia Burthen and the legacy of slavery in Canada / Andrew Hunter.
Names: Hunter, Andrew, 1963- author.
Description: Includes bibliographical references.
Identifiers: Canadiana (print) 20210288795 | Canadiana (ebook) 20210288825 | ISBN 9781773102191 (softcover) | ISBN 9781773102214 (EPUB)
Subjects: LCSH: Burthen, Sophia. | LCSH: Women slaves—Canada—Biography. | LCSH: Slaves—Canada—Biography. | LCSH: Slavery—Canada. | LCSH: Slave trade—Canada. | LCSH: Slaves—Canada—Social conditions. | LCSH: Slaves—Emancipation—Canada. | LCSH: Freedmen—Canada—Biography. | LCSH: Imperialism—Social aspects. | LCSH: Postcolonialism—Social aspects. | LCGFT: Biographies.
Classification: LCC HT1051 .H86 2022 | DDC 306.3/62092—dc23

Goose Lane Editions is located on the traditional unceded territory of the Wəlastəkwiyik whose ancestors along with the Mi'kmaq and Peskotomuhkati Nations signed Peace and Friendship Treaties with the British Crown in the 1700s.

Goose Lane Editions acknowledges the generous support of the Government of Canada, the Canada Council for the Arts, and the Government of New Brunswick.

MIX
Paper from responsible sources
FSC® C103567

For Reighen Grineage, colleague, mentor, and friend,
who accompanied me on this journey.

History is not the past. History is the present. We carry our history with us. To think otherwise is criminal.
  —James Baldwin[1]

Since at least the seventeenth century, Africans arrived in Canada in bondage. Their forcible relocation from Africa, or other parts of the Americas, was facilitated by their designation, first as cargo, and subsequently as chattel, a strategy that excluded them from the category of settler. That these histories — spanning over two-hundred years and two empires (British and French) — are overwhelmingly disavowed is a result of Canada's national myth of racial tolerance and, concomitantly, the profound failures of Canada's education system. However, it does not take much digging to uncover the lie of our blinkered, heroic, national self-aggrandizement as the territory to which enslaved African Americans fled.
  —Charmaine Nelson[2]

All struggles are essentially power struggles. Who will rule? Who will lead? Who will define, refine, confine, design? Who will dominate? All struggles are essentially power struggles, and most are no more intellectual than two rams knocking their heads together.
  —Lauren Olamina, in Octavia Butler, *Parable of the Sower*[3]

A journey is called that because you cannot know what you will discover on the journey, what you will do with what you find, or what you find will do to you.
  —James Baldwin[4]

CONTENTS

CHAPTER 1
WHAT'S IN A NAME?

...carried us to a vessel, put us in the hold, and sailed up the river. I know not how far nor how long — it was dark there all the time.

—Sophia Burthen (Pooley), in 1855[*]

She carries three names. The first, Sophia, is common. Its Christian meaning is "divine wisdom." To Muslims, it means "beautiful." Let's think of her in these dignified terms. Her last name, Pooley, she took from the man she married in freedom. *Pooley* refers to a pond or a pool of water (from Old English *pōl*, from Dutch *poel*) that is located next to a *ley*—an area of pasture or grassland.[1] *Ley* can also refer to a *ley line*, "a supposed straight line connecting three or more prehistoric or ancient sites, sometimes regarded as the line of a former track and associated by some with lines of energy and other paranormal phenomena." *Pooley* is riparian, as in fed by or living near the banks of a river. Wise and beautiful, she sits by water, at the edge of a field. I am searching for the ley lines which still pulse, linking her across time and space to this moment. It is her maiden name, her enslaved name, Burthen, that carries the most weight and casts the longest shadow.

Burthen is an archaic English word that will become *burden*, the *th* morphing into a single *d*. It now means a physical thing one carries or a psychological weight

---

[*] From an interview (reproduced in full in the appendix of this book), in Benjamin Drew, *A North-Side View of Slavery. The Refugee: or the Narratives of Fugitive Slaves in Canada. Related by Themselves, with an Account of the History and Condition of the Colored Population of Upper Canada* (Boston: John P. Jewett; Cleveland, OH: Jewett, Proctor and Worthington; New York: Sheldon, Lamport and Blakeman; London: Trübner, 1856), 192. All quotations by Sophia used throughout these chapters are from this interview.

In most cases, I will refer to Drew's book as *The Refugee* (the primary title embossed on the first edition). Drew used the name *Sophia Pooley*, whereas I have chosen to refer to her as *Sophia Burthen (Pooley)*.

(of anxiety, trauma, or depression) that can or will be passed on to others, becoming a responsibility ("the burden of proof") and maybe a curse lingering in the past and shading the future. But originally, it was a very specific nautical term referring to a ship's measure or capacity. A ship's *tuns* (tons) *burthen* defined the very weight and quantity of what it could hold and convey,[2] its maximum cargo, as it was used in the text of the following fugitive-slave advertisement: "Run away about 10 o'clock Thursday last from John Cannon, New York City, three Negroes with a sloop belonging to said Cannon, burthen about 35 tons. Whoever takes up and returns said Negroe Men and the Sloop shall receive Twenty Pounds and all reasonable charges from John Cannon."[3] The average burthen of ships plying the Middle Passage[4] was much more than 35 tons. The 125-foot ship *Diamond*, for example, launched in 1798 by Patrick Beatson & Co. with construction overseen by Henry Baldwin, was the first large cargo vessel built in Quebec since the British ended French rule of the colony in 1763. Upon changing ownership in 1801 to Parry & Co. of London, it was retrofitted, its hull sheathed with copper and the cargo hold divided with a second deck, its burthen reduced from over 500 to 443 tons. Under Captain James Clark, *Diamond* sailed from London to West Africa, and then made two known deliveries of enslaved Africans to the West Indies: in 1802, 391 persons were transported to Trinidad; in 1803, 389 persons were transported to Cuba (44 died on each of the two voyages).[5] *Diamond*'s time working the Middle Passage was brief; it was refitted for whaling in 1804. There was another *Diamond* (Danish built, sailing from Liverpool and London under Captain William Jameson) that transported 986 enslaved persons in total from Onim/Lagos on three voyages (1804, 1806, and 1807), with the total deaths of 111 on route, to Kingston, Jamaica (twice), and Grenada.[6] In the British Empire, An Act for the Abolition of the Slave Trade, passed in 1807, ended the international trade and made it illegal for British vessels to continue shipping human cargo across the Atlantic. But this did not change Sophia's enslaved status, as the sale of enslaved people within specific colonies was not stopped. Britain also continued to trade and manufacture materials and products and to otherwise profit from a global economy dependent on enslaved labour.

The term *burthen* has echoes in a ship's berth — a place to moor a ship and unload its cargo. If it's a living cargo, then the berth signifies a landing where the next stage of the journey begins, and the space within the ship where a person sleeps. Sophia carried this term as part of her name, as did her parents, Dinah and Oliver, whose first names are mentioned in her interview, and her sister, who remains otherwise unnamed in the historical record. But where did this name come from? Who burdened them with a name pointing to a past filled with journeys in the holds of various vessels, in bondage? How far distant in Sophia's ancestry is the Middle Passage that forced twelve to fifteen million persons into migration across the Atlantic, of whom nearly two million perished — and were in effect murdered? Did previous generations of her family come directly to the coast of North America, or did their journey happen in stages, via the Caribbean or South America or maybe with stopovers south of New York, around the Gulf of Mexico, Georgia, the Carolinas, Virginia, Maryland, the shores of Chesapeake Bay? How long were the Burthens and their ancestors trapped in the Triangle Trade of Europe to Africa to the Americas? Do their roots go back to the early 1600s, when the Dutch West India Company imported Africans to New Amsterdam (later renamed New York City), or to the first slave auction held there in 1655?

"Slaves rarely had a surname," Charmaine Nelson tells me. Nelson's expertise includes the long history of slavery in Canada and the country's deep economic and social embeddedness in the slave trade over centuries. Now the Canada Research Chair in Transatlantic Black Diasporic Art and Community Engagement and Director of the Institute for the Study of Canadian Slavery at NSCAD University (Halifax), she was previously a professor at McGill University — the first Black tenured professor of art history in Canada. "If enslaved people did know their surname," she continues, "it was likely that of their owner," and this may be the source of *Burthen*, possibly the name of a past owner of Sophia's ancestors. For Sophia and her parents, however, I believe their owner would be Harris (sometimes spelled Herris), the name of a particular family that remains unburdened by the Burthen family's spirits and memories. This Harris family tree spread and still flourishes, while Sophia would pass on alone. Harris is such a common name, there is a family of prominence carrying that name in almost every Canadian city. It is a proper WASP name, like Johnson/Johnston, Brown, or the family names I carry, from Birmingham and Glasgow: Allen and Hunter. I can think of many prominent Black families and individuals with these names; the most common British names are also the most familiar names of those who trace their lineage to enslavement.

In 1855 Sophia tells Benjamin Drew, a Bostonian who has come north, that she is in her nineties, but an 1851 census lists her as 75, putting her year of birth at around 1775, at the beginning of the American Revolution (she likely died in the 1850s or early 1860s). According to Nelson, "most former slaves did not know their birthdate," a fact Sophia's neighbour John Little demonstrated when he tells Drew: "At the time of the sale, I was about twenty-three, but being a slave, I did not know my age."[7] The Harriet Tubman Historical Society says that the American abolitionist and activist born into an enslaved family "must have been between 88 and 98 years old when she died. She claimed in her pension application that she was born in 1825, her death certificate said she was born in 1815 . . . her gravestone indicated that she was born in 1820."[8] Nelson affirms, "So slaves often believed they were older than they were"[9] — and why wouldn't they? Time must have progressed at an insufferably slow pace for someone trapped without the freedom to choose an existence that might feel rewarding and joyous, the freedom to shape a life so satisfying that it makes time fly.

In that 1851 census from Peel Township, Sophia appears as "Sophia Polly,"[10] but even though *Pooley* has become *Polly*, it is obviously her, living in the Queen's Bush settlement, Wellington County, Peel Township, Canada West (previously Upper Canada and now Ontario).[11] *I find plenty of people in the bush to help me a good deal,* she says to close the interview with Drew, completing the single, thin narrative documenting the arc of her complex corporeal existence. In the census, she is listed as coming from the United States via Brantford — the town once known as Brant's Town (or Brant's Ford), named for the Haudenosaunee/Kanyen'kehà:ka (Mohawk) leader Thayendanegea, a British Loyalist who was also called Joseph Brant.[12]

My master's sons-in-law — let's leave them unnamed for a while — *came into the garden where my sister and I were playing among the currant bushes,* Sophia tells Drew, *tied their handkerchiefs over our mouths, carried us to a vessel, put us in the hold, and sailed up the river. I know not how far nor how long — it was dark there all the time. Then we came by land.* Taken as cargo, the sisters are literally burthen now, not just a trace of their ancestors carried in an obscure name. Held and transported on a sloop up the Hudson River, then over land, their passage projects lines of meaning onto the enmeshed landscapes of New York and Canada today, with branches extending out across the continent and the globe. These ley lines are faint and fading, and the traces that remain can be stubbornly cryptic. Describing some of her research tracing the Atlantic slave trade, Saidiya Hartman writes:

The archives contained what you would expect: the manifest of slavers; ledger books of trade goods; inventories of foodstuffs; bills of sale, itemized lists of bodies alive, infirm, and dead; captains' logs; planters' diaries. The account of commercial transactions was as near as I came to the enslaved.... In every line item I saw a grave. Commodities, cargo, and things don't lend themselves to representation, at least not easily. The archive dictates what can be said about the past and the kinds of stories that can be told about the persons catalogued, embalmed, and sealed away in box files and folios. To read the archive is to enter a mortuary; it permits one final viewing and allows for a last glimpse of persons about to disappear into the slave hold.[13]

For Sophia Burthen (Pooley), the hold has been *The Refugee* and the 1851 census.

One can imagine her name or at least a description of her existing elsewhere, and one can imagine the same for her parents and sister, who remain even more elusive. In her various owners' business papers, for example. They'd be anonymous, a number, listed as chattel, like furniture, equipment, or livestock. Or they'd each be described as a *slave*, a *Negro(e)*, or with their true status hidden behind an apparently neutral term like *servant*. When a child, Sophia would be described as a *girl*, when a woman, a *wench*. If she had run away, we might find her in fugitive-slave advertisements. But the truth is that it was beneficial for slave owners to obscure the presence of the enslaved: they were taxable property, so many existed without a trace and do not appear in archives. This is especially true if, like Sophia, an enslaved person was born during the chaotic beginnings of a new nation that lacked an ordered bureaucracy.

Generations of white scholars and educators have used these absences to further erase and deny the existence of slavery in the northern "free" states and in Canada. They often try to dismiss slavery as something "common" to all human societies, as if the monumental scale and scope of the system that enslaved the Burthens has any true equal.[14] They go further and claim that slavery outside of southern plantations was somehow more humane, and that the enslaved were better off, as if there was a "nice" version of being owned and treated as disposable property.[15] "Enslaved girls everywhere began laboring as young as four or five," Margaret Washington states in *Sojourner Truth's America* (2009), which meant they "had little opportunity for regular interaction with other black women, and endured a cultural isolation rarely experienced in the American South."[16] Maureen G. Elgersman Lee argues that, for enslaved women like Sophia, such isolation worsened their vulnerability:

> It appears very probable . . . that some Black women enslaved during the British regime lacked significant opportunity to create social bonds with other Black women based on shared gender, race and legal status. Such isolation would have made it impossible for many Black women to go to other Black women for respite from the degradation of physical or sexual abuse, for assistance in raising children, or for celebrating religious or labor holidays. It is highly possible that where Black women lacked such support systems, they may have found the slave system even more trying than for women who had such support.[17]

Those who perpetuate racist theories that dismiss the horrors of chattel slavery are merely justifying the extreme expansion of a so-called "common" human evil that is the foundation of their society. Dawn settlement[18] resident William Henry Bradley, also interviewed by Drew, bluntly dismisses the basis for such justifications: "If a man could make slaves of mud or block, and have them work for him, it would be wrong,—all men came to life at the hand of the Almighty; every man ought to have life, and his own method of pursuing happiness."[19]

Sophia was birthed into the continuing tragedy of colonial North America, in the heart of the traditional Algonquin territories of the Wappinger and the Muh-he-con-neok/Mahican (Mohican) people. She traversed the foundations of the interconnected nation states of modern Canada and the United States that emerged from, and remain tethered to, empires of slavery and the systemic assault on Indigenous peoples and their lands. Enslaved children knew their status. They worked from as young as four years old, were hired out and traded. They were punished and constantly exposed to loss, trauma, and violence, as were their parents. In Dutchess County, New York, where Sophia was born, "the threat of sale was a source of constant anxiety; actual separation produced gut-wrenching anguish."[20] Sojourner Truth (born Isabelle Belle Baumfree in 1797 in nearby Swartekill, in Ulster County) recalled that her mother, Mau Mau Bett, "saw most of her children sold away."[21] Sojourner herself never knew several of her older siblings, but she knew her status: she was sold three times in one year. Sophia would have known hers too.

Near the end of her life, Sophia's stories came into Drew's possession, under his claim that he "will endeavour to collect, with the view to placing their [his interviewees'] testimony on record, their experiences of actual workings of slavery —and such statements...bearing upon the weighty subjects of oppression and freedom." Weighty subjects, yet he misses the true weight of Sophia's unique narrative, as she had not, as he declares, "fled from the North and the South into Upper Canada to escape the oppression exercised upon them by their native countrymen."[22] She did not come to Canada a fugitive or free, but as chattel. She does not fit Drew's narrative, which will nearly erase Sophia as her history becomes buried beneath well-burnished myths of the Underground Railroad and its promises of freedom in Canada, and a present-day Canada that believes it is free of the legacies of slavery and systemic racism.

Such trauma plays out in Sophia's recollections with Drew, filtered through wounds, time stretching, places merging. *I know not for how long*: I hear her speaking the truth and read the various discrepancies (of dates, names, places) in her narrative as coming from trauma and as a result of Drew's failure to transcribe her telling accurately. I am trying to see Sophia at all stages of life. I also seek to understand my relationship to her *master's sons-in-law* (*the white men*, who sold her and her sister, *at Niagara*); to their families; and to Samuel Hatt, the *Englishman at Ancaster*, who paid Thayendanegea/Joseph Brant $100 for her alone. And what about Thayendanegea/Joseph, whom Sophia called *old Indian Brant, the king*? A polarized (and polarizing) figure, he is the most complicated presence at the heart of her journey from Fishkill, where she notes she was born, to the Queen's Bush settlement where she gave her interview. A man of two worlds: a Kanyen'kehà:ka (Mohawk) leader dedicated to his people, equally shaped by British Christian ideas and ideals. Thayendanegea/Joseph was defined by his Indigeneity yet colonized by whiteness. I am seeing myself in all of these intense manifestations of whiteness. *Canada was then filling up with white people*, Sophia tells me. I cannot be innocent.

What a surprise Sophia, a woman brought enslaved to Canada, and sold here, must have been to Drew, a man born during the War of 1812 who lived to see the twentieth century dawn. But perhaps she wasn't a surprise to him at all. That this woman was enslaved in Canada, however, would prove to be a revelation for future generations—for us, now. Did Drew explain his project to her? Did he articulate to her, as clearly as he does to his readers in his introduction, his intention "to visit those Americans who have fled from the North and the South into Upper Canada to escape the oppression exercised upon them by their native countrymen"? Did he assure her that she had, as he writes, "the sympathies of many friends in the United States"? Did he advise her in the same tone, which reads in his introduction as condescending and patronizing, that her "good conduct and success in life may have an important bearing on the destinies of millions of their [your] brethren...who have the misfortune to be descended from slave mothers"?[23] I cannot help hearing "misfortune" as Drew condemning Sophia's mother, Dinah, and her ancestral mothers rather than looking into himself and seeing that her real misfortune was to "descend" in another sense, within a system of chattel slavery from which he cannot self-righteously distance himself.[24]

> The dismemberment of Africa happened in two stages. During the first of these, the African personhood was divided into two halves: the continent and its diaspora. African slaves, the central commodity in the mercantile phase of capitalism, formed the basis of the sugar, cotton, and tobacco plantations in the Caribbean and American mainland. If we accept that slave trade and plantation slavery provided the primary accumulation of capital that made Europe's Industrial Revolution possible, we cannot escape the irony that the very needs of that Industrial Revolution—markets for finished goods, sources of raw materials, and strategic requirements in the defense of trade routes—led inexorably to the second stage of the dismemberment of the continent.[25]

Canada was both focus and platform for the European colonial enterprise. "For over 200 years," prior to Confederation in 1867, "New France and British North American colonies held Africans in bondage and Canadians helped suppress Caribbean slave rebellions," Yves Engler reminds us in *Canada in Africa: 300 Years of Aid and Exploitation* (2015).[26] He quotes Natasha L. Henry from her book *Emancipation Day: Celebrating Freedom in Canada* (2010): "Very few Canadians are aware that at one time their nation's economy was firmly linked to African slavery through the building and sale of slave ships, the sale and purchase of slaves to and from the Caribbean and the exchange of timber, cod, and other food items from the Maritimes for West-Indian slave-produced goods."[27] To borrow from wa Thiong'o's description of European practices in Africa,[28] Canada too has been fertile ground for "planting European memory," narratives that nurture the selective erasure of the past as well as justify the nation's continuing participation in the business of natural-resource extraction and in the dismemberment of communities.

Sophia Burthen (Pooley) embodies this erasure. To follow her is to follow the ley lines she traced and crossed, which expose the realities of the transatlantic slave trade as the bedrock of the British Empire and hence of Canada. The much-vaunted United Empire Loyalists (UELs) brought enslaved people here. Caribbean-based slaveholders used their "compensation" (discussed further, below) to acquire land and fund new businesses in Canada. The source of materials and trade feeding industry in Canada (sugar and cotton coming in; furs, fish, timber, liquor, and cloth going out) were products of slavery. Sugar barons and lumber merchants in Montréal, shipbuilders in the Maritimes, leaders of industry in Upper Canada / Canada West, the first banks — they all accumulated vast wealth from the slave economy. Their tainted wealth flowed into the infrastructure of a modernizing Canada, post-Confederation. It lingers in the assets of leading banks that for years refused to give mortgages to non-white citizens, as Engler explains:

> Much of the capital used to establish the current incarnation of the Canadian Imperial Bank of Commerce (CIBC) came from supplying the Caribbean slave colonies. The Halifax Banking Company was the first bank in Nova Scotia and the founding unit of today's CIBC.... One of the eight founding shareholders of the Halifax Banking Company was steamship pioneer Samuel Cunard. In the early 1800s, Cunard's vessels brought cod and lumber to the West Indies and returned with rum, molasses and sugar.... The first President of ScotiaBank [Bank of Nova Scotia], William Lawson, "had extensive dealings in the West Indies" when the bank opened in 1832.[29]

As it clearly declares in a news release, CIBC is proud to recognize Halifax as home to their first bank.[30]

The stories we tell in Canada obscure and erase, are virulent and toxic. Too often Black history emerges as a blank page, a clean white sheet. "How many times

have you been told there were no Black people here in the past?" I ask Reighen
Grineage, eighth-generation descendant of the first settlers who joined Reverend
Josiah Henson at the Dawn settlement in Upper Canada, as we walk down the
main street of Dresden, Ontario, in April 2018, "How many times have you been
asked where you're from?"

"Too many," she says, "too, *too* many."

"There is a great deal of prejudice here," William Henry Bradley states bluntly
in his interview included in the "Dresden/Dawn" section of Drew's book. Bradley,
who escaped from Maryland, would have known Grineage's ancestors and he likely
arrived with the first Dawn settlers. Like many fugitives, he had changed his name.
"In slavery I was known as Abram Young," he says, which indicates another reason
it can be difficult to trace the genealogies and journeys of enslaved peoples. Bradley
says he "prospered well in freedom...I have fifty acres of land, bought and paid
for by *my own energy and exertions* [emphasis added], and I have the deed to my
house." He truly paid for his prosperity. It wasn't granted to him; that privilege was
reserved for white people who came north and from across the Atlantic. He proudly
declares, "I own two span of horses, twelve head of hogs, six sheep, two milch
[milk] cows, and am putting up a farm barn."[31] But where are his descendants?
There are no Bradleys in the area now, and there is no longer a Dawn settlement.

I am sitting with Reighen and her grandparents Peggy and Paul Robinson, in
their home in Dresden, a few miles from the site of the long-abandoned Dawn
settlement and the grave of Reverend Josiah Henson. The Grineage and Robinson
family are the last Black family living in the town. We talk about the Black
communities that once dotted Upper Canada/Canada West.

"Imagine how different it would be now," Paul wonders aloud, "if those
communities had been allowed to flourish?"

Peggy asks, rhetorically, "And where did everyone go?"

Peggy and Paul may not know precisely where people went, but it is clear from
our long conversation that they know why. It was clear also to a journalist writing
for a national magazine in 1949:

> The Canadian who looks down on the Southern United States for
> "Jim Crow" racial segregation will suffer a rude shock on visiting
> the sleepy agricultural centre of Dresden, Ont., 300 of whose 1,700
> citizens have Negro blood. Although Dresden's citizens do not like

to talk about it, Negroes cannot eat at the town's three restaurants serving regular meals, cannot get a haircut in the four regular barbershops, cannot send their wives to the only beauty parlour.[32]

Peggy and Paul experienced such treatment from whites in their community first-hand.

"Peggy's father said I would have sat there for days and not been served," Paul says. He is recalling the time he'd come to Dresden from nearby Chatham to woo Peggy (around 1960), and was left waiting at Kay's Meals Lunches Sodas for almost an hour—ignored because, as Peggy's father told him, everyone in Dresden knew that "Kay's doesn't serve coloured people." The local whites whom Sidney Katz interviewed a decade earlier for his article "Jim Crow Lives in Dresden" put it more bluntly: "'Look mister, would you like a nigger to marry your sister?' and 'Well, I'm against discrimination—but I got to think of my business.'" [33] That was in 1949, when one fifth of the population of Dresden was Black, and the grave of the Reverend Josiah Henson (popularly referred to as "Uncle Tom" after Harriet Beecher Stowe based this character on Henson's life)[34] was already a tourist draw, particularly for African Americans. It would be a mistake to think Dresden an aberration in the Canadian experience. Canada has been very selective about the histories it honours, the stories it continues to invest in telling. One such story is the Battle at Stoney Creek.

Drew would have been just one year old on June 6, 1813, when that battle raged as the War of 1812 continued. Sophia recalls that *the cannonade made everything shake well.* Today a stone tower marks the site, now a National Historic Site with a museum called Battlefield House. Every year enthusiastic, costumed re-enactors restage the battle. In the 1830s, plantation owner Robert Neilson came north from Trinidad. With the money he received from the British government as compensation for his loss of property—the people he owned and the land they worked—when slavery was abolished, he purchased the battlefield property. There has been no compensation for the formerly enslaved in the British Empire. There has been a lot of investment in maintaining a story of the Battle of Stoney Creek (with its UEL war heroes), but not in narratives of slave owning, of compensation, or of the enslaved. No one is dressing up and re-enacting those histories.

In 1813 Sophia, still enslaved, was *seven miles from Stoney Creek.* Stoney Creek is now part of Hamilton, where I was born and raised. Back in 1813, Sophia would have been standing where I am now, at Dundas (now also part of Hamilton), just a few blocks from Old Ancaster Road. The Hatt brothers, Samuel and Richard, carved this route through the bush from their properties atop the escarpment and down into the valley that would become Dundas.

I'm following in Sophia's footsteps, desperate to find her presence. With *old Brant we caught the deer*, she says. *It was at Dundas at the outlet.* She mentions *white people in the neighbourhood, John Chisholm and Bill Chisholm*: her memory is clear. It leads me to find out that the latter was born in 1788; he was a colonel. They *would come and say 't was their hounds* who caught the deer, she recalls, *and they must have the meat. But we would not give it up.* I follow William Chisholm further along the north shore of Lake Ontario. He was a founder of Oakville. That man willing to claim what was not rightfully his is well honoured: a local school bears his name.

I'm standing, *at Dundas at the outlet,* by the water, at the edge of a field, searching for ghosts and shadows, the burden of proof. I'm standing where the waters of Cootes Paradise narrow into a thin, straight channel that leads to the turning basin of the long-defunct Desjardins Canal. *Cootes, Desjardins*: more names of settlers branded onto Indigenous lands, obscuring all those who truly laboured here. Further west, Cootes Drive will cross York Road. Turn left, and you will come to Hatt Street. I grew up around here. In my earliest memories, a rail line ran up the centre of Hatt Street. It passed factories and served what was once an industrial town. It all started with the mills along Spencer Creek owned by Richard and Samuel Hatt.

Sophia was sold to Samuel Hatt and *lived with him seven years* before she took her freedom, presumably heading west into Waterloo Township, and eventually to the free Black settlement of Queen's Bush. How many Black bodies, "servants" and "labourers" skilled in the building of roads and mills, toiled on behalf of the Hatts? The brothers were well connected, they didn't earn by their "own energy and exertions," like William Henry Bradley. Imagine what Sophia, with her hard-earned knowledge and survival skills, could have done with even a modest land grant. ("Imagine," Paul Robinson wondered, "how different it would be now if those communities had been allowed to flourish?") Imagine how different it would be if Sophia had flourished here.

Here—sold and lived enslaved here. Sophia had not found freedom at the terminus of the Underground Railroad, that epic journey Canada claims as a foundational narrative and nurtured to distinguish it from neighbours south of the border. Sophia was sold and bought as a slave here, where I again live. She walked the ground where Hatt Street runs. The names of those who owned enslaved people are inscribed on this landscape, on the signs for streets, towns, and buildings. Many came north from New York. They had roots, like Sophia, along the Hudson River, in Dutchess and Ulster Counties, and at Albany. And what of those who owned the Burthens, stole and sold them? They came here too. Their names are also spelled out on signs and heritage plaques, while Sophia's lies buried, her sister's erased, in shadow, here.

Dear Sophia,

Your interview is a puzzle, a complex weaving of fragments. At times it seems you were several ages at once, that between your birth in Fishkill and passage out of slavery decades later, you move through time fluidly and you are channelling the memories of more than one person. At times you seem too old, then too young, but then you give us much to align and triangulate, markers to navigate from—names, relationships, dates, places. You have divined connections (you who are named for divine wisdom). From the eve of the American Revolution in the mid-1770s you witnessed: Governor John Grave Simcoe's 1793 An Act Against Slavery;[35] An Act for the Abolition of the Slave Trade in Britain and the Act Prohibiting Importation of Slaves in the United States, both in 1807; the War of 1812, that ran through 1815; the British Slavery Abolition Act, passed in 1833, enacted in 1834; and the United States' Fugitive Slave Act of 1850. Did you live to see the American Civil War break out in 1861, and witness the Great Emancipation in 1863 at the war's end? Were you present at the birth of Canada in 1867, and if so, where were you? Did you read the words of formerly enslaved persons—Frederick Douglass, Sojourner Truth, William Wells Brown, and many others? Were you given the opportunity to learn to read? Did you hear Reverend Samuel Ringgold Ward, the prominent Black freeman from the United States who was an executive officer of the Anti-Slavery Society of Canada, which supported Drew's book? Did you ever encounter Reverend Josiah Henson? How often, if ever, did you frequent the African Methodist / British Methodist Episcopal Church in the Queen's Bush? Did you live to see the dissolution of the community of over one thousand Black settlers, where Drew encountered you, when they were pushed off the land they'd cleared, all while *Canada was filling up with white people?*

CHAPTER 2
ON WHITENESS

*Is it that by its indefiniteness it shadows forth the heartless voids and
immensities of the universe, and thus stabs us from behind with the thought
of annihilation, when beholding the white depths of the milky way? Or is
it, that as in essence whiteness is not so much a color as the visible absence
of color; and at the same time the concrete of all colors; is it for these reasons
that there is such a dumb blankness, full of meaning, in a wide landscape
of snows—a colorless, all-color of atheism from which we shrink?*
        —Ishmael, in Herman Melville, *Moby-Dick; or, The Whale* (1851)[1]

I am a white man. I realize that many BIPOC (Black, Indigenous, People of
Colour) readers do not need to hear another white man's words, particularly words
shaped by the life of a Black woman who lived enslaved in Canada that draw on
the writings and cultural expressions of BIPOC voices. I know that there will
also be white people who don't want to hear the critique of whiteness that runs
throughout this story. To BIPOC individuals and communities: I hope that you
will take up this narrative and come to see it as a valuable contribution. To white
people, particularly Canadians: you need to read this or any book that discomforts
us in trying to get beyond feel-good narratives of our histories; we are implicated;
we cannot continue in innocence or feigned ignorance of a damning legacy that
we continue to benefit from and defines our place in the world. We need to
accept a past that has shaped, and that we continue to reshape in, the present. As
writer James Baldwin cautions, "An invented past can never be used; it cracks and
crumbles under the pressures of life like clay in a season of drought."[2]

White as a category of race is, like race (or gender), subjective. The skin
privilege of whiteness—the privileges associated with being white—is a fact.
It exists. It intersects with the fact of racism (and other facts, like transphobia,

homophobia, and misogyny). These all exist and intersect; whiteness and racism (like transphobia, homophobia, and misogyny) are facts that intersect. "Race is an *idea*, not a *fact* [emphasis added]," American historian and artist Nell Irvin Painter declares in *The History of White People* (2010), "and its questions demand answers from the conceptual rather than the factual realm."[3] In *How to Be an Anti-Racist* (2019), scholar Ibram X. Kendi declares that "race is fundamentally a power construct of blended difference that lives socially."[4] He goes on: "Race creates new forms of power: the power to categorize and judge, elevate and downgrade, include and exclude. Race makers use that power to process distinct individuals, ethnicities, and nationalities into monolithic races.[5] Kendi ties the idea of race directly to transatlantic chattel slavery: "The first global power to construct race happened to be the first racist power and the first exclusive slave trader of the constructed race of African people."[6] He is referring to the fifteenth-century Prince Henry the Navigator (Dom Henrique of Portugal, Duke of Viseu). Those of us who are white often try not to identify as such, to claim not to "see" race. We point out that there is no scientific evidence to support the division of humanity into invented categories based on skin colour. Dismissing (uncritical) race theory does not nullify racism, or dissolve whiteness as a fully functioning worlding[7] that offers the "privilege of being inherently normal, standard and legal."[8] Those who deny their whiteness in these ways also deny the lived realities of Blackness, denying identity, community, and agency to all held outside of the policed boundaries of whiteness. In Canada, Black and Indigenous peoples continue to be criminalized and stigmatized. In *Policing Black Lives* (2017), Robyn Maynard accurately defines Canada as a country that, "in the eyes of many of its citizens, as well as those living elsewhere, is imagined as a beacon of tolerance and diversity," a resilient fiction contradicted by "an untold story of Black subjection in Canada." Maynard adds that "Black lives in Canada have been exposed to a structural violence that has been tacitly or explicitly condoned."[9]

Denying racism by dismissing race as an idea (an idea produced by whiteness no less) is a privilege of the historic normativity of whiteness. Over generations, communities included in whiteness have greatly expanded; it was not that long ago that to be Irish, Italian, or Portuguese (like Prince Henry the Navigator), for example, was to be considered "ethnic," a vague categorization, neither white nor Black.[10] At the same time, "poverty in a dark skin endures," Painter wrote in the final paragraph of her vital study, "driven by an age-old social yearning to characterize the poor as permanently other and inherently inferior."[11] Race endures, overlapping with class, caste, and gender, maintaining and multiplying the communities whiteness seeks to oversee and control.

The denial of whiteness has a flipside: the grasping for difference where no evidence exists. Despite the growing acceptance that race has no basis in biology, some still cling to racist legacies of the likes of one Dr. Collins, a nineteenth-century British physician and plantation owner: "There are many striking variations between the temperaments of the whites, and those of the Negroes, sufficient almost to induce a belief of a different organization, which the knife of the anatomist, however, *has never been able to detect* [emphasis added]."[12]

Canadians continue to overwhelmingly praise prime ministers John A. Macdonald, Wilfred Laurier, William Lyon Mackenzie King, and Pierre Trudeau, considered by many Canadians to have been the country's best leaders, conveniently ignoring their racism. Macdonald was the first prime minister and a nation builder; he also initiated the residential school system and established a race-based immigration system. King was longest-serving and was also known to admire Hitler in advance of the Second World War. Trudeau, who embraced multiculturalism, was also behind the 1969 White Paper, which proposed to abolish legal documents concerning Indigenous people, such as the Indian Act and all treaties. Laurier is seen to have established an independent, modern Canada, and yet in 1911 he made it clear who Canadians are, when he introduced an order-in-council banning Black persons from coming to Canada: "Canada is free, and freedom is its nationality.... We are here a nation, or we want to be a nation, composed of the most heterogeneous elements—Protestants and Catholics, English, French, German, Irish, Scotch, every one, let it be remembered, with his traditions, with his prejudices."[13] Laurier stated that "the Negro race...is deemed unsuitable to the climate and requirements of Canada,"[14] a persistent, unfounded idea that continues to inform anti-Black racism.[15] Indigenous people, immigrants from backgrounds other than those named, and refugees, including those Black people who fled enslavement, were not considered Canadian by the prime minister. In 2016, *Maclean's* magazine ranked Laurier as one of Canada's "best" prime ministers.[16] In 2010, newspaper editor and columnist Neil Reynolds argued that "by restoring Laurier's lost tenets, this century could be ours."[17]

The dominant ideas about Canada (multicultural, diverse, free of racism) I was raised on have long been set in opposition to ideas about the United States, the latter a "melting pot" of overtly coerced assimilation, a nation defined by the exclusion and incarceration of those not considered "normal, standard, and legal" citizens. The distinction between the nations, however, is really just in methodology; Canada's preferred image of racial tolerance and innocence regarding slavery has created more challenging barriers that sustain a nation where "a discernible lack of awareness surrounding the widespread anti-Blackness," as Maynard states in *Policing Black Lives*, "continues to hide in plain sight, obscured behind a nominal commitment to liberalism, multi-culturalism and equality."[18]

"We shouldn't believe the hype that we are a nation of grand cultural tolerance and equality," advises Charles Officer, director of *The Skin We're In*, a 2017 documentary that takes its title from its subject, the 2015 essay (now a book) by journalist and activist Desmond Cole.[19] The few BIPOC students who attended my elementary school (Mohawk Trail School) were always introduced as being from somewhere else and encouraged or required to perform their ethnicity and otherness. Officer demands that whiteness consider what it is like to enter spaces always "aware that there is someone who thinks of you as 'other' or 'lesser'."[20]

In following Sophia, I am also necessarily writing of whiteness and of erasure, carrying an inheritance of flawed memories weighed down by the absence and the spirit of a fellow human being nearly lost, intentionally obscured, extirpated. In trying to find her, I inevitably find whiteness, because whiteness has documented itself and not her; I cross the troubled paths of too many nineteenth-century white abolitionists who carried white supremacist and racist ideas out of Emancipation, who wanted slavery to end but Black people sent back to Africa; I encounter too many white voices maintaining privilege. I find whiteness too often surfacing in my own language.

I have worked to progress in dialogue with and following the lead of those deeply invested in filling the void, writing into the archive, believing that there are so many stories untold and that the absence of Black lives in history is a void in all histories, that these Black lives should truly matter, to everyone. I struggle to know how to engage Sophia's experiences without appearing to claim her through language. I am trying to honour her by following her passage across and in time, hovering in the places and moments she points to through language no doubt shaped by her interviewer Benjamin Drew, another white man, knowing there is much in those details—names, places, time and memory, disturbed chronology.

I cannot gain Sophia's permission to tell this story, so I have approached her journey in conversation with a generous circle of colleagues, mentors, and editors, who have consistently challenged the *how* and *why* of my telling. Their feedback has addressed both my recurring doubts about proceeding, and my missteps in trying to position Sophia, and myself, in this narrative. Professor Charmaine Nelson made it clear to me that, "The history of slavery is all of our history. This isn't just Black history; we all have responsibility to do this hard work."[21] Artist, educator, scholar, and poet Chantal Gibson challenged me to better understand my place of responsibility, reminded me that "this work is hard, it should be difficult for you."[22] We spoke at length about my place in the "wake work" articulated by the professor of literature and Black studies Christina Sharpe,[23] and the need to unpack my relationship (in whiteness) not just to the *wake* as she uses the term, but (to extend the metaphor) also to the vessel, the hold, the current, the *wake*, and turbulence. You will encounter their voices regularly throughout this book, along with many others who continue to inform and critique my progress and help to hold me accountable.

My background is art making and curating. Reading as well as telling stories with text, images, and objects forms my critical foundation, as does place-based research. I ground myself in the landscapes of those I am engaging with, and so I've travelled back and forth over Sophia's landscape, a geography I also have deep connections too. Reighen Grineage, also deeply connected to the region, was a regular presence on these journeys, and so she appears consistently throughout this story. A graduate of the University of Western Ontario (where we first met) and eighth-generation Canadian, she had the courage to share with me her experiences in the wake of Sophia's life. My circle has introduced me to the work of writers and artists, and they have also sent me back to re-engage with material, including films, published narratives of the formerly enslaved, and — most important — many BIPOC writers (historical and contemporary), including James Baldwin, who was the first writer I read in depth.

As I've grown older, I have come to understand that what makes me uncomfortable and often appalls me are the fundamental values of whiteness, a worlding that dominates, colonizes, and hoards, while normalizing coercive and self-serving hierarchies of power. *White*, as a racial category, is an evolving and unstable fiction that absorbs and excludes, and while it can be dismissed as scientifically unsupportable, whiteness (as with racism) is a fact, an all too real looming presence. Whiteness is a self-perpetuating disease, like a cancer, a virulent sickness that is, ironically, a selfish and self-destructive trap for those who celebrate (or willfully deny perpetuating) whiteness. In his novel *Moby-Dick*, Herman Melville saw the abhorrent whiteness of Ahab infecting the whale, saw Moby-Dick as the manifestation of the United States' imperialist capitalism. His narrator, Ishmael, states: "It was the whiteness of the whale that, above all things, appalled me."[24] In *Moby-Dick*, I see the "appalling" whiteness of a way of being that is virulent and spreads, infecting others, colonizing the bodies of those who, like the harpooners on the whaling ship *Pequod* in the novel, are absorbed into an exploitative allelo-pathic system (I will return to this idea in relation to Thayendanegea/Joseph Brant in chapter 16, "Numbers"). It is the whiteness of Ahab (his aggression, arrogance, and imposing wilfulness), not the imagined evil projected onto the whale, that is most "appalling."

While appalled by whiteness, I know I cannot escape, write, or perform my way out of it. I am tethered to it, and it defines me, and so I try to worry whiteness from within. Many who embody whiteness believe they have a choice about confronting the past; too often they choose to defend, excuse, or simply ignore it. In trying to write of Sophia, I feel I am responding to Baldwin's demands of whiteness to not abdicate responsibility, which Eddie S. Glaude Jr. quotes and expands upon:

> "Not everything is lost. Responsibility cannot be lost; it can only be abdicated. If one refuses abdication, one begins again." Begin again is shorthand for something Baldwin commended to the country in the latter part of his career: that we re-examine the fundamental values and commitments that shape our self-understanding, and that we look back to those beginnings not to reaffirm our greatness or to double down on myths that secure our innocence, but to see where we went wrong and how we might reimagine or recreate ourselves in light of who we originally set out to be. This requires and unflinching encounter with the lie at the heart of our history.[25]

There are many white voices throughout this story, which I necessarily en-counter although I am seeking Sophia. I felt it was necessary to incorporate Drew, and I have worked to reveal details of his biography to trouble his legacy and to accept that I must see myself in Drew, as I must see myself in the trajectories and manifestations of all the embodiments of whiteness I engage. I have taken the same approach to all white voices, to expose them and, by extension, the historic moral choices and values of whiteness. Unlike Sophia, whose life was manipulated *by* whiteness, I have been shaped *in* whiteness, as Drew was, and as the white men who held Sophia in bondage were. I cannot fully separate myself from them.

Thayendanegea/Joseph Brant baffles a binary of racial identity. His identity is complicated by both Indigeneity and Britishness. In recent years, Canadian narratives and representations of him have tended to emphasize his Haudenosaunee/Kanyen'kehà:ka (Mohawk) ancestry, while downplaying the reality that he embodied colonial British ideals. He was a commissioned British officer, a Mason, Anglican, and a landowner. Downplaying this enables many scholars to see his slave owning (for example, of Sophia) as an extension of an imagined pan-Indigenous traditional practice, rather than a privileged engagement with a European colonial model that exclusively enslaved the people in the African diaspora.

Whiteness denies and defends itself, then blames, as can be heard in statements often directed at BIPOC individuals and communities, such as: "It's history, get over it!" But *it* is not some distant past, *it* is very present, *it* is whiteness. How does one get over something they are still living in, that is still *here* and *now*, enforcing its supremacy with violence?

The abolitionist and women's rights activist Sojourner Truth summed up the experience of living enslaved and its afterlife: "When I go before the throne of God, and God says, 'Sojourner, what made you hate the white people?' I've got my answer ready" — she would then reveal her heavily scarred back — "I hated them. I had my cause."[26] More than a century and a half later, artist, scholar, and co-founder of Black Lives Matter (Toronto), Syrus Marcus Ware emphasizes this past that is not past:

> Our ancestors were working on the abolition of slavery, and many say that the abolition of prisons and police is just the continuation of that unfinished project — that we didn't actually finish abolishing slavery and that this is the final step. . . . I think what we have to be careful of is that the message doesn't get watered down or co-opted into a story about reform. We're not asking for reform: we're asking for abolition.[27]

The unfinished project of abolition links to the valid demand that the promise of reparations be fulfilled. Reparations are more than financial compensation; they also encompass a reckoning with the past and a commitment to fundamental change in the present. As Simukai Chigudu puts it: "Ignorance of history serves many ends. Sometimes it papers over crimes of the present by attributing too much power to the past. Perhaps more often, it covers up past crimes in order to legitimize the way society is arranged in the present."[28] Whiteness wants to set the terms of reparations, as well as the conditions of change in order to maintain privilege, to continue its cover-up. Those of us who embody whiteness have a moral responsibility to work against this momentum and unmake this worlding.

My efforts cannot just be about adding Sophia onto, or inserting her into, a history that is ultimately still primarily defined by whiteness, to become just another appalling enhancement through "inclusion," simply reproducing whiteness, albeit annotated. I am struggling through not only the *what* but the *how* of channelling a story shaped by the traces Sophia left. I've been told that doing this work is "being an ally," but I am cautious of the roots of that term in the strategic alliances made for national and military self-interest and self-preservation. Too often whiteness has simply allied itself with "others" to benefit itself, without giving up space or resources or privilege, never really making room at the table. As Malcolm X put it: "Sitting at the table doesn't make you a diner, unless you eat some of what's on the plate."[29]

I have a seat at this table. I have been able to live with my family, to be raised and nurtured by (and ultimately to care for) my parents, to know my siblings, to be a son, and to become a parent. My parents encouraged me to know my ancestry and to critically value history and stories, to question and keep learning that life is *my* journey. For Sophia, such relationships and opportunities were severely limited, if not fully denied: to be a sister and a daughter, to be of a family and a community, to see life as *her* journey, and to have the freedom to lead and, as Baldwin stated, "discover…what you will do with what you find, or what you find will do to you."

I won't do better by insisting on leading. If I'm lucky, I'll be allowed to continue to watch and learn, to be invited to be mentored, maybe to even participate, and to be welcomed beyond this all too necessary time of reckoning.

Dear Sophia,

Time is fluid. I find an opening in what at first appears a closure: in 1851, a time long past your birth and journey out of enslavement, the year you first appear in the written record. In 1851, Sojourner Truth, known for her eloquence and sharp wit, projected her powerful and sophisticated language before a stunned audience at the Ohio Woman's Rights Convention, only to have her words filtered and reduced to plantation dialect in print by privileged white witnesses as "Ain't I a Woman?" According to The Sojourner Truth Project, "it is questionable that she said the words, 'Ain't I a Woman?' or even 'Ar'n't I A Woman?'"[30] In 1851, Frederick Douglass's authenticity is being doubted and he is being criticized by former abolitionist allies because of his command of the written word, his oratory, and his independent position that will not accept passivity and instead embraces a robustly physical challenge to slavery and racism. The Anti-Slavery Society of Canada will be formed in Toronto in 1851, and Douglass will come to Canada that year for the North American Convention of Coloured Freemen. In 1851, the Reverend Josiah Henson will travel from Canada to stand before Queen Victoria and her entourage in the Crystal Palace at London's Great Exhibition, the same year he will be reduced to the "original Uncle Tom" by Harriet Beecher Stowe.[31] It was also the year Herman Melville published *Moby-Dick*, with its chronicling of appalling whiteness (Ahab's, not the whale's), written a short journey north and east of your birthplace, in a house bought with a loan from his father-in-law, the Massachusetts Chief Justice Lemuel Shaw. In 1851, Shaw's influence in the shaping of Black lives was not restricted to the *Sims* case. His ruling in favour of slave owners in the infamous case confirmed the legality of the Fugitive Slave Act and sent the fugitive Thomas Sims back to a Georgia plantation; the ruling caused many others to flee even further

north across the border.[32] In 1851, on the north shore of
Lake Ontario, an obscure woman named Nelly Outwater
(née Harris) died in Adolphustown, in a well-established
community where United Empire Loyalists from the Hudson
Valley have prospered. And in 1851, blue-black ink flowed from
the pen of an anonymous hand onto a lined and gridded page,
declaring your presence here, in Canada.

CHAPTER 3
ALLELOPATHY—OF BLACK WALNUT

Perhaps my complexion attracted attention, but nearly all who passed,
paused to look at me, and at themselves, as reflected in my large black
walnut framed mirrors.
　　—Reverend Josiah Henson, at the Great Exhibition of the
　　Works of Industry of All Nations, London, 1851[1]

In 1851, the year Sophia's presence was being confirmed in the census of Peel Township, the Reverend Josiah Henson travelled to London to exhibit products made from black walnut timber from trees grown and harvested on the banks of the Sydenham River in Canada West (now Ontario), expertly processed at a lumber mill near the Dawn settlement. The Dawn Mill had been designed and built by former and fugitive slaves and freemen who had come north with Henson. They established the British American Institute for vocational training and founded their own community (the Dawn settlement). Their ambitions were similar to those of the Elgin settlement at North Buxton, founded by the Reverend William King, 40 kilometres away. Canada West was home to numerous significant Black populations, including many who settled before white people. By the mid-nineteenth century, however, Black people came up against racism as well as laws limiting their freedoms. In 1851, the Reverend Samuel Ringgold Ward challenged his predominantly white associates in the Anti-Slavery Society of Canada for failing to acknowledge that slavery and racism were distinct evils. He foresaw that the end of slavery would not guarantee equal rights for Black people and was painfully aware that few of his fellow abolitionists would fight for equality. Many were promoters of "colonization" plans that would send Black people back to West Africa or to the Caribbean.

Dear Sophia,

I am trying to imagine Queen Victoria's reflection in one of Josiah Henson's monumental mirrors at the Great Exhibition in London, within the Crystal Palace, designed by Joseph Paxton and filled with "raw materials, machinery, manufacturers and fine arts" from across the globe.[2] One can imagine Henson had much to say to the Queen, but she did not speak directly to him, choosing instead to ask her guide if this man standing before her was "indeed a fugitive slave?"[3] She'd heard of him. *The Life of Josiah Henson, Formerly a Slave, Now an Inhabitant of Canada, as Narrated by Himself* appeared in 1849.[4]

I can imagine Victoria contemplating her reflection in his large mirror. Standing near Henson, who resides "freely" in one of her colonies, is she filled with pride at leading a nation that abolished chattel slavery, or does her reflection confront her with the hard truths of empire and colonial exploitation? If only Henson could have fixed her image in the glass, captured the thoughts, even, of this physical embodiment of an expanding global power that was, like the dark wood of the mirror's frame, allelopathic: it suppressed the growth of what attempted to live with it.

More than half of the material on display in the Crystal Palace was representative of Queen Victoria's vast empire. Many saw the Great Exhibition as marking a new age of peace and global culture that would break down class and racial barriers. The former American colonies were harshly criticized for the expansion of their *peculiar institution* and the recent implementation of the Fugitive Slave Act (1850), which legally obligated free states to return into bondage Blacks seeking freedom. Even Henson was vulnerable in Canada. The perspective of many abolitionists was clearly articulated in the Boston press:

My Dear Sir,

An interesting anti-slavery demonstration took place at the Great Exhibition on Saturday last. . . . The same idea appears to have arisen simultaneously in the minds of [several] abolitionists — the propriety of exhibiting...some specimens not merely of hams, locks, revolvers and firearms, but of the more peculiar staple produce of America —Slavery.[5]

The arrogance of presenting Hiram Powers's sculpture *The Greek Slave* (1843) at the heart of the United States' section of the exhibition was taken by many as an insult and provocation. A nude female, demurely posed, her hands strategically positioned and shackled in delicate chains, was presented on a rotating pedestal backed by a red velvet curtain that gave the pure white marble a pink hue. This slave "blushed" (according to William Wells Brown).[6] John Tenniel offered a succinct visual damning of "the Americans." His cartoon *The Virginian Slave, Intended as a Companion to Power's [sic] "Greek Slave"* depicts a Black woman similarly posed at auction. A decade later, Tenniel's concept would be made real

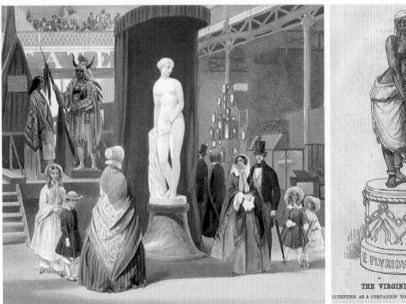 

Left: Illustration showing the sculpture *The Greek Slave*, 1843, by Hiram Powers, on display at the Great Exhibition of the Works of Industry of All Nations, London, in 1851
Right: Cartoon by John Tenniel, *The Virginian Slave (Intended as a Companion to Power's "Greek Slave")*, published in *Punch, or the London Charivari* 20 (January–June 1851): 236

by the artist John Bell, whose bronze *The American Slave — Scene on the Shore of the Atlantic* (1862), countered Powers's marble figure, but also a similar sculpture by Erastus Dow Palmer titled *The White Captive* (1857–58; carved 1858–59).

It is not known the degree to which Henson engaged with the many abolitionists and formerly enslaved people present in London, but there was certainly a critical mass moving throughout the city in the summer of 1851. "It was on the first of August, 1851," African American scholar and abolitionist William Wells Brown declared in his 1852 memoir, "that a number of men, fugitives from that boasted land of freedom, assembled at the Hall of Commerce in the City of London, for the purpose of laying their wrongs before the British nation, and at the same time, to give thanks to the God of Freedom for the liberation of their West India brethren."[7] Brown used his opening address to praise the British Crown and condemn the American states, referring to England as "a noble example to America." He declared that "Americans boasted of their superior knowledge, but they needed not to boast of their superior guilt."[8] He then praised "a band of fearless men and women in the city of Boston, whose labours for the slave had resulted in good beyond calculation."[9]

Benjamin Drew has long been considered one of Boston's "fearless." He came to Canada West from Boston in 1855 to collect the stories of "refugees" — fugitive slaves and free Blacks who had settled throughout what is now southwestern Ontario, in St. Catharines, Toronto, Hamilton, Galt, the Queen's Bush settlement, Chatham, the Elgin settlement, the Dawn settlement, Windsor, and Sandwich. He interviewed Harriet Tubman (often referred to as "the General") at St. Catharines[10] and visited the Dawn settlement. The publisher John P. Jewett would draw on the unexpected wealth gained from publishing *Uncle Tom's Cabin* (1852), the monumental bestseller by Harriet Beecher Stowe, to publish Drew's *A North-Side View of Slavery. The Refugee* (1856). Stowe claimed her novel, which lined the pockets of Jewett, was inspired by Henson's 1849 memoir. The publisher would republish Henson's memoir and market it by explicitly linking Uncle Tom to Henson, despite the character being a gross misrepresentation of the man.

Drew's goal was to produce a powerful counter-narrative to a publication by fellow Bostonian Nehemiah Adams, *A South-side View of Slavery; or, Three Months at the South in 1854,* and others defending the institution of slavery who were bolstered by the Fugitive Slave Act.[11] Even in Canada fugitive slaves were at risk of being captured or kidnapped and returned to slavery. If so, they were often resold

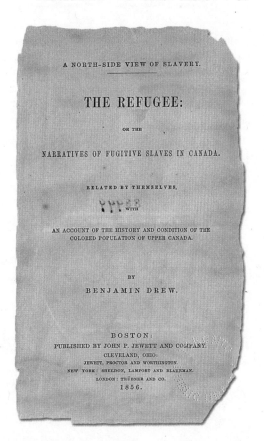

Title page of Benjamin Drew's book, photographed by the author

as plantation slavery spread toward the Pacific and the United States continued on its path of belief in manifest destiny in the lead-up to the Civil War. Freemen were at risk of being taken — or sold by their white neighbours — as famously documented by Solomon Northup in *Twelve Years a Slave* (1853).[12] Living on the "north side" close to a fluid border was still risky, as those who hunted fugitives were not averse to making the crossing, aided by whites in Canada. Drew's stories of Black people who had fled north to Canada offer a stark contrast to any claims that the enslaved were better off as chattel. But the compelling anomaly in this collection of over one hundred narratives is the story of Sophia Burthen (Pooley), by then an elderly woman, whose life bridges the American Revolution and the abolition of slavery, and who lived for nearly three decades enslaved, *in Canada*.

Drew was not publishing carefully edited academic history. He was anxious to get these narratives out into the world. There are discrepancies and factual problems in his book; dates and places don't add up, leading to impossible scenarios in Sophia's story. The "errors" that emerge speak of an elderly woman's memory damaged by a lifetime of trauma, as well as the rushed compilation of oral histories. *I know not how far nor how long — it was dark there all the time*, Sophia says. It's as if she were describing a lifetime of trauma and loss — not just the journey upriver then overland away from her parents, but an epic journey of even more family members vanishing into darkness, becoming shadows.

Dear Sophia,

I am imagining myself gazing into one of Henson's plate-glass mirrors, the silver nitrate coating that backs it is deteriorating, distorting my image, making my skin appear scarred and my limbs to hang torqued and deformed. I hover in an atmosphere that is hazy, pitted, and pockmarked, grey, not bright. It's as if the surface is now absorbing, not reflecting, me. Yet the dark wood frame remains solid and dignified, well crafted, maintaining the deep brown of black walnut timber from which it has been shaped.

Juglans nigra is a deciduous tree of the walnut family Juglandaceae native to eastern North America. It is a riparian species (thrives near water) and grows from the Florida-Georgia border, north to Southern Ontario, west to the Dakotas, and south to Texas. Draw these lines out on a map and you'll see territory that overlays the sprawling terrain of chattel slavery at its peak, when cotton was king in the United States. Over these disputed territories, the ancestral lands of Indigenous peoples, black walnut lines the banks of deep pooling waters, frames the flow of rivers and creeks. The water's surface reflects the sky, becoming a shifting film of shadows and memories. Can the film be rewound? If I step into the current, will the ripples disrupt time?

Black walnut contains the compound Juglone that seeps into the ground and stunts the growth of and eventually kills other plants. It has evolved to limit what can thrive around it on land it has claimed. In its shadow grass often dies, and a silhouette of toxic soil spreads out, lined by exposed roots and rotting mast. The grooved nuts, cracked open, seem like tiny skulls emptied of brains. What were they thinking?

I have crafted a frame from black walnut harvested at Dundas at the outlet, to frame a tiny decaying mirror. The wood stains my hands; once you touch it, you are marked by it. Juglone bleeds into my advancing vitiligo, the condition patching my skin with an intense whiteness ("Not so much a colour but an absence of colour," says Ishmael) that bleaches out all pigmentation, creeping up my forearms. In the sun, my skin burns easily, turns pink and blushes. You can produce fabric and hair dyes from *Juglans nigra* and inks for printing and writing. What stories can be written in allelopathic inks, inks that reveal and also obscure?

[...] and all these years I have looked through your limbs
to the river below and the roofs and the night
and you were the way I saw the world[13]
—from W.S. Merwin, "Elegy for a Walnut Tree" (2014)

CHAPTER 4
"A GOODLY PORTION OF THE LIFE
OF BENJAMIN DREW" (AND MINE)

His pen was always acutely pointed, and age and use did nothing to dull it.
—from his obituary, titled "A Goodly Portion of the Life of
Benjamin Drew" (1903)[1]

Dear Sophia,

I'm assuming that Benjamin Drew did not tell you very
much about himself—where he was from, his family roots,
or his work. He worked in the technical side of the newspaper
trade (printing and copy-editing) and as a writer and political
satirist. He was also an educator and school administrator.
His book that includes your interview was his first. He would
publish only two others, *Pens and Types* (1872) and *Burial
Hill, Plymouth, Massachusetts* (1894).[2] Drew was a man deeply
immersed in text, but his first and last books are really acts of
curation: the collecting, editing, and organizing of material
within a contained narrative structure. This is just one of my
connections to him. I want to tell you a little about myself.

My work has largely been curation, my writing shaped by
a curator's logic and privilege (the ability to travel widely and
gain access to valuable material culture and rare documents,
to have a platform to speak and add to the public record). It
was through curating that I first encountered Drew's book a
number of years ago, but it took me a while to recognize the
significance of your story within it. My path to curating was

accidental, but my impulse to search for erased and obscured
narratives, individuals, and communities is deeply personal.
It emerges out of a sense of loss and absence, a constant
feeling that there is always something missing, that there are
stories not being told and connections being severed. I see
this impulse to search for such narratives as a response to
those, including to my own self, holding power and privilege.
Encounters with power and privilege exacerbate my mental
illness, which I now recognize first appearing when I was quite
young. Professionally, they inform my curatorial work, but
these things are not separate. By telling you about Drew, I'm
also telling you much about myself.

The modern usage of *curator* evolves from the Latin: *cura* meant to *care*, and
curators were the *caretaker*s who supervised aspects of Roman territories. Curating
was and is essential to empires. Within the church, as "a priest of the lowest rank,
especially in the Church of England, whose job is to help the vicar,"[3] the curate has
responsibilities in the care and healing of parishioners' souls. A parish curate also
cares for written records, relics, and church property. Over time, this aspect of the
role of the *curate* became the main role of the *curator*. Curators were responsible
for organizing private collections of the wealthy, and then shifted to have this role
for public museums (which have never distanced themselves from the wealth and
power of individuals or the state, whose collections they are founded upon).

For decades now, curating has incorporated the creative act of articulating
material and intellectual holdings, often framed by a distinct world view of dominance. Many curators want people to believe their work is independent and objective,
embodying theoretical and academic rigour, and that they possess special knowledge and insight. What they do, however, is highly subjective: an act of controlling
knowledge through what is and what was collected and held in an institution, what
is selected to be presented to the public, and what is determined valuable enough
to be spoken of. It sets the limits of knowledge sharing. Collections develop out of
their own histories, with previous decisions continuing to be enhanced. Too often,
they remain watched over by elite wealth and power reflected in governing boards,
who in turn hire an institution's directors. An essential skill of many curators is
the ability to obfuscate through impenetrable, specialized language — or stubborn

Portraits of Benjamin Drew (1812–1903).
Left: Age 32–35, in Boston, Massachusetts, ca. 1845,
daguerreotype, unknown photographer, private collection
Centre: Age 46, in Plymouth, Massachusetts, 1858, *carte de visite*,
W.S. Robbins & Co. (Plymouth), collection of the Minnesota Historical Society
Right: Age 88, in Plymouth, Massachusetts, 1900, unknown photographer,
collection of Ohio State Library, Wilbur H. Siebert Collection

silence—hiding behind their supposed eye for genius, their informed taste, and their allegiance to their governing boards (and the authority bestowed on themselves by these "vicars"). In this way, curators seem to present the same authority as priests, and have the magic and wisdom of wizards or druids.

As mentioned earlier, *curator* is strongly associated with *caretaker*: "Caretaker (noun): one that gives physical or emotional care and support; one that takes care of the house or land of an owner who may be absent; one temporarily fulfilling the function of office. Synonyms: custodian, guardian, janitor, keeper, warden, watchman."[4] These dictionary definitions are relevant and revealing, as they point to profound contradictions. Rather than providing care and support, museum curators are too often agents of trauma who perpetuate ideologies of exclusion and erasure. Instead of working for the purported "owner who may be absent"—the public—as they are meant to, curators usually work for the wealthy: political and social elites who dominate and benefit from institutional agendas. It is often forgotten that the curator is "one temporarily fulfilling the function of office"; curators tend to hold (and defend) their position as gatekeepers for far too long.

Their role doesn't bring to mind a person working "in the service of" (as implied by the roles of *custodian*, *guardian*, or *janitor*, for example) but rather a person working to restrict and control (like a *keeper*, *warden*, or *watchman*). These latter characteristics have been dominant in the role of curator in my experiences, and they have increased exponentially in the larger and more prominent institutions I've worked in. Like the colonial empires that produced them, these institutions are concerned with growth, expansion, accumulation, and control. This is their fundamental wiring. I believe they are based on faith in untenable ideologies.

Before I was a curator, I was actually a caretaker, a substitute school janitor responsible for cleaning and maintaining older schools throughout the north and east ends of the city of Hamilton in the early 1980s. It was in this role that I first became aware of erasures within institutions, not just in the daily maintenance work but also in the books being discarded from libraries and the items removed from view and soon forgotten in a school's basement or attic (class records, framed documents, and pictures). Many of the discarded books were those published just after the Second World War, before Canada's official policy of multiculturalism was implemented and expounded in the boxes of new textbooks I delivered to the library and classrooms. I was based out of Memorial School, built at the end of the First World War, and where my father attended in the 1930s. The names of all the First World War battles that Canadians fought are painted on the walls, along with these words: "That our youth will ever remember the valiant men of Hamilton who died in the Great War, this school is a memorial." According to a plaque erected in 2007 on the lawn of the school, at the official opening in 1925, General Sir Arthur Currie said the school was "a torch that will burn up ignorance!"

One day, I came across two large picture frames leaning against a damp basement wall. I brought them into the light and wiped the dust from the glass. They were plaques, one for each world war listing the names of the students from the neighbourhood who'd been killed or were missing in action. The background was printed with a sword evoking a Christian cross, a Union Jack, a maple leaf, and thin black horizontal lines where the names of those who "sacrificed" themselves for the great cause of empire and country were to be written. The names were handwritten, like Sophia's in the census of 1851. The decision to remove those plaques from view was an act of curation.

Both my grandfathers fought in the First World War. My paternal one, Thomas Hunter, died before I was born; my mother's father, Herbert (Bert) Allen, died when I was ten. Bert never spoke about the war (few survivors of the Great War did). Just before he died, he burned a box containing his personal photographs, including pictures of the family he'd left behind in Birmingham, England, and his friends from the war. Those hidden plaques brought that box of photographs to mind. I rehung the plaques in the school's lobby, and I have come to understand this as my first act of curation—this intervention addressing absence, done without permission, within an institution built to shape memory and to carry the baggage and waste of empire. In the void left by my grandfather's silence and his burnt photographs, I always believed something meaningful remained that could be revealed if I found the right tools or if I regularly returned to the right sites, felt the ground, looked for signs, waited. I also believed that if I approached things the "wrong" way, I would find what lay hidden. Whichever way, I felt the importance of my deliberate choice and of discerning what and when the "right" tool or the "wrong" approach would best be used. I learned that from my father's mother, Marion Crawford Hunter.

When I was young, Marion would take me to the old Art Gallery of Hamilton. She would encourage me to just look at whatever interested me and to imagine stories. The bronzes *Panthère saisissant un cerf* (*Panther Seizing a Stag*, 1847) and *Lion au serpent* (*Lion and Serpent*, 1835), by French sculptor Antoine-Louis Barye haunted me, and I was fascinated by *View of Hamilton* (1862) by local painter Robert Reginald Whale. Whale's view was from a mystery location atop the Niagara Escarpment above Dundas. It would inspire my lifelong obsession with the traces of landscapes buried beneath heavy industry. My first job as a curator was at the Art Gallery of Hamilton; my first exhibition included these works by Barye and Whale.

Marion had grown up in Barrowfield, a very poor area in the east end of Glasgow, Scotland. Her primary school was a brick hulk on the bank of the River Clyde, surrounded by cotton and dyeing mills. When not in school or working, in a biscuit factory, she would visit Glasgow Green where the People's Palace and Winter Gardens stand. The People's Palace was one of the first "local history" museums in the British Empire: "A palace of pleasure and imagination around which the people may place their affections and which may give them a home on which their memory may rest," declared Lord Archibald Philip Primrose, 5th Earl of Rosebery at the official opening in 1898.[5] While I wouldn't have expressed it in such language, his description is how I saw museums as I wandered with my grandmother. We also went for walks in local parks, which included the Hamilton Cemetery. The agenda there remained the same: wander, look (in the cemetery, at the headstones), and imagine buried lives. One of my favourite grave markers is still a flat grey slab with "Lost At Sea" etched in the stone.

Drew's grave marker in the Oak Grove Cemetery, Plymouth, Massachusetts, is a simple grey block with just his name and life dates: November 26, 1812, to July 19, 1903. It offers very little to stir the imagination, no iconography or inspirational quote, no recognition of accomplishments. *Drew* is a common surname throughout Britain. It can mean *descendant of the Druid* (in Ireland), or *manly* (to the Scots, from Greek).[6] It is the current preferred short form of *Andrew*. So along with the profession of curator and writer, I share a name with Drew. He also spent some of his career in public schools, more time than I did, but he was a superintendent and a teacher; I was a caretaker.

> Dear Sophia
>
> I have found an obituary for Drew, published in the *Old Colony Memorial* of Plymouth, Massachusetts, the same newspaper where he once apprenticed. Here is what stands out for me: he was a descendant of Plymouth settlers who arrived in 1660 and had an ancestor who was knighted by Queen Elizabeth I in 1589. He wrote political satire for *The Carpet-Bag* (a Boston periodical) under the *nom de plume* Ensign Stebbings. He taught public school in Boston for thirty-five years and (after meeting you just before the American Civil War) he moved to Saint Paul, Minnesota, continuing to work in education. He took a job in Washington, DC, that led to him publishing *Pens and Types*. After retiring, he travelled to China (around 1882, when "he passed his seventieth birthday anniversary") for an extended stay with his son Edward Bangs Drew, "a mandarin in the Imperial Chinese Customs service." He remembered "boys running through the streets shouting, 'Peace, Peace,'" at the end of the War of 1812. Like me, he spent time in cemeteries, cataloguing and writing about the interred. The work that he is most remembered for is mistitled in his obituary as *The North Side of Slavery*, and beyond the

vague phrase, "written in a crisis of the country," we are offered
nothing more about Drew's involvement with abolitionist work
in Boston or Plymouth.

The arrival of English Puritan settlers at Plymouth from aboard the *Mayflower*
is a most favoured creation story for the United States of America. Having departed
from the River Thames, the *Mayflower* headed west through the English Channel,
passing high chalk cliffs, which changed to spectacular layers of rock—would
eventually come to be known as the Jurassic Coast, its fossil-packed geology
dramatically disturbing understandings of the age of the earth, the evolution of
life on the planet, and faith in an all-seeing God. The ship passed the mouth of the
River Exe, flowing down from Broadclyst, ancestral home to the Drews/Drewes.
"One-fifth of early New England Puritans were indentured servants," Nell Irvin
Painter states in *The History of White People* (2010), "including eight who died while
crossing on the *Mayflower*."[7]

The Puritans, or Pilgrims, brought a severe form of Christianity (distinctly
independent and anti-papist) and advocated for piety in personal and commercial
affairs. Their initial relations with the local Indigenous people in Massachusetts
remain debated. Did the Pilgrims steal food and desecrate sacred sites, as Nathaniel
Philbrick claims in his book *Mayflower: A Story of Courage, Community and War*
(2006), or did they join in friendship for a first Thanksgiving, as often told? Either
way, their diseases decimated Indigenous populations. The decision to install the
ship's cannons above their settlement to defend against attack tells us much about
the nature of the relationship and set a pattern of future engagement. The Puritans'
guns fired cannonballs, measuring over three inches in diameter and weighing
over six pounds, up to a mile.[8] By 1636, there was open warfare with the Pequots,
Indigenous peoples whose lands are now Connecticut.[9] Many Pequots, following
their defeat, were sold into slavery (or traded for enslaved Africans) in the West
Indies. As Douglas Harper points out on his website Slavery in the North:

> Christianity was no barrier to slave-ownership....Puritans regarded
> themselves as God's Elect, and so they had no difficulty with slav-
> ery, which had the sanction of the Law of the God of Israel. The
> Calvinist doctrine of predestination easily supported the Puritans in
> a position that blacks were a people cursed and condemned by God

to serve whites. Cotton Mather told blacks they were the "miserable children of Adam and Noah," for whom slavery had been ordained as a punishment.[10]

By the end of the 1600s, ships sailing out of Massachusetts were working the slave trade with Madagascar, the West Indies, Virginia, and throughout New England.

Drew's ancestor knighted by Queen Elizabeth I was Sir Edward Drewe of the Killerton estate, in Broadclyst, Exeter (Devon), and the Grange estate in Broadhembury (Devon). A Serjeant-at-Law, he was the Member of Parliament representing various seats (Lyme Regis, Exeter, and the City of London), and the Recorder of the City of London (basically a circuit-court criminal-trial judge). The stone effigy on his tomb in St. John's Church, Broadclyst, depicts a bearded man with a receding hairline and prominent nose, a stiff linen ruff encircling his neck. ("Ruffs were highly luxurious garments," states fashion historian Katy Werlin. "Anyone who could afford to wear and maintain a ruff was clearly not doing any manual labor."[11]) Four generations bridge our Drew to the first Massachusetts Drew(e)s. Their genealogy is well documented. Such documentation was an impossibility for Sophia's family. "Genealogical trees do not flourish among slaves,"[12] Frederick Douglass declared, in the same year Sophia was interviewed by Drew.

There is nothing ostentatious about Drew in the *carte de visite* photograph taken in 1858 in Plymouth. He looks "professional" in his dark suit with a precisely knotted cravat bow tie. He is only forty-six and in his final years of teaching in Boston — just three years on from his encounter with Sophia. By today's standards, Drew looks much older than mid-forties. His greying beard and haggard expression, with eyes a little sunken, the lids heavy above a fixed wistful stare, make him appear gaunt.

Drew worked for thirty-five years teaching in Boston before moving to Minnesota around 1860. Three of the schools he taught at were primary schools in the heart of Boston. The Phillips Grammar School, named after Boston's first mayor, John Phillips, father of abolitionist Wendell Phillips, was one of them. A historical description of the school notes that:

> The Phillips Grammar School [originally] educated only white male children.... Black Bostonians fought tirelessly for equal school rights.... In 1847 Benjamin Roberts [a Black resident] attempted to

have his daughter Sarah admitted to the school closest to their home, but his request was denied.... Frustrated, Roberts brought Sarah to the door of the Phillips School, which now educated both males and females, but entrance was denied by Principal Andrew Cotton. Ironically, when Boston schools were finally integrated in 1855, by an act of the Massachusetts legislature, the Phillips School became one of the first integrated schools in Boston.[13]

One would assume, based on *The Refugee*, that Drew was an advocate for the desegregation of Boston schools, and that the passing of the act in the year he travelled to Canada made him optimistic for the future, but in 1859 he relocated to Minnesota, taking on the role of superintendent of schools, Ramsay County and City of Saint Paul, a position he held until 1872. "By 1856," state Stephen and Paul Kendrick in *Sarah's Long Walk* (2004), "black children in St. Paul who sought formal instruction were being discouraged from attending public schools, and anti-Black sentiments appeared in editorials in the city's papers. Finally, in November 1857, the St. Paul Board of Education resolved to formally segregate."[14] Drew would be hired soon after. After the Civil War, Democrats of that time fought hard against equal rights for Black residents, and while state support for Black suffrage was high, it was voted against by a significant majority in Saint Paul. "Without state action," notes William D. Green, "segregation in St. Paul schools would likely have continued for a long time."[15] All the above transpired under Drew's stewardship. His scolding of one of his teachers makes clear that he acted to support the Saint Paul majority: "When Benjamin Drew, hired to head the city's schools, discovered in 1859 that a 'quadroon' boy was attending a white school, he told the teacher that 'she had done wrong to receive him, as [the boy] would not be allowed to remain.'"[16] Saint Paul would honour Drew by naming a new school after him. Built in 1895, "the three-story [*sic*] building was made of cream-colored brick with white stone trim. Pilasters extended the length of the building. A large Palladian window lit the front stairway landing. It had detailed brickwork and window trim."[17] It was torn down in 1974, the same year protests broke out in Boston over desegregation and bussing.

Canada was not immune to systemic racism that led to school segregation. Post-Confederation, Ontario and Nova Scotia maintained segregated schools for Black children. The last one to close in Ontario was the S.S. #11 in Harrow, Essex

County, in 1965, and the last in Nova Scotia, Lincolnville School, in Guysborough, closed in 1984. Historical researcher James Bradburn explains, "The majority of segregated schools (in Ontario) were located in Essex and Kent counties, where Black communities had been established during the Underground Railway era. S.S. #11 grew from the Matthews Settlement which was founded in the 1820s."[18] This is compelling evidence of the prejudice in Canada that led many former fugitive slaves and free Blacks to return to the United States in the wake of the Civil War.

Knowing all of this, Christina Sharpe's concept of being "in the wake" is a potent description of racism and the legacies of slavery: "Racism, the engine that drives the ship of state's national and imperial projects...cuts through all of our lives inside and outside the nation, in the wake of its purposeful flow."[19] While the ship of state carries on generating turbulence, the wake spreads, its waves rippling out to break on shorelines, eroding them, as whiteness remains comfortably on board.

> Dear Sophia,
>   Drew was clearly entrenched in segregationist institutions of the ship of state before and after he published your story. *The North-Side View of Slavery. The Refugee* did not make him one of "the band of fearless men and women in the city of Boston"[20] that William Wells Brown acknowledged in 1851. But let's leave him adrift for now, I want to go to where your journey begins, in that purposeful flow out of the Fishkill Mountains.

CHAPTER 5
LEY LINES: AT FISHKILL

*Bondage in Dutchess County could be brutal and violent, and household
slavery in the countryside could be extraordinarily oppressive.... Scars and
disabilities attested not only to the harsh reality of life and labor in the
eighteenth-century Hudson Valley but also to the violence of an institution
that grew more brutal over time.*
— Michael E. Groth, *Slavery and Freedom in the Mid-Hudson
Valley*[1]

Kill and *hook*. The terms sound brutal, as if they are naming acts of violence or
pointing to the finality of the grave. But these terms, which echo across the former
New Netherland, around what is now New York State and along the Hudson River,
are Dutch: *kill* means creek, stream, river, or inlet; a *hook* is a spit or point of land.
Fishkill (originally Vis Kil), Catskill (sometimes Katts Kil), Peekskill, Freshkills,
Kill Van Kull, and Bronx Kill equal Fish Creek, Cat's Creek, Peek's Creek,
Fresh Creeks, Creek of Kull, and Bronx Creek. (*Bronx* comes from Dutchman
Jonas Bronck who settled the area in the 1600s). Sandy Hook, Red Hook, and
Kinderhook combine English and Dutch words (in English these names would
be Sandy Point, Red Point, and Child Point). Acknowledging their roots, these
names still speak to me of violence. They project a bleakness, perhaps because so
often places near the water's edge become sites of industrial filth, and home to
the destitute and working poor. In many places, like Hamilton where I grew up,
such places were buried in landfill in order to build factories and piers, railyards
and roadways along the harbour once defined by numerous inlets and abundant
wildlife. These rivers and streams continue to flow underground, to eventually
resurface to flood streets and basements and to collapse roadways. These *kills*
destabilize the foundations of the present. It is hard to permanently bury the past.

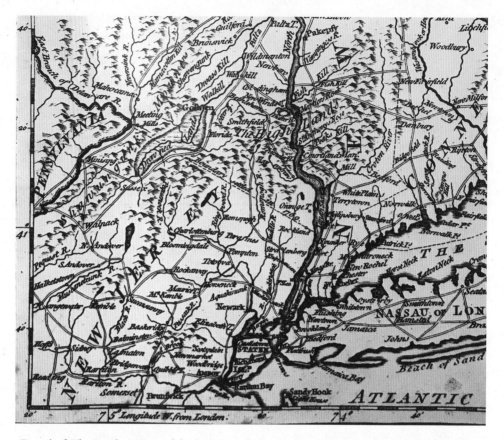

Detail of *The Southern Part of the Province of New York: with Part of the adjoining Colonies, By Thomas Kitchin and Sons, Hydrographer for His Majesty,* printed for R. Baldwin at the Rose, Pater Noster Row, London, 1778, collection of Albany Institute of History and Art

The village of Fishkill in Dutchess County, New York, was defined by land, not water. It grew like adjacent communities because of the rich soils for farming in valleys surrounded by some of the oldest mountains on earth. It has views of the Hudson Highlands and to the distant Catskill Mountains across a wide Hudson River, which Sophia called *North River,* just *twelve miles* away. The highlands were named for Henry Hudson, another English mariner on a colonial quest. Fishkill Creek (having forgotten the meaning of *kill,* the English unwittingly repeat the word) empties into the Hudson south of Dennings Point. From the landing at Beacon just north of there, boats would ship and receive chattel, heading up, down, and across the water—over to Kingston, south to New York City, and north to Albany (once called Fort Orange). In its meanderings from east to west, flowing out of the Fishkill Mountains, Fishkill Creek carries the waters of the Sweezy, Christine, McKinney, and Furnace Ponds; Frog Hollow Brook, and Sylvan Lake; as well as Sprout, Wiccopee, and Clove Creeks, among other smaller rivulets and streams.

Fishkill is in the heart of Dutchess County, just south of Poughkeepsie. Roughly an hour north of Manhattan by today's roads, its current population is just over 2,100. It occupies the lands of the Wappinger people who were largely driven from their lands, first by Dutch forces allied with the Haudenosaunee/Kanyen'kehà:ka (Mohawk) and later by a flood of British settlers. The last Wappinger sachem, Daniel Nimham (or Ninham), travelled to England in 1766 to plead for the return of their traditional lands. The royal Lords of Trade heard his plea and declared that "the conduct of the lieutenant-governor and the council [of New York] ... does carry with it the colour of great prejudice and partiality, and of an intention to intimidate these Indians."[2] Yet the Lords of Trade did nothing. A later decision by the New York provincial governor Sir Henry Moore decided "that returning the land to the Indians would set an adverse precedent."[3] By the end of the eighteenth century, the Wappinger people were dispersed, absorbed into other nations, including their old enemies the Haudenosaunee/Kanyen'kehà:ka (Mohawk).

Were Sophia's parents born at Fishkill, or brought there via what she called *North River*? Were they even born in New York? Slaveholders in the Mid-Hudson Valley often bought in the markets at New York City, or at Albany or Poughkeepsie, where many of the newly arrived people from the Caribbean and West Africa were auctioned. "Colonial New York contained the North's largest enslaved population; it grew by 70 percent between 1750 and 1770," Margaret Washington explains in *Sojourner Truth's America* (2011). "By then, merchants imported captives directly from Africa."[4] In Dutchess County, slaves were constantly being sold, or hired out for extended periods by one neighbour to another or passed on within a family from generation to generation. Sophia's ancestors may have been in the area for decades. She says she was seven when her abductors *came into the garden*. How much could she have known of her ancestry? How well did she know her parents? At least she told us their names. When she recalls, *My sister and I were playing among the currant bushes*, where were Dinah and Oliver at that moment that preceded the tragedy of their children being kidnapped? No doubt they were preoccupied labouring for their masters. I can only imagine the loss of their daughters to have been devastating.

The details suggest that the sale of the girls needed to be hidden, that there was another further shady layer on top of the reprehensible base act of selling human beings. Why have I come to this conclusion? Because slavery was ubiquitous in Dutchess County; the regular sale of enslaved individuals was a constant practice in a community where the white practice of owning one to three Black people was the norm, even among those of limited means. It is a myth that only rich people owned slaves. With the exception of elite, wealthy families who enslaved many, most only "required" (or could afford) a few, which meant enslaved families were regularly broken up. As high as 75 percent of enslaved parents, spouses, and children lived separated and with minimal contact. "Throughout the colonial period," Michael E. Groth reminds us, "the slave family enjoyed no legal protection; not until 1809 did state law recognize slave families. The threat of sale was particularly salient in the Hudson Valley."[5] Breaking up families generated revenue for owners, prefiguring the all too common practice of destroying families in selling the enslaved from northern states to southern plantations, which emerged as the nineteenth century progressed. The demand for slave labour from northern states had dramatically increased following the passing of the Act Prohibiting Importation of Slaves in 1807 and the adoption of Eli Whitney's cotton gin (or cotton engine, which mechanized the separation of cotton fibre and seed) on southern plantations.[6]

One of the most misguided ideas about slavery is that, for those held in bondage where numbers were relatively low (that is, in the northern states/colonies and in what became Canada) the experience of enslavement was somehow more humane. A related concept is that "domestic slaves" who worked in the home were "privileged." Scholar Christy Clark-Pujara destroys that myth: "Domestic labour *is* labour — not *status* — labouring in the home was *essential* to survival."[7] Even those who acknowledged the harshness of conditions, often suggested that bonds were formed in the close-knit settings where masters and the enslaved lived under the same roof. Helen Wilkinson Reynolds, author of *Dutch Houses in the Hudson Valley Before 1776* (1929), states that the enslaved, "were quartered in the cellars and attics of the master's dwellings or in out-buildings nearby and received practically no consideration in connection with provision for light and air," only to undermine any sense of empathy: "But the personal relations between the two races were kindly and, allowing for an *occasional* owner of irascible disposition and an occasional black of *incorrigible* tendencies, good will prevailed and often deep attachments [emphasis added]."[8] Evidence shows the opposite. Such bonding was extremely rare and "occasional"; the loyalty and deference to masters arose mainly in what Margaret Washington described as a "form of defence."[9] Such defences thinned when confronted by the brutality of slavery in a region that remained pro-slavery beyond the Revolution and discouraged manumission well into the nineteenth century. Sojourner Truth's heavily scarred back gave her cause to hate white slaveholders in the Hudson Valley. Drew would witness Sophia's numerous scars and "cicatrices of wounds,"[10] as he confirms in a note in her interview, and one can imagine others he would not have seen or recognized, marks that were both physical and psychological.

Here are some other hard numbers from government records.[11] In the second half of the eighteenth century the number of Black people in Dutchess County was the highest in the whole colony of New York (growing by nearly 300 percent) reaching a population of 2,300 (of which 1,856 were enslaved). The first *Federal Census of the United States*, in 1790, reveals that 75 percent of enslaved people lived in Clinton, Fishkill, Poughkeepsie, and Rhinebeck. Fishkill was home to almost one-third of all the known enslaved in Dutchess County: 10 percent of residents of Fishkill were enslaved, and 20 percent of Fishkill households held enslaved people.[12] There was clearly a well-established slave trade in the Fishkill area. Had they not been stolen, the Burthen sisters would not need to be silenced, taken discreetly to the landing, hidden below deck, and snuck upriver for a long journey west through dangerous and hostile territory. To then be sold to an infamous ally of the British living at Niagara, at the peak of Revolutionary tensions and when Fishkill was at the heart of "Patriot country," sounds deeply suspicious. It is not Sophia's recollections I find suspicious; it is the actions of her captors.

> Dear Sophia,
>   There is more unpacking to do to clarify this moment in your life and to attempt to settle the foundations of your story. Too many things just don't align for this to have happened *long before the American Revolution* as Drew claims you stated. Perhaps he misunderstood and blurred events of the War of Independence (1775–83) and the War of 1812 (1812–15), the latter war being the continuation of the unfinished former

conflict, pitting the same old adversaries against each other to
settle all that was left unresolved during your childhood. On
top of your enslavement, you are trapped in these uncertainties,
these decades of conflict and intrigue, when nothing was
stable or predictable, which makes understanding Drew's
transcription of your truths complicated today.

ᔕ

I'm with my eldest child, twenty-two-year-old Max, driving south from Albany.
We are following Highway 9 and its old rolling tributaries that skirt closer to the
edge of the Hudson River, punctuated by numerous historic plaques, made of cast
iron and painted the signature blue and golden yellow of New York State, that
speak of George Washington's movements and about the homes of Patriots from
the era of the Revolution. At Poughkeepsie, we veer east, the road ascending as we
progress away from the river, through Wappinger Falls and finally to Fishkill. At
the crossroads of highways 9 and 52, the First Dutch Reformed Church (founded
in 1716 and built in 1736) still dominates. It is surrounded by weathered gravestones
and fronted by the DuBois House (named for the founder of the church, who
actually never lived here).

From sunny skies along the river, we have emerged into cold wind, grey clouds,
and drizzle. The conditions are befitting the highlands. In the churchyard we scan
the faint inscriptions and admire the cartoonish renderings of angels and death
skulls that top the headstones. We walk over to the Trinity Episcopal Church
(founded in 1756 and built over the winter of 1768–69). According to the plaque
above the entrance it "was erected about 1769 — Occupied by the Provincial
Convention . . . [in] 1776 — Used for a military hospital by the army of Gen
Washington until disbanded . . . [in] 1783." It was in Fishkill that the postmaster
Samuel Loudon printed the first New York State Constitution that, for all the talk
of freedom among the Patriots, maintained the British model of slavery. "Resistance
to emancipation," Groth states in his book, "was nowhere more pronounced than
in the Hudson Valley."[13]

We follow Old Main Street down to Sarah Taylor Park, a wide expanse of
mowed lawn featuring a sports field and fenced-in playground, and named for
the town's former mayor. Taylor, according to a 1970 *New York Times* article,

was a self-described "hippie" from New York City who'd once run a tearoom in Greenwich Village. Her election platform emphasized keeping the village "clean and tidy" and maintaining a "grass roots American aura."[14] Fishkill Creek defines the southern edge of the park. We observe it flowing fast with spring runoff around subtle bends and under the bridge that carries Highway 9 to Interstate 84, which heads west to the southward turn to New Jersey and east to Connecticut. We reach the edge of the creek; the drizzle has turned to rain. A sign states "No Swimming"—a warning that seems unnecessary considering the shallowness of the uneven and rocky bed before us.

"The river is everywhere at the same time," Siddhartha declares in Herman Hesse's eponymous novel, "the present only exists for it, not the shadow of the past nor the shadow of the future."[15] This may be true for the flow of water, but this specific artery we see is given form by its weighted rocky bed and more rigid banks that shape it *here*, where the underlying geology consists of sedimentary rock. The Paleozoic era in its Cambrian and Ordovician periods reveals itself in these rocks from roughly 450 million to 540 million years ago. And there are older rocks here too, formed more than a billion years back in the earliest, Precambrian, geological era.

> Dear Sophia,
>   I want us to return to this later, these geological details that I am certain would have baffled and been found blasphemous by your Christian parishioner–masters. Those people looked for unquestionable truths in their bibles, and they found justification for your enslavement in their scripture. I want to come back to this continual shaping of landscape, like that of the water shaping and revealing rocks over millennia. I want us to divine the ley lines, held in deep time, in the ground beneath our feet. This creek is more than just the water that is slowly shaping the adjacent ground. It is a site of history and events, of lives lived and endured and darkened by shadows of the past and future.

Coming out of the woods we slowly circle the playground. A police cruiser idles just beyond the adjacent picnic pavilion. The dome of a climbing structure echoes the profile of a distant mountain from where the cold wind and persistent rain descend. A chain-link fence encloses the playground, limiting the children's freedom of movement, a thin contemporary rampart against outside threats. *My sister and I were playing among the currant bushes . . .* [they] *tied their handkerchiefs over our mouths.* As we reach the park entrance, Max stops to photograph a sign that boldly declares: "KEEP AMERICA AMERICAN. REPORT ANY AND ALL ILLEGAL ALIENS. THEY ARE *CRIMINALS*." It is the work of the white supremacist Patriot Front promoting their version of keeping things "clean and tidy" and maintaining "a grassroots American aura." And how are these "aliens" to be identified? I'm assuming by the colour of their skin.

"People of colour in the countryside could not escape into the anonymity of the city to become 'unrecognized' and 'unrecognizable' among other black, brown and yellow faces," Groth states.[16] He adds that "ultimately, the experience of slavery in the North, the ordeal of northern emancipation, and the emergence of white supremacy in the nominally Free States are as vital to understanding racial formation in the United States before the Civil War as the expansion of slavery across the Lower South."[17] How much has truly changed? These experiences, too long hidden beneath the surface of history, continue to inform the present. They flow where currents of white supremacy and racial hierarchies persist with virulence, in historic regions where, as historian Ira Berlin described throughout *Many Thousands Gone* (1998), a "society with slaves became slave societies."[18] Chattel slavery became the bedrock of economic growth, currents of the slave trade became a currency, here.

Enslaved people "were present in every facet of the economy," scholar Christy Clark-Pujara has made clear.[19] "Slavery enabled the take-off of capitalism. . . . The landowner can shift their labour to other things if slaves worked the land,"[20] scholar Joanne Melish added. Imagine the benefit to the tradesperson who invested in just one slave. Imagine, Clark-Pujara asked, what it meant to "have somebody who you don't have to pay wages to who is not going to become a competition for you" and who will become "better and better at what they do every year."[21] Slavery touched everyone—anyone not enslaved benefited from the system. Owners profited not only from the coerced physical labour of the enslaved but also by stealing their deep skills and profound knowledge.

From The Commons at Fishkill gated housing complex (which is actually private and *not* part of "the commons"), we follow Sophia's path of abduction out of Fishkill and into the town of Beacon, via Beekman Street, named for Gerard W.

Beekman who, "In October 1778," writes Groth, "purchased an African coachman for 200 pounds and in 1779, acquired an African 'cuper' (cooper), who could also 'shave and dress haire,' for 1000 pounds."[22] We come to the landing where a ferry still crosses to Newburgh on the western shore of the Hudson. During the second half of the eighteenth century, an enslaved man named Quam captained a ferry service belonging to his owners, Martin Wilts and Son, here. "He conducted the service between towns on the Hudson by means of a rowboat and a piraqua, a two-masted vessel without a jib," according to A.J. Williams-Myers, who refers to Quam's duty as "prestigious" work.[23] Was Quam present when Sophia and her sister were escorted to the vessel's berth with, as Sophia recounts, *handkerchiefs over our mouths*? Did he witness them being loaded below deck?

They were playing by the currant bushes when they were taken into new currents. We are so lucky that Sophia named them, these *white men*, the *sons-in-law*: Daniel Outwaters and Simon Knox. Now we can step into the current that is flowing south from Albany, past the landing at the outlet of Fishkill Creek, and on to New York City.

> Dear Sophia,
>   It is curious to me whom you name, but more so whom you don't. Certainly, the omission of your sister's name leaves a potent absence. Not naming your family's "master," however, is unfortunate as this name is foundational to reconstructing the web of your life. Was it you who left that family unnamed, or was it Drew — or whoever transcribed and edited his book? Your sister's name I can only guess at. Since your name, and your parents' names, have spiritual weight and biblical significance (like Sojourner Truth's birth name, Isabelle, suggests to her biographer roots in Catholicism that Portuguese slavers introduced to the West African homeland of her grandparents),[24] I imagine her name being of similar origin. Reighen Grineage suggests *Sarah* (meaning "princess" or "noblewoman") or *Deborah* (the "prophetess," the "bee"). I want to know this to honour her. But as for the "master" family, I want their names as evidence.

RUN away from the Heirs of Barent Van Cleek, of Poughkeepsie, deceased, on Tuesday the 23d Instant March, a Mulatto colour'd Negroe Man Slave, named Tom, pock-broken, about 5 Feet 10 Inches high, a well-set likely Fellow, plays well on the Fiddle, and can read and write; perhaps he may have a false Pass: Had on when he went away, a red Plush Breeches, a full-trimm'd Coat, a Cloth Jacket, and it's suppos'd several other Clothes: Took with him a bay Horse about 13 Hands and a half high, with a Star in his Forehead, Bridle and Saddle: Whoever takes up said Negroe, and delivers him at Poughkeepsie, or secures him in Goal, and gives Notice thereof to Leonard Van Cleek, or Mynderi Veile, of Dutchess County, shall receive FIVE POUNDS Reward, and all reasonable Charges, paid by LEONARD VAN CLEEK, and MYNDERT VEILE.   m. 30.

A MULATTO NEGRO, NAMED Tom, Run away from Joseph Harris, of Beekman's Precinct, in Dutchess County, being the same Fellow formerly advertised, that then belonged to the Heirs of Barent Van Kleck, deceased, and a Reward offered by Mynder Viele and Leonard Van Kleck, who since sold him to said Harris; he went away on the first Instant, and had on a half worn Beaver Hat, a blue and white Cotton Cap, a greenish Homespun Coat, a blue Cloth Jacket, a white Linen Shirt; he took also with him a Linen Jacket and Breeches, also a red plush Breeches; he is lusty and well built, full of Freckles, talks English and Dutch, can read, write and Cipher, play well on a Violin; Whoever takes up said Negro, and secures him in any Goal, shall receive Five Pounds, York Currency, and all reasonable Charges paid; and if any takes extraordinary Trouble and secures him, an honourable Allowance shall be further made by   Jju 23.   Joseph Harris.

RUN away from Joseph Harris, of Beekman's Precinct, in Dutchess County, on the 3d of September last, a Mulatto Fellow, named Tom, about Five Feet eight Inches high, is thick and well set, can talk good Dutch and English, and can play very well upon the Fiddle,--can read, write and cypher, and has some Freckles. He first listed himself in the Boston Forces, and was seen in Albany about a Fortnight ago with the Forces, so that it is likely he is gone towards Boston, or other Parts of New-England: Whoever takes up and secures the said Servant Fellow, so that his Master may have him again, shall have TEN POUNDS, New-York Currency, Reward, and all reasonable Charges paid by Joseph Harris.
N. B. Whoever secures him, send Notice to Baltus Van Kleck, in the City of New-York; or to the said Joseph Harris.

"Run Away Slave" advertisements for Tom from the
New-York Gazette, Or, the Weekly Post-Boy, March 30,
1755; June 23, 1755; and December 13, 1756,
all on page 3, collection of the New York Public
Library, original newspapers photographed
by the author in 2019

CHAPTER 6
"SO THAT HIS MASTER MIGHT HAVE HIM AGAIN"

The figure of the runaway is tremendously compelling as they embody rebellion in a very particular way. Their resistance restores their identity. ...Effectively, to even consider the possibility to run away despite the suffocating levels of surveillance around Black bodies, one would require an aptness for futurity and imagination to dream oneself out of enslavement. The future, it would seem, is the location of freedom.
— Raven Spiratos, "Defying Systems of Surveillance"[1]

Between the early spring of 1755 and the winter of 1756–57, there were three advertisements placed in the *New-York Gazette, Or, the Weekly Post-Boy* for a man named Tom. Tom had "run away," and his owners—first "the Heirs of Barent Van Cleek, of Poughkeepsie," then "Joseph Harris, of Beekman's Precinct, in Dutchess County"[2]—were anxious for his return. Tom was highly skilled, and he had left with much property. These very detailed ads tell us much about him and reveal much about the interconnected families who were searching for him. These related families were prominent in business (farming, trading, land speculation), the Dutch community, and the church, and they are directly linked to Sophia. Tom may, in fact, have been a relative of hers.

Notices for fugitive slaves from the Hudson Valley were usually placed in the city papers of New York City and Boston. These were common destinations for runaways as it was easier to blend in with the many enslaved and freemen in these densely populated, diverse urban centres. It was also where they could ultimately find passage out of the region. The *New-York Gazette* was published in New York City, the heart of the rapidly growing multicultural settlement that was a major centre of shipping and trade. The paper's masthead was adorned with the city's original seal: a pale-skinned sailor and a dark-skinned Indigenous warrior supporting between them a shield featuring two beavers, a pair of barrels, and the four-bladed "propeller" of a windmill, all topped with a large crown (replaced with an eagle in 1784). The sailor holds a plummet (used for sounding depth); the Indigenous figure holds a bow and has a quiver of arrows slung over the shoulder. "With the freshest Advices, Foreign and Domestick," completes the ornate header.

Most of each issue's four pages were taken up by advertisements: for local goods (produce, livestock, furs, and game from the Hudson Valley, for example); for imports (rum and sugar from the Caribbean, crockery and millinery from Britain, silks and fine china from Asia, spices from the South Pacific); and property available in the region — including enslaved people (considered property or chattel, not persons). Prominent throughout are ads for individuals who had "absented" themselves from their masters' service. Some were indentured servants, a few were apprentices, but most were enslaved, a status often hidden to contemporary readers but obvious during that period in the term *servant* preceded by a racial qualifier (*Negro* or *mulatto*). The actual term *slave* was not always employed. In fact, the term *Negro* alone was enough to identify an enslaved individual, as in a very long advertisement, listing "two lively young Negroes" which was placed by Robert Savage of Middletown Point in April of the same year Tom went missing.[3] A similar posting earlier that year announces: "Three houses and lotts of ground together or separate, in Montgomerie Ward: Also a right in the Patent of Minisink; and Two Negro Boys, and Two Negro Women."[4]

In the months preceding the first advertisement for Tom, there are numerous "to be sold" advertisements mixed in with the "to be found" ones placed.[5] In the ad searching for "A Negro Girl 14 years old, she has had the Small Pox and Meazles, This Country Born," the girl described would have likely been noticeably scarred by smallpox and measles, which was often called out in ads, and "This Country Born" makes it clear she was born in the region, of an enslaved mother.[6] Ads for "A Likely Sturdy Negro Lad about 16 Years of Age, Fit for Either Town or Country" and "A Likely Healthy Negro Wench, Aged about 20" run for several weeks.[7] The phrase "Fit for Either Town or Country" defines the "lad" as already skilled in a number of ways; able to work in the home, in the city or on the farm, he may also have had a trade. The common use of terms like "lad" and "fellow" is jarring. These friendly terms offer another way to obscure the brutality of the relationship between the enslaved and the enslaver.

The following advertisement is typical in content and format, listing precise details of appearance of the person and the items (mainly clothing) they absconded with — property that was also of high value to the advertisers that often impacted the amount of the reward. However, we can see in the following that the return of "property" includes the person sought after:

> Absented from Master's service, on the first instant January, at night, a High Dutch German Woman named Ann Janse, aged 36 Years, of tall stature, very well set Otherwise, has a Full Face, and is a Fair Complexion. Has on when She Went Away, Four Striped Petticoats, and a [illegible], short Callico Gown, Check Apron, Handkerchief and Linnen Cap, has no Bonnet with her. Master may have her again, shall have Twenty Shillings Reward and all Reasonable Charges, Paid by Peter Waldron.
> N.B. If She comes back, Her Offence will be Overlook'd.[8]

That Janse's indiscretion would be "Overlook'd" by Waldron was a generous gesture sometimes offered to indentured white servants, but rarely to enslaved Black people, who would usually face punishment, confinement, or greater physical restrictions on their movements once captured. Such treatment could be severe, as detailed in the following advertisement from the autumn of 1756:

> Run away the 26th day of this instant [most recent] August, from Isaac Freeman of the township of Woodbridge, in East New-Jersey, a middle-sized thick squat Negro Fellow named Caesar, aged about 22 years: had on when he went away, an old Beaver Hat, an old Wig, a tow-cloth Shirt, and tow-cloth Trousers, a dark coloured homespun woollen Jacket, and an old pair of shoes: when he went away he had a pair of Iron Pot-Hooks round his neck, with a chain fasten'd to it, that reached down to his feet, but may possibly have got it off. Whoever takes up said Negro, and secures him, and gives notice, so that his Master may have him again, shall have Twenty Shillings reward, or if he is brought home to his Master, Forty Shillings reward, and all reasonable charges, paid by Isaac Freeman.[9]

The iron pot-hooks would be "S" shaped, attached to a metal collar around Caesar's neck, the chain tethered to his ankles. Their presence suggests he was a flight risk, and had likely run away previously. We can assume he "got it off" this time, as he likely would not have been able to travel far with these highly visible restrictions. And what of the name *Caesar* (evoking a powerful, independent leader)? Such a sad and insultingly ironic sobriquet for a man held in bondage, yet one that was commonly assigned by slave owners, like *Primus* and *Hercules*, or the generic *Tom*. It would be a mistake to think that these were the names their families had known them by.

Tom first ran away on March 23, 1755, and the following appears every week until April 21:

> Run away from the Heirs of Barent Van Cleek, of Poughkeepsie, deceased, on Tuesday the 23d Instant March, a Mulatto Colour'd Negro Man Slave, named Tom, pock-broken, about 5 feet 10 inches high, a well-set likely Fellow, plays well on the Fiddle, and can read and write; perhaps he may have a false Pass: Had on when he went away, a red plush breeches, a full trimm'd Coat, a cloth Jacket, and it's suppos'd several other clothes: took with him a bay Horse about 13 hands and a half high with a star on his forehead, bridle and saddle: whoever takes up said Negroe, and delivers him at Poughkeepsie, or secures him in a gaol, and gives notice thereof to Leonard Van Cleek, or Myndert Veile, of Dutchess County, shall receive five Pounds Reward, and all reasonable charges paid by LEONARD VAN CLEEK and MYNDERT VEILE. [10]

The above appears consistently paired with the following ad:

> Run Away the 21st inst. from Godfrey Mallbone, Esq., and Capt. Robert Stoddard, Two Mulatto Fellows, in Company with Each Other; One Named Jeremy, the Other Anthony: the First mention'd carried with him, Two Blue Coats, Turn'd up with Red, and a Silver-Laced Hat, with Sundry other Clothes; One of his Hands is Considerably Less than the Other; Supposed to be About 21 Years of Age, and 5 Foot 10 Inches High. The Other had on a Darkish

Bearskin Coat, Light Cloth Jacket + Breeches, and a Blue Jacket with Brass Buttons, a Pair of Red Breeches, and a Castor Hat, with Sundry other Clothes; about 18 Years of Age, Supposed to be About 5 Foot 8 Inches High. Both Speaks Good English. Whoever Shall Take Up Said Runaways, and Bring them to Their Above-Mention'd Masters, Shall have Twenty Pounds Reward for Each, and all Necessary Charges Paid By Godfrey Mallbone, and Robert Stoddard.[11]

Here, the advertisers employ the archaic "Castor" instead of the more common "beaver" hat, but many of the details of clothing in the above are ubiquitous; the occasional sartorial quirks that stand out (a "Silver-Laced Hat") would help identify the fugitive. Lists of clothing, however, were more than just tools for identification: advertisers want such itemized property (which, in Tom's case, includes a large bay horse) to be returned. Specific physical distinctions ("pock-broken," meaning pockmarked, or the unusual "One of his Hands is Considerably Less than the Other") and characteristics of behaviour or gait were essential to aid in the chase. Samuel Foster of Rockaway, Long Island, defines the "High-Dutch Servant Man" he is searching for as "a well-set middle-siz'd fierce looking man."[12] Joining the above in the April 14 issue are detailed ads for the "Negro man," Primus, as well an indentured Englishman, Thomas Smith, who is characterized by a common phrase, "down look," implying a person either subservient or untrustworthy.

These texts reveal something of further significance: the skills of those being sought, such as "speaks good English," "can work at the Gold Smith's business,"[13] or, in Tom's case, "plays well on the Fiddle…can read and write." In June, when a new advertisement appears for Tom—who had been caught, then sold, and run away again—his resume will be enhanced:

A Mulatto Negro
Named Tom, Run away from Joseph Harris, of Beekman's Precinct, in Dutchess County, being the same Fellow formerly advertised, that then belonged to the Heirs of Barent Van Kleck, deceased, and a reward offered by Mynder Viele and Leonard Van Kleck, who since sold him to said Harris; he went away on the first Instant, and had on a half worn Beaver Hat, a blue and white Cotton Cap, a greenish homespun Coat, a blue cloth Jacket, a white linnen Shirt: he took

also with him a linen jacket and breeches, also a red plush breeches; he is lusty and well built, full of Freckles, talks English and Dutch, can read, write, and Cipher, play well on a Violin: Whoever takes up Said Negro, and secures him in any gaol, shall receive five Pounds, York Currency, and all reasonable charges paid, and if any takes extraordinary Trouble and secures him, an honourable allowance shall be further paid by Joseph Harris.[14]

Tom is now simply a "Mulatto Negro" and a "Fellow," not a "Mulatto Colour'd Negro Man Slave." He has become "lusty and well built," and his skills now include speaking Dutch and knowing "Cipher" (either code writing or arithmetic). The fiddle has become a violin. The author is Tom's new owner, Joseph Harris. The ad runs for six weeks and appears consistently with another one offering a reward of "FOUR PISTOLES" (pistols) for the capture of another fugitive Englishman whose owner suspects is heading on a circuitous route to the port of New York, "in order to ship himself for England." Where Tom was heading on his second known escape is unclear.

More ads appear in July alongside Joseph Harris's for Tom. A "Servant Man named Christian Medsher" is described as having a "black complexion," although it is not clear if this means he is considered "Negro" or "mulatto." In an ad for "Peter" in his "bearskin coat" and "pair of old turn'd pumps," we encounter the oft-repeated phrase "so that his Master may have him again," an all too polite articulation of entitlement and privilege.[15]

Tom was not successful in his second attempt to run away from Joseph Harris, for Harris advertised for his capture again in late 1756, stating that he ran away "on the 3d of September last" — which means he was caught before that. This was the same period when "A likely Bermuda born Negro Wench, about 25 Years of Age, fit for any Household Work" was offered for sale; Caesar attempted to escape in chains from Isaac Freeman (how painfully ironic the master's surname); Duke, a skilled goldsmith, tried for freedom; a jilted husband, David Morehouse, complained of the actions of his errant wife Rebecca; one Solomon Hays defended his character against "several scandalous Jews" by offering pistols as reward; and the English servants Bednam and Jones escaped to try their fate as "pirates."[16]

On December 13, 1756, the third and final advertisement for Tom appeared, and ran for several weeks into the first month of 1757:

Run away from Joseph Harris, of Beekman's Precinct, in Dutchess County, on the 3d of September last, a Mulatto Fellow named Tom, about 5 feet eight inches high, is thick and well set, can talk good Dutch and English, and can play very well upon the fiddle, can read, write and cypher, and has some Freckles. He first listed himself with the Boston Forces and was seen in Albany about a fortnight ago with the Forces, so that it is likely he has gone towards Boston, or other Parts of New-England. Whoever takes up and secures the said servant fellow, so that his Master might have him again, shall have Ten Pounds, New-York currency, and all reasonable charges paid by Joseph Harris.

N.B. Whoever secures him, send notice to Baltus Van Kleek, in the city of New-York; or to the said Joseph Harris.[17]

Still described as a "Mulatto Fellow," Tom is now two inches shorter than he was described in March of 1755, has "some Freckles" (not "full of Freckles" as Harris previously expressed), and his violin is back to being a lowly "fiddle." Harris sounds less enthusiastic about Tom, but he has increased the reward, doubling it to ten pounds (although this may simply reflect the wild fluctuations in the value of unstable currencies in the colony). Tom has a new story of escape: he appears to have sought out a situation — military service — where his writing, language, and cipher skills might be more highly valued. It may have been hard for Harris, given the chance, to extract him from service during an active colonial conflict (France and England were at war again), and Tom was clearly capable of producing alternative proof of his identity and status (back in March of 1755 it was suggested he carried a "false Pass"). Perhaps Tom was able to escape into a better situation. Perhaps not.

Over the course of these notices for Tom, the spelling of names is inconsistent. *Van Cleek* shifts to *Van Kleck*, then *Van Kleek*, while *Myndert Veile* becomes *Mynder Viele*, but these are clearly the same people. Another Van Kleek (Baltus) surfaces in the last ad. Again Tom, who was highly skilled (as many people enslaved in the Hudson Valley were), in combination with the extra property he carried, was obviously of significant value. His persistence in repeatedly running away must have been an affront, not just an inconvenience. One cannot dismiss the insult to the "masters" Tom's actions would have represented; he challenged their authority and power, and continues to undermine any idea that slavery was good for, and accepted by, the enslaved and that conditions in the northern states were positive. The "good will" and "deep attachments" Helen Wilkinson Reynolds insisted on, in her book on the Dutch houses of that region, are once again revealed as a convenient myth.[18] Reproduced in Reynolds's book is a grainy black and white image of the lintel stone from the Baltus Barent Van Kleeck house (the fourth variant of the spelling) in Poughkeepsie with date and initials "1702 BVK TVK" (for Baltus Van Kleeck and Trintje Van Kleeck). The house was demolished in 1835, but a descendant of BVK and TVK saved the lintel stone. Here, the memories of enslavers remain preserved in hard rock, while Tom's trajectory slips into obscurity and the ambitions of those Boston Forces.

We are left to wonder: was Tom was ever captured a third time? This was at the beginning of the so-called French and Indian War (1755–63), an extension of Britain's latest European conflict with France known as the Seven Years' War (1756–63). During this period, prominent and influential figures, including General Frederick Haldimand and Sir William Johnson, would emerge. (We will encounter them later in Sophia's journey across New York and into Canada.) The French and Indian War began with mixed results for the British in 1755. They successfully captured Fort Beauséjour (at the top of the Bay of Fundy on the border between present-day New Brunswick and Nova Scotia), while General Braddock's forces failed miserably in their attack on the French and their "Indian" allies at Fort Duquesne in the Ohio Country. (Braddock, shot in the back, died on the return march to Virginia.) This loss taught the British that they needed to adopt "frontier" warfare, and abandon the strict dress and formalities of traditional engagement. (George Washington served under Braddock, and what he witnessed informed his future strategies.) New regiments were formed, led by British officers and composed primarily of colonials. Recruiting was aggressive in 1756 to build this army. These are the Boston Forces mentioned in the notice for Tom; the fact that he would have been in Albany "about a fortnight ago"—a couple of weeks before the early-December advertisement—is consistent with the well-documented movements of these forces in November 1756.

Whether Tom wholeheartedly volunteered or was "encouraged," and where his enlistment took him to, we'll likely never know. These colonial troops were spread throughout the frontier, and some went north to support the forced expulsion of Acadians from the region that would become Canada's Maritime provinces (New

Brunswick, Nova Scotia, and Prince Edward Island). Tom vanishes, either taken back into slavery with Harris, or absorbed into the brutal existence of a colonial soldier, possibly in Nova Scotia—a region that will become a primary destination for both free and enslaved Blacks following the American Revolution. The Boston Forces may have been his path to freedom, but more likely he would have found a premature death in a system all too willing to exploit his vulnerability. Tom, like many other people in the above advertisements, is consistently defined as "mulatto," and it is worth noting the significance of his mixed racial heritage. He is likely the son or grandson of white slaveholders. Was he in fact, a Van Kleeck? Was Sophia of similar mixed ancestry?

Joseph Harris is, I am convinced, the "master" that Sophia left unnamed. Joseph Harris (1727–1790) was the husband of Annatje/Annie Joanna Veile (1731–1780). They lived in the Fishkill area and were the parents of Neeltje/Nelly Harris (1756–1851), who married Daniel Outwater II (1755–1827), son of Daniel Outwater and Elizabeth Kniffen. The younger Outwater couple honoured Tom's original owner by naming their son Barent Van Kleeck Outwater, and Daniel's sister Tryntje Catherine Outwater married Tom's original owner's son Barent Baltus Van Kleeck. And who was Annatje Veile? She was the daughter of Myndert Veile named in the above ads.

The *white men* Sophia recalled three-quarters of a century on from Fishkill are Daniel Outwater II (she says *Outwaters*; it is sometimes spelled Oudewater, from old Dutch—Daniel's ancestors would have arrived from the Netherlands in the early 1600s—and becomes Atwater in some places) and Simon Noxon (sometimes spelled Knoxon, Noxen, Noxin, or, as she says in the interview, *Knox*; the latter is the name of a prominent Dutchess County family). These are the sons-in-law, the relatives, of Joseph Harris (whose names occasionally appear as Joseep or Josep and Herris). The deep connection over generations of the Harrises, Noxons, and Outwaters extends to other leading local families of Dutch heritage, including, most importantly, the Van Kleecks and Veiles. All were members of the Dutch Reformed Church and often appear, linked through intermarriage, in the church's records.

In 1774, Neeltje/Nelly Harris married Daniel Outwater II at the Hopewell Reform Church, Dutchess County. Her parents, Joseph and Annatje/Annie Harris, also had a son Balthus Harris (1758–1828). He married Anna Noxon (1761–1861), who shares a family name with Simon Noxon. But Simon is hard to pin down, though he does occasionally surface. A Simon Noxon is recorded in 1776 as an "Enlisted Man, 2nd Regiment, Dutchess, New York."[19] As Anna Noxon's relative, Simon Knox/Noxon might not have been a son-in-law to Joseph Harris, but these families are interlinked. In fairness, how precise can we expect Sophia's knowledge of these families to be? It is remarkable that she was able to recall what she did, particularly since all of these white people may have spoken Dutch as well as English, and it is unclear whether she did too—although the fact that Tom, Sojourner Truth, and most enslaved persons in the Hudson Valley at this time could speak Dutch suggests she may have as well.

Joseph and Annatje/Annie Harris also had a son Joseph (1769–1841). In the 1790 federal census he appears as living in Beekman next to Fishkill.[20] There is only one Joseph in the census (as Joseph Sr. was dead by 1790), and he is listed as owning two slaves. Had the two enslaved people in the younger Joseph's household been passed down from his father? Are they Sophia's parents, or other unnamed relatives? Could they be descendants of Tom? The 1790 census records a total of 601 enslaved people living in Fishkill Town. Some masters far exceeded the average of owning two or three individuals per slaveholding household. Many owned seven or eight enslaved people; Phillip Ver Plank, Jacobus Swartwout, and Matthew Van Benschoten each owned twelve; Catharina De Witt owned thirteen; and Gysbert Schenck, seventeen.

After the Revolution, many residents from Dutchess County would head north to what would become Canada, including the younger Joseph Harris, who possibly went with the two enslaved people. He would be joined by Nelly and Daniel Outwater II and their relatives Balthus, Peter, and Knoxon Harris. They will all petition for land and claim to be good Loyalists, even though most were Patriots.

Dear Sophia,

These lives are hard to trace in the thin and buried records of Dutchess County in the 1700s, a time of deep conflict and upheaval. There are constant shifts in dates, the spellings of names of people and of places, and identities. Not everyone wants to be truthful about their lives in such precarious times. Specific first names persist formally, but may not be the common or familiar name used. A first son will have his father's name, but will go by a middle name—there are many

Josephs and Peters known by other names, for example. Often spellings shift from Dutch to English.

We will come back to the Harris/Outwater/Noxon trajectories, and will consider then the true values of the many United Empire Loyalists so heavily praised in Canadian history. I don't want the complex details of all these white lives to overshadow the focus on your journey out of Fishkill. And I will let something else linger, another question of values to return to. Why would the *sons-in-laws* of Joseph Harris steal you and your sister from him?

What a tangled web! But there is clearly enough to triangulate. There is compelling evidence of future trajectories for these Dutchess County slaveholding families that, in their paths north, parallel your journey. This all reinforces the importance of knowing your story in Canada. All of these interconnected lives assert that, in the late 1700s and early 1800s, the border between Canada and New York was fluid; these landscapes, cultures, and histories were contiguous and in turmoil—as are their legacies.

Albert Robertson, *7 Miles Below Albany*, 1796, pencil and ink on paper
(drawing from sketchbook), 25 cm × 30 cm (approx.),
collection of the Albany Institute of History and Art

CHAPTER 7
ON THE "NORTH" RIVER

From the landing on the eastern shore, around 1783, a modest vessel has pushed off with the Burthens held in darkness. It is being maneuvered out into open water by its skipper. Let's hope it isn't Quam, the enslaved "captain" of the Wilts and Son ferry. Let's wish that his "prestigious" role (as A.J. Williams-Myers referred to it[1]) didn't include ferrying north a captive Sophia and her sister. Are they bound as well as gagged? What else fills that hold? What shadows appear and move about them? This sturdy sailing vessel slips through calm water, tacking into a good breeze, its sails full, its hull heaving slightly, zigzagging north into the wind, against a current pushing south. The river will carry on past West Point, through the rapids known as Horse Race at Peekskill, past Sing Sing (named for the Indigenous Sinc Sinck or Sint Sinck, Wappinger people; the prison opened in 1828[2]) and into the Tappan Zee (named for the Tappan Delaware/Lenape people; *zee* is Dutch for *sea*). But the vessel with the Burthens heads in the opposite direction.

I imagine it appearing like one of the sloops depicted in Albert Robertson's sketchbook, in the precise ink renderings by this Scottish artist who followed the Hudson River north from Manhattan and west along the Mohawk River in September of 1796. He made his journey two decades after the sisters', but little had changed in the passing landscape. The middle of Robertson's journal reveals hints of the sisters' journey, scenes they would however not witness from the hold as they progressed to Albany. Let's imagine their sloop travelled at 4 to 5 knots over 150 kilometres. Allowing for tacking into the wind, cargo, and the constant press of the current, this becomes a journey of around 24 to 30 hours. *It was dark there all the time.*

Robertson titles each of his drawings in the 1796 sketchbook with descriptions that pinpoint places on the journey as it closes in on Albany: *Hudson* and *On the Hudson River a Little Above Hudson*; *Kinderhook*; (counting down) *12 Miles Below Albany*, *8 Miles Below Albany Looking Up*, *7 Miles Below Albany*, and *Overslaugh Near Albany*; and finally the capitol, at *Albany*. In *Albany—from the North*, Robinson looks down from a hill to the dense town, packed with churches, emerging from behind a series of ridges. Let's look downriver with him and see, as his drawing shows, the masts of many boats evident along the shore, while full sails and a pennant flapping atop a single spar reveals another sloop to the left, its hull concealed by fields as it carries onward north to the Mohawk River, on a journey the sisters would not take. At Albany: *Then we came by land.*

The territory Robertson passed through was well described by the 1770s. On Thomas Kitchin Sr.'s map *The Southern Part of the Province of New York, with Part of the adjoining Colonies* (1778), Poughkeepsie is *Pakepsy*, Catskill is *Kats Kill*, and the *Great Beaver Kill* and *Lit [Little] Beaver Kill* to the west of the *Katskill Mountains* are reminders of what brought the Dutch here in the first place: *Castor canadensis*, the beaver. On Captain Holland's remarkable map *The Provinces of New York and New Jersey; with parts of Pensilvania, and the Province of Quebec* (1776), he identifies the *Endless Mountains* and *The Great Swamp* and *Coughsaghrage or the Beaver Hunting Country of the Confederate Indians*. The latter is shown as a vast area east of Lake Ontario reaching to the western shore of the Hudson and north to the St. Lawrence River and Montréal. At the end of the last ice age, much of the southern section of this area was submerged until the rising waters of Lake Iroquois (an expanded version of Lake Ontario) drained through the outlet in what is now Rome, New York, and followed a course south along the Hudson Valley. The meltwater from the receding glaciers, which once crushed this region in a blanket of ice over two kilometres thick, shaped this land. The land is still rising from the weight of those glaciers.

"The Confederates, called by the French Iroquois," declares the bold text on Holland's map,

> surrendered this Country to the English at Albany the 19th of July
> 1701; and the Cession was confirmed the 14th of September 1724.
> It belongs to New York and is full of Swamps, Lakes, Rivers and
> Drowned Lands; a Long Chain of Snowy Mountains, which are seen

from Lake Champlain, runs through the whole Tract North and South. This Country is not only uninhabited but even Unknown, except towards the South where Several Grants have been made since the Peace.

Names of places continue to be refined to this day, and the dates and details in Holland's map are flawed. The Deed from the Five Nations to the King, of their Beaver Hunting Ground is today known as the Nanfan Treaty (John Nanfan was the acting colonial governor of New York). It was amended on September 14, 1726 (not 1724 as stated on the map). The original treaty of 1701 did not include the area defined as the "Beaver Hunting Grounds" in Holland's rendering; they are part of the latter amendment. The colonizers were truly rendering the ground (diagramming it), but they were also rending and rendering it (as in cutting up and processing meat). They were not planting a Great Tree of Peace[3] (the foundation of the Great Peace, signed at Montréal in 1701 between the French and many Indigenous nations[4]). Their plantings were once again allelopathic, and there were and are many such planters, plantings, and plantations, constantly branching out, spreading, and erasing. Settlers are constantly imagining this ancient place as empty of people and culture. They are remaking the land, and they will use many tools—enslaved bodies burdened with labour and colonized bodies infused with imposed ways of being in the world.

Landscape comes from Frisian/Dutch *landschop*. *Schop* means *shovel*, so we get "*shovelled land*, land thrown up against the sea,"[5] according to John R. Stigloe, professor of the history of landscape at Harvard, a reference to dyke building in the Netherlands. Were Dutch settlers conscious that the land they settled on here was once submerged and inundated with water? They would not have known that the mountains of Appalachia and the Adirondacks that cut through this region are formed of the same rocks that define most of the British Isles and parts of the coast of the great bulge of West Africa (as well as much of Newfoundland and Labrador, the east coast of Greenland, and the Caledonian Mountains of western Scandinavia). They wouldn't know these places were divided when the Atlantic Ocean emerged in the gap that broke apart the supercontinent Pangaea (formed over 375 million years ago) into our current arrangement of continents (a process that began about 175 million years ago).

These are deep-time memories of catastrophic changes buried in the ground beneath our feet. This ground is rising up to confront us with memories of flooded lands and wrenched and rendered and rent mountain ranges, all deeply embedded in the complex creation narratives of many Indigenous cultures. Other narratives are compressed in the timelines of Abrahamic faiths brought here, and they impose a new cultural bedrock favoured by the European nations who would reconnect this rent geology through the Triangle Trade of chattel slavery. From the so-called "New World," more money and trade goods were returned to European shores, and the cycle continued, for generations. Sometimes the trade flowed in reverse. Rum produced in Montréal was shipped to the Caribbean, while the rough textile ("slave cotton") produced in northern mills of Britain and the United States was sold back south to clothe the enslaved, who picked more cotton. Millions of people made into property, sent as cargo — *Burthen*. Such an enterprise has no parallel in human history. It cannot be compared to any other system of enslavement that has been a sad characteristic of many human societies. This was slavery on a monumental, almost unfathomable, scale. Like the rending of continents and the birthing of oceans, it has shaped and redefined the ground we walk on.

To contemporary English speakers, *to landscape* literally means to form and shape land. *A landscape* is also a type of image, a representation of a place (real or imagined), initially (from a European perspective) from the sea, from a ship approaching the land. It was likely sailors who brought the term to England from encounters with the Netherland's north coast, the *landschop* holding back the sea. The genre of European landscape painting followed — refined in France in the seventeenth century by Claude Lorrain, and in England in the early nineteenth century by the likes of John Constable and William Turner.[6] These artists influenced nineteenth-century painters in the United States, including Frederic Edwin Church, Asher Brown Durand, Albert Bierstadt, and Thomas Cole, who will become known as the principal members of the much beloved Hudson River School of painting. Their overly romantic, spiritually evocative, sublime, and deeply Christian views *captured* "America" in more than one sense: their scenes also *captivated* settlers with scenes that held Indigenous people in a "primitive" state, while erasing the presence of the enslaved. They focused first on this land we are currently travelling through (hence the school's name), then eventually moved on to the American West. Their imagery is the landscape of a belief in manifest destiny, fuelling more expansion and further conquest. Their paintings drew future photographers, filmmakers, and tourists to places like Yosemite. Several of these

Robert S. Duncanson, *Cincinnati from Covington, Kentucky*, ca. 1851,
oil on canvas, 63.5 cm × 91.5 cm, lent to Cincinnati Art Museum
by Cincinnati Historical Society (long-term loan)

artists also produced dramatic views of Niagara Falls—we will follow them there soon.

Bierstadt, Church, and Cole are the most famous of the Hudson River School. Their paintings hang packed together, salon-style, in many museums. The persistent vision they present continues to be widely embraced as representing an "ideal America," the "New Eden." Robert Seldon Duncanson (born in 1821 at Seneca, Albany County, New York) was an African American freeman who taught himself to paint by copying them, producing numerous landscapes of the Hudson River region. He moved west to Cincinnati, Ohio, where he was considered a leading artist. A painter of portraits and landscapes (and a skilled daguerreotypist), he toured Europe and visited Scotland, a country he was deeply inspired by. During the Civil War, he spent several years in Montréal, where his work was praised. The influential nineteenth-century photographer William Notman produced

Robert S. Duncanson, *Uncle Tom and Little Eva* (detail), 1853, oil on canvas,
69.2 cm × 97.2 cm, Detroit Institute of Arts, USA © Detroit Institute of Arts/
Gift of Mrs. Jefferson Butler and Miss Grace R. Conover/Bridgeman Images

a handsome portrait of Duncanson in Montréal in 1864, and the artist's major
paintings include such classic Quebec subjects as *Montmorency Falls* (1864) and
Mount Orford (1864).

Prior to these sojourns, Duncanson produced several works addressing slavery,
including *Uncle Tom and Little Eva* (1853; a scene from *Uncle Tom's Cabin*) and
an intriguing reworking titled *Cincinnati from Covington, Kentucky* (ca. 1851), of
a print by an unknown artist. Duncanson's reworking represents the view from a
slave state to a free state. In translating the print to painting, he changed several
white figures in the Kentucky landscape to enslaved people, replacing these whites
at leisure with Black working bodies. Ohio freedom beckons from across the
waters. The painting was completed in 1851; the Fugitive Slave Act (1850) had made
Ohio freedom precarious.[7] The Ohio-born African American poet C.S. Giscombe
described the Ohio-Kentucky border as "the color line" in his long poem *Here* (in
which Duncanson features prominently):

2. *Duncanson's "View of Cincinnati, Ohio from Covington, Kentucky"*
(1848)

The wide eye corporeal &
at the time sane, both —

but on the remotest edge

of description, at an exaggerated pinnacle

of the color line,

at no rest, no rest, no Campground

to come between the long stare across

& the big pale sky

no place for the eye to rest on, soul's

opaque surface

or the river sloped down *to*
by Covington houses

or Ohio's dim self of hills & smoke, another economy[8]

Giscombe's poem closes with a concise encapsulation of the emerging metropolis of Cincinnati, its burgeoning economy clearly distinct from the rural scene across the river/border.

In 1855, the year Sophia was being interviewed by Benjamin Drew, Duncanson worked out of the Cincinnati gallery of the pre-eminent African American daguerreotypist J.P. (James Presley) Ball, who was born in Virginia. Although he primarily worked in the studio retouching photographs, Duncanson also exhibited paintings. Under the direction of Ball, he contributed to the production

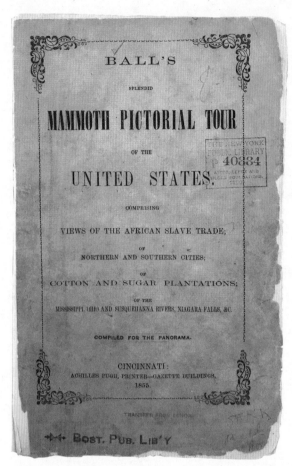

Cover of program for *Ball's Splendid Mammoth Pictorial Tour of the United States*, published in 1855, collection of the Schomburg Center for Research in Black Culture, New York Public Library

of a panorama painting, four yards high and six hundred yards wide, titled *Ball's Splendid Mammoth Pictorial Tour of the United States Comprising Views of the African Slave Trade*. This work, accompanied by an anti-slavery booklet/program for audience members, consisted of a canvas wrapped around two large spindles that would be unspooled before paying audiences to the accompaniment of an orchestra, and with dramatic lighting and a narrator describing the changing scenes. *Ball's Splendid Mammoth Pictorial Tour* travelled the country, advertised as: "Painted by Negroes." Sadly, as with almost all such ambitious scroll paintings, one can only find fragments of these visionary efforts that prefigure the experience of cinema.[9] Fortunately, a few tattered copies of Ball's pamphlet do survive.

Totalling fifty-six pages of numbered texts, the rare pamphlet is the only existing record of the presentation. It provides brief descriptions of the thirty distinct scenes that appear to have comprised, as it says, the "2400 square yard" scrolling painting, but no illustrations. In it Ball (referring to himself in the third person) states that: "He has endeavoured to avoid the insertion of any thing that cannot be substantiated as truth," further claiming to be "unbiased," and that there was "nothing extenuate, nor aught set down in malice."[10] Much of what Ball described is consistent with other representations, and he gave a sound "unbiased" description of the specifics of the slave trade in "The Niger" (West Africa) and of enslaved people's arrival into the United States, as well as the horrors facing fugitive slaves and conditions in the border states and northern cities. As those attempting to escape, or "conduct" fugitives north, required secrecy to succeed, Ball devoted minimal space to the Underground Railroad. He focused on the precarious situation in the United States, where he remained.

Of all the descriptions in Ball's volume, two in particular stand out in relation to Sophia's journey, "Wyoming Valley" and "Boston." That Boston is included is hardly surprising. Wyoming Valley, on the other hand, seems an obscure location to emphasize, until one reads the tale of a fugitive slave's presence and harrowing escape from a town Ball condemns in his narrative. He praises Boston for being the "head-quarters of a noble band that . . . pointed the American people to the wrong and danger of slavery." There is, however, a "but." Ball makes it clear that, even in this progressive northern city, there is no true equality or freedom: "The Fugitive Slave Act has made Massachusetts slave territory, and the Bostonians have submitted. . . . Simms [Thomas Sims] and [Anthony] Burns, have been successfully torn away, and plunged into slavery, the Bostonians have gotten used to seeing human rights disregarded."[11]

Thomas Sims had escaped bondage in Georgia, arrived in Boston in 1851, and was then caught, tried, and returned south where he was sold to a Mississippi plantation. His trial was the first test of the 1850 Fugitive Slave Act. While many were outraged by his fate, they could do little but protest in solidarity as he was marched under guard to a waiting ship. Anthony Burns escaped from Richmond, Virginia, by ship and arrived in Boston in 1854. Also quickly captured, he too was tried and sent back into slavery. In the end, both found freedom. Abolitionists purchased Burns's freedom and he returned to Boston, studied at Oberlin College, and eventually moved to St. Catharines, Ontario (where Harriet Tubman resided), to preach. He died there in 1862, a year before Sims managed to escape again and return to Boston.

Massachusetts Chief Justice Lemuel Shaw presided over Sims's trial. The judge's son-in-law was Herman Melville. As Melville's *Moby-Dick* was published that year, 1851 was a landmark year for all three men, and it can be argued that Shaw's decision was one factor in Melville transforming what began as another ripping yarn about life at sea into what he published that autumn: a political tome of an "appalling" white leviathan. Many literary critics have identified *Moby-Dick*'s "cousin" in Cornelius Mathews's *Behemoth: A Legend; Or, the Mound-Builders* (1839),[12] a strange tale with "striking parallels" to Melville's novel.[13] In Mathews's narrative, a monstrous mammoth/mastodon wreaks havoc on "an Ancient American race."[14] Three decades earlier, another "monstrous" figure was depicted. The Kanyen'kehà:ka (Mohawk) leader Thayendanegea/Joseph Brant was described as a mammoth, terrorizing white settlers at Wyoming Valley:

> The mammoth comes — the foe — the Monstrous Brant
> With all his howling desolate band
> These eyes have seen their blade, the burning pine
> Awake at once, and silence half your land.
> Red is the cup they drink, but not with wine…[15]

Ball's story "Wyoming Valley" as reproduced in the spectacle pamphlet surfaces Thayendanegea/Joseph Brant, and he paints a convincing picture of a settler community long mired in vicious conflict and in political divisions. He recalls the events of the Battle of Wyoming, in 1778, as "a dreadful tragedy" and a "merciless massacre," perpetrated during a period when Loyalists settlers and their Haudenosaunee allies were raiding settlements across central and western New York. Thayendanegea/Joseph fought to protect the Haudenosaunee (called Iroquois) Confederacy's homelands and was consistently blamed for atrocities. Patriots took to calling him "the Monster Brant." Ball, however, describes the skilled military leader sympathetically as "celebrated" and "a man of intelligence and energy." He states that while the "chief blame" is usually attributed to "Thayendanegea, or Joseph Brandt [sic]," it is really the Whigs and Tories (Loyalists and Patriots) who engaged in brutalities. Ball makes the common error of identifying Brant as "half breed."[16] He also, like Campbell quoted above, perpetuates the myth that the

Kanyen'kehà:ka (Mohawk) War Chief was at Wyoming Valley; he was not.[17] But Ball tells this backstory to establish that Wyoming Valley was a malicious place, a town historically infused with a vicious streak of violence and cowardice.

Had he known that Thayendanegea/Joseph Brant enslaved people, would Ball still have described him so sympathetically? Judging from the effort he made to see the complexity of situations, I'm guessing he would have contemplated Brant's actions in the wider context of the impacts of colonization on Indigenous peoples and of his existence between British and Indigenous cultures. Ball described African slave traders and revealed that many women were also slave holders. He sympathized with the Natchez "irretrievably defeated" by the French in 1772.[18] He called out Boston for its complicity.

Ball and Duncanson were successful artists and businessmen well known in their day, yet both faded into obscurity, largely erased from the landscape of art history. Duncanson's paintings in Canadian museums are rarely seen, where his influence is diminished to an occasional footnote. Ball left many single-portrait photographs, including one of Frederick Douglass, taken in Cincinnati in 1867. Compared to the younger Douglass's intense presence in earlier daguerreotypes, Ball's image of him reveals a thin and weary man, his hair almost fully grey. At the time of the portrait, Douglass was two years beyond the passing of the Thirteenth Amendment, but his gaze remains clear and focused, still determined, deeply aware that Emancipation did not equal the erasure of systemic racism.

Douglass was arguably the most photographed person of the nineteenth century; Sojourner Truth was also consistently photographed. She made extensive use of *cartes de visite* to promote and fund her speaking tours. One from 1864 carries her catchphrase: "I Sell the Shadow to Support the Substance." Of all the images of her, this is one of the most powerful for its simplicity and directness. The focus of the close-up portrait is sharp and has the uncanny depth of a daguerreotype. She seems to project out from the surface and the emphasis remains on her, not on her clothing or props, and not just on her face but her eyes, free of the wire spectacles that obscure her stare in many images. She fixes you in her gaze, and one must truly witness her presence, her substance: a distinct person carrying wisdom, who speaks the truth.

In the Hudson River School landscapes featuring the terrain of Sojourner Truth's birth in Ulster County, just across and upriver from Sophia's Dutchess County, such "substance" is consistently missing — if there are figures they are

I Sell the Shadow to Support the Substance.
SOJOURNER TRUTH.

Sojourner Truth: I Sell the Shadow to Support the Substance (ca. 1860), *carte de visite*: albumen print, 5.8 cm × 8.9 cm, mounted on a card, 6.4 cm × 10.2 cm, collection of the author

tiny and peripheral, and they are almost always white. Occasionally, an Indigenous person appears, depicted helplessly watching what is unfolding on their ancestral homelands, about to exit the scene (imagine the giant spindles turning the panorama of painted history and these people disappearing as the canvas rolls onto itself, sealed into darkness). The settler-colonial state was crafting its narrative, shaping the landscape free of those who were displaced along with the enslaved legions forced to labour to build a nation that will consistently reject them. They insist, as Captain Holland wanted us to believe, "This Country is not only uninhabited but even Unknown," and the many representations of Indigenous and Black bodies that existed outside of the sublime scenes of Bierstadt, Church, Cole, et al., perpetuated racist ideas.

"I sell the shadow," declared Sojourner Truth — her shadow as both a surface representation of identity and the identity itself that at times conformed to stereotypes (a polite conservative Christian lady in refined gowns and shawls, the elderly matron in wire-rimmed glasses, unthreatening), but from that shadow harsh truths would emerge, "to support the substance." That other shadow, a physical trace or image, was the photograph — a thing literally defined by the chemical fixing of shadows on a specific piece of paper. It seems necessary to say this now, to consciously remember that a photograph was a *thing*. In the eighteenth century it was an object that occupied space that one held in the hand. It had weight (physical and in memory). Put in a frame or made into a tangible and tactile *carte de viste* (a paper print glued to a heavy card), it also cast a shadow. It was fixed in time, to be passed forward as evidence.

> Dear Sophia,
> I try to imagine the conditions below deck. In darkness your space was potentially infinite, and I am haunted by that infamous image of the Liverpool slave ship, *Brooks*, published in 1788 with its stacked bodies, precisely fit to fill its burthen. Did you think of your ancestors in the Middle Passage? How distant in time were they from you? Were they carried from Africa across the Atlantic, perhaps to the Caribbean and then north, making their way, over generations, in stages, to finally make the journey on this same river from Manhattan to Dutchess County? Or was their passage more recent, direct from West Africa to New York as the importing of slaves direct from the "Guinea" coast expanded along the Hudson in the later eighteenth century? Were your parents African, African American, African Caribbean, possibly "mulatto"?...

Charmaine Nelson argues that the concept of the Middle Passage needs to be expanded in time and space, and that we need to take into account the many journeys of the enslaved over generations — journeys through alternating locations and forms of chattel slavery and shifting identities. Nelson defines the Middle Passage as "a central concept of Trans-Atlantic Slavery, [that] is at once a territorial location, a site of genocide, a locus of diasporic remembrance, and a means of theorizing the diasporization of Africans."[19] She goes on to ask: "Although it is geographically defined as part of the Atlantic Ocean which was crossed by slave ships from Africa to the Americas with their cargoes of enslaved Africans, is it not an erasure of another site of the Atlantic that we have yet to explore the routes, practices and customs of the slavers that sailed from the Caribbean and other southern ports, north to Canada?"[20] It is not a stretch to add to this expanded view the transportation, in bondage, of enslaved people along other routes: Sims and Burns shipped back south, Sophia and her sister in the hold on the Hudson.

> ...I tried to imagine what it would be like for you and your
> sister in the hold. I realized, in doing so, I know too little
> about your lives and I cannot possibly imagine your experience.
> To imagine the shadows, to attempt to steer events toward
> some invented clarity and suggest the conditions, your personal
> experiences—this is not my place. My ancestors are not with
> you in the hold, in the wake; they are up on the deck of this
> vessel trailing turbulence. So I step back from the boat and
> watch it progress upriver through a wide landscape, positioning
> your vessel in the broader narrative of history.

Sophia exists in words filtered through others—Drew and those of all who have referenced *The Refugee*. How much did he alter her interview? Judging from the diversity of voices and language in the published book, her interview does sound distinct—the record of an individual, dropping names only she would know—but as previously noted, there are many obvious discrepancies concerning dates and time in her story, making it seem as though the book was rushed and leaving one to wonder about the accuracy of other interviews. If only Drew had been accompanied by a photographer in 1855! The idea of a photograph of Sophia might seem like a stretch, since the *carte de viste* had only been introduced in 1854. But touring Canada West to interview over a hundred people and then publishing the results within a year is a rather ambitious enterprise. To have photographed even a few individuals surely was possible. The first known photograph taken in Canada dates from 1840 (a remarkable image of Niagara Falls by Englishman Hugh Lee Patterson) and, as Katherine Tweedie and Peggy Cousineau point out: "In Toronto, several studios flourished for short periods of time, but their output is now lost. However, from 1847 until about 1870, Eli J. Palmer produced daguerreotypes and the popular *cartes de visite*."[21] There is a surviving photograph of Reverend Samuel

Ringgold Ward taken in Toronto in 1855. If only there had been a photographer present to meet Sophia, an image of her, and of the Queen's Bush settlement, could reveal much to me. I wonder if Drew carried any images, pictures of Brown, Douglass, Henson, Truth, or Tubman, and wonder what Sophia knew of them. Did Drew even think to ask her? Did he know anything about Thayendanegea/ Joseph — his people and their fate?

Minus these details, we continue in shadow, heading into the current toward a complicated encounter with a truly complicated figure. Thayendanegea (meaning "Two Sticks Bound Together for Strength"), Joseph Brant, Chief Brant, Captain Brant, "the Monster Brant," or *the old Indian Brant, the king* (as Sophia called him): he is a man who may be one of the most contested figures in the histories of Canada and the United States, a man who continues to stir up heated debate. Thayendanegea/Joseph Brant's biographical details are critical to clarify when Sophia's journey took place, and her age. But first we need to stop at Albany, the White City.

CHAPTER 8
THE WHITE CITY

Once again, Max and I are on a landing witnessing two captive women, but no longer by the river exposed to the elements imagining captives from the past. We are indoors, looking at art. Having left that landing near Fishkill, where we'd tried to imagine the departure of the vessel carrying the Burthen sisters, and its slow progress upriver, we've arrived in New York's capital. Albany takes its name from the ancient Latin *Albanus* (*of Alba*, the ancient city *Alba Longa*), meaning *of White*. The downtown is at the intersection of State and Pearl Streets, as it was on the day Sophia and her sister arrived, but there is nothing left of the old Dutch architecture they witnessed. When this settlement was known as Beverwijk (or *Beverwyck*, and meaning "Beaver District") prior to the English takeover in 1664, State Street was Joncaer Straet, and Rom Straet (now Maiden Lane) ran parallel to the ferry landing.

The landing we now stand on is sheltered, held on the inside. We have ascended the steep rise of State Street past the site where Fort Orange (*Fort Oranje*) once stood strategically positioned on the high ground. The site is now dominated by legislative buildings — the Capitol (built 1867–99) and the Governor Nelson A. Rockefeller Empire State Plaza (built 1965–76). The latter displays full-on the architectural style known as brutalism, with its single massive skyscraper attended by The Egg (a performing arts centre that resembles a cross between Noah's ark and alien spaceship) and a quartet of monolithic towers perfectly aligned to dominate an open square with its reflecting pool. This is all watched over by the New York City State Museum, an inverted pyramid on a wide pedestal. This complex was erected over a neglected inner-city neighbourhood known as "The Gut," home to immigrants and a large Black population, echoing the kind of classic urban renewal program practiced across North America that targeted the neighbourhoods of the disenfranchised left after "white flight" to the suburbs. As intended, Rockefeller's bold white structures can be seen for miles around.

The landing Max and I currently occupy features white honeycomb tilework, marble steps, and deep blue walls with glossy white trim. Elegant iron balustrades (that were cast in a foundry on the riverside) top varnished oak railings. This is a resting place between floors in the Albany Institute of History & Art (AIHA). Founded in 1791, the AIHA "is one of the oldest museums in the United States," according to their website, and "the genesis of the institute began with the Society for the Promotion of Agriculture, Arts, and Manufactures, founded in New York City in Federal Hall."[1] The AIHA began as an amalgam of various entities including archives, records offices, and a few "learned" societies.

Max and I have just passed through the main gallery dominated by Hudson River School paintings. A group of Black high school students are being toured through by an older white woman, a docent ("one allowed to teach," from the Latin *docene*, "to make to appear right"). The students are being monitored closely by museum staff and teachers. They are being spoken to, not spoken with. Having exited that sombre gallery of dark walls and warm spotlighting, we are confronted by two figures, sisters if you will, of similar age and complexion. They face each other on the landing, bathed in natural light. Like the towers in the plaza, these figures glow in reflected sunlight, their pristine white surfaces appear unblemished. Sculpted around 1853–56 and in 1857–58, they point us, once again, to a time concurrent with Sophia's interview and the publishing of Drew's book.

Indian Girl, or The Dawn of Christianity (ca. 1853–56) and *White Captive* (1857–58) are by one of Albany's most famous artists, Erastus Dow Palmer. Life-size figures, they stand protected and highly valued and yet they are also unprotected, literally exposed. *Indian Girl* has dropped her garment to reveal her naked upper torso as she stares—captivated—by the crucifix in her hand, while *White Captive* stands fully nude, her hands bound to a modest tree stump. She looks away, frightened and ashamed.

The artworks also expose, and preserve, the legacies of Puritan settler values and the beliefs the sculptures embody as allegorical figures. The former articulates the forced Christianization of Indigenous peoples, while the latter reflects the obsessive

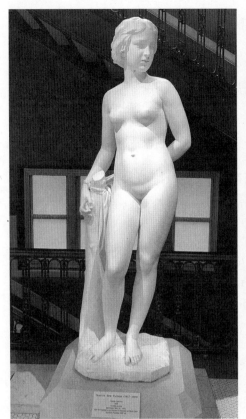

Left: Erastus Dow Palmer, *White Captive*, 1857–58, plaster, 165.1 × 51.4 × 43.2 cm,
collection of the Albany Institute of History and Art, photographed by the author in 2019
Right: Erastus Dow Palmer, *Indian Girl, or The Dawn of Christianity*, ca. 1853–56, plaster,
152.4 × 50.2 × 56.5 cm, collection of the Albany Institute of History and Art,
photographed by the author in 2019

fear of unconverted "savages" stalking white womanhood. They are related in their
fundamental disrespect for the Indigenous peoples of this place.

White Captive is Palmer's take on *The Greek Slave*, the infamous sculpture by
Hiram Powers exhibited in London in 1851 that infuriated abolitionists (discussed
in chapter 3). Palmer's overly sexualized slave figure depicts a much younger
woman, barely a teenager (as if the representation weren't disturbing enough). She
appears to be in genuine fear of her *actual* observers — an older male artist and

his intended audience. These figures embody the violence of a scene, but not the violence considered by Palmer and understood by his "enlightened" audience (an audience, sadly, not limited to his era—there are still many prurient "Victorians" who think themselves enlightened). Having imagined other sisters, captives hidden in the shadow of a vessel's hold, we now witness the continuing preservation of an overvaluing of whiteness (in this case notions of white womanhood) that protects and directs attention away from the male gaze, the colonizer, and the subjugation of "others."

These figures encapsulate the persistent and perpetual flaw in the institution of museums—one cannot keep preserving and valuing such works of art separate from the histories, economies, and ecologies they emerged from and carry forward. Such content and context will cast these works in a more complex and troubling light, no matter how hard institutions labour to shelter them by consistently resetting the conversation to tradition, taste, and exclusive expertise. Too often, honouring and preserving the intentions of the artist and the hierarchies of academic art history takes precedence over the honouring of the many who are unacknowledged and under-represented in a system that carries on burdened by its colonial genesis. The encounter between students and docents feels like a confrontation between the protection of the status quo and youth who are being controlled in their behaviour and are the focus of a process of indoctrination. Too often the docent-audience relationship is about preservation, taking "others" onboard the coercive and hierarchical vessel of the museum, its leadership unwavering in their commitment to staying on course of "making to appear right."

I don't know what the students felt, confronted by Black absence in the painted landscapes of New York or by Palmer's *White Captive* as they were ushered quickly past. What difference would it have made if they had also encountered John Bell's sculpture *The American Slave—Scene on the Shore of the Atlantic* (1862) with her gold earrings and silver shackles hanging in stark contrast to the brown patina of her body, or if John Tenniel's 1851 *Punch* cartoon of *The Virginian Slave* (both discussed in chapter 3) were present on this landing? These latter representations are still the work of white male artists, and who would determine their placement, and how permanent would these gestures be?

Looking at the silver shackles in a photograph of Bell's sculpture, I can't help but think back to Fred Wilson's *Mining the Museum: Metalwork 1793–1880* (1992), a truly ground-breaking curatorial intervention at the Maryland Historical Society, now the Maryland Centre for History and Culture (MCHS). Wilson displayed ornate silverware (pitchers and goblets) of the white ruling class, typically collected and displayed in such institutions, together with the brutal metalwork used on the enslaved (shackles, collars, and thumbscrews, for example) that made the accumulation of wealth by slaveholders possible. His project influenced many artists and curators, and may be the most referenced artist's intervention in the field of curatorial and museum studies—a model for disrupting and calling out institutions. Yet nearly three decades on, how much have institutions like the MCHS changed?

The MCHS's strategic plan, *Path Toward Preeminence* (2016–21),[2] states that the institution "operates in an environment of radically different demographics than its founders or the leaders of the last 173 years could have imagined," then goes on to identify the African American population of Maryland as the fourth largest in the United States, referring to this community in the possessive, as "*our* largest minority [emphasis added]." In fact, these demographics are not "radically different" from 1790 (the beginning of the period covered by Wilson's intervention) when over 32 percent (103,000 persons) of the population of Maryland were enslaved Blacks (and this doesn't include freemen,[3] an additional 8,000). It is hard to imagine all that remained invisible to the authors of *Path Toward Preeminence*, all that remains "marginalized" and "minoritized." What they did choose to imagine only appears defined in ways to be monetized and to protect their privileged position as overseers of culture and history. Such institutions seem more concerned about strategically incorporating the diversity they have only recently acknowledged into their unaltered core *missions*, continuing to engage in a form of coercive missionary practice, their *missionary position*.

In critiquing the MCHS (and by extension many museums) I am not criticizing Fred Wilson; his work continues to have a profound impact on engagements with the persistence of white supremacy. It is not Wilson's fault that institutions and museum professionals are often lacking in their commitments, unwilling to honestly comprehend and act on the challenges posed by him (and by many more individuals and communities). Wilson profoundly influenced my career as a curator in public museums, but I'm deeply aware that too often while employing such a model of disruption my privileged position was maintained as I remained supported by the very system I sought to disrupt. My identity within institutions was often enhanced by a "progressive" agenda that benefited me and the organization while (unintentionally? naively?) the agenda continued to marginalize communities as "other" — communities that are only "marginal" in the eyes of whiteness. Too often, in their awakening to diversity, established organizations continue to obscure a complex multiplicity of pasts and deny their own limited genealogy, failing to be accountable for creating and maintaining so many margins and barriers.

There were no paintings by the New York–born Robert Duncanson in the AIHA, and there were no historic works by Black artists on display there either. What if the percentage of artists and artworks reflected the historic Black presence in this region, reflected that the 1790 population of Albany (3,500) included 572 enslaved and 26 freemen, or 16 percent of the population — a number consistent with the current African American population in New York? To do so would challenge the museum to open itself to an expanded conception of art, cultural production, and what it means to be seen as an artist. But there is a need to push things even further. What if museums, archives, libraries, and educational institutions met the disturbingly high bar of overrepresentation set by other federal and state institutions: over 30 percent of those incarcerated in New York are Black—more than double the general population.[4] We are not immune to these disparities in Canada, where "Blacks are overrepresented in federal prisons by more than 300% vs their population, while for Aboriginals [sic] the over representation is nearly 500%."[5] These are the sad paths I wander down in searching for Sophia, too often ending up mired in appalling numbers and categories, depressing demographics and statistics, hard-pressed to come upon more potent and poetic traces — the artistry, beauty, and "divine wisdom" of her presence here. If only I could encounter her walking toward us and hear from her, on her own terms, about who she encountered passing through Albany. In the vaults of the AIHA, there are hints.

James Eights was not widely known as an artist; his legacy is one of science, engineering, geology, and medicine. Born in Albany, he managed to secure the position of naturalist/geologist on the South Sea Fur Company and Exploring Expedition to Antarctica in 1829. While the Eights Coast in Western Antarctica was named for him, he never secured another position on such a voyage. He remained in Albany to teach engineering and practice medicine. For some reason, around 1850, he decided to produce a series of watercolour illustrations based on his childhood memories from around 1800.

Eights's precise scenes depict the centre of Albany and feature detailed renderings of buildings, with annotations. These works are invaluable records of a

James Eights, *The East Side of Market Street (now Broadway) between Maiden Lane and State Street Looking South as It Appeared in 1805* (detail), 1805, watercolour on paper, 26 cm × 38 cm, collection of the Albany Institute of History and Art

built environment now completely erased (which was likely his inspiration for doing them: many buildings he depicted were already gone by the mid-nineteenth century). Among the buildings and along the cobblestone streets of early Albany, he included a few figures to enliven the scenes — well-dressed citizens, children at play, a man on a white horse. In several scenes there are Black figures: a boy stands on the road speaking to a man on a hotel veranda; a mother and child, pestered by a small dog, face densely packed facades on the north side of State Street; three people (a family?) watch a white man in white knickerbockers and long blue coat emerge next to a substantial three-storey residence that features the stepped roof design common throughout the town. The most compelling figure, however, is a woman in a blue dress striding toward us along Market Street (now Broadway) at Maiden Lane. The side of the Dutch Reformed Church is just visible in the distance. Dominating the centre of the very broad Market Street, is Market Square with its covered pavilion. It was here that the enslaved were sold and sometimes brutally punished. In Eights's scene, two well-dressed men and a pair of elegant ladies occupy the veranda.

Who is this woman in blue? What is her status—is she enslaved or free? Is she a distinct individual in Eights's memory, or the embodiment of several Black women he recalls seeing about the town? She appears to be unescorted and moving with confidence, her blue dress flowing and revealing bare arms and shoulders, her head uncovered. She glances to her left and smiles at a white man clothed in white knickerbockers, a red waistcoat, and long brown tailcoat. He is eying her in return, but moves constrained, with his thin walking stick and black hat. These two individuals appear connected, and they are being observed by the two ladies sitting in the shade of the veranda of the nearby pavilion. In most of Eights's images, tiny figures appear as mere details, yet here he constructed a mini drama. (Even though these figures are also tiny, their features and gestures appear intentional, not just some accident of scale.) What is Eights asking us to witness?

If only we could imagine the likelihood that this woman moved in freedom... but this is Albany, New York, in 1805. While New York State passed a law of "gradual abolition" in 1799, the enslaved were not fully "free" until 1827, so we are two decades from abolition in New York, six decades from it in the country. Full freedom is distant for those in a region with one of the largest enslaved populations in the north and that discouraged manumission. The woman in the blue dress is likely enslaved. Possibly, she moves along the street having been sent on an errand.

Maiden Lane leads down to landings, docks, and wharves on the river, as does Manhattan's Maiden Lane. It may have been named after a street in central London, near Covent Garden. The British settlers had renamed Dutch streets with English terms that recalled their homeland, and they also brought their way of seeing, mapping, and representing the world. The landscape painter William Turner was born in a house on London's Maiden Lane in 1775. Turner's paintings with their tactile romanticism would influence the Hudson River School, although none of the latter's would be as experimental and modern in their approach. In 1840, he would exhibit *Slavers Throwing Overboard the Dead and Dying—Typhoon Coming On*, now often referred to as the *Slave Ship*.

Joseph Mallord William Turner, *Slave Ship (Slavers Throwing Overboard the Dead
and Dying— Typhoon Coming On)*, 1840, oil on canvas, 90.8 cm × 122.6 cm,
Museum of Fine Arts, Boston, Henry Lillie Pierce Fund 99.22.
Photograph © 2022 Museum of Fine Arts, Boston

In Turner's painting, with its spectacular glaring sun and swirling technicolour
clouds of a coming storm, a slave ship founders in the distance, stripped of its sails,
trapped in a turmoil of waves and churning white water. One cannot see any "slavers throwing," as they are all obscured in the atmosphere of cloud and sea spray,
just as their victims have vanished beneath the waves. There are a few remnants of
chains in the foreground, and the trace of a single figure, a leg with a shackle still
attached to it in the lower right corner of the canvas. This body is being devoured
in a frenzy of imagined sea creatures. Approaching them, jaws agape, is the type
of beast often depicted on early maps, a hybrid of whale and sea monster. In a few
seconds it will swallow the remains of the slave's body whole. If only that person

would be carried on alive, like Jonah in the belly of the whale, to be deposited on some dry coastline. While this was not the fate of those people who were thrown into the sea, for Christina Sharpe they remain: "This is what we know about those Africans thrown, jumped, dumped overboard in Middle Passage; they are with us still, in the time of the wake, known as residence time."[6]

Back in Market Square, we witness the woman in the blue dress surrounded and observed by *whiteness*. Will she reach us before she is, like the figure in Turner's painting, swallowed up? This tiny fragile figure, rendered in delicate watercolour that will fade if exposed to too much light, remains held in the museum's vaults while those more robust renderings, the oil paintings and solid sculptures, continue to hold the privileged space above. Her presence is all too rare in the visual art of the United States and Canada; a Black person on the ground, here to be witnessed, a historical presence many are constantly searching for. Does she think of freedom? Like the enslaved women of New Orleans, who are the focus of law scholar Emily Owens's work, "freedom may not have been relevant," or the primary "organizing principle of their lives." Owens suggests other priorities: "Belonging and street names. [Women would ask themselves,] Do I know people who have my back? Do I have the ability to move about?"[7] The woman in blue is moving quickly in the midst of various white characters and under their watchful eyes. It is unlikely that any of them "had her back."

Sophia and her sister were only children when they passed through Albany. It seems they, too, would have thought less of being free and more of their safety, their parents, and the loss of whatever fragile conception of family and home they'd had. They, too, were surrounded and constrained by the shackles of *whiteness*, both the physical restraints and the laws and conventions of colonial society. The white men likely escorted the sisters up Maiden Lane from the river and passed through Market Square. Did they attempt to sell them there, or was it always their plan to take them further west? I think the latter: it may have been easy to sell them in Albany, but such a transaction would have been hard to hide from Joseph Harris if the sisters had been taken without his permission.

I see Sophia and her sister's passage across New York transpiring in the latter years of the American Revolution, certainly a tumultuous time, but following the American victory at the Battle of Saratoga, where British General Burgoyne surrendered his army (in October 1777), the Hudson Valley and Albany were relatively calm. The major decisive battles would now take place elsewhere. In New

York State, the skirmishes between Patriots and Loyalists with their Indigenous allies were progressing westward throughout 1778. These were mostly "raids," small-scale confrontations compared to battles, which involved armies, but they were equally devastating to the combatants and communities implicated. In 1779, General Washington was determined to exterminate the Haudenosaunee, to push them from their traditional lands, which he largely accomplished with troops under the leadership of generals Sullivan and Clinton that summer. These conflicts drove Loyalists and most of the Haudenosaunee people to cluster around Fort Niagara at the outlet to Lake Ontario.

Dear Sophia,

We will retrace your path across this terrain, adding details of Daniel Outwater II's activities during the war to solidify our understanding of when you were sold to *old Indian Brant, the king*. But first, we need to venture east, on a short diversion to Boston. We'll return across Massachusetts, following the Mohawk Trail, then south into the Berkshires and across the Hudson at Rensselaer, to pick up the trail again at the Albany landing.

CHAPTER 9
ON THE MOHAWK TRAIL

This then, I thought, as I looked around about me, is the representation of history. It requires a falsification of perspective. We, the survivors, see everything from above, see everything at once, and still we do not know how it was.
—from W.G. Sebald, *The Rings of Saturn*[1]

As Benjamin Drew once had, Turner's painting *Slave Ship (Slavers Throwing Overboard the Dead and Dying, Typhoon Coming On)* (1840) now resides in Boston. Its home is the Museum of Fine Arts (MFA), just a short walk along the Fenway from the Massachusetts Historical Society (MHS). Max and I leave the MFA having viewed Turner's painting. I took the information on the painting's label—"Turner (born 1775–died 1851)"—as a sign that this diversion from Sophia's path would be productive. The renowned English artist's life ran concurrent with Sophia's (ca. 1775–ca. 1860). And there was that date again, *1851*, the year Sophia appeared in the census, with her recorded age, *75*, an echo here too. Having glanced one last time at the frenzy of fish and the lone shackled leg, we head to the MHS's elegant mansion at the corner of Boylston Street and the Fenway.

In the 1850s Boston was home to many abolitionists, "the band of fearless men and women" that William Wells Brown praised and whom J.P. Ball also identified as a "band."[2] It was home to William Lloyd Garrison and his newspaper the *Liberator*, as well as the Massachusetts Anti-Slavery Society. The Boston Lyceum regularly presented debates and lectures, including ones by Frederick Douglass and Henry David Thoreau, and numerous African American abolitionists resided in the Boston area. The city also had its share of those indifferent to the plight of the enslaved, if not distinctly pro-slavery, such as the minister Nehemiah Adams, whose *A Southside View of Slavery* defended the institution of slavery in 1854. It was in Boston that Chief Justice Lemuel Shaw confirmed the legality of the Fugitive Slave Act with his decision in the 1851 case of Thomas Sims to return the captured fugitive to the slaveholder. The MHS holds extensive records of this period, including Drew's diaries and papers, and this is what has enticed us here, to see what further evidence of Sophia and her sister might reside in the archives.

The author's preface to *The Refugee* states that: "Many who furnished interesting anecdotes and personal histories may, perhaps, feel some disappointment because their contributions are omitted in the present work.... The manuscripts, however, are in safe-keeping, and will, in all probability, be given to the world on some future occasion."[3] I had hoped the place of "safe-keeping" was the MHS, but like others who have followed this tantalizing lead, we are disappointed. The manuscripts seem to have vanished. Drew's diaries were of little use as he never mentions the trip to Canada. Max and I decide to return to Albany via a less direct route than the Massachusetts Turnpike.

J. Disturnell's *Traveller's Map of the Middle, Northern, Eastern States and Canada* (1849) claims to be (as the title continues) *Showing all the Railroad, Steamboat, Canal, and Principal Stage Routes*. Compared to maps from the period of Sophia's birth identifying territories "uninhabited" and "unknown," this 1849 map reveals how voracious settlement was across Indigenous territories. One need only hold an image of this map in mind when reading the histories of endless treaties and commitments to Indigenous nations to visualize how disingenuous those agreements were. On the 1849 map, Fishkill is still only accessible by river and stagecoach, and this is also true for the journey between Albany and Manhattan, but a route for the future rail line along the Hudson is marked in a dashed line as "proposed." The rough trail Sophia and her sister would have followed west from Albany had become a stagecoach route by the mid-nineteenth century, and new rail lines and the Erie Canal run parallel. Max and I take Highway 2, which follows the train's path across Massachusetts as far as Greenfield. Near Turner Falls, it takes on the name *Mohawk Trail*. Having paused at a traffic light, I spot a prominent stone marker.

Turner Falls was named for Captain William Turner, who, the stone marker informs us, "with 145 men surprised and destroyed over 300 Indians encamped at this place May 19, 1676." This was during Metacom's War (or King Philip's War). Metacom was a Wampanoag sachem (called King Philip by English colonists) and his "war" was a resistance by Indigenous people desperately trying to defend their homeland against settler incursions, an effort repeated many times and by many nations in the coming decades and centuries across Turtle Island. The site of the massacre was Peskeompskut, a traditional fishing spot where the river cascades over prominent rocks. It was considered a safe space by the Wampanoag and their allies, but turned out not to be for the "over 300" Turner "surprised" and likely doesn't feel like one to any Indigenous person reading the stone marker today. According to the Historic Deerfield Museum: "Many of the *enemy* [emphasis added] were killed at first fire...others, in their confusion plunged into the torrent hoping to swim to safety, only to be swept over the cataract and drowned....The scene was one of smouldering wigwams, smashed canoes, and broken bodies—people, many of whom were women and children, dying violently." Turner was also killed in the melee.

Highway 2 / Mohawk Trail traverses a landscape of trauma, as do many roads following historic routes cutting through the states of Massachusetts and New York, including the old NY 5, a state highway that runs along the Mohawk River and splits the eastern side of the Haudenosaunee Longhouse (not a building but a social, political, and cultural worlding that defines the Haudenosaunee Confederacy[4]). Past Syracuse, Highway 5 bends south to merge eventually with US Route 20 that skirts the northern tips of the Finger Lakes (eleven in all, they include, west to east, Canandaigua, Seneca, Cayuga, Owasco, and Skaneateles Lakes—all named by or for Indigenous peoples). Across this meandering route, highways are known as Cherry Valley Turnpike, Mohawk Turnpike, and Revolutionary Trail, while Seneca Turnpike offers an alternate route from Chittenango to Skaneateles. Along the way, we pass endless reminders of who was here before the settlers came, as many places retain old Iroquoian names; the current urban and rural landscape is literally constructed on the metaphorical foundations of the Longhouse. These highways link what Europeans commonly referred to as the "castles" of the original Five Nations of the Haudenosaunee (Iroquois) through their current map names: the Kanyen'kehà:ka (Mohawk) at Canajoharie (known as Upper Castle) and Caughnawaga (Lower Castle), in the east, and then the Onʌyoteʔa·ká (Oneida, for which the village of Oneida Castle is named); the Onóńda'gega' (Onondaga, for which Onondaga Road at Syracuse is named); the Gayogohó:nǫ' (Cayuga; the town of Cayuga is near Auburn); and the Onödowa'ga (Seneca, from which the city of Canandaigua and the hamlet of Seneca Castle derive their names).

This is the likely route the *sons-in-law* followed to take Sophia and her sister from Albany to Niagara, and we will follow it soon, encountering along the way many historic plaques marking sites of raids by Loyalists and their Haudenosaunee (Iroquois) allies in 1778, the Sullivan-Clinton Campaign of reprisal in 1779, and the counter raids that continued into 1780–81. Sophia was carried along in the wake of these battles, following the bloodthirsty momentum of Washington's forces that must have appeared, to the harassed and depleted Indigenous populations, an enraged and vengeful leviathan assaulting their selves and their land. It was, in a way, an act of *landscape*, land being "thrown up against the sea" of colonial violence.

> Dear Sophia,
>
> When you passed through Albany, did you look southwest and see, rising out of the forest, a wall of white and grey rock? This is the Helderberg Escarpment, formed of many layers of ancient seabed, built up over millennia. Fossilized in these rocks are long-extinct flora and fauna, and the escarpment features a natural "ladder" leading up to a long path that winds across the Catskill Mountains and further southwest to where a large Iroquoian village once stood on the Susquehanna River. Called Onaquaga (sometimes Oghwage or Oghwaga⁵), the village was destroyed in 1778 by colonial forces under the command of Lieutenant Colonel William Butler. Until then, the village was home to Thayendanegea/Joseph Brant. But you would not meet him there; the path to Onaquaga is not the route you followed. You will move along a trail heading northwest out of Albany, along the shore of the Mohawk River.

On top of the Helderberg Escarpment, we took in commanding views of the Hudson Valley to the east and the Mohawk Valley to the north. *Then we came by land,* Sophia says, and so she will follow the Mohawk River for a while, passing just south of the grand home of Sir William Johnson, 2nd Baronet (British major general and superintendent of Indian Affairs) that still sits high on a hill a few kilometres above where the river bends briefly southward before continuing west as it comes in to Canajoharie. This is the very heart of the Cherry Valley. Had Sophia been able to venture up onto an adjacent mountain, she would have observed a territory of staggering beauty—rolling hills thickly treed above a lush green flood plain, a clear and meandering river fed by many creeks. It is a view that remains stunning, echoed all the way to the Genesee River and north to Niagara. This landscape is cradled by two escarpments, the Onondaga Formation (of which the Helderberg Escarpment is a small part) and the Niagara Escarpment, running parallel to the north. These formations are rich in flint that is ideal for tool making. The Kanyen'kehà:ka (Mohawk) are "the People of the Flint," Onʌyoteʔa·ká (Oneida) are "the People of the Standing Stone," the Onoñda'gega'(Onondaga) are "the People of the Hills," the Gayogohó:nǫ' (Cayuga) are "the People of the Great Swamp," and the Onödowa'ga (Seneca) are "the People of the Great Hill." The original Five Nations of the Haudenosaunee are, literally, the people of the earth we are traversing.

I think of my ancestors in Ireland and Scotland, colonized and displaced by the English who will extensively employ the Scots as the soldiers, administrators, and missionaries of colonization and Christianity. In many ways, England rehearsed its colonial empire in its own backyard. Thayendanegea/Joseph's life will be dominated and shaped by the values and ideologies of Britain. While maintaining his Haudenosaunee identity, he will yet absorb and practice the King's religion, adopt the settlers' model of land tenure and ownership, engage settlers' business practices and economic system, fight alongside them, and embrace class hierarchies. He will become close with a number of colonial officials and settlers, all to try and advance the well-being of the Haudenosaunee, and at times his own interests. His British ways will feed tensions within his own community and make other Indigenous Nations, of the Longhouse and beyond, suspicious of his status and motives. And like so many in this period who will flee north after the Revolution to start over and seek stability in what would become Canada, owning enslaved people was a part of the British scenario he accepted.

Moving across the foundations of the Longhouse, we will pass numerous reminders of Thayendanegea/Joseph's martial activities from the late 1770s into the beginning of the 1780s. And while we contemplate his determination to defend his homeland and maintain the status of his people, I will worry about his central place in Sophia's narrative, trying to comprehend the complexities and contradictions of Thayendanegea/Joseph and his third wife, Ohtowaʔkéhson/Catharine, and their place in the scenario of colonial chattel slavery that held her.

CHAPTER 10
"AND THEN WE CAME BY LAND"

Dear Sophia,

It must have been brutal to make that journey by land, struggling along a rugged footpath, even given the possibility of horses or ox cart aiding the journey. You were children. What time of year was it? What kind of weather? Did you know how far you were going to travel? From Albany to Niagara is nearly 500 kilometres: it would take weeks, if not well over a month. I imagine you being strong, that you had the stamina to keep going, yet I am certain the white men were not above physical coercion to make you keep up the pace. What did you know of the landscape, or the people encountered? Focused on surviving, and no doubt traumatized by being taken from your parents who are growing far distant, I doubt you took in the richness of your surroundings. The wilderness that was threatening and frightening to them nonetheless suggested great opportunities for exploitation to the white men — to watch, observe, catalogue, and map all they could possess, and those they could dispossess.

In the same pages of the *New-York Gazette* featuring the notices for the fugitive Tom from 1755 through 1756, an advertisement appeared for Mark Catesby's *The Natural History of Carolina, Florida and the Bahama Islands* (1754).[1] An ideal addition to the library of any colonial planter (or investor who wished to remain in Britain), it described the fertile lands awaiting development and extraction. These details of land for the taking was the appeal and direct link to colonization of such natural history books. Much of what Catesby revealed would be harvested, eradicated, and reduced, as building material and fuel, and to make way for the labour-intensive cultivation of introduced plants and animals. There is no mention of whose lands these are, and little of who will undertake the labour.

> Dear Sophia,
>   A century after Catesby, John James Audubon produced his monumental *Birds of America* (1827–38, in four volumes). A black walnut tree is the setting for his "common crow," the bird staring mischievously at us with one shiny black eye. It appears to be smiling, ready to steal the eggs from a hummingbird's nest. I wonder if, progressing across New York, you were able to take in the vast menagerie of birds or register their songs and calls in the dense forests where war parties had and would pass, where armies of conquest seeking revenge marched, and where refugees fled west to Fort Niagara.

At the heart of those battles, Haudenosaunee/Kanyen'kehà:ka (Mohawk) War Chief Thayendanegea/Joseph Brant, along with the Loyalist Butler's Rangers, engaged in a form of guerrilla warfare outside of the direct command of the British. Thayendanegea/Joseph and his allies made many enemies. They were accused of atrocities and massacres during raids. The Haudenosaunee lost a lot as a result of the Revolution; the Longhouse was almost completely destroyed.[2] Even those who sided with the Americans (particularly the Onʌyoteʔa·ká/Oneida), or who tried to remain neutral, ultimately lost. The Longhouse had to be rebuilt elsewhere — a monumental task that defined the life of Thayendanegea/Joseph.[3] Thayendanegea/ Joseph's parents were Margaret Onagsakearat and Peter Tehowaghwengaraghkwin, both Kanyen'kehà:ka (Mohawk) and Protestant. After Peter died, while the family was living on the Ohio River, Margaret returned to the Mohawk Valley with her infant Joseph and his sister Konwatsi'tsiaiénni/Mary (Molly).[4] The family settled at Canajoharie where Margaret married Kanagaradunkwa/Nickus Brant, "a Mohawk believed to be part Dutch, who lived and dressed in European style." The couple were leading figures in Haudenosaunee/Kanyen'kehà:ka (Mohawk) society, their high status linked to Margaret being a descendant of Theyanoguin (a chief, "also known as King Hendrick, Hendrick Peters, or White Head"),[5] and named *Sa Ga Yeath Qua Pieth Tow* "King of the Maquas" in one of the "Four Indian Kings," painted by Jan Verelst in 1710, when they visited England to meet Queen Anne.[6]

By 1778, Thayendanegea/Joseph's base for military actions appears to have been the predominantly Onʌyoteʔa·ká (Oneida) village of Oghwage/Onaquaga on the Susquehanna River. Situated near present-day Windsor, on the western edge of the Catskill Mountains, the site is about a two-hour drive from Fishkill or Albany today. Brant lived there with his second wife Susanna Dekayenesere and his two children (Isaac and Christina from his first marriage to Neggen Aoghyatonghsera/Margaret, Susanna's half-sister, who had died in 1771).[7] The village was abandoned in 1778 following a raid lead by Lieutenant Colonel William Butler of the 4th Pennsylvania Regiment (not to be confused with the Loyalist Butler's Rangers, formed under John Butler). Between 1779 and 1784, Thayendanegea/Joseph was based at his newly acquired farm at Lewiston, just west of Fort Niagara. He had married Ohtowaʔkéhson/Catharine (Susanna died in 1778), and they were a powerful political partnership. Sophia and her sister met them at Niagara, possibly as early as 1780. They reached Niagara having crossed a disturbed *landscape* of land "thrown up against the sea" of colonial violence,[8] clearly described on a large roadside plaque erected in 1961 by the Education Department of the State of New York (Department of Public Works), located at US Route 20 (the Cherry Valley Turnpike) and NY Route 80:

> HISTORIC NEW YORK—Cherry Valley
> The overland route westward from Albany which crests the divide between the Mohawk and Susquehanna valleys was an invitation to settlers. George Croghan, Indian agent and western land speculator from Pennsylvania, in 1768 staked out a large tract near Otsego Lake. During the Revolution the frontier settlements suffered from British Tory and Indian raids from Canada. The most famous was the Cherry Valley Massacre of November 11, 1778. In 1779 the troops of General James Clinton were floated down the Susquehanna from Otsego Lake to join General John Sullivan's men at Tioga. The Sullivan-Clinton Expedition devastated Indian lands and secured the frontier.

In the 1740s, the village now known as Cherry Valley was called Lindesay's Bush; it had been established by Scotsman John Lindesay who had been sheriff of Albany and served in the British military based at Oswego and had the role of "Indian Commissioner." When Lindesay died in 1751, he had accumulated over 8000 hectares. The small community was renamed Cherry Valley in 1778 by Reverend Dunlop. On November 11 of that year, forty-seven settlers were killed in what became known as the "Cherry Valley Massacre." A large stone monument in the Cherry Valley Cemetery states: "SACRED TO THE MEMORY of those who died by MASSACRE in the destruction of this village at the hands of the Indians & Tories under BRANT & BUTLER, NOV. AD 1778."

This village sits in Kanyen'kehà:ka (Mohawk) territory, at the eastern door of the Haudenosaunee Longhouse, so one can understand why it was a significant target. Its presence was an affront to Kanyen'kehà:ka (Mohawk) sovereignty and also considered anti-Loyalist. That said, Thayendanegea/Joseph would have known many living there. George Croghan, named in the Historic New York plaque, was the father of Ohtowaʔkéhson/Catharine, who would become Thayendanegea/Joseph's third wife (and Sophia's "mistress"). The "massacre" or "defensive raid" (the terminology depends on allegiance) would be a catalyst for Washington's decision to mount a campaign to wipe out the Haudenosaunee in 1779.

Unlike many other raids that he was not present at, yet blamed for, Thayendanegea/Joseph definitely participated in the surprise attack on Cherry Valley. Contradicting the moniker of "Monster" Brant, he was praised by his enemies for his empathetic treatment of the wounded and of prisoners:

> Brant in particular was dismayed to learn that a number of families who were well known to him and whom he had counted as friends had borne the brunt....Accounts surrounding the capture of Lieutenant Colonel Stacy report that... "[Brant] saved the life of Lieut. Col Stacy, who [...] was made prisoner when Col. Alden was killed. It is said Stacy was a freemason, and as such made an appeal to Brant, and was spared."[9]

Accounts of his compassionate actions would make him a respected figure in the region beyond the war, as is captured in the paintings produced by leading British and American artists who represented him as a noble and heroic leader, including

Left: Gilbert Stuart, *Portrait of Thayendanegea (Joseph Brant)*, 1786,
oil on canvas, 76.2 cm × 63.5 cm, collection of the Fenimore Art Museum, Cooperstown,
New York. Gift of Stephen C. Clark, N0199.1961. Photograph by Richard Walker.
Right: Ezra Ames, *Joseph Brant*, 1806, oil on canvas, 88.9 cm x 73.7 cm,
collection of the Fenimore Art Museum, Cooperstown, New York.
Gift of Stephen C. Clark, N0421.1955. Photograph by Richard Walker.

Gilbert Charles Stuart's *Portrait of Thayendanegea (Joseph Brant)* (1785) and Ezra Ames's *Joseph Brant* (1806). Versions of these two canvases (each artist did several versions for different people) reside in the Fenimore Art Museum in Cooperstown, at the southern tip of Otsego Lake just over a low mountain from Cherry Valley.

In a slightly distorted video documenting a C-SPAN interview from 2001, Stuart's portrait of Thayendanegea/Joseph is prominent in the background, hovering over the right shoulder of the chief curator of the Fenimore Art Museum.[10] The Kanyen'kehà:ka (Mohawk) War Chief is a silent witness through the extended thirty-minute interview. The curator emphasizes some of the key institutional highlights: the American art collection; the significance of the site and artefacts connected to James Fenimore Cooper; and the prized Thaw Collection of American Indian Art. Through it all, Thayendanegea/Joseph lingers, yet the

Philip Thomas Coke Tilyard,
Portrait of a Child, ca. 1815–25,
oil on canvas, 61 cm × 49.5 cm,
collection of Fenimore Art Museum,
Cooperstown, New York.
Gift of Stephen C. Clark, N0250.1961.
Photograph by Richard Walker.

painting and its subject are never mentioned. It is hard not to imagine incredulity creeping into his fixed expression. The day I visited the museum in 2019, the space Thayendanegea/Joseph's portrait held in 2001 is occupied by another, a face that also hovers shrouded in ambiguous institutional language.

The portrait hangs before me on a curving wall in the central stairwell. Her gaze is direct, a strong light reflects off her smooth skin and heightens the intensity of the whiteness of the capelet draped over the shoulders of the puffed sleeves of her high-waisted yellow dress. This modest portrait is now titled simply *Portrait of a Child* (it was formerly titled *Black Child*) and was painted by Baltimore artist Philip Thomas Coke Tilyard. Placed high up on the wall, the portrait is a distant image when I view it, and the information on the label is evasive, never addressing the basic omission: What was her name? How hard would that have been for the artist to inscribe on the back, on the stretcher, or the minimal gold frame?

"Perhaps a young girl, this honest, compassionate representation of an anonymous African American child is unusual for an early 19th century white artist," the permanent-collection label states. "Was the well-dressed child a favoured slave, the child of a free African American family, or the charge of a white abolitionist family? The child's gender, class and social position remain uncertain." To call this portrait, "honest, compassionate representation," is pure projection and far too subjective an opinion to be offered in the anonymous authoritative voice of the institution. I want to know who the author of this label is and where they speak from to come to such a conclusion. There is no ambiguity about the gender suggested by the child's clothing — the sitter is presented as a young girl.

Like the artist Tilyard, this child was likely living in Baltimore, the state where Josiah Henson, Frederick Douglass, and Harriet Tubman were all born enslaved in 1789, 1818, and 1822 respectively, and from where each escaped. She is likely around ten or twelve years old so, as the painting is dated circa 1815–25, she would have been born sometime between 1805 and 1815. In 1810, the enslaved population of Maryland was 111,502, or 29.3 percent of the state's total population. Only 9 percent of the overall population was considered "free non-white."[11] The odds are that this girl was enslaved, and the type of clothes worn suggest she was likely working in a home. The quality of the clothing may have less to do with being "favored" and more to do with her domestic role in a house and accompanying her master/mistress around the city. She may have been present while one of Tilyard's more privileged clients sat for their portrait. There is also the possibility that she may have been owned by Tilyard himself. Her expression is stoic, and she looks constrained by the stark white capelet and the *whiteness* of the society within which she exists, that weighs on her, holding her in place. What was her future? Like Sophia's sister, we are given nothing else to go by in imagining her fate.

The two portraits of Thayendanegea/Joseph that belong to the Fenimore Art Museum were not on display when I visited. Both were painted from life. The one by Stuart was painted in England when Thayendanegea/Joseph visited there in 1785, and he sat for the one by Ames in Albany in 1806, the year before he died. It is understandable why the Stuart portrait is better known: unlike the older man stiffly posed in Ames's work, he appears the energetic visionary leader befitting his reputation at the end of the Revolution. Sophia's description of him as *a good looking man — quite portly,* sounds more like the Ames image of an aging diplomat than Stuart's vibrant warrior who, in 1785, had only recently been racing back and forth across a wide territory engaged in mortal combat.

The Fenimore Art Museum is named after James Fenimore Cooper, author of *The Last of the Mohicans*. Published in 1826, a time when the "vanishing race" myth, which posited the extinction of the "Red Man," was starting to take hold among white populations (the term would continue and grow well into the twentieth century, thanks to the Edward S. Curtis images, one of which was called *The Vanishing Race*),[12] this historically based fiction is replete with stereotypes and racist tropes. Through his central characters, he praises the noble Muh-he-con-neok/ Mahican (Mohican) and Lenape (Delaware) peoples, all while crafting a portrait of the Kanyen'kehà:ka (Mohawk) — and Wendat (Huron) — people as deceitful and "snakelike" savages. Hawkeye calls the Wendat (Huron), "a thievish race," and declares, "A Mohawk! No, give me a Delaware or a Mohican for honesty."[13] Subtitled *A Narrative of 1757*, Fenimore Cooper's novel draws on records of the siege of Fort William Henry by the French forces of General Montcalm (Louis-Joseph de Montcalm-Grozon, marquis de Montcalm de Saint-Veran) and their Indigenous (primarily Wendat, called Huron) allies who descended from Canada. Even though the Haudenosaunee were allied with the British, Fenimore Cooper casts the character of Magua, a Kanyen'kehà:ka (Mohawk), as the central representative of deceit and evil. The young Major Duncan Heyward has been entrusted with the safety of Cora and Alice Munro, the daughters of Colonel Edmund Munro, commander at Fort William Henry. Heyward mistakenly trusts Magua, choosing him as guide on the secret journey with the sisters.

The Last of the Mohicans is the story of captive sisters being led on a precarious journey into the Longhouse, and so we are in familiar historical territory within the fiction of the novel, even encountering characters who will influence the lives of the Burthen sisters. In the context of the Burthen sisters, there is a detail concerning the daughters of Munro that takes on added significance. Cryptically revealed in the novel, but not incorporated in later film versions, is the fact that the sisters have different mothers. Munro describes his first wife as a woman from the West Indies, "a lady whose misfortune it was to be descended, remotely, from that unfortunate class who are so basely enslaved to administer to the wants of a luxurious people."[14] In short, Cora would have been considered "Negro."[15]

Leaving the Fenimore Art Museum, I drive back through the village of Cherry Valley, passing the cemetery, then spot a sign for a yard sale. I stop to browse, and acquire a stack of old schoolbooks, including: *Botany for Young People and Common Schools: How Plants Grow* (1858), *Essentials of Geography* (1916), and *Building Our America* (1958). *How Plants Grow* has been well used. The wood engravings are very detailed, and the "Index to the Names of Plants in the Popular Flora" reads like a poem of the beautiful, odd, and sinister: apple-of-Peru and adder's tongue; bladder-cucumber and beaver poison; coltsfoot and carrion-flower; dianthus, dockmackie, and Dutchman's breeches; and so on, to end with zantholoxylum.

The endpapers for the two volumes of *Essentials of Geography* are illustrated with four "American" moments: Columbus landing on a beach observed by three Indigenous men hiding in the bushes; labourers picking apples (the labourers are all white and the reference, Johnny Appleseed); Davy Crockett in his coonskin cap, leaning on a pine tree, while a long line of covered Conestoga wagons head west; a long train and a giant freighter meeting below grain elevators on the Great Lakes. In "Section 93: Our Early History," the division of people into racialized groups is plainly articulated: "As the people of the world are divided into large groups, or *races*, and the races are named by the color of the skin, the Indians are called the *red race*. Most of the people of Europe and North America, as well as many people in other parts of the world, belong to the *white race* [emphasis in original]."[16] A page later, in the same disturbing racist logic, we are told:

> But not all people of our country are descended from these first early [white] settlers.... Early in our history, also, negroes, or people of the *black* race, were brought here from Africa as laborers. There are now many negroes in different parts of the country, especially in the South. People from China and Japan, in Asia, who belong to the *yellow* race, also came to our country. They are not now allowed to come so freely as they once were.[17]

The book includes portraits of four middle-aged men to illustrate each racial type.

Though published decades later, *Building Our America* seems to actually "build" on the above in the following passage about Lincoln, the lead-up to the Civil War, and slavery:

> The nation was becoming more and more bitter over slavery. Slavery did not pay very well in the North. Free men worked harder than slaves. When the owner built a warm house and bought warm clothes for a slave, it sometimes took more than the slave earned. In the South, where the weather was warm, the slaves could make money for their owners by working in the cotton fields.

Slavery was not allowed in the states north of the Mason-Dixon Line (the boundary between Pennsylvania and Maryland), or north of the Ohio River. There was trouble when new states came into the Union. The people in the North wanted the new states to be free. Those in the South wanted them to be slaves. The feeling between North and South became bitter. *Uncle Tom's Cabin* was a book showing the evils of slavery. It became very popular in the North. Southerners said that the book wasn't fair. Most slave owners were kind to their slaves.[18]

It's clear that such virulent propaganda was widely absorbed and continues to surface and fuel ignorance.[19] Similar writing is typical of schoolbooks published concurrently in Canada, with the additional praising of all things British. Easily found at yard sales in Ontario, these books honour the monarchy and its empire, the Commonwealth, colonies, and dominions,[20] and let pupils know that "Canada's Indians" were always treated kindly.[21]

As I leave the Cherry Valley yard sale, I notice a massive white pine tree across the road, dead and stripped of its branches and bark, topped with the US flag, the familiar stars and stripes. I imagine a different flag flying here: the white-on-purple of the Hiawatha Wampum. The white squares and central white pine date from the time of the Peacemaker, and the belt is described on the website of the Onoñda'gega' (Onondaga) Nation like this:

This belt is a national belt of the Haudenosaunee. The belt is named after Hiawatha, an Onondaga who was the Peacemaker's helper in spreading the good words of Peace.... The Hiawatha Belt is extremely old. This belt was created at the beginning of our confederacy of peace. We do not know when this belt was created, but we know we have had this belt long before the French, Dutch and English explorers made their way to our lands.

When the peace was made between the 5 nations, the Peacemaker told us to think of us all living together under one longhouse. Just like a longhouse, every nation will have their own council fire to govern their people. But they will govern their people under one common law, one heart, and one mind.... The Hiawatha belt is comprised of

5 symbols joined together and when reading the nations of the belts, we follow the path of the sun, starting in the East.

The first nation on the belt and the first nation to accept the peace is the Mohawk, our Eastern Doorkeeper of our common longhouse.... The next symbol represents the council fire of the Oneida, the People of the Standing Stone.... The third symbol (the tree) represents Onondaga. Here the Peacemaker uprooted the tallest white pine, the Tree of Peace, which leaders buried their weapons of hate, jealousy, and war beneath it (they buried the hatchet).... The fourth symbol is that of the council fire of the Cayuga, the People of the Swamp.... The fifth symbol belongs to the council fire of the Seneca, the People of the Great Hill. The Seneca Nation is the Western Doorkeeper of our common longhouse.[22]

This is now the flag of the Six Nations of the Haudenosaunee (Iroquois) Confederacy.[23] It can be regularly seen flying proudly on contested territory overlapping the Canada-United States border, across what is also Sophia's "prophetic" landscape. The flag reminds us of histories erased and demanding to be seen, like the history of Black people in North America. As professor and designer Walter Hood points out:

Black landscapes matter because they are prophetic. They tell the truth of the struggles and the victories of African Americans in North America.... These landscapes are the prophecy of America; they tell us our future. Their constant erasure is a call to arms against concealment of the truth that some people don't want to know or see. Erasure is a call to arms to remember. Erasure allows people to forget, particularly those whose lives and actions are complicit.[24]

Soon, with Reighen, I will cross back into Canada, over a border defined at the time of Sophia's crossing.

CHAPTER 11
IN THE LONGHOUSE

At the time of Sir William's death, the 1774 probate inventory lists the building as the "Negroe Room West Stonehouse." Slaves living in this Stonehouse were probably household servants given the structures proximity to the main house.

— From an interpretive plaque at Johnson Hall, Johnstown, NY

I am back in the Mohawk Valley and on my own again as Max is back at university in Montréal, and Reighen is studying in London, Ontario. I'm driving from Canajoharie to Johnson Hall, a short distance of just over fifteen miles. A mansion of wood that has been finished to appear as stone, it is over 250 years old and is immaculately restored. At the south end of Sir William Johnson Park, there is a statue of Johnson with the following inscription: "A man of strong character. A Colossal Pioneer. One of the greatest men of his time. Sole Superintendent and Faithful Friend of the Six Nations and their Allies. Their *Warraghiyagey*. Founder of Johnstown. He established here the first Free School in the State. Born in Ireland, 1715. Died in Johnstown, 1774." Johnson had numerous relationships with many different women, but never formally married any of his partners. Following numerous documented and rumoured relationships and offspring, he settled at Johnson Hall with Konwatsi'tsiaiénni/Molly Brant. They were joined there by her younger brother, Thayendanegea/Joseph.

Johnson is considered a heroic figure of the pre-Revolutionary era in New York, a skilled diplomat who encouraged positive relations between British settlers and the Haudenosaunee (Iroquois) Confederacy, keeping the Covenant Chain "polished," as it were.[1] He also owned enslaved people, possibly as many as sixty (the most in the New York colony),[2] as the upkeep of his grand home, with a constant schedule of diplomatic and social events, would not have been viable without a substantial number of people to do the work. Johnson was a gregarious man who loved to entertain, and he had great respect for the Kanyen'kehà:ka (Mohawk) people, particularly those who embraced Christianity and British ways. Johnson supported Thayendanegea/Joseph's education at Eleazar Wheelock's Moor's Indian Charity School in Connecticut where Thayendanegea/Joseph learned to write and studied mathematics, classics, and agriculture. Johnson planned for him to continue studies at King's College (now Columbia University, New York City); however, those plans did not come to fruition. The outbreak of Pontiac's Rebellion/ War (1763) drew Thayendanegea/Joseph back into a warrior's role. The Odawa leader Obwandiag (Pontiac) had gathered together people of various Indigenous Nations from the Great Lakes and Ohio Valley regions who were disaffected by British treatment following the French and Indian War. It was a conflict that would haunt the British for decades, a reminder that their Indigenous allies were not afraid to assert their independence.

The Kanyen'kehà:ka (Mohawk) were the first of the Haudenosaunee to establish relations with the British, and it both enhanced their status and strained relations within the Longhouse. Throughout his life, Thayendanegea/Joseph would struggle to balance his place within the overlapping dynamics of these two cultures, some-times with great success, but often with the feeling of being on the outside ("in between worlds" is a phrase often used to describe him). He clearly believed, like many Indigenous leaders before and after him, that the best future for his people involved a hybrid existence, maintaining independence by adopting and trusting aspects of colonial culture. In far too many cases this trust was, and continues to be, betrayed.

Thayendanegea/Joseph encountered enslaved Blacks from a very young age, and he also witnessed Black soldiers. He must have understood the lowly status imposed on these people brought into his homeland, as they had been a presence for over a century. While the early Dutch and French enslaved Indigenous people, this practice was largely phased out by the British. By the time of Thayendanegea/ Joseph's adulthood, the colonial norm was the exclusive enslavement of people of African descent. This fact, combined with the ongoing practice that held many poor British, Dutch, German, and other Europeans in indentured servitude, provided the essential labour of colonization. Indigenous people knew the incredible power and numbers of the colonizers as their own populations had been devastated by the war, disease, and transformation of the natural environment that had occurred since the arrival of European settlers. A number of Indigenous leaders had also visited Europe. Stressed and under duress, these communities were committed to maintaining their status as equals, to be treated as independent nations and not become subservient. They witnessed the treatment of the enslaved and understood the cost of being dominated.

One can see parallels in West Africa, where rigid class divisions and historic practices of enslavement were grossly expanded to feed the demands of colonial powers. Some communities turned on neighbours in order to protect themselves, a reality Saidiya Hartman described, while following the path of the Sisala ("the ones who come together"), as happening in Ghana prior to the abolition of slavery in the British Empire:[3]

> On foot they had fled from the slave raiders and traders...they dreamed of a place without royals and where they would never again hear the word "barbarian," "savage," or "slave."...The ones who came together were still the prey of the powerful....The new terrors to be faced were part and parcel of the global trade in black cargo....To hand over enemies or unsuspecting strangers captured along the road as tribute to a powerful state or freebooter was one thing, but delivering your brother, wife, and children was another matter....Powerful men as far away as Britain, France, the Netherlands, and Brazil and as close as Asante, Gonja, Dagomba, and Mossi had forced their hand, decided the rules of the game, and dictated the terms of continued existence.[4]

In colonial America, some Indigenous peoples similarly adopted the "rules of the game"; this became central to the imposed terms of their continued existence.

It bears repeating that while a form of slavery was practiced in many Indigenous societies (the result of conflict between rivals and the capture of prisoners), there is no comparison with the economic system of chattel slavery imposed on African peoples by colonial powers. A slave of the Haudenosaunee could certainly be held in bondage for their lifetime, but many were adopted into the communities of their captors, and there are numerous examples of individuals linked to Thayendanegea/Joseph who experienced this transition.[5] Chattel slavery came with the pressure to assimilate and adopt British and European agricultural models of settlement.

Thayendanegea/Joseph adopted the settler notion of a reliance on farming and that farming was unsustainable without enslaved labour, at least until many more immigrants were willing to come from across the Atlantic. He also aspired to the status of his mentor Sir William Johnson, and this clearly included owning enslaved people who would be in service in the home, ideally a grand gentleman's home like Johnson Hall.

> Dear Sophia,
> I have been contemplating for a long time the *sons-in-law*, and wondering how far they would have journeyed with you and your sister across New York. I doubt they knew the landscape beyond the Hudson Valley well. Did they pass the two of you on to an intermediary who had a connection to Thayendanegea/Joseph? I am assuming that there would have been a knowledgeable guide who journeyed with you who knew languages and the best route beyond Albany. I'm also thinking, as your parents may have been living in the Hudson Valley during the French and Indian War, that violent encounters between the colonizers and colonized may have deeply influenced your parents' understanding of Indigenous people and the dangers in the surrounding landscape. As you traversed the remains of the lands of the Longhouse, I wonder what thoughts you carried about the People of the Longhouse, the Haudenosaunee? What did you know of these diverse people and their precarious situation?
> There is another reason for wondering about how far Daniel Outwater II would have wanted to travel and potentially encounter the Kanyen'kehà:ka (Mohawk) War Chief in person at Niagara. Outwater had served as a lieutenant in the Patriot forces, stationed at Fort Montgomery in 1775 and 1776, under a Captain Fowler (also from Fishkill), and he served until the end of the war as a lieutenant in the Dutchess County Militia. He remained deeply committed to the Revolutionary cause and a knowledgeable informant and observer concerning the activities of Loyalists. This evidence comes from numerous

witness statements, all submitted with a petition filed long
after his death by his widow, Nelly Outwater, for a pension
from the United States government.[6] I have reasons to
question the accuracy of these accounts (which I will address
in chapter 18) but what resonates is the fact that I could find
many narratives of this white man's life in the American
Revolutionary War pension petitions that appear to bend the
truth for his widow's benefit, while you linger in only one first-
person narrative. That said, your story projects an authenticity
through its directness, lacking in these suspiciously consistent
tales of Outwater's early years by aging and distant relations.

Once again I backtrack, heading south out of Johnstown and then west following in Sophia's footsteps. The highways leading to the Genesee Valley are dotted
with NY State historical markers, many placed since the 1920s. The first marker
I encounter is from 1928: "CAN-A-GOR-HA 1666–1693 Mohawk Indian Castle
burned by French and Indians 1693." This is a reminder of the initial wave of
assault on the Longhouse, to be repeated nearly a century later by Washington's
forces. The next sign I see (erected in 1978) is at Fort Plain, just past the Iroquois
Lanes bowling alley and Flint Liquors: "1779 CLINTON MARCH Col. Lewis
Dubois with 5th New York Regt. and artillery left Ft. Plain for Otsego Lake."
This refers to the beginning of the Sullivan-Clinton Expedition. Two more plaques
(from 1928) are reminders that the fight was far from over in 1779: "FORT PLAIN
1776–1786 Northern limit of raid by Brant's Indians [and] Tories 16 killed — 60
captured, 100 buildings burned, Aug. 2 1780" and "SAND HILL Dutch Reformed
Church, first built 1750, burned in 1780 raid." The reality is that nothing was
"secure" in the landscape Sophia and her sister journeyed across until well beyond
the War of 1812.

Not far past the site of the former Sand Hill Dutch Reformed Church (a further
extension of the denomination of those who'd enslaved Sophia), I pass the restored
Indian Castle Church ("Erected by Sir William Johnson in 1769," as a plaque says)
and then the pristine and imposing stone church at Fort Herkimer. The former
is an elegant white-painted wood structure reminiscent of the Mohawk Chapel
Thayendanegea/Joseph will build on the Grand River in 1785. There are more
historic plaques along the way, and signs for roadside businesses and towns, streets,

and roads that all reference the Iroquois Confederacy. Just beyond the limits of the village of Oneida Castle, what looks like a homemade version of a NY State historical marker draws my attention. Beneath a maple tree a bronze plaque, green with age, is affixed to a memorial stone. Erected by the Shenandoah Chapter of the National Association of the Daughters of the American Revolution in 1912, it makes the following declaration and finishes with a quote:

> This marks the site of the last home of SKENANDOAH Chief of the Oneidas "The White Man's Friend." Here he entertained Governor DeWitt Clinton 1810, and many other distinguished guests, and here he died in 1816 aged 110. He was carried on the shoulders of his faithful Indians to his burial in the cemetery of Hamilton College, Clinton, N.Y. and laid to rest beside his beloved friend and teacher Reverend Samuel Kirkland. "I am an aged Hemlock, the winds of a hundred winters have whistled through my branches: I am dead at the top. The generation to which I belonged have run away and left me." — Skenandoah[7]

Skenandoah was a Susquehannock (called Conestoga by the British), adopted by the On∧yote?a·ká (Oneida). He met the Connecticut-born Reverend Samuel Kirkland in the 1760s. Kirkland was a Presbyterian missionary who counselled Haudenosaunee to fight with the Americans, much to the displeasure of Thayendanegea/Joseph, who knew Kirkland from Moor's Indian Charity School. Skenandoah commanded as many as 250 warriors during the Revolution, fighting against other people of the Longhouse. The above quote comes from a long speech he gave near the end of his life. His statement concerning the generation that "have run away and left me," may be a reference to the rift in the Iroquois Confederacy caused by spilt allegiances due to the Revolution that saw the Longhouse divided and on opposite sides of the border. Skenandoah was buried alongside Kirkland, not among his own people.

My route bends south, skirts the sprawl of Syracuse, crosses the intersection of the West Seneca Turnpike and Onondaga Road, and eventually joins US Route 20 just before Skaneateles. I have entered the Onoñda'gega' (Onondaga) territory and pass above the largest of the Finger Lakes traversing Gayogohó:nǫ' (Cayuga) and Onödowa'ga (Seneca) lands, to come to what I think of as the western door of the Longhouse. A rusting sign greets me: "SULLIVAN'S CAMPAIGN One mile west Col. Butler Crossed Cayuga lake and Destroyed Cayuga Village of Tichero." This is the same Butler who destroyed Oghwage/Onaquaga. Beyond the village of Cayuga, the Seneca River continues to meander, cascading over Seneca Falls just beyond where Tichero once stood. Before reaching Canandaigua, a sign for Seneca Castle Road points to the village of the same name. The city of Canandaigua is the seat of Ontario County, New York. It takes its name from the historic Seneca village Ganondagan ("At the Chosen Place") that was destroyed by French forces in 1687; survivors rebuilt nearby and had at least twenty-three longhouses by 1779 when the Sullivan-Clinton Expedition arrived. A plaque just west of the city states: "CANANDAIGUA Indian Village Destroyed by Sullivan 1779."

What is striking about these plaques is their bluntness, with their limited details and fragmented sentences, suggesting the expectation that readers will know the history and understand who all the various parties are, their motives, and the details of the events referred to. Perhaps this was once true, but it seems unlikely today. Do contemporary travellers (particularly recent immigrants) actually understand who "Brant's Indians and Tories" were, why a Colonel Butler "destroyed" a Cayuga village, or why Sullivan would obliterate an "Indian Village"? Some travellers might even be confused that today *Cayuga* and *Canandaigua* refer to settler communities, not the historic Iroquoian communities. I imagine that for Haudenosaunee these signs must feel like an extension of the violence inflicted on their ancestors, and of the violence of racism perpetuated in textbooks and historical notes produced more recently, and I doubt the signs encourage empathy or understanding amongst non-Indigenous people.

The first time I encountered the "CANANDAIGUA Indian Village Destroyed by Sullivan 1779" sign, I was travelling with Reighen Grineage. Her ancestors had come out of slavery via Ohio to join the Reverend Josiah Henson at Dawn. She is one of seven siblings (six young women with a brother in the middle). We met in 2018 when she was a student at Western University (formerly the University of Western Ontario) following my lecture about Canadian artists doing work concerning the erasure of Black and Indigenous histories. I also spoke about Sophia, although I was only at the beginning of my research. Reighen had approached me because, as she said later, "That was the first time I've heard anyone speak about Black history in this region, or Canada, at this school." I share this to acknowledge the reality of an education system that remains ignorant of, or continues to marginalize, many. Following a few visits in Ontario to London and Dresden, and some investigations together around Waterloo and Wellington County, we decided to undertake a research trip around western New York, a trip that approached Canandaigua from the opposite direction of the trip I've described thus far.

A year before my trip with Max, Reighen and I crossed from the Canada side of the Canada-US border, into Lewiston, New York, then headed south toward the Genesee Valley, following side roads through a landscape that truly is incomparably beautiful (*Genesee* means "beautiful valley" to the Onödowa'ga/Seneca). We pass the Tonawanda State Wildlife Management Area and the Iroquois National Wildlife Refuge. On the approach to Canandaigua, we are confronted by the Sullivan sign, engulfed by bushes in a narrow corner of a wide lawn anchored by a farmhouse and immaculately maintained flower gardens. A small creek flows past it. To the north, Woodlawn Cemetery occupies the site of the former Onödowa'ga (Seneca) village, the land divided by Sucker Creek.

Further on, we come to Pioneer Cemetery (established in 1790) and West Avenue Cemetery, which face each other across the road. We park beneath a large chestnut tree. It is sunny and incredibly hot, the grass tall and dry. One of my favourite Victorian designs was among the many substantial and ornate headstones: a large stone tree trunk with a scroll naming the deceased. The family plots are large, and the first we encounter is for *Atwater*.

"I'm always looking for signs that I'm on the right track," I tell Reighen as we pause at the line of graves. "*Atwater* is a variation of *Outwater*, one of Sophia's 'white men.'" The patriarch of the Canandaigua clan was Dr. Moses Atwater (1765–1817).

"In this cemetery are interred the remains of many leading men and women," the sign at the entrance to the Pioneer Cemetery informs us, "and at least one family's slave... 'OLD PHYLLIS' Slave in the family of Dr. Moses Atwater." We begin to wander in search of this enslaved woman, calling out names to each other until we find *Phyllis*, isolated in the back corner of the cemetery. Her modest headstone leans back, tilting a little to one side. We almost miss it as the few words etched in the thin grey stone were worn to faint traces. If not for the raking sunlight that gives the surface some contrast, we would have passed what appears to be a blank marker.

The words "OLD PHYLLIS" surface, a tactile whisper; above was the barely discernible "NIG JACINTA." We speculate on the meaning of this. Is it another name or a religious phrase? We search online from our phones, trying a number of variations, getting the occasional hits on the Greek variation of *Hyacinth* (*Jacinth*) meaning beauty, and the Portuguese name *Jacinta*, which resonates as many enslaved Africans carried Portuguese names, traces of the significant Portuguese Catholic presence in the slave trade. We wonder if Phyllis was African born and if Jacinta was her original name. The term *nig* seems all too obvious. "Old" speaks to the level of disrespect for this woman, repeated even in the modest attempt to honour her presence. Once again, a hint of a life surfaces, a person's status obvious in a few words, only to have the life quickly slip away.

Everything in Canandaigua seems oversized and overbuilt; the city exudes confidence and purpose in its permanence. The Ontario County Courthouse dominates the main intersection, across the street is Atwater Park, on the site of the doctor's home and office. This was where Phyllis lived. If only she had been remembered on this prominent corner. Atwater came from Connecticut in 1791.[8] He was one of the town's first settlers and Phyllis may have arrived with him. It's unlikely that she was the only enslaved person in the settlement. *I remember when we came to Genesee — there were Indian settlements there, — Onondagas, Senecas, and Oneidas*, Sophia recalled. The land between Canandaigua and the Genesee Valley is the traditional territory of the Onödowa'ga (Seneca), so if she encountered these other nations, it would have been after they had been pushed west: further evidence that her journey took place around 1780.

We don't linger in Canandaigua for long. On the way north, we pause to see the reconstructed longhouse at Ganondagan, trying to imagine the 150 of these large structures, housing many families, that were wiped out by the French in 1687, and then the over 20 longhouses being decimated by Sullivan's attack a century later. There are no images of these massacres, but I visualize the devastation through all the archival photographs I have seen of such violence: Matthew Brady's Civil War images, the victims at Wounded Knee, the carnage of the Somme battlefields where both my grandfathers saw action. This landscape grieves, for all its beauty.

I tell Reighen that I remain deeply conflicted about what I am doing, that I'm struggling with the challenge of trying to tell Sophia's story from *whiteness*, that this story, and I, are still very much a work-in-progress. She reminds me of what Charmaine Nelson told me: "The history of slavery is all of our history." We are heading for yet another landing by a river, where many crossed, both willingly and coerced, and always under duress.

CHAPTER 12
A NOW AS WELL AS A THEN

Reighen and I have been sitting at the landing by the river, watching the floating detritus race by: sticks, logs, and plastics, carried along on the Niagara's momentum past Lewiston, New York. The village of Lewiston was founded in 1818, but the European presence here dates back to the French in the early 1600s. This would be such a hard river to cross, I think to myself while looking over at a small dock on the farther shore, in Canada, near the Queenston Heights. In what season did Sophia ford this deep channel? We are now at a nearby picnic table positioned close to a sculptural tableau on the theme of the Underground Railroad: four bronze figures and a rowboat on a stone base. Reighen is silent, reflecting on Sophia's interview, searching for the words to articulate what resonates in her story.

I look at the bronze figures, then across to the far landing, and recall another transfer of bodies on this stretch of river, a different exchange described on an Ontario Heritage plaque located on the Niagara River Parkway (near the intersection with Line 8 Road in Queenston, Niagara-on-the-Lake, Ontario):

> On March 14, 1793, Chloe Cooley, an enslaved Black woman in Queenston, was bound, thrown in a boat and sold across the river to a new owner in the United States. Her screams and violent resistance were brought to the attention of Lieutenant Governor John Graves Simcoe by Peter Martin, a free Black and former soldier in Butler's Rangers, and William Grisley, a neighbour who witnessed the event. Simcoe immediately moved to abolish slavery in the new province. He was met with opposition in the House of Assembly, some of whose

members owned slaves. A compromise was reached and on July 9, 1793, an Act was passed that prevented the further introduction of slaves into Upper Canada and allowed for the gradual abolition of slavery although no slaves already residing in the province were freed outright. It was the first piece of legislation in the British Empire to limit slavery and set the stage for the great freedom movement of enslaved African Americans known as the Underground Railroad.

Peter Martin described "a violent outrage committed by one [Vrooman]...residing near Queens Town...on the person of Chloe Cooley, a Negro girl in his service, by binding her, and violently and forcibly transporting her across the [Niagara] River, and delivering her against her will to persons unknown,"[1] who waited to receive Cooley where Reighen and I are sitting on the American side of the border. Those persons need to be witnessed here still. As in Canada, the narrative of the Underground Railroad overshadows the much longer history of enslavement in New York. We know the names of those who held Chloe Cooley as chattel, and they should be mentioned on this plaque as well, as should the fact that Martin had been enslaved before the Revolution by that same John Butler who led the Rangers. Martin gained his freedom by serving for the British. The man who sold Cooley across the river, Adam Vrooman, was of Dutch descent, born in 1753 in the traditional Kanyen'kehà:ka (Mohawk) territory of Schoharie, just west of Albany, below Canajoharie and east of Cooperstown and Cherry Valley. Having also served in Butler's Rangers, Vrooman fought alongside Martin (as well as Thayendanegea/ Joseph) during the Revolution, then moved north to settle at Queenston around 1784 with other United Empire Loyalists (UELs). Vrooman had purchased Cooley just before the incident Martin witnessed, from Benjamin Hardison, who operated a mill and distillery at what is now Fort Erie, Ontario. Born in Maine in 1761, Hardison fought as a Patriot, was captured and then sent to Fort Erie, where he chose to settle upon his release. Unlike his UEL neighbours, Hardison arrived with no property, so he would have purchased Cooley while living in Upper Canada (later Canada West and now Ontario). Vrooman claimed that he "had received no information concerning the freedom of Slaves in this Province," then claimed ignorance, stating that, "if he has transgressed against the Laws of his Country by disposing of Property...it was done without knowledge of any Law being in force to the contrary."[2] The case was dismissed. The complaint made by Martin

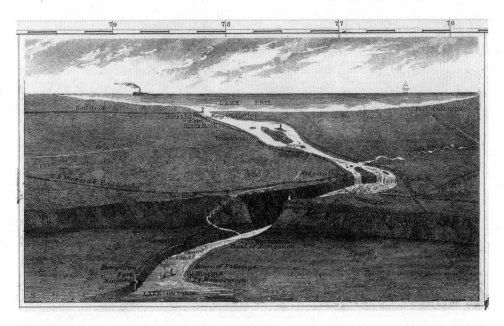

"Niagara River and Surrounding Country, Showing the Proposed Ship Canals, Rail Roads, &c, Drawn by the late Captain W.G. Williams, U.S. Topographical Corps," detail from *Traveller's Map of the Middle, Northern, Eastern States and Canada. Showing all the Railroad, Steamboat, Canal and Principal Stage Routes* (New York, 1849)

inspired Simcoe to draft his act, but this had very limited relevance to the likes of Cooley and Sophia, as those who were enslaved in 1793 would remain so, as would their offspring. The site on the river where Cooley was cast off is still known as Vrooman's Point. Cooley's fate is unknown.

Chloe Cooley may have come from New York and may already have known the shadowy figure waiting on the Lewiston side. Her name has its roots in the Anglicized Irish Gaelic names *Mac Cuille* or *Mac Giolla Chuille*, morphing into *Cooley*, but it also carries a deeper meaning, a label, like *Burthen*, that resonates with the identity of those who carry it. *Cooley* derives from "a nickname for a swarthy person, from the Old English pre 7th Century 'colig', dark, black, a derivative of 'col', (char)coal."[3] This name will resurface in Sophia's story (chapter 19).

"Family," Reighen finally says. "I think about Sophia's parents left behind, and what family would have meant to her. What was her conception of a family, having been taken at such a young age and sold here? I think she saw the Brants as a kind of family that she was a part of, had been *adopted* into, as she claimed Brant stated when he criticized Catharine for assaulting her."

Reighen falls silent again, so I wait, mulling over Sophia's detailed description of escalating abuse by Ohtowaʔkéhson/Catharine:

> *Brant's third wife, my mistress, was a barbarous creature. She could talk English, but she would not. She would tell me in Indian to do things, and then hit me with any thing that came to hand, because I did not understand her. I have a scar on my head from a wound she gave me with a hatchet; and this long scar over my eye, is where she cut me with a knife. The skin dropped over my eye; a white woman bound it up. . . . Brant was very angry, when he came home, at what she had done, and punished her as if she had been a child. Said he, "you know I adopted her as one of the family, and now you are trying to put all the work on her."*

I believe these incidents happened when she was still a child, as she likely learned to speak the Kanien'kéha (Mohawk) language early on; she tells Drew that *I used to talk Indian better than I could English.* Such physical abuse was all too common for the enslaved, particularly when young, and as Drew notes, Sophia had many noticeable scars, the worst of which he attributes, in his annotation, to "civilized (?) men." I'm assuming he means *the sons-in-law,* or *the white men,* and those she encountered in the Hatt household. I'm thinking this over while contemplating the narrative playing out in the nearby sculpture: a distressed Black woman precariously standing in a rowboat, her arms extended, hands reaching out for a child being handed to her by a white man, while an elderly Black man (frail and hunched, supported by a cane — the child's father or grandfather?) is being directed by a woman standing on the shore (her clothing and hairstyle suggesting she is meant to be understood as Indigenous) who is pointing across the river to freedom. We know that crossing this river didn't mean freedom or safety to Sophia.

"I think," Reighen breaks the silence again, "that because I come from a close family, a family of seven siblings, that I think about family *a lot.* So, I can't help thinking about Sophia's parents, and her sister who simply disappears from the narrative."

"I keep thinking about her too," I comment. "She said that 'the white men sold *us*,' so clearly, they were still together. But then she shifts to the singular, '*I* guess *I* was the first colored girl brought to Canada, and, *I* lived with old Brant,' so it seems her sister never left here."

"Was her sister sold to someone else, or did she die?" Reighen wonders. "How old was she?"

The fate of her sister remains one of the deepest voids in Sophia's recollections.

And Ohtowaʔkéhson/Catharine will also remain distant and little understood, a rarely acknowledged or remembered presence among many of the Kanyen'kehà:ka (Mohawk) of Six Nations.

"How is she remembered?" I ask the award-winning artist and filmmaker Shelley Niro (Kanyen'kehà:ka/Mohawk/Turtle Clan).

"She isn't," Shelley replies. "I don't know much about her.... She was not a nice person....I was told Brant divorced her."[4]

The response of other Haudenosaunee colleagues is consistent with Niro's response.

Back in 1791 to 1792, however, the Scottish traveller Patrick Campbell was quite enchanted by "Mrs. Brant," when he encountered her at the Brants' Grand River home that winter.[5] He was entranced by her cultivated appearance, confident presence, and demeanour while revealing throughout his narrative a profound ignorance about her:

> Here we found two young married ladies...on a visit to the [Brant] family, both of them were very fair complexioned and well looking women. But when Mrs. Brant appeared superbly dressed in the Indian fashion, the elegance of her person, grandeur of her looks and deportment, her large mild black eyes, symmetry and harmony of her expressive features, though much darker in the complexion, so far surpassed them, as not to admit of the smallest comparison between the Indian and the fair European ladies.... Her person about five feet nine or ten inches high, as straight and proportionable as can be, but inclined to be jolly or lusty. She understands, but does not speak, English.[6]

Campbell describes a woman who is notably tall, dressed in "Indian fashion" (a hybrid mix of Indigenous and European styles at this time), reflecting her ancestry (she was of Kanyen'kehà:ka/Mohawk and Irish descent) that he did not appear to be aware of. While she did "not speak English" in his presence, she could and clearly chose not to (*She could talk English, but she would not*). The encounter reveals what surfaces in other anecdotes about Ohtowaʔkéhson/Catharine: that she was deeply committed to emphasizing her Indigeneity and downplaying her Irish roots. She emerges as a woman who is truly confident in her position, highly intelligent, and who understood the importance of embodying a strong, at times intimidating, presence.

The Brants' hybridity is significant and needs to be examined. Sophia's understanding about Thayendanegea/Joseph is a common mistake. She says, *Brant was only half Indian: his mother was a squaw*. Both his parents were Haudenosaunee/Kanyen'kehà:ka (Mohawk), although his distinct hybrid dress, and adoption of Britishness, certainly suggested to many that he was of two cultures.[7] His relationship with Sir William Johnson, and the fact that Ohtowaʔkéhson/Catharine's father was the Irishman George Croghan, may have also contributed to confusion. His mother, Margaret Onagsakearat, died around 1782 at Niagara; she didn't live long enough to make the journey into Canada after the Revolution. Sophia states that, *I saw her when I came to this country*, which suggests that she understood Fort Niagara and the area now known as Lewiston, New York, as British Canada and that she was sold to the Brants around this time. Thayendanegea/Joseph, and his mother, were not based at Niagara until 1779. Soon after arriving, and with his second wife having passed away, he married Ohtowaʔkéhson/Catharine. She was a Turtle Clan Mother with the right to name the Tehkarihoken, the principal hereditary sachem of the Kanyen'kehà:ka (Mohawk). The couple began a family by 1782 (their first daughter, Margaret, was born that year; a son Joseph would be born in 1784). They would have wanted a young woman to help around the home and with child rearing, a role Sophia would fulfil throughout her many years of enslavement.

During this period at Niagara, Thayendanegea/Joseph continued to lead raids and war parties, and to travel extensively on diplomatic and strategic missions, so Sophia would have primarily been under the supervision of Ohtowaʔkéhson/Catharine and would have remained so for most of the years she spent with the Brants. At Niagara, Haudenosaunee warriors were regularly preparing to go out on raids, and Sophia offers a vivid description of their preparations: *I liked the Indians pretty well in their place; some of them were very savage, — some friendly. I have seen them have the war-dance — in a ring with only a cloth about them, and painted up. They did not look ridiculous — they looked savage, — enough to frighten anybody. One would take a bowl and rub the edge with a knotted stick: then they would raise their tomahawks and whoop.*

In his annotations, Drew reveals his racism towards Indigenous people, referring to "Indian savages." While Sophia also uses the term savage, she uses it in its original sense as meaning "fierce" or "wild" (from the Latin *silvaticus*, meaning "of the woods") and in the context of warriors preparing to raid. Because she qualifies "savage" with "and not ridiculous," her statement doesn't read as derogatory, but as an honest understanding of the powerful effect the warriors wished to project. According to Sophia, Thayendanegea/Joseph *never would paint* but she notes that *He had his ears slit with a long loop at the edge, and in these he hung long silver ornaments. He wore a silver half-moon on his breast with the king's name on it, and broad silver bracelets on his arms.* Her wording that *I liked the Indians pretty well in their place* (emphasis added), implies a respect for the culture, place suggesting "world" or "traditions," as opposed to "knowing their place" in a hierarchy. And her description of rubbing the knotted stick in a bowl evokes the ceremony of smudging,[8] evidence that she was observing the details. Sophia was deeply immersed in Haudenosaunee culture for at least twenty years, from a very young age and well into adulthood. Had she been adopted, she would have been considered Kanyen'kehà:ka (Mohawk), a member of a complex culture that, during her time, was under great strain and being rebuilt, a state echoed in a household torn between distinct worldings.

Standing at the site of Thayendanegea/Joseph's Lewiston farm, I contemplate a grey decaying bone I've pulled from the soil—the leg bone of a deer (was it killed by a human hunter or a coyote, or did it simply die from sickness or age?). I think of Sophia's sister, where do her bones rest? I look up at the escarpment, grey stone peeking out between a curtain of bare trees. It feels so familiar, like so many views from Dundas at the outlet, the continuation of this geology across the border and around the lakeshore to the Head-of-the-Lake.[9] I am trying to write a story shaped by Sophia that I want to be more than just an additional layer in the growing strata of contested memories, all that has been stacked up that is still weighed down, crushed, pressed, fossilized by whiteness. These structures linger unstable, and the sub-layers spill out to disrupt the present, and whiteness scrambles to explain away what is exposed, to frantically stabilize its narratives, and heal over wounds it has inflicted. I think again of what James Baldwin said about responsibility: "Not everything is lost. Responsibility cannot be lost, it can only be abdicated. If one refuses abdication, one begins again."[10]

The dominant narratives concerning Abolition, Emancipation, and the Underground Railroad have long been overly shaped by the views, goals, and needs of white people, in order to repudiate not only slavery but anti-Black racism as well—as if these were one and the same thing. These narratives seek to absolve whiteness, while still maintaining its enabling racism. This is the reality that Drew fails to directly address in his encounter with Sophia. There is a dissonance between her vivid recollections of continued enslavement and the book that contains them, which seeks to emphasize fugitive freedom in the North. Sophia haunts Drew's volume.

The few contemporary individuals who have drawn attention to Sophia's story often employ it to primarily problematize Thayendanegea/Joseph's legacy, and to emphasize the "barbarous" treatment of her by Ohtowaʔkéhson/Catharine, not to address the continuation of chattel slavery by many settlers and UELs in what will become Canada.[11] *There was but one other Indian that I knew, who owned a slave,* Sophia says, but even one appears to be enough to divert attention away from the far wider colonial system. In the context of reflecting on her life with the Brants, Sophia states: *I had no care to get my freedom*—a startling confession that Drew failed to acknowledge in his annotations.

Reighen wonders what Sophia imagined family to mean, and if she found some sense of fragile security in that precarious familial structure with the Brants. Equally, she is troubled by what "freedom" meant to Sophia, and if she ever truly found it.

"I don't read Sophia's words as revealing her acceptance of enslavement," Reighen explains, "but as a declaration that *freedom* represented a daunting unknown, as it was a condition she had no real experience of." How would Sophia's freedom play out in a land that will deny her rights and will refuse to generously grant her the lands and resources being freely given to white settlers? Freedom might just be a ruse, as whiteness will change the rules regularly for its own benefit.

Such treatment is the foundation of the continuing "racial wealth gap" across North America. In Canada, Quebec and Ontario have the greatest income gaps based on race, with the most significant gap between "Caucasians and Indigenous people."[12] In the United States, Black wealth is about 7 percent of that held by whites, and is still lower for Indigenous people.[13] Abraham Lincoln had promised to grant all people freed from enslavement "forty acres and a mule,"[14] but this promise was rescinded soon after his assassination. According to Dr. Martin Luther King Jr., if Lincoln's promise had been fulfilled, the wealth generated by African Americans would have been $800 billion during his time — in the trillions of dollars today.[15] Instead, the United States government gave slave holders $300 compensation per freed individual (about $6,000 to $8,000 in 2019 currency) that would grow exponentially over time, while giving nothing at all to the enslaved. The British did the same when they abolished slavery in the Empire.[16] These facts have been consistently ignored by whiteness, by all who continue to believe they've just worked harder, are smarter, and have earned their status and privileges.

Sidney March, *United Empire Loyalist Monument*, 1929, unveiled on Empire Day 1929, bronze, approximately 2.5 m tall, Hamilton, Ontario, photographed by the author

CHAPTER 13
"THE PEN-AND-INK WORK"

We are now straitened, and sometimes in want of deer, and liable to many other inconveniences since the English came among us, and particularly from the pen-and-ink work that is going on at that table.
　　—Canasatego, from a speech made at the Treaty of Lancaster (1744)[1]

The patriarch in his tricorne hat wraps his arm around his wife's shoulders. A tiny daughter, a toddler, grips the tail of the man's coat. On the opposite side of the parents, a boy leans back against his mother's skirt. He holds an axe and a hoe, and his posture is strange, twisting, turning back, looking behind at the land they've left behind in the United States. Is he pining for home or turning in fear of the ghosts that may follow? His mother reaches to bring him closer, her hand on the small of his back draws him into the family fold. Cast in bronze, they form a solid family unit—one of the many things Sophia was denied.

Planted in the garden in front of Hamilton's *United Empire Loyalist Monument* is a small cast-metal sign that twists history and misrepresents Haudenosaunee status and motives. "Dedicated to the Defenders of Upper Canada during the War of 1812, the United Empire Loyalists and the Six Nation [*sic*] Indians whose courage to uphold Crown, God and Country led to the beginning of a new Nation," it spells out in navy blue text on a bright white background, topped with the Union Jack. The Six Nations (some, not all) were actually fighting as allied nations with the British and for *their own rights*, as they had for generations, continuing to operate within a fragile and strained relationship that had been clearly established in the seventeenth century and reaffirmed many times. The British, the UELs, and later, the Canadian government, always found it convenient to believe the

Haudenosaunee were content to exist as a subservient people and to ignore the reality that settlers inherited treaty obligations that are still binding today.

Haudenosaunee leaders had long been struggling to maintain equality and understanding with the British, reminding them repeatedly that they were bound together by the Covenant Chain (a series of agreements dating from the early seventeenth century) that obligated both parties to respect boundaries, share defined territories, and support each other as equals and "Brethren."[2] From the Haudenosaunee perspective, the British clearly misunderstood the numerous agreements, interpreting them as land transfers open to unlimited settlement. Settler usage of land and resources was not supposed to cause the Haudenosaunee to suffer. When they did, the Covenant Chain became metaphorically tarnished. Like other treaties such as the Dish With One Spoon (or One Dish One Spoon, which dates back to the 1100s) and the Gä-sweñta' (Two Row Wampum, originally a treaty with the Dutch, 1613, adopted by the British: two purple bands on a white background representing two canoes carrying distinct peoples travelling down one river together, separate but equal), the Covenant Chain employs a succinct and elegant visual metaphor: in this case, a (British) ship protected by being tethered to Haudenosaunee territory. With the war drawing to a close in 1783, Thayendanegea/ Joseph Brant addressed the British general and lieutenant governor Frederick Haldimand at Quebec, calling him "Brother." He described broken treaties and strained relations, reminding Haldimand of his obligations: "We fastened your ship to a great mountain at Onondaga, the Center of Our Confederacy."[3]

The Haudenosaunee never thought the British would lose the war, and they certainly didn't expect to be abandoned in the Treaty of Paris (1783), to have their lands in New York State forfeited to Britain's "rebellious children," the Americans. Their understanding, from the long treaty relationship and Haldimand's more recent commitment to compensate for any losses, had been that they wouldn't be abandoned. As it took a long time for the news of the treaty to travel across the Atlantic, Thayendanegea/Joseph Brant likely didn't hear the details until early in 1784, though he heard rumours before that the British had not maintained "Permanent, Brotherly Love and Amity," as he stated in a speech he made to Frederick Haldimand on May 27, 1783.[4]

The 1784 Haldimand Proclamation (or Haldimand Treaty) emerged as part of the solution, but it was a divisive process as the Longhouse was broken, and not everyone wanted to leave New York or move to the land along the Grand River.

Some stayed around Niagara, others (including Konwatsi'tsiaiénni/Molly Brant) moved to the north shore of Lake Ontario at the Bay of Quinte.

It was at this time that Sophia and her sister were sold to the recently married Thayendanegea/Joseph and Ohtowa'kéhson/Catharine. Although still quite young, she would have been witness to the strains on the Haudenosaunee: the winters were brutal, and food and lodging were scarce for the approximately three thousand Indigenous people gathered around Fort Niagara. There would have been other enslaved people there too, including in Konwatsi'tsiaiénni/Molly's household, and they, like Sophia, would end up in Canada, where the strain would continue. The Haldimand Proclamation came with strings attached, its intended scope was almost immediately challenged, and there were white settlers already on the land purchased from the Mississaugas even before Thayendanegea/Joseph led a fragmented confederacy to Grand River in 1785. Sophia would travel with them from Niagara, without her sister. And with the move to Upper Canada, the Mississaugas would be drawn further into complex and precarious relations between the British and the Six Nations. A speaker named Pokquan addressed Lieutenant Colonel John Butler and Thayendanegea/Joseph Brant on behalf of the Mississaugas on May 22, 1784:

> Father & Brethren Six Nations: We have considered your request.
> Father,
> We the Mississaugas are not the owners of all the Land laying between the three Lakes, but we have agreed and are willing to transfer our right of soil & property to the King our Father, for the use of his people and to our Brethren the Six Nations.... We are Indians, and consider ourselves and the Six Nations to be one and the same people.... We are bound to help each other.
> Brother Captain Brant, we are happy to hear that you intend to settle at the River Oswego with your people, we hope you will keep your young men in good Order, as we shall be in one Neighbourhood, and live in friendship with each other as Brethren ought to.[5]

Pokquan uses the phrase "our right of soil & property" of a land they are "not the owners of." This can be interpreted in various ways, but based on their own traditions, the Mississaugas would not have understood this to mean a *land sale* as the British did, as one cannot literally "own" the earth. The Mississauga had rights to live (in all that entails) in this place, as the Haudenosaunee and others had in the past. The territory was in fact defined as the "Beaver Hunting Ground of the Five Nations of the Iroquois" in the Nanfan Treaty (1701 and 1726) and the Great Peace treaty (Montréal, 1701) between New France, the Wendat (Huron), Haudenosaunee (Five Nations of the Iroquois), and Anishinaabeg (Algonquin) would have covered the shared presence of multiple Nations on a river that Pokquan called *Oswego*. The British first referred to the Grand River as the *Ouse*, taking the name from numerous rivers in Britain. *Ouse* comes from the old Celtic *Ūsa*, meaning "water." The redundancy of *Water River* echoes the naming of *Fishkill Creek*, in which *kill* also means "creek." Thayendanegea/Joseph understood that the "Mississauga Surrender" of the Haldimand Tract (described in the Haldimand Proclamation) included the entire length of the Grand River, six miles back from each shore, but this would be challenged and contested by others, and remains largely unresolved today.

During all her years with the Brants, Sophia would have witnessed a man and community under constant duress, continuing to struggle under the same settler pressures that had plagued them in New York, of land grabs and misleading negotiations and patronizing and manipulative government interventions that rarely benefited the Haudenosaunee. Thayendanegea/Joseph, tired, bitter, growing old, and disenchanted with the British, would be constantly travelling, mediating, advising, and negotiating, caught up in fundamental issues of land tenure.

> Dear Sophia,
> I first came to understand the complex history of the Haldimand Tract from artist and curator Jeff Thomas, a member of the Six Nations of the Grand River, born in Buffalo, New York. Jeff self-identifies as "Urban Iroquois," a reflection of his efforts, as he puts it, at "finding a balance between the Iroquois identity my Elders at Six Nations instilled me with as a teenager and the agency of survival in the city."[6] He combines his original photography with archival imagery and historic works of art, "weaving a new story from the fragmented cultural elements left in the wake of North American colonialism." His series Scouting for Indians records

his "journey to find traces of Indigenous presence in the city," and The Bear Portraits — featuring his son, musician and activist Ehren "Bear Witness" Thomas (Cayuga First Nation), who goes by "Bear" — "explores the loss of male role models by using Bear as a marker of Indian-ness in sites where it does not exist."

One of Jeff's first projects was for Library and Archives Canada, researching photographs of Indigenous peoples taken during the period when reservations were established, Indigenous cultures were actively suppressed, and children were being taken from their families and sent to residential schools or put up for adoption. Jeff was struck by "the absence of images produced by aboriginal people," adding that, "I was frustrated by the silence and challenged to stimulate conversations that did not exist."[7] Jeff's photography and archival research often incorporates historic images of the Haldimand Tract and the people of Six Nations, including the 1807 painting of Thayendanegea/Joseph by William Berczy. In his 2019 *Europeanization — Broken Treaties: 1613–* he positioned Berczy's portrait with three of his own images, including this one.

Jeff's *OH CANADA — We fought for You!* was taken at Six Nations reserve. The flags of the Kanyen'kehà:ka (Mohawk) Warriors (seen in the window) and the Hiawatha Wampum (above the stop sign) bracket the billboard. Positioning the portrait of Thayendanegea/Joseph in relation to this photograph grounds the past as still present. That unstable moment of arrival when you first came here with the Haudenosaunee has never closed as the manipulations of whiteness continue to destabilize the foundations of communities they broke alliance with. Jeff's imagery clarifies and reveals what still occupies this landscape.

In 2020, the Six Nations' Land Defenders set up road blockades on the Grand River at Caledonia, Ontario; they were attempting to stop another housing development on

Jeff Thomas, *OH CANADA— We fought for You!* (2019),
black and white photograph, size variable,
reproduced with permission of the artist

unceded Haudenosaunee territory. This is the latest in a long
history of disputes along the Haldimand Tract that date back
to when you came here. The Hamilton region is a very land
developer–driven place; the pattern of settler behaviour has
hardly changed since 1785. You said, *Canada was then filling
up with white people*, and today whiteness continues filling up
this country.

The lengthy florid statements bolted to the granite base of Hamilton's *United
Empire Loyalist Monument* fail to mention the Six Nations or any other Indigenous
peoples who fought alongside the British. The front plaque's language of high
praise focuses exclusively on the heroic sacrifices and accomplishments of the UELs:
"Neither confiscation of their property, the pitiless persecution of their kinsmen in
revolt, nor the calling chains of imprisonment could break their spirits, or divorce
them from loyalty almost without parallel." A second plaque on the side of the

monument further embellishes: "They set the stamp of their character in the institutions of this country and handed them on to succeeding generations glorified by their sacrifices, enriched by their labours and made sure by their indomitable spirit." And as if this weren't enough verbiage, there is another lengthy declaration on the back: "FOR THE UNITY OF THE EMPIRE," blustering on:

> The United Empire Loyalists believing that a monarchy was better than a republic and shrinking with abhorrence from a dismemberment of the Empire, were willing, rather than lose the one and endure the other, to bear with temporary injustice. Taking up arms for the King they passed through all the horrors of civil war and bore what was worse than death, the hatred of their fellow countrymen, and when the battle went against them, sought no compromise, but, forsaking every possession excepting their honour, set their faces toward the wildernesses of British North America to begin amid untold hardships, life anew under the flag they revered.

This is followed by one more layer of exuberant praise from a UEL descendant.

It is tempting to annotate the above declarations. We should add "and the exploitation of the enslaved" to the statement "enriched by their labours." "Forsaking every possession excepting their honour" should include "and those enslaved." "A monarchy was better than a republic," should be rewritten as: "A class-based system of privilege was better than a representative democracy." Finally, "set their faces toward the wildernesses of British North America," should be amended to, "set their faces toward more lands of Indigenous peoples to the north."

This *United Empire Loyalist Monument* was unveiled on May 23, 1919, to mark Empire Day in Hamilton, with the original Wentworth County Courthouse looming behind, both situated on land donated by city founder George Hamilton in 1816 for a courthouse and jail built to serve the District of Gore. Born in nearby Queenston Heights in 1788, Hamilton was educated in Edinburgh, Scotland, and like many in his circle of political and business elites in the region (including the Hatt brothers) he served in the War of 1812. He acquired his land at the Head-of-the-Lake in 1815 from James Durand. George was the son of Robert Hamilton, one of nine members of the Legislative Council of Upper Canada (of which there were fourteen total) who were also slave owners or members of slaveholding families.

Thayendanegea/Joseph was just one of many who brought or purchased enslaved persons in Canada. A *Canadian Encyclopedia* entry states: "Around 3,000 enslaved men, women and children of African descent were brought into British North America. By the 1790s, the number of enslaved Black people in the Maritimes (New Brunswick, Nova Scotia and Prince Edward Island) ranged from 1,200 to 2,000. There were about 300 in Lower Canada (Québec), and between 500 and 700 in Upper Canada (Ontario)."[8] Enslaved people represented 5 to 8 percent of the population at the time of the Constitutional Act of 1791 that defined Upper Canada. Here, as in the Hudson Valley, slave owning was common and touched all levels of society, with not only the wealthy, but tradespeople and farmers, merchants and traders, politicians and the clergy, all engaged in chattel slavery. "To encourage White American settlers to immigrate north, the government passed the *Imperial Statute of 1790*, which allowed United Empire Loyalists to bring in 'negros [*sic*], household furniture, utensils of husbandry, or cloathing [*sic*]' duty-free."[9] Many slave owners who settled on free land given by the Crown came from the very regions where Sophia was born and traversed on her journey to Niagara: Dutchess and Ulster Counties, along the Hudson River and at Albany.

> Dear Sophia,
>   There is much in Hamilton Cemetery to remind us that this city emerged as an extension of Britain. There are markers here for those whose remains vanished or lie buried far distant—too many soldiers of various conflicts of the British Empire to mention. I come here often to look for memories and stories, to search out faint traces and read between the lines, waiting to encounter unsettled ghosts. I continue to wonder where you lie buried, Sophia, as well as your parents and sister. If only I knew where to look for your graves, where to feel, as I walk, the shallow impressions of your bodies absorbed into the soil, and to mark them well.
>   *I was seven miles from Stoney Creek at the time of the battle — the cannonade made everything shake well,* you said. That's roughly the distance from the battlefield to where I now stand. At the heart of this cemetery are the snaking

ramparts built by the British stationed here during the War
of 1812. You would have been close by when the troops from
these heights raced to confront the Americans on June 5, 1813.

In 1862, painter Robert Reginald Whale (born in Cornwall, England) produced *View of Hamilton* roughly based on the view from Rock Chapel looking down at a creek flowing toward Cootes Paradise, Burlington Bay (now Hamilton Harbour), and Lake Ontario with a hint of the Niagara Escarpment above Stoney Creek lingering in the far distance. The view would have been familiar to Sophia. Raised in Burford, just west of Brantford, Whale, like his contemporary the artist Robert Duncanson, was self-taught and worked in portraits and landscape. He was inspired and influenced by many of the same artists as Duncanson was, from France, England, and the United States. Whale would produce numerous images of the Grand River and the Haldimand Tract, which was quite fragmented and parcelled off by his time. Another painting by Whale, also called *View of Hamilton* (1853) shows the landscape from the east. It reveals the details of the escarpment: an eroding cliff face and a large protruding fragment of rock beneath ragged trees. Hamilton is seen spreading out before a family of settlers, their modest log cabin rests in a clearing carved out of the hillside. There is a lone woman sitting further up the hill, separate, wrapped in a red shawl. She appears to be writing, reading, or painting; if only we could see what she is holding, the story she wants to tell, the tale she is absorbing, the view she is constructing. I think of Sophia when I look at this woman, distant from the family group (a mother, father, and two children, like the family in the *United Empire Loyalist Monument* downtown). The spires of various churches (still extant) are barely visible in the city centre. In Whale's paintings, with views from opposite sides of the city, Hamilton Cemetery is always in the middle—dead centre, so to speak.

Today, above the spot where Whale painted his 1853 *View of Hamilton* looking west, sheets of chain-link fencing make a feeble attempt to hold back the disintegrating face of the escarpment. The limestone and shale crumbles, exposing fossilized shells, plants (and plant/animal hybrids) trapped in layers of seabed, the endless rumbling of traffic noise and the rain and buried creeks seeping into cracks in the rock, to freeze, expand, and break it down. Below, the city has sprawled to conceal all traces of the land below.

Robert Reginald Whale, *View of Hamilton*, 1853, oil on canvas, 90.6 cm x 120.8 cm,
National Gallery of Canada, purchased 1949, photo: NGC

In the deep time of geology, the territory from which Sophia came and this
terrain she was brought to are inseparable, borderless, as are the constantly evolving
generations of flora and fauna here. Indigenous peoples' overlapping presence
stretch back through millennia of allegiances, conflicts, and adaptations, existing
within an endlessly expanding and contracting sense of place and belonging,
grounded in stories and memories and ways of being in the world. But the culture,
which was the same in the two geographies of Sophia's life — of New York and
Upper Canada under the rule of the British — is a disruption of this space. What
was continuous became contiguous. I see the finite geographies of British colonial
rule in New York severed and transplanted here. A hard border came to divide
Upper Canada from the United States, yet the key players who shaped Sophia's
early life were transplanted from one side to the other; even the Harris/Noxon/

Outwater families crossed north. It seems that Sophia never left the landscape of her childhood. She remained in constant dialogue with the legacy of slavery on the Hudson River and the dismantling of the Longhouse; the devastations of both were lifted up and transported here. The momentum of whiteness sprawls across surfaces, blanketing and obliterating, rooting in the earth only in order to extract, looking skyward only for further space to conquer.

Dear Sophia,

There is a poem I am fond of that reveals through erasures a deeply concealed truth, Tracy K. Smith's "Declaration." Smith, winner of the Pulitzer Prize for poetry and named poet laureate of the United States in 2017, describes this as an "erasure poem drawn from the text of the Declaration of Independence."[10] It ends:

In every stage of these Oppressions We have Petitioned for
Redress in the most humble terms:
                                        Our repeated
Petitions have been answered only by repeated injury.

We have reminded them of the circumstances of our emigration
and settlement here.
                        —taken Captive
                                        on the high Seas
                                                to bear—[11]

These extracted lines from the nation's foundational text, in which white men outlined their collective grievances in making their case for their exclusive independence and freedom, are brought to the surface and voiced anew to carry the muted petitions of all the enslaved whose rights and freedoms were denied, who were valued only as chattel ("value" they will not inherit) and for their labour that was the new nation's economic foundation, as it was for the Empire they broke from and that hovered to the north. And in these extracted words shaped by Smith, I hear the echo of the poetry of your words, Sophia.

It is time to pick up the trail of those who held you and your family in bondage, to follow you to other rivers, and into those scattered ruins of empires.

CHAPTER 14
OF BLACK CURRANT

Black currant's genus is *Ribes* (meaning "currant" in Latin, "rhubarb" in Arabic). Currant comes from the French *raisin de Corinthe* ("grapes of Corinth," the city in Greece). According to *Botany for Young People and Common Schools: How Plants Grow* (1873), one of the books I picked up at a Cooperstown yard sale, black currant plants can be described as "shrubs with alternate rounded and radiate-veined leaves; the tube of the calyx coherent with the one-celled ovary, and continued above it into a cup which is often colored, like a corolla,"[1] "Seeds many," it continues with a precise botanist's cadence, "with a pulpy outer coat, borne upon the walls of the berry and two thickened lines (*parietal placenta*)." In early English, *ribe* often referred to a scrawny or thin person or animal, which makes sense in relation to a shrub that is defined by pencil-thin branches and modest clusters of dark seedy berries prized by birds.

The ~~currant bushes~~ Sophia mentioned were most likely garden black currant (*Ribes nigrum*), the most commonly cultivated in the region, an introduced species that grows wild in Britain, northern Europe, and across Russia and into China —all places where it has long been actively cultivated. One bush can produce up to ten pounds of fruit. Multiple plants are essential if one desires a proper harvest that will produce preserves, dried berries, dyes, and traditional medicines. The fruit can be used in sweet and savoury dishes, baked or boiled, and made into syrups, juices, and alcoholic beverages. Very high in vitamin C, black currant has significant antioxidant traits, is anti-inflammatory and anti-rheumatic, and has long been used in treating osteoarthritis, gout, and painful ligaments, tendons, and joints — ailments afflicting the elderly, especially those who have lived a life of constant physical labour. *I am now unable to work*, Sophia declares, *and am entirely dependent on others for subsistence: but I find plenty of people in the bush to help me a good deal.* Did these people provide her with extracts and tinctures of black currant to soothe her pain?

All of the above would probably have been familiar to Sophia; she would have learned these essentials, like so many things about working around the home and in the gardens, fields, and adjacent woods, from her parents, and carried this knowledge over a lifetime, for the benefit of others who would have perceived her knowledge as something they owned. "They are *red* when they're *green*," my colleague and friend Lisa Hunter remembers her grandmother telling her, "I pretended I knew what she meant, that black currants are green, as in *not ripe,* when they are *red*. You must pick only the darkest ones."[2] I remember how starlings, cedar waxwings, and cardinals would strip the plants of the last desiccated berries in late fall at my grandparents' farm.

> Dear Sophia,
>
> I will always associate black currants with the farm of my maternal grandparents, Florence and Herbert "Bert" Allen. In addition to the line of dishevelled black currant bushes that marked the boundary between their distinct plots of flower and market gardens with crops in labelled rows, there were two other plants defined by distinct purple and black details: massive irises and clusters of black tulips. Their rhizomes and bulbs were dug up, divided, and shared with my mother, to thrive in her garden, and some were transferred to me.
>
> Florence and Bert loved to work in their garden, finding freedom in their property, and this work of cultivating and harvesting, preparing and preserving, was a pleasure for them. They passed these labours of love on to my mother, and she did her best to pass them to me. I remember transplanting black currant from the farm to my parents' yard, and my mother making jam from the fruit, but now the bushes are

gone, and my mother can't remember when that happened.
When we speak of her parents and the farm, she will slip into
oft-repeated stories, of a young man who lived with them and
who was killed in the Second World War, and of her assault,
as a young teen, by the man next door.

My mother, Anne, is now in her eighties, as you were when
you met Benjamin Drew. She is in the second progressive
stage of Alzheimer's disease. Her old memories fading, new
memories no longer form, she seems haunted by specific
incidents of trauma from her life, as if these persistent
memories are the deepest. My psychiatrist tells me that "as the
individual struggles to form new memories, older, embedded
memories, those that seem firmly laid down, surface and
repeat." For many, these are often "extreme" memories,
sometimes of joyous moments, "but often of traumatic events
that one may have long buried." My psychiatrist describes the
fragile "vulnerability" of an individual unable to control their
emotions—"Their reactions to 'triggers' can be extreme and
uncontrollable"—and repeats, with emphasis, that they are
profoundly vulnerable when faced with being asked to discuss
their memories, saying, "It is as if they have no defences or
control of their thoughts."

When I'm with my mother, I think of you, *unable to
work and entirely dependent on others*. How much did you
struggle with disrupted memories and the trauma you carried?
I think of Drew appearing out of nowhere, a white man
asking you questions, and wonder how sensitive he was to your
vulnerabilities or what his probing might bring to the surface
in your mind.

My grandmother, Florence (or "Flowery" as Bert called her),
chose to come to Canada from England with her sister Bee,
imagining her own place, so that she no longer had to work as
a maid for others. She made a hard choice to leave her family,
but it still was her choice. Her strength, determination, labour,
and independence are all foundational to my privileges. If only

you had been free to make such choices, to set the foundation
for a family and a distinct pattern to your life, free of coercion
and judgement.

"The man next door," Mom begins to tell me the story again, "he came at me
in the garden…my father was livid…confronted the man and his wife…I didn't
have to work there anymore…"[3] My mother's story reminds me: Sophia's father
was denied the right to protect and defend his daughters, and the system of slavery
distorted their relationship, broke down the essential and cardinal elements of
nurture and security. The detail and clarity of Sophia's recollections gives me hope
that she remained lucid in her old age, and that she could choose the memories to
share, to deliberately leave the details of her time with the Hatts a blank slate, and
offer her description of hunting deer with Thayendanegea/Joseph and the children
as a strong positive memory of deep meaning.

William Berczy, *Thayendanegea
(Joseph Brant)*, ca. 1807,
oil on canvas, 61.8 cm × 46.1 cm,
National Gallery of Canada,
purchased 1951, photo: NGC

William Berczy's *Thayendanegea (Joseph Brant)* was painted around the time of the subject's death (ca. 1807). A small painting, it places Thayendanegea/Joseph above a wide river, pointing to the distant terrain. He is wrapped in a bright red blanket, holds a long rifle, a George III Indian Peace Medal around his neck, a pipe and tobacco pouch slung under his arm, and, as Sophia described, *broad silver bracelets on his arms*. The landscape is imagined, but it is likely the Haldimand Tract / Grand River country, and one can also read aspects of the outlet at Dundas where Spencer Creek flows into Cootes Paradise. A small, short-haired hound watches him intensely. Light brown and white, its pointed ears, sharp nose, and frozen stare, are all locked on its *master*. It is easy to imagine Thayendanegea/Joseph directing the deer hunt described by Sophia. There would be more hounds, moving free and loose under his direction, and he would be dressed in rough clothing, in a much happier place, with family, not arguing with the British and Americans, or caught in disputes with his own people about how he may be personally benefiting in his relations with the whites.

I lived with old Brant we caught the deer. It was at Dundas at the outlet. We would let the hounds loose, and when we heard them bark we would run for the canoe —— Peggy [Margaret], *and Mary, and Katy* [Catharine], *Brant's daughters and I. Brant's sons, Joseph and Jacob, would wait on the shore to kill the deer when we fetched him in. I had a tomahawk, and would hit the deer on the head — then the squaws would take it by the horns and paddle ashore. The boys would bleed and skin the deer and take the meat to the house.* (editorial insertions in the original)

Here she is, with five of the eldest Brant children and their father, their efforts described as a collaborative endeavour that she was clearly part of, bringing more skills of survival into the mix, not only working at home. At this moment, based on the approximate ages of the children, who would have had to be old enough to participate in the hunt, *the house* would be the grand house built on land acquired from the Mississaugas in 1797, as explained on the website of the Mississaugas of the Credit First Nation: "Brant chose a tract of land containing 3450 acres [1400 hectares] on which the present day city of Burlington, Ontario is located. Governor Simcoe of Upper Canada gave instructions that the land chosen by Brant was to be purchased from the Mississaugas of the Credit by the Crown and then granted to Joseph Brant."[4]

The Kanyen'kehà:ka (Mohawk) leader "lived in a genteel English style," according to the *Dictionary of Canadian Biography*—likely modelled on Sir William Johnson's lifestyle and the design of Johnson Hall. The dictionary also claims that he "had about 20 white and black servants, kept a well-stocked table, was waited on by black servants in full livery, and entertained graciously."[5] They are likely the men Sophia spoke of: *Brant had two colored men for slaves: one of them was the father of John Patten, who lives over yonder, the other called himself Simon Ganseville.* Sadly, these men were not interviewed, but Sophia shares another critical detail: *There was but one other Indian that I knew, who owned a slave.* We will return to these numbers in chapter 16.

They would have travelled by canoe to the outlet from the house at the far corner of the bay, where the area now known as Burlington / Hamilton Beach forms a border with Lake Ontario. Hugging the bluffs along the north shore, Sophia's hunting party would pass Willow Cove, and proceed around a thin narrow point to head into a sheltered bay. Once known as Rock Bay, this location is now called Carroll's Bay, and the point, Carroll's Point, named after Peter Carroll, president of the Great Western Railway.[6] Carroll had made a fortune by land surveying and speculating and in business, and built a substantial house on the point made of stone quarried at Queenston. The "castle" as it was known burned down in 1908. The land is now the Woodland Cemetery, where my father's parents, Thomas and Marion Hunter, are interred. Some of the last remnants of the oak savannah habitat that was extensive in Sophia's day can still be seen along the bluffs and shoreline today.

From Carroll's Bay, they would have followed an inlet that eventually entered the marsh at its northeast corner. This route is now blocked, having been infilled with earth for a road and to form a foundation for rail lines. From there, the hunters would have paddled across shallow waters to reach the mouth of Spencer Creek, *at Dundas at the outlet,* where the hounds will drive the deer into the water, and where Sophia would be waiting. She would have been surrounded by the sights and sounds of nature in all its abundance and diversity, particularly the once-incredible array of avian species that lived in or frequented the Hamilton area.[7]

Back on the water, around 1802, I see Sophia wielding her tomahawk. She is the one striking the animal with enough force to nearly kill it, and it will be the

Brant sisters (Sophia refers to them as "squaws"[8]) who seize the beast and *take it by the horns* (clearly this was a large animal) and head for shore. They will all stand up to the white men who arrogantly claimed that *'t was their hounds, and they must have the meat.* As she proudly states: But we would not give it up. In this brief moment of power in the face of *whiteness,* I feel closer to understanding Sophia's troubling declaration, *I would not have chosen freedom* and closer to the truth in her memory of those potent words of Thayendanegea/Joseph, spoken when scolding his wife for her treatment of Sophia: *Said he, "you know I adopted her as one of the family, and now you are trying to put all the work on her."* Hunting the deer, Sophia appears to truly be part of a family. This leaves her fate of being sold to *the Englishman at Ancaster* a troubling puzzle to resolve.

Those incidents with Ohtowaʔkéhson/Catharine continue to overwhelm Sophia's narrative; her mistress striking her with *a hatchet* (she does not say "tomahawk," but uses the word for the white man's tool), then *a knife,* leaving *this long scar over*

Shelley Niro, *Portrait of Sophia Burthen (Pooley),* 2021, acrylic, pencil, and ink on paper, 76.2 cm × 57.2 cm, collection of the author (reproduced with permission of the artist)

my eye. So much blood flows out from the head of this child Sophia *because I did not understand her.* An older Sophia, who says she *used to talk Indian better than I could English,* and who had the strength and skill to take on a deer, might not have been so vulnerable. The hunt for the deer stands out as a coherent and powerful memory, yet the incident in the garden amongst the currant bushes, and the description of the repeated assaults by her mistress, are the ones I fear haunted her more as she aged, surfacing repeatedly and out of her control.

CHAPTER 15

"THE INTERIOR INHABITED PARTS"

The author set out... to explore the interior inhabited parts of North America, attended with an old faithful servant, a Dog, and gun, only. As he travelled such in wilderness, and in birch bark canoes, through lakes and rapid streams, where the mind could not at all times be inattentive to safety, and wrote in these canoes, and on the stumps of trees occasionally, as he went along...

— Patrick Campbell, *Travels in the Interior Inhabited Parts of North America. In the Years 1791 and 1792*[1]

"The Author in his Travelling Dress," states the caption below a distinctly unflattering portrait of Patrick Campbell.[2] A brown and white dog of unknown breed accompanies him as he stands on a landscape of vague, stubbled ground, populated with just two small tree stumps. Campbell wears a ruffed waistcoat beneath a jacket that falls short of his knees, his leggings and moccasins (for which he writes "magazines" in his book)[3] look more like ballet tights with carpet slippers. His hat is truly spectacular: a large marshmallow of beaver fur with a massive puff of a red fox tail that flops down the back, ending in a white tip at his shoulders. "The Foxes here are of various colours, black, red, and grey," Campbell states, describing the wildlife around the future city of Hamilton. "They are caught in traps, and I have been told of one man who since last fall had taken about sixty."[4] There were numerous individuals like Campbell writing of their wanderings about North America at this time. His stated goal is to "direct those bent on leaving their country to the proper object";[5] no one needed encouragement. *Canada was then filling up with white people.*

The Scotsman visited a number of locales across Sophia's landscape: Hudson Valley, Albany, Mohawk Valley, Niagara, Brant's Town or Brant's Ford (he called it "Mohawk"), and the Hamilton area. Campbell passed through the Genesee country, noting the presence of "Indian" communities (the scattered remains of the Longhouse, which Sophia also noted). Travelling by sleigh from Niagara in winter, his route followed the base of the escarpment to Stoney Creek. He describes the general trip first: "This Mountain begins in the Genesee country, and stretches along until it crosses the river Niagara at the Grand Falls; from thence in a serpentine form to the head of the small lake, called by the Indians, *Ouilquetou*, and known to the white people by that of Geneva."[6] Then Campbell says he "drove along a fine beach until we came to the neck of land which separates the two lakes, the Grand Ontario from the Geneva." He passed close to where Thayendanegea/ Joseph will build his last home, then veered west, crossing Burlington Bay (*Lake Geneva*), "about ten inches deep on the ice."

Artist unknown, *The Author in his Travelling Dress*, from Patrick Campbell's *Travels in the Interior Inhabited Parts of North America in the Years 1791 and 1792* (1793), iii–iv, reproduction of watercolour on paper (dimensions of original unknown)

Campbell encountered several Mississauga men (he writes "Messessagoe") fishing for "Pickerel, Maskanongy [muskellunge], Pike, and other kinds of fish, inhabitants of, and particular to this and other Canadian waters." He admired their fishing nets: "I am of the opinion that nets of the same construction, but on a larger scale, might be used to advantage in Scotland for catching Salmon of small rivers." It does not occur to Campbell that larger nets would deplete small rivers. The colonial impulse is always for *bigger* and *more*, and to Campbell and others like him, nature was infinite — something the Mississaugas understood to be false, even before settlers over-consumed the natural resources they relied on. Campbell eventually arrived at the Burlington Heights and the home of Richard Beasley, was "entertained with the highest hospitality" by the well-established trader and land speculator from Albany, then headed to Brant's Town/Ford. Campbell claimed to use stumps as seats to pause and write; I imagine him perched upon these little stools (like those in the watercolour illustration of him), his knees jutting up, balancing his notebook, while black walnut stains his bottom, or the resin from a newly felled white pine sticks to his leggings. From wherever the Scotsman sits, stories will spread and stain, stories that will stick, overwrite, and push to the margins of his vision mere fragments and faint anecdotes of *others*.

Margin is an old English term from the Latin *margo*, meaning "border," first used in English in the fourteenth century to refer to "the empty space at the side of a written or printed page; the part that is not included in the main part of a group or situation." *Marginalia* comes much later. First used around the time Sophia took her freedom in the second decade of the nineteenth century, it means "the notes written in the margin; facts or details that are not very important." *Marginalized* appeared in the 1970s: to be pushed to the edges, outside the main body of matter (one could say what or who was historically "not very important," and remained outside the "main group"). To write from whiteness about "marginalized" communities and individuals is to maintain privilege, while crowding the space within with endless variations and repetitions of narratives and imagery of dominance, *filling it up with white people*, keeping many silent, down in the hold.

Dear Sophia,

All that I don't know isn't marginal but is held, redacted,
within the body of the text that's defined me. Strangely,
redact first meant "to bring into organized form," then "to
put in writing," then "to select or adapt," and now, in its most
common usage, "to remove information from a document
because you do not want the public to see it." All those pages
of precisely delineated dark shadow seeking to extirpate lives
held within—hold them up to the light, and stories will bleed
through these allelopathic gestures.

On a recent visit to the location of the Dawn settlement,
near Dresden, Ontario, Reighen and I harvested black walnuts.
I've made black walnut ink, a deep-brown tincture with subtle
hints of green. I've been giving it away to writers and artists,
and trying, myself, to produce some images of absence, to
fill within the margins themselves, within my own borders
(erasures on maps, in old texts, producing silhouettes of
ghosts). I tell people it will stain their clothes and to not get it
on their hands, as it will also stain their skin. It does not turn
white skin brown; my fingers end up tainted a yellowish green,
making them look terminally diseased. You cannot wash it off;
you have to wait until it slowly fades over time.

I often wonder what you would do with this ink, Sophia?
What you'd put into your own story? What would you add to,
or obscure from, Drew's text? What would you redact from
mine?

I am standing once again in Hamilton Cemetery, close to where Campbell
spent that evening, back in 1793, being entertained by Beasley. Trains are shunting
in the railyards below; the steel mills with their massive blast furnaces loom in the
distance. Many societies around the globe had smelted iron in "blast furnaces" for
centuries when, in 1709, Abraham Darby of Bristol, England, succeeded in smelting
iron using coke as fuel to make a high-quality pig iron. The iron trade expanded, a
major factor in the birth of the Industrial Revolution. The steel mills on Hamilton
Harbour still dominate the view from Thayendanegea/Joseph's former property.

Now mostly automated, their furnaces continue to spew clouds of pollutants into the air and water, while lighting up the night sky with the blue flames from waste gas stacks that exhale their burnt-off toxic breath. These leviathans on buried inlets of Hamilton Harbour's south shore evolved from Darby's prototype.

As early as the late seventeenth century, ships were leaving Bristol to fill their holds with enslaved Africans, their live burthen held in Bristol-made iron restraints. Bristol investors in Darby's initiative were already profiting from transatlantic slavery by 1709. Enslaved Africans were long familiar with the heavy metal Darby advanced: their societies had been iron smelting to make fine tools, weapons, and ceremonial objects for over two thousand years before the Portuguese initiated the Middle Passage. Their iron was formed in pits dug into the earth. As history professor and public historian Madge Dresser further points out: "The legacy of slavery continues in a more tangible form in Bristol. Many of the city's public buildings, educational and economic institutions...owe their origins to the wealth created by the trade in enslaved Africans and slave-produced commodities."[7]

What can be said of Bristol can be said of Liverpool and many other British cities that prospered during the Industrial Revolution and at the peak of the slave trade, including Glasgow, where such leading scholars as Marenka Thompson-Odlum and Sir Thomas Devine have done much to reveal the profound economic impact of the Triangle Trade.[8] "The Merchant City," as the economic heart of Glasgow is known, "was founded on exploitation. Its grandest thoroughfares...are named after the traders who made their money through slave-run tobacco and sugar plantations; the neoclassical mansions that grace them were built with the fortunes they amassed."[9] The shipyards at nearby Greenock built Glasgow merchants' vessels. So many of the resources brought to Canada to fuel its prosperity flowed from Great Britain. In an industrial region like Hamilton (including Ancaster and Dundas), the connections to Bristol, Birmingham, Glasgow, and Liverpool are deep and foundational; Canadian cities, businesses, institutions, and political and family legacies are rooted in the profits directly tied to the slave trade. Hamilton once called itself "the Birmingham of Canada," but I doubt civic leaders were looking to emphasize connections to slavery (Birmingham having once been a major producer of iron chains, restraints, and implements of punishment used in the slave trade).

George III gave Thayendanegea/Joseph many gifts, including a steel officer's dagger (or *dirk*) that the latter praised to Campbell for its brutal efficiency in dispatching one's enemies. It was better than the tomahawk, he claimed, that was prone to inflict glancing blows.[10] Sophia received such a blow from Ohtowaʔkéhson/ Catharine, and then a more precise cut from a knife that she was lucky to have had properly treated. Such a wound could turn fatal, as Thayendanegea/ Joseph's eldest son, Karaguantier/Isaac, discovered. Born in 1766 at Canajoharie to Thayendanegea/Joseph and his first wife Neggen Aoghyatonghsera/Margaret (Peggy), Karaguantier/Isaac appears to have always been troubled. He drifts in and out of many narratives about his father. Sophia did not mention him, leaving me to wonder what she made of the following tragic incident.

The story goes that the "Indians" had gathered at the Head-of-the-Lake to receive what is too often referred to as "gifts" (what they were owed by the Crown).[11] At one of the local taverns or stores (possibly the King's Head Inn on the beach, or Beasley's store at Burlington Heights) Karaguantier/Isaac attacked his father. His anger may have reflected years of father-son tension, or he may have been acting out the wider grievances of many Haudenosaunee who were frustrated by Thayendanegea/Joseph's land dealings and close bonds with whites. There were likely many factors. In self-defence, Thayendanegea/Joseph struck his son on the head with that fine steel dagger. Karaguantier/Isaac refused medical treatment and the wound turned septic; he died a few days later.[12]

Karaguantier/Isaac died in 1802, the year that Sophia moved to Burlington, as Thayendanegea/Joseph distanced himself from the tensions on the Grand River. From there, she ventured out to *hunt the deer*. The Scotsman John Norton (later Teyoninhokarawen), Thayendanegea/Joseph's adopted nephew, later witnessed the dagger hung on the wall above his elder's sickbed; he claimed that the ailing man would look upon it and weep. Thayendanegea/Joseph died in 1807, the same year the Englishman at Ancaster got married.

> Dear Sophia,
>
> Thayendanegea/Joseph is still not at rest. He remains a highly contested figure, and his name will continue to surface in your narrative, as his dealings with all those who settled here were extensive. First buried at Burlington, he will be reinterred on the grounds of the Mohawk Chapel on the Grand River, next to his son Ahyonwaeghs/John Brant, their graves marked by a massive boulder and enclosed by a cast-iron fence. There is a newer, black granite marker for Ohtowaʔkéhson/

Catharine next to it. She died in 1837, five years after her son Ahyonwaeghs/John had succumbed to cholera. *She was a pretty squaw: her father was an English colonel,* you said (he was actually Irish), and *She hid a crock of gold before she died, and I never heard of its being found.* Ohtowaʼkéhson/Catharine died *the year the stars fell.*

CHAPTER 16
NUMBERS

Sophia Pooley's early experience in Canada allowed her to construct her experience as the first, but the last decades of the eighteenth century witnessed a significant increase in the visibility of Black slave women, if only in printed advertising offering their sale or soliciting opportunities for their purchase. The Upper Canada Gazette *advertised the following notice in July of 1795:*

"For sale, for three years from the 29th of this present month of July, a Negro Wench, named Chloe, 23 years old, understands washing, cooking &c. Any gentleman willing to purchase, or employ her by the year or month, is requested to apply to ROBERT FRANKLIN, at the receiver general's."

— Maureen G. Elgersman Lee, in *Unyielding Spirits* (1999)[1]

It bears repeating Maureen Elgersman Lee's words from the very beginning of this book, that Sophia would have "lacked significant opportunity to create social bonds with other Black women based on shared gender, race and legal status," and that "it is highly possible that where Black women lacked such support systems, they may have found the slave system even more trying than for women who had such support."[2] This is a stark reminder of the reality that being enslaved in Canada was not the "kinder, gentler" version so many claim it to have been.[3]

It is likely that Sophia's only significant relationship with other Black people growing up was with her mother, father, and sister, all of whom vanished from her life before the age of ten. During her time with the Brants, she may have encountered other individuals; she tells Drew that Thayendanegea/Joseph *had two colored men for slaves* and that she knew of *but one other Indian . . . who owned a slave.* Sophia makes no mention of any meaningful contact with other enslaved people—a revealing detail in her interview as a number of writers and historians have confidently claimed that Thayendanegea/Joseph held anywhere from 20 to 40 enslaved people. This "fact" (as it is framed in the following) needs to be addressed:

> DID YOU KNOW?
> Five years before moving to Burlington, Ontario in 1784, Joseph Brant began to own black slaves, possibly as many as 30 people. While still living on the United States side of the border near Niagara, he bought a kidnapped black slave girl named Sophia Pooley, whom he claimed to have adopted as "one of the family." He brought her and other slaves with him when he moved to Burlington Bay, where she hunted deer with his children and travelled with the family for many years.[4]

The egregious errors in this prominent "pop out" feature of *The Canadian Encyclopedia*'s online listing for Thayendanegea/Joseph are numerous: he did not move to Burlington in 1784 (he moved to the Haldimand Tract in 1785, and Burlington around 1802); the territory around Fort Niagara was still British territory at that time he lived there (the British held a number of border forts after the Revolution); Sophia did not assume the name *Pooley* until her later marriage, so she should be referred to as Sophia Burthen. *The Canadian Encyclopedia* does not provide a specific source for "as many as 30 people," and none of the books listed at the end of the article under "Further Reading" provide supportive evidence.

In the numerous cases where this high number is stated, either no primary source is listed to support it, or a sole source is listed: that of Isaac Weld Jr. Dublin-born Weld travelled extensively in eastern North America from 1795 to 1797, and met both George Washington and Thomas Jefferson. In his widely read *Travels through the States of North America and the Provinces of Upper and Lower Canada* he stated that, at the Kanyen'kehà:ka (Mohawk) village on the Grand River in 1795,

> he [Thayendanegea/Joseph] has no less than thirty or forty negroes, who attend to his horses, cultivate his grounds, &c. These poor creatures are kept in the greatest subjection, and they dare not attempt to make their escape, for he has assured them, that if they did so he would follow them himself, though it were to the confines of Georgia,

and would tomahawk them whenever he met them. They know his disposition too well not to think that he would adhere strictly to his word.[5]

Weld calls out the wrongs of slavery in his writings. Reflecting on his time with Thomas Jefferson in Virginia, he states: "It is immaterial under what form slavery presents itself, whenever it appears there is ample cause for humanity to weep at the fight, and to lament that men can be found so forgetful of their own situations, as to live regardless of the feelings of their fellow creatures."[6] His sympathies, however, rarely extended to Indigenous people. In fact, his description reveal his presumptions of their heartless nature, all setting the scene for his encounter with Thayendanegea/Joseph. He prefaces his sharing of second-hand details of the killing of a captured slave by an "Indian woman of some consequence," with this racist and unsubstantiated generalization:

> The Indians have the most sovereign contempt for any set of people that have tamely relinquished their liberty; and they consider such as have lost it, even after a hard struggle, as unworthy any rank in society above that of old women.... You could not possibly affront an Indian more readily, than by telling him that you think he bears some resemblance to a negro; or that he has negro blood in his veins: they look upon them as animals inferior to the human species, and will kill them with as much unconcern as a dog, or a cat.[7]

Weld is hardly a reliable source, and his line "unworthy any rank in society above that of old women" is an absurd statement in the context of predominantly matriarchal societies where older people are honoured as Elders. Weld consistently accepts hearsay (from biased white settlers and soldiers) as truths; his sources, and his retellings, are clear exaggerations. Much of his narrative should be dismissed as yarns.

Just a few pages before claiming that Thayendanegea/Joseph had "no less than thirty or forty negroes," Weld states that "at Detroit, Niagara, and some other places in Upper Canada, a *few* [emphasis added] negroes are still held in bondage."[8] Patrick Campbell, who spent several days at Brant's Town on the Grand

River before Weld and whose observations were not limited to inside the house, mentioned only the "two handsomely attired Negro slaves waiting on the table."[9] Later writers cite Campbell, and also repeat elements of Weld's narrative. Isabel Thompson Kelsay, in her 1984 biography *Joseph Brant, 1743–1807: Man of Two Worlds*, claims that, at Lewiston: "Joseph already had the beginnings of a *retinue* [emphasis added] of slaves whom he had captured or who had run away to join him."[10] *Retinue* is rather imprecise, and Kelsay oddly cites only Campbell, whose encounter was at Brant's Town a number of years later than Thayendanegea/Joseph was at Lewiston. "If any of these expected an end to their labor," she continues, "they were mistaken...it was always said of Joseph that he would tolerate no nonsense from his slaves."[11] Again Kelsay cites only Weld.

To own "no less than thirty or forty negroes" would have been unprecedented in this context. At Fort Niagara, people were starving and suffering from disease, severe cold, and the many depredations brought on by war. It can be easily argued that the Haudenosaunee suffered most with the recent destruction of the Longhouse. Thayendanegea/Joseph's people would not have taken kindly to suffering further while one of their leaders was supported—and on his private land—by dozens of enslaved people. While the Brants were certainly spared the extremes, maintaining an enslaved workforce would have been impossible. How would such numbers be housed, clothed, and fed, and did Thayendanegea/Joseph even have enough land under cultivation to need such labour? At Brant's Town, and later at Burlington, these same issues of sustaining a significant enslaved labour force would hold true. As in New York, slavery was common, but the number of enslaved per household was low, with the exception of the likes of Sir William Johnson (whose wealth far exceeded anything Thayendanegea/Joseph ever achieved).

The enslaved Black individuals "who had run away to join" Thayendanegea/Joseph would have been treated as fellow combatants as the British promised freedom to enslaved men who ran away to fight for the Crown (although many found this hard to secure). There were Black soldiers on both sides in the war: "In the little known 1779 Battle of Minisink fought between the combined forces of British agent Colonel Joseph Brant, the famous Mohawk chief, and those of Colonel John Harthorn of Warwick, New York, African Americans were combatants on both sides," A.J. Williams-Myers states in his 1976 book *Long Hammering*.[12] Though he elevates Thayendanegea/Joseph to colonel (he was a captain),[13] Williams-Myers does provide sound sources. The presence of Black fighters among the British forces, including those "loaned" by their Loyalist owners, is well documented.

In the "Thayendanegea" entry of the *Dictionary of Canadian Biography* online, Barbara Graymont states that: "He lived in a genteel English style, had about 20 white and black servants, kept a well-stocked table, was waited on by black servants in full livery, and entertained graciously," seeming to back away from the term *slaves* to use the more ambiguous *servants*, but still providing no source for these details.[14] Finally, Linda Brown-Kubisch, in *The Queen's Bush Settlement* (2004), asserts that: "Nothing more is known of her sister, but Burthen became one of the many slaves owned by Brant," citing only the Drew interview, which mentions only two (Simon Ganseville and the father of John Patten).[15] Brown-Kubisch also makes the inaccurate claim that Sophia's life with the Kanyen'kehà:ka (Mohawk) was a "nomadic" one, a very unfortunate misrepresentation of Thayendanegea/Joseph's situation.[16] The combined accumulation of misinformation and poor sources in the biographical accounts of Thayendanegea/Joseph leads to a profoundly misleading representation of Sophia's life—a life we don't know enough about.

It feels strange to be arguing that the number of enslaved held by Thayendanegea/Joseph has been significantly inflated in a narrative that seeks to address Sophia's absence, as well as the erasure of Black lives. I am not defending Thayendanegea/Joseph, but I believe the repetition of Weld's questionable claim undermines the realities that many are striving to bring to the surface, and that perpetuating these falsehoods becomes a convenient distraction from the widespread presence of a British legal system of slavery in Upper and Lower Canada.

As I've previously stated, there is a persistent tendency to diminish white, colonial accountability for a global economic system by making such statement as "Slavery has been present in many human societies" or "Many Indigenous people held slaves too." Both statements are true; however, the scope and scale of chattel slavery that held the African diaspora in bondage across colonial empires is a particular creation of European states, occasionally practiced by colonized peoples. "The one thing I will say," the artist and member of Six Nations of the Grand River Jeff Thomas tells me, "is there was a very different mindset in the way Indigenous people used so-called slaves from Euro-North Americans. It was largely a result of war with other Indigenous enemies. The reason the Haudenosaunee were able to maintain a fighting force for so long was because of adoption."[17] Thayendanegea/Joseph absorbed many aspects of Britishness, including concepts of land ownership,

Christianity, genteel domestic life, and chattel slavery. It is not necessary to exaggerate the numbers to make him the ultimate holder of enslaved people in Upper Canada—a status more likely held by Peter Russell (member of the executive council, a legal counsel, and the receiver general of Upper Canada) and William Jarvis (the provincial secretary of Upper Canada) of York, both of whom opposed the ending of slavery in Upper Canada (discussed further in the next chapter). It seems no different than the exaggeration of his actions during the Revolution, or calling him "Monster" Brant.

Ultimately, I look to Sophia (who lived with Thayendanegea/Joseph for over twenty years) as the most reliable source for understanding his slaveholding. Sophia would likely have spoken of such a staggering number of fellow enslaved peoples had they been present at Niagara, Brant's Town, or Burlington. Peter Martin, compelled to protest at the treatment of Chloe Cooley (see chapter 12), would not have been silent about such a substantial slave presence either.

CHAPTER 17
"BEATEN OR SHAPED BY HAMMERING"

*Hamiltonians are unique! They are a rare breed, with an all-fired loyalty to
their city. . . . There's pride in Hamilton's firsts, and her beloved sons. . . . Let
someone else claim an outdoor market, borders of farm land, woods and
water; or, speak about the might of industrial giants, halls of learning, a
place of opportunity, and he will have a fight on his hands. The Ambitious
City has them all! Better still, let these pictures tell their own story.*
— from *Up and Down in Hamilton* (1971)[1]

Up and Down in Hamilton, 1770's to 1970's: A History in Pictures was written by T.M.
Bailey and C. Carter and published to mark the city's 125th anniversary by "The
MacNab Circle" (a group of Hamiltonians dedicated to the city's heritage, named
for Sir Allan MacNab). It claimed that the collected images "are as representative
of the city as Gore Park. However, if some aspect of her [the city of Hamilton's] life
has been omitted, it was for good reason: either a lack of space, or want of a good
picture."[2] These are such common excuses for the public erasures of so many lives,
and indicate a failure to query where those "other" images could be or why they
don't exist. The first image in the book is a hand-drawn town plan, titled *Sketch
of Burlington Bay, Hamilton, and its Vicinity* (1846). Like the selective history that
begins this volume, it is cropped to fit the page, cutting off the west end of the town
of Dundas (itself to the west of Hamilton), much of the escarpment to the south,
and the areas east of the city core that were farmland. Dundas is marked on the
sketch by a small cluster of black squares for prominent buildings. The Governor's
Road and the King's Road (now Highway 8) heading northwest to Waterloo, as
well as Old Ancaster / Old Dundas Road (built by the Hatts and running roughly
south from Dundas), are cut off. What's labelled the *Dundas Canal* or *Des Jardins*
(Desjardins) *Canal* makes a straight channel through the marsh after following

a natural path around the north end of the Iroquois Bar / Burlington Heights.[3] (The map predates the channel cut to join the marsh to Burlington Bay.) On the Heights, now occupied by Hamilton Cemetery, military buildings are identified: *Old Barracks, Magz* (for the magazine, storage for ammunition), *Battery, Old Lines* (meaning the ramparts of 1812), *Old Blockhouse*, then *Dundurn Castle* (the grand home of Sir Allan MacNab). The small area of water where Chedoke Creek ends is labelled *Coot's* (Cootes) *Paradise*. If you follow the line of the creek south and inland, it will traverse the property of *Wm. Beasley Esq.*, whose family name is attached to so much land in this region where Sophia lived.

In the sketch Hamilton is laid out in a grid between what is now Dundurn Street in the west and Victoria Avenue in the east, the labelled *Brickworks* and *Barracks* on the harbour to the north and Aberdeen Avenue at the base of the escarpment to the south. The only features identified in the core are *English Church* (Christ's Church Anglican Cathedral), *Market Place* (where Hamilton Farmers' Market and the Hamilton Public Library's Central Library now stand), and *Courthouse* (the John Sopinka Courthouse, now Ontario Offenses Offices and Provincial Court of Justice, and the location of the *United Empire Loyalists Monument*; see chapter 13). The caption on the sketch states: "Where Hamilton Began. After explorers like Brûlé and La Salle (1669), the Head-of-the-Lake began to be visited in the late 1770's by Loyalists from the States to the South." *Visited*—what a strange choice of term for the wave of settlers who took over the region. On the reverse page, two photographs are reproduced, with the question posed *Our First Settler?*: Robert Land's grave (*Died July 1818, aged 82 years, THE FIRST WHITE SETTLER IN HAMILTON*) is contrasted with Richard Beasley's *Fur Cache* (a stone cellar beneath Dundurn Castle, labelled *Hamilton's Oldest Architecture*). These men didn't come here alone—and neither was the "first."

Gore Park (sometimes called "The Gore") sits in the heart of today's Hamilton, a thin parcel of ground running two blocks between James and John Streets, split by Hughson Street. Its northern and southern borders are called King Street (the south is also known as Maiden Lane). It narrows to a point at its eastern tip, where the pedestal for a recently toppled statue of Sir John A. Macdonald remains.[4] A massive statue of Queen Victoria, by prolific Montréal artist Louis-Philippe Hébert, has watched over the west end of the park since 1908. She is posed on a granite pedestal, the lion symbolizing the British Empire rising at the base. The dedication reads: "Victoria Queen and Mother / Model Wife and Mother / May

Children of Our Children / Say she Wrought Her People Lasting Good / The Women of Hamilton in Affectionate Admiration / Have Raised This Monument." *Wrought*: among the various meanings of this word is "beaten or shaped by hammering."

The Gore was once the property of city founder George Hamilton. "Hamilton, from whom the city by the bay earned its name, was a wealthy merchant from Queenston (Niagara) and a slave-owner," historian and curator Adrienne Shadd states, adding, "his wife Maria Lavinia Jarvis... also came from a prominent slave-owning family."[5] The land holdings of George's father, Robert (who was born in Bolton, Scotland, and died in Queenston, Upper Canada) were vast: "If contiguous, his lands would have stretched one township deep from the Niagara River almost to Burlington Bay."[6] He held an astounding 321 655 hectares and was owed over £68,000 New York currency when he died. He had an extremely profitable business supplying the British military with materials, equipment, and foodstuffs, and a portaging business that shipped furs to the Todd McGill company of Montréal, a lucrative partnership of Irishman Isaac Todd and Glasgow-born James McGill. The founder of McGill University, as academic Charmaine Nelson reveals, profited extensively from shipping, sugar, rum, and financing—all profit-making ventures deeply imbedded in the slave economy.[7] Like McGill, Robert Hamilton was a pure capitalist. He believed the entrepreneurial class, not government, should lead colonial development, a position his son, George, and grandson, Robert Jarvis, shared. They were typical laissez-faire Scottish capitalists (their views consistent with those of another Scot, economist Adam Smith).

George Hamilton's spouse Maria Lavinia was the daughter of Connecticut Loyalist William Jarvis, who, after first fleeing back to England following the Revolution, came to Upper Canada with John Graves Simcoe, in 1792 or 1793. Jarvis was appointed provincial secretary and registrar. Like Peter Russell, Jarvis is honoured with a street bearing his name in current-day Toronto. These two men both sat on the executive and legislative councils of Upper Canada, and both were the most prominent slave owners in the region, When George Hamilton died intestate in 1836, his son Robert (whose middle name was Jarvis) returned to the city to take over his father's estate and business interests. He fought with local political leaders over the future of The Gore, and successfully blocked their ambitions to build on it.

Through a sequence of definitions in the *Oxford English Dictionary*, we can follow the evolution of *gore*. The first entry for it as a noun defines *gore* as "a triangular piece of land" or of fabric or metal (as in a sail or spearhead). As a verb, it can mean "(of an animal such as a bull) pierce or stab (a person or other animal) with a horn or tusk," which relates to another definition for the noun form: "Blood that has been shed, especially as a result of violence." The *Cambridge Dictionary* enriches these definitions, with the noun form meaning "blood that has come from an injury and become thick," and the verb form, "(of an animal) to cause an injury with the horns or tusks."[8] The word comes from the Old English *gor* ("dung, dirt") "of Germanic origin; related to Dutch *goor*, Swedish *gorr* 'muck, filth.'"

The sharply pointed east end of Gore Park forms a triangle. The city was the administrative centre for the district named for Francis Gore, from London, England, who was lieutenant governor of Upper Canada from 1806 to 1811. Previously, Gore was governor of Bermuda, where a woman named Mary Prince was born enslaved, in 1788, at Brackish Pond, on land next to a pool or pond (the land riparian, like the name *Pooley*). She was sold in the Caribbean many times and lived in London, England, where her narrative, *The History of Mary Prince*, was published in 1831. Her words resonate with Sophia's: "It was night when I reached my new home. The house was large, and built at the bottom of a very high hill; but I could not see much of it that night. I saw too much of it afterwards. The stones and the timber were the best things in it; they were not so hard as the hearts of the owners."[9]

The geometry of Gore Park, like the accumulative progression of the term "gore" (from a shape, to a weapon, to acts of violence, to the thickening of blood), embodies the progress of colonization, from policy, to physical presence, to land claimed, shaped, and weaponized, occupied through violence, leaving conflicts, wounded land and wounded people, carrying the thick scars of trauma, all calculated and triangulated. Rooted in trigonometry, triangulation, a primary technique of cartography and navigation, has taken on a psychological meaning as a preferred toxic and manipulative strategy of the psychopath, sociopath, or narcissist. The strategy of triangulation is used, even institutionalized, by police states and totalitarian regimes. *Narcissistic triangulation* describes how a manipulator plays two parties off or against each other, creating rivalry and trauma for their own benefit (think of the divisions among the Haudenosaunee that colonial powers nurtured). It is easy to see how triangulation can be used as a preferred coercive and manipulative weapon of capitalism.

A massive water fountain, cast locally in iron, anchors The Gore. A wide bowl forms the lower tier into a shape reminiscent of a collapsing tulip, filled by arching streams of water projected from below. When the bowl is filled, sheets of water spill over its lip, cascading back down into the pool at its base. The thick veil of white water obscures the fountain's base, forming a true *cataract*. The word is derived from the early fifteenth century from the Latin *cataracta*, meaning "*waterfall*." The alternative meaning comes from Latin and probably passed through French to the English, "a medical condition that affects the lens of the eye so that you gradually lose your sight." The escarpment that runs through Hamilton and defines the Dundas Valley hosts over one hundred waterfalls, leading many to call this the "Waterfall Capital of the World."[10] I think of Hamilton as a place of cataracts, where an accurate view of history has been obstructed.

Flowing water is energy. It drew early entrepreneurs to this area, to build their mills (paper, timber, grist, cotton) that relied on water-based energy. The industries of James Crooks and the Hatt brothers were fuelled by the momentum of Spencer Creek. Crooks (born in Kilmarnock, Scotland) built mills atop the escarpment on Spencer Creek, above Webster's Falls, in an area now known as Crooks' Hollow. Crooks became a prominent figure in business and politics here. Back in 1792, James Crooks and his brother William were shopping for help: "Wanted to purchase, A NEGRO GIRL from 7–12 years of age, of good disposition — For further particulars apply to the subscribers. W & J Crooks."[11] Crooks acquired land through purchase from Elizabeth Russell, who had inherited property from her brother Peter, the slave owner in York (now Toronto).

Unlike most Indigenous people Thayendanegea/Joseph Brant was able to personally acquire properties through land grants and purchases, while the Hatts, over a number of years, received *multiple* land grants (as did most white settlers), and they were given blanket permission to develop and exploit the local environment for their own benefit. UELs who flooded north were compensated for their losses through land grants, and many loyal subjects who made the journey from the British Isles also obtained free property. Grants were generously handed out to whites only, officially signed by the powerfully positioned Peter Russell. The Irish-born former army officer once claimed as a gambling win a "462-acre tobacco plantation 42 miles west of Williamsburg [in Virginia]," states his entry in the *Dictionary of Canadian Biography*, where he lived "hiding from his creditors and longing for capital to enter the lucrative slave trade. To raise funds he tried gambling, but again lost; to pay his Virginia debts he had to sell his estate and return to England."[12] An aging, inveterate gambler who served time in London's Fleet Prison (released under the Insolvent Debtors Relief Act), seems a strange choice to become a judge, particularly as he had no legal training, or to become receiver and auditor for Upper Canada (giving him seats on the legislative and executive councils, a salary, and over 2400 hectares of land), but Russell had close friends and supporters, including John Graves Simcoe, who recommended him to these positions, and the chief justice at that time, William Osgoode. Russell also owned enslaved people in York where Peter Street, in the heart of the city of Toronto, and Russell Street and Russell Hill Road are all named for him.

On February 8, 1806, around the time Sophia was sold to Samuel Hatt, Russell placed this ad in the *Upper Canada Gazette*:

> ## TO BE SOLD,
> A BLACK WOMAN, named PEGGY, aged about forty years; and a Black boy her son, named JUPITER, aged about fifteen years; both of them the property of the Subscriber.
>
> The Woman is a tolerable Cook and washer woman and perfectly understands making Soap and Candles.
>
> The Boy is tall and strong of his age, and has been employed in Country business, but brought up principally as a House Servant—They are each of them Servants for life. The Price for the Woman is one hundred and fifty Dollars—for the Boy two hundred Dollars, payable in three years with Interest from the day of Sale and to be properly secured by Bond &c.—But one fourth less will be taken in ready Money.
>
> PETER RUSSELL.
>
> York, Feb. 10th 1806.

The *Dictionary of Canadian Biography* entry for Russell, though it mentions his longing to "enter the lucrative slave trade" does not mention Peggy and Jupiter—a glaring omission considering Russell's high status in Upper Canada. The open advertising of his intent to sell them is clear evidence that slavery remained an acceptable practice more than a decade after the passing of An Act Against Slavery (1793).

I was a woman grown when the first governor of Canada came from England; that was Gov. Simcoe, Sophia states. She would have been around about eighteen or twenty years old when Simcoe arrived in 1792, with his wife, Elizabeth, and daughter, *Sophia*. In an address to the Legislative Assembly, Simcoe declared: "The principles of the British Constitution do not admit of that slavery which Christianity condemns. The moment I assume the Government of Upper Canada under no modification will I assent to a law that discriminates by dishonest policy between natives of Africa, America or Europe."[13] Simcoe's Act, however, had no impact on Sophia's status and was hardly generous. It did not abolish slavery; it outlawed the import of slaves but maintained the status of those already enslaved ("servants for life," as Russell wrote) and held their children in bondage for twenty-five years, an approach to "gradual" emancipation similar to other jurisdictions, including several northern states. The Wikipedia entry (at the time of this writing, January 20, 2021) for the 1793 Act wrongly states that, "Slavery was thus ended in Upper Canada long before it was abolished in the British Empire as a whole. By 1810, there were no slaves in Upper Canada, but the Crown did not abolish slavery throughout the Empire until 1834."[14] (While I acknowledge that as an open-source resource Wikipedia is not necessarily reliable, this article cites multiple academic sources, and I cite it as a primary source of information available to the public, like many of the sources I call into question throughout.) Until the British Parliament's passing of the Slavery Abolition Act in 1833 (implemented in 1834), Simcoe's Act remained fully enforced.

Much is made in Ontario about the supposed "abolition" of slavery in 1793 under the leadership of Simcoe, but this consistently distorts the true impact of his Act. Sophia witnessed a phenomena that was the leading factor in the decline of slavery here: *Canada was then filling up with white people*. With the great influx of settlers to work the land, chattel slavery was no longer a viable and "necessary" business model. Ultimately money, more than empathy or conscience, was the "value" that determined slavery's decline.

Simcoe's tenure in Upper Canada was brief, less than half a decade, and his next posting certainly tainted his anti-slavery credentials. Having returned to England due to illness in 1796, Simcoe was assigned to lead British troops in San Domingo (what the Americans and British called Saint-Domingue, now Haiti) where he found himself fighting against General François-Dominique Toussaint L'Ouverture, leader of an epic slave revolt. Writer and historian C.L.R. James described the French colony as "the greatest individual market for the European slave trade";[15] it relied on five hundred thousand slaves. Simcoe joined a British expedition of sixty thousand men with their charge to establish British control and re-establish planter dominance, reversing L'Ouverture's historic victories. As James points out: "It was a critical moment in world history. If the British could hold San Domingo, the finest colony in the world, they would once more be a power in American waters. Instead of being abolitionists they would be the most powerful practitioners and advocates of the slave trade."[16]

Like other attempts to quell the rebellion over a twelve-year period by local French and Spanish whites, the British failed. Simcoe returned to England and soon died, unable to take up an appointment that he was offered in colonial India. He is hardly the heroic fighter for freedom he is commonly consider by many Ontarians.

It seems appropriate here to cite the words of the influential Haitian scholar Michel-Rolph Trouillot, who has written extensively about the troubled history of the country where Simcoe ended his career, away from witnesses in Upper Canada and so deeply embedded in the machinery of colonial repression: "The ultimate mark of power may be its invisibility; the ultimate challenge, the exposition of its roots."[17]

It is not just the *past* practice of intentionally erasing the lives of the enslaved in Canada (from archives, print sources, school curricula, and public institutions) that is deeply problematic, it is the continuing practice of intentionally overlooking or omitting the evidence and avoiding the opportunities to put these histories forward at every opportunity. It leaves Black writers, scholars, and artists the work of seeing through the voids and absences, to worry the traces of lives, bringing meaningful portraits of these individuals and communities back to the surface of this landscape, remapping the geography of this not-so-great-White-North. This energy put into having to constantly remind and correct, repeat and reiterate, in an age when facts are consistently ignored, magnifies the demands on BIPOC scholars and artists.

"We must create from what has been made invisible," artist and curator Anique Jordan states, "we must assume the responsibility of thinking through the consequences of erasure and the multiple ways in which we must construct meaning from what is absent."[18] Jordan's photographic work, *94 Chestnut* (2016), challenges the under-representation of Black people in Canadian culture, as well as their overrepresentation in the criminal justice system. She says, "Blackness and Canadian-ness seem to be at odds. If I am Black, I am not Canadian. If I am Canadian, I am not Black. When I deliberately join these identities, *I am uneasy* [emphasis added]."[19]

Anique Jordan, *94 Chestnut* (detail), 2016,
digital photograph, size variable, one of a sequence of four images,
collection of the artist/reproduced with permission of the artist (original in colour)

In the centre of Toronto, on Chestnut Street, a half block north of the city hall, a British Methodist Episcopal (BME) church once stood, one of a number of historic Black churches in the city. Most are long gone, buried beneath such dominant structures as St. Michael's Hospital and the Sheraton Centre hotel. When the BME congregation at 94 Chestnut Street shrank and moved elsewhere, the building became a synagogue, then a Korean church, before being torn down and covered by a parking lot, and is now the site of a massive Ontario Court of Justice. For Jordan, that an institution of judgement and incarceration, consistently excessive in its focus on Black people, should be built on this spiritual site, was appalling and tragically ironic; an irony heightened when she was denied access to the construction site to produce a work honouring Black presence. Jordan's work emerges from these tangible barriers.

Jordan's four images record the calling into presence of an Ancestor, and the activation, through symbols drawn on the construction hoarding, of an intersection of time and space. A lone woman in Victorian mourning dress, her face partially obscured by a hat and veil, hovers before the tall plywood hoarding, then rotates to the four cardinal points. As Jordan was, the Ancestor is denied access, but her presence disrupts the barrier and all that has been hoarded inside. Too often, the presence of Blackness in cities is perceived as a troubling disruption of public space; it is read by whiteness as threatening, as a sign of individual and societal illness. Yet here, the powerful presence of the Ancestor reveals the threat and virulent sickness to be held within the hoarding.

Spring Creek that powered the Hatts' first mill (the Red Mill) still runs through a heavily treed valley separating west Hamilton from Dundas. The valley has been partially filled in, for the railway that once crossed it and for the roadbed of Main Street West, leaving the creek to be channelled underground and through culverts. The rail line was pulled up years ago. Its bed is now a trail running east through the city and up the escarpment, and is called the Hamilton to Brantford Rail Trail heading west into the countryside, to Brantford. Near the Mohawk Chapel in Brantford the trail connects to the Grand River Trail heading north to the towns of Paris, Galt, and then Blair where the Speed River flows in. This is the edge of what was known as the Lower Block of the Haldimand Tract. The Iron Horse Trail cuts through Kitchener and Waterloo, known as the Upper Block. Keep following the Grand River north and you'll come to the Conestogo River, in the heart of the former Queen's Bush.

The street I lived on back in Dundas dead-ends at the Hamilton to Brantford Rail Trail heading out of town and is separated from a valley and Coldwater Creek (formed by the merging of Sulphur and Ancaster Creeks) by a post-war shopping plaza. This land once belonged to the Hatts. Over its northwesterly progress, the rail trail traces Sophia's journey out of Dundas into a precarious freedom, never outside contested landscapes, bracketed by Thayendanegea/Joseph's legacy, all marked by official manipulations, deceptions, and settler/colonial *hoardings*.

In 1810 as Sophia approached freedom, Daniel Outwater II and his wife Nelly (née Harris) first appear in the records of Upper Canada. Having followed their relatives north, they chose to settle in Hastings County, near Nappanee, west of Kingston—toward the east end of Lake Ontario. On the eve of the War of 1812, they received one lot, in Adolphustown, near Hay Bay. Outwater's petition for land was supported by a testimonial from a man named Thomas Dorland (who paid the necessary fees as well) affirming Outwater's loyalty to the Crown: "I have been acquainted with Daniel Outwater Junior upwards of eight years & believe him to be an honest & Industrious Man & a Loyal Subject."[20] The receiver general was Thomas Ridout; archival records include his signed statement: "There are several vacant & grantable Lots in the Village of Adolphustown. I do not find that the petitioner has been located for any."[21]

The Outwaters got their lot, and had many children to support on it. In 1849, long after Daniel's death in 1827, Nelly petitioned for a US veteran's pension. Like their petition for land, Nelly's application was well supported by testimonials, in this case confirming Daniel's service in the Patriot cause. As Sophia had learned as a child, the Outwaters and their kin were quite comfortable taking what they wanted and working the system for their own benefit.

Nelly reached the age of 95, passing in that tantalizing year of 1851. The family lived for decades near Adolphustown, among many UELs and new immigrants from Britain, including the Glasgow-born, debt-ridden merchant Hugh Macdonald and his wife Helen (née Shaw), and their son, who was five when they immigrated in the 1820s. The son's name was John Alexander, who grew up into fame as Sir John A. Macdonald, Canada's first prime minister. The original Parks Canada heritage plaque marking the Macdonald property overlooking Hay Bay stated: "From this soil, home of the Loyalists, he drew inspiration to weld together the weak and scattered colonies of his day into a strong and ambitious Dominion, equal partner in the far-flung British Commonwealth." It was replaced with: "His National Policy and the building of the CPR [Canadian Pacific Railway] were equally indicative of his determination to resist the north-south pull of geography and to create and preserve a strong country politically free and commercially autonomous."[22]

Parks Canada appears to have superb skills at presiding over selective memory and obfuscating language, exemplified in such phrases as "to resist the north-south pull of geography" and "a strong country politically free and commercially autonomous." It is probably too much to expect, in the heart of Loyalist country, acknowledgement of Macdonald's foundational racist policies; his ideas remain entrenched, obscuring more complex truths. Contemporary artist Camille Turner's work troubles the narrow brackets of Canada's selective history, just as Sophia's presence troubles Benjamin Drew's "refugee" narrative:

> My Toronto neighbourhood actually dates back to 1793, when the town of York was founded. Some of the first Black residents of the area arrived as part of the military or as the property of white Loyalists. This history was, until recently, largely unmarked and un-acknowledged in official accounts of the area. Since then, I have made it my mission to un-silence the stories of the people of African descent who arrived here before me.[23]

Turner here speaks of the Ward (St. Patrick's Ward), the same downtown neighbourhood at the heart of Anique's *94 Chestnut*. It was from Turner that I first learned to interpret the coded language of slave ads (see chapter 6). Her work reveals the complex interconnections of slavery across time, space, borders, and economies; she travels into history and archives, assuming that, "in most museums and heritage institutions in Canada, I will find the evidence of slavery."[24] She is usually profoundly prescient, revealing the presence of enslaved people in histories of numerous heritage homes, and exposing the building of slave ships in Newfoundland, for example. In the WANTED series (a collaboration with artist Camal Pirbhai), we witness dreamings. The artists' statement explains: "WANTED draws from detailed descriptions in 'runaway slave' ads.... Rather than portraying these freedom seekers in the past where their lives are constrained by the violence and inhumanity of institutionalized bondage, we presented them in the future space of possibility they dreamed about as they set off on their journey to freedom."[25] The scholar Raven Spiratos observes this of the series:

> Through diasporic and historical imagination, speculation becomes employed in service of healing.... Pirbhai and Turner are not imagining what those of African-heritage would have been like had colonialism never happened. Instead, WANTED is working through the genocidal past to perform the all-important representation of self-sovereignty. It also speaks to the fact that while these individuals

were enslaved, they were never slaves. This de-conflation of race and the condition of slave is paramount as it de-links those of African-descent from the status of subhuman both past, present and future.[26]

In the summer of 2017, one of the WANTED images appeared, monumental in scale, on illuminated screens at Toronto's Yonge–Dundas Square, an outdoor public venue in the heart of the city located near possibly one of the busiest intersections in Canada. It featured a woman in a formal gown and bright red overgarment, an interpretation of an original slave ad, whose words ("black Gown and red Callimanco petticoat") are reproduced on the image. The screen shows the woman slowly curling dumbbells at the gym, her strength matched by the bold statement *NOT FOR SALE* on the adjacent screen.

Charmaine Nelson sees the WANTED series (and fugitive slave ads in general) as portraiture,[27] while Raven Spiratos argues these images should be understood through the genre of history painting, as monumental depictions of significant figures and events.[28]

Camal Pirbhai and Camille Turner, *Unnamed Woman*, from the WANTED series, 2017, digital photograph, size variable, collection of the artists/reproduced with permission of the artists (original in colour)

Black gown and red callimanco petticoat

I've been thinking back to a summer night in Yonge–Dundas Square, in July 2017, Canada's sesquicentennial. It was late, but the intersection was crowded and noisy. Every thirty seconds the *Unnamed Woman* appeared, towering over tourists and shoppers, a proud troubling of the nation's birthday. Now, I am trying to imagine how Turner and Pirbhai would represent Sophia, who was not a fugitive, and whom we have no description of, save for Drew's comments about her scars. I think of Jordan's *94 Chestnut,* and wish Sophia would materialize to say more about what happened in the void she left after moving out of enslavement and away from Dundas. She summed up those forty years in just a few sentences: *Then I lived in what is now Waterloo* —Where, exactly? *I married Robert Pooley, a black man* —Where did you meet him? *He ran away with a white woman* —Who was she? *He is dead* —When? How?

> Dear Sophia,
>   In the end, you said, you found *plenty of people in the bush to help me a good deal.* This is how you closed your conversation with Drew (or I assume you did; who knows what he chose to redact from your memories). I will always wonder what you felt upon leaving Dundas. Did it feel like freedom, were you hopeful, was that even possible?

CHAPTER 18
"DECUS ET TUTAMEN
(AN ORNAMENT AND A SAFEGUARD)"

Keep It Beautiful…Yours to Discover…Open for Business / A Place to Grow
> —The province of Ontario's slogan, evolving over time[1]

At twelve years old, I was sold by Brant to an Englishman in Ancaster, for one hundred dollars — his name was Samuel Hatt, and I lived with him seven years: then the white people said I was free, and put me up to running away. He did not stop me — he said he could not take the law into his own hands.

Dear Sophia,

Here we enter a void, a space of silence lacking the details and potent anecdotes that have so far provided points of connection and landings to step off from. All you say about life with the Brants is shadowed by the little you offer about the Hatts. Their "chapter" opens and closes quickly. *At twelve years old,* you begin; this is an obvious error that I attribute to Drew. Having spent over two decades with the Brants, you were closer to the age of thirty. I believe that you joined the Hatt household near the end of Thayendanegea/Joseph Brant's life, when Samuel married Margaret Thompson in 1807, and that you likely did *live with him seven years.* This coincides with the end of the War of 1812, before the Hatts moved to Chambly, in Lower Canada (Quebec), where they prospered.

You say, *I was seven miles from Stoney Creek at the time of the battle*, which also puts you here, in the Hamilton area, in 1813.

While what you describe of this area comes mostly from your time with the Brants, it is a period that overlaps with the Hatts' arrival. Between 1797 and 1807 they established themselves here while you lived in the landscape they shaped. The Hatts asked, and were given permission, to access more land and bought up property along the creek that flows through the Dundas Valley, out of the gorge to the west and into the outlet, where you hunted deer with Thayendanegea/ Joseph and his children. Since the children would have had to have been old enough to participate in a hunt, and the five you name were born between 1782 and 1796, the events you describe likely took place after the move to Burlington in 1802.

During that period of overlapping presence, did you ever encounter the Hatts? There were so few people here then. I imagine you knew of the *Englishman at Ancaster* before you were sold to him. Hatt, Beasley, and Jean Baptise Rousseau and James Wilson (whom I'll get to soon), these are men who continue to be positioned at the pinnacle of local history. All had regular dealings with Thayendanegea/Joseph. I see you moving in their orbit as they work to occupy this place, like those *white people in the neighborhood, John Chisholm and Bill Chisholm*, who were so confident to *come and say . . . they must have the meat.* Had Samuel Hatt observed you, a strong, highly skilled woman who knew the area well and what it took to survive here?

Were you at Brant's Town to observe Patrick Campbell, the Scotsman who came to the house at "Mohawk" in the winter of 1792? He mentioned "two handsomely attired Negro slaves."[2] Were they the *Simon Ganseville and the father of John Patten* that you mentioned? If you were there at the same time as he, I assume you went unseen by Campbell. You were likely not in the same room but preparing food or minding the youngest children, while Ohtowaʔkéhson/Catharine, your "mistress," entertained unaware she was being compared to those "fine European ladies" in Campbell's recollection. As much as I wish to encounter you in more than the 1851 census and Drew's book, I know Campbell would have only seen you in the superficial terms he applied to the "slaves," "Mrs. Brant," and the many things he clinically catalogued in these "Interior Inhabited Parts," as he called them.[3] We can be spared you being drawn into degrading comparisons.

The Hatts claimed the well-established path that the Attawandaron (as they were called by the Wendat; called Neutral by Europeans), Wendat (called Huron), Mississaugas, and Haudenosaunee (called Iroquois) had long followed, and that fur traders would come to exploit and covet, to reach the Grand River to travel south to Lake Erie. That hidden portage route carried whiteness into the wilderness, setting it on its familiar extractive progress. The portage led out of the valley, up to streams and cataracts. Campbell witnessed one of the first mills (built by James Wilson and Richard Beasley) on this route, and it paled in comparison to the facilities back home in Scotland. This mill, "was greatly admired by my fellow travellers, who protested it to be one of the finest contrivances they had ever seen . . . requested that I take particular notice of it in my journal," Campbell stated, "but I told them it was not new to me, though it was to them."[4] The Hatts would bring such technological advances as made in Scotland and England to the village of Cootes Paradise. The settlement was first named for Lieutenant Thomas Coote, a British officer who found "paradise" in the slaughter of waterfowl in the marsh. The village was fuelled by the heavy flow of Spencer's Creek (formerly called by other names: Flamborough, Crooks, Fletcher's, Sanderson's, or Wilson's) that dropped over the escarpment at Webster's Falls (known formerly as Flamborough, Spencer's, Fisher's, or Hatt's). All these white names, filling up the land. In expanding their operations, the Hatts substantially altered the creek to suit their needs. They channelled it into a millrace or millrun.

The white people said I was free, and put me up to running away, Sophia states. Who were these white people who didn't know her status? As one born and brought to Upper Canada enslaved, and held in bondage when John Graves Simcoe passed An Act Against Slavery (1793), she was not legally free. True freedom for her could only come through manumission as the language of the act made clear. An article from an early twentieth-century journal explains: "Those who were lawfully slaves remained slaves for life unless manumitted and the statute rather discouraged manumissions, as it provided that the master on liberating a slave must give good and sufficient security that the freed man would not become a public charge."[5] Samuel Hatt could have "taken the law into his own hands" and truly addressed Sophia's freedom, but he chose to do nothing to stop her running away. More significantly, he chose to do nothing for her. How onerous would it have been for Hatt to transfer some land or resources to her? Whites would put Sophia up to running away, but not offer meaningful support for her to live. If they believed she was free, why did they not actively support and protect her against the Hatts in the same area, to avoid her having to relocate yet again?

Sophia said, *I would not have chosen freedom,* and we need to understand what freedom meant in her time. Escaping enslavement meant moving into isolation, beyond the borders of the main "text" of colonization and settlement that did not see her as anything more than chattel and labour, in a region where there was no significant free Black community to welcome her. She may not have "chosen" freedom, but that doesn't mean she chose enslavement. In the early 1800s, there was no other place offered her than where she was. Sophia was trapped between two evils, neither truly the lesser.

Her break from the Hatts was not clean or final, she had to make a run for it in the mid-1810s, and that effort no doubt added to the scars she carried. Was she aware of Benjamin Drew's observation (in which he refers to himself in the third person) that "the scars spoken of were quite perceptible, but the writer saw many worse looking cicatrices of wounds not inflicted by Indian savages, but by civilized (?) men." It is hard to imagine wounds worse than the one she describes inflicted on her forehead. Were the Hatts amongst those "civilized" assailants? *Cicatrix* (plural *cicatrices*) comes from the Latin word *cicatricem* ("a scar") and can refer to the mark left on plants as well as persons. Sophia's silence about the Hatts leaves a prominent scar here, on this branch of the family tree grown in whiteness, to be worried. What did she know of her ancestors, her own family tree? What did she know of the Hatts' own privileged past?

Now partially hidden in England amongst London's bland office buildings is the original home of the Worshipful Company of Cutlers of London (founded 1624), one of 110 livery companies that "comprise London's ancient and modern trade associations and guilds."[6] The dagger presented to Thayendanegea/Joseph by the king, George III, would have been made by a member of this guild. Close by the Cutlers home is the site of the original Worshipful Company of Feltmakers of London (founded 1604), a guild representing hatmakers and milliners. Its coat of arms features a knight's helmet topped with a "dexter arm embowed proper" (a left arm bent up) holding aloft a black hat with an azure band.[7] This helmet is repeated on the "arms" (a shield) below, featuring a red hand (the Badge of Ulster) underneath. The motto of the feltmakers' guild is *Decus et Tutamen* ("an ornament and a safeguard"). The Anglo-Saxon surname *Hatt* has its roots in the Old English *hætt* (or *haet*); unlike other names that have revealed deep memories and potent trajectories, *haet* and *hatt* just mean *hat,* suggesting the person so named comes from a line of makers or sellers of headwear. The name Hatt appears throughout northern Europe and England (with the largest concentration in London). Not particularly common in general, it is still certainly far more so than the name Burthen. According to an index of London inhabitants within the city walls in 1695, there were seventeen Hatts (plus their servants) living in the city.[8] The control of vast wealth has remained in London, where major institutions that serviced the slave trade were born, as a BBC video about the slave trade details:

> The thriving British economy after 1660 was made possible mainly because of Britain's financial institutions.... The expansion of overseas trade, especially in the Atlantic, relied on bills of credit... which were at the heart of the slave trade. Similarly, the maritime insurance, which was focused at Lloyds of London, thrived on the Atlantic slave trade.
>
> Provincial banking emerged in the 18th century because of the need for credit in the long-distance Atlantic slave trade. For example, Liverpool merchants involved in slave trading later formed Heywoods

Bank, which eventually became part of Barclays Bank.... The Bank of England was also involved. When it was set up in 1694, it under-pinned the whole system of commercial credit, and its wealthy City members, from the governor down, were often men whose fortunes had been made wholly or partly in the slave trade.[9]

London's financial district is in the ward of Cornhill, one of three ancient hills in London (the others are Tower Hill and Ludgate Hill, where St. Paul's Cathedral looms). At Cornhill, nine streets converge on the Bank of England and Mansion House (home to London's lord mayor), including King William, Threadneedle, and Cornhill Streets. The churches of St. Michael Cornhill, and St. Peter-upon-Cornhill, designed by Christopher Wren, are located here; the latter stands at the corner of Cornhill and Gracechurch Streets where (the church website says) "it is widely held that there has been a Christian place of worship...since 179 AD when Lucius, the first Christian King of Britain, founded it as the first church in London."[10]

Numerous members of one London Hatt family worshipped, were christened, married, and were eulogized at St. Peter-upon-Cornhill. Richard (born 1769) and a brother named Samuel (born 1772) were christened there. Following the death of this Samuel, another brother (born in 1776 to the same parents) was christened Samuel, at Wormley in Hertfordshire, between London and Cambridge. Neither surviving brother remained in England; both married, and were laid to rest, in Canada.

Even before they arrived in Canada, this generation of Hatts were not hatmakers but were involved in various businesses before renting properties in Wormley to pursue agriculture, in which the father, Richard Sr., proved highly successful, becoming a leading figure in the community. The Hatts may have moved to get away from competitive London, a particularly unhealthy city. In their new home they grew their wealth and cultivated valuable connections. James Cecil (7th Earl and 1st Marquess of Salisbury) and William Henry Cavendish-Bentinck (Duke of Portland) provided the Hatts with "letters of introduction," *ornaments* of priv-ilege to *safeguard* their future in Canada. The Demerara sugar plantations of the Cavendish and Bentinck families were generating significant wealth at this time. A colony in the Guianas in South America, ceded to Britain in 1815, Demerara was famous for its brown sugar from cane fields worked by enslaved Africans and Indigenous peoples.

Richard Hatt Jr. came to Upper Canada in 1792, settling at Niagara as a merchant. In 1795, he petitioned for land for himself, as well as his now-widowed father and siblings. The family claimed they would come to Canada with the means to prosper, as a letter from Richard Sr. to his son makes clear:

> Dear Richard—I am now come to the resolution of coming out to Upper Canada, with all my Family & Six young men as Indented Servants, since the Decease of your Dear mother I have nothing to detain me here in England....I shall expend as much money as will obtain a good Settlement in upper Canada, as we are Farmers. Your Brothers & I can manage a considerable Tract, we will take Care to bring proper Letters of recommendation &c with us. You will make application in a proper manner, to his Excellency Governor Simcoe, for the proportion of Land we are Intitled to Receive as Loyalists. That is, for Richard Hatt Sen[r], Rich[d] Hatt J[r], Augustus Hatt, Samuel Hatt, Mary Hatt, and Susannah Hatt, with Six Indented Servants.[11]

Richard, Samuel, their brother August(us), and father Richard each received grants of 486 hectares, and would receive further grants and rights to lease Crown and Clergy Reserve lands in other areas around Lake Ontario: Niagara, Ancaster, Glanford, Scarboro (now Scarborough), and Cootes Paradise. From 1797 to 1798, Richard Jr. and Samuel began their tenure in Ancaster Township (which included much of the Dundas Valley), going into competition with Beasley, Rousseau, and Wilson. The Hatt brothers ran a general store and operated their newly built Red Mill just below the escarpment near the sharp bend, known as "the Devil's Elbow," in the road the brothers extended to Cootes Paradise in an attempt (which failed) to draw customers to their grist milling operation. The "elbow" remains, still a treacherous turn on the Old Dundas Road, just above a recently erected heritage plaque, put up by the Ancaster Township Historical Society, Hamilton Historical Board, that begins "Richard Hatt became one of the most influential men in this region" and continues:

To obtain a source of water power, Richard and his brother Samuel purchased this site on Ancaster Creek in 1798 and built a gristmill and sawmill 200 feet downstream on the western edge of Old Dundas Road. They painted the structure red with the only available paint.... The mill served farms from as far away as Galt, Guelph and Woodstock.

The Hatt brothers widened a section of "Indian trail" to Dundas [what settlers called the long established Indigenous route from the Grand River to the valley] to improve business, but in 1804, they sold the mill and moved down to Dundas where they eventually purchased mills and water rights on Spencer Creek.

From this point, Richard's trajectory is very well documented and honoured; Samuel's not so much. The younger brother became a side note to Richard, if mentioned at all. Samuel is often dropped from descriptions of early developments in which he played a central role, particularly by the Dundas Historical Society (DHS) and the Dundas Museum and Archives. A line in a 1965 DHS museum guide captures the dismissive tone of most descriptions of Samuel who, it says, "appeared very briefly in Dundas history because he sold his quarter share of Dundas Mills on August 7, 1807, to his brother Richard.... He served as a captain in the War of 1812, and after the war he moved to Chambly, Que., where he built mills, prospered, died, and was buried."[12] In two recent DHS publications (of 2016 and 2019),[13] Samuel has been completely expunged and it is only Richard who is repeatedly credited with the development of infrastructure in the valley. Yet Samuel was a full partner in the Red Mill operation, as well as the construction of the road to Dundas and the initial phase of mill developments. He also served through 1815 in a number of official capacities in the area, and his land holdings were extensive.

Together, in 1804, Richard and Samuel purchased an existing grist mill (built by Edward Peer in 1800) in Cootes Paradise (now Dundas), then obtained more properties and rights to build on and alter the landscape (including the construction of a millrace, lots for houses in Cootes Paradise, and permission to build a wharf and storehouse on the distant Burlington Beach (near Thayendanegea/Joseph's home). Their attorney would write repeatedly (beginning "Humbly herewith" and "Having the Honour Respectfully") to the receiver general of Upper Canada, Peter

Russell, and lieutenant governor of the Province of Upper Canada, Peter Hunter, Esq., to fill their needs. Thomas Ridout, who acted as the Hatts' attorney, also had climbed the ranks from clerk in 1793 to surveyor general of Upper Canada by 1810, and concluded the numerous petitions with: "Your excellency will be pleased to grant him a lease thereof and your petitioner as in duty bound shall ever pray."[14] (We will return to Ridout shortly.) Richard became sole owner of the Dundas mill operations in 1807. While it is often suggested that the brothers had a falling out at this time, their 1808 partnership with Teyoninhokarawen/John Norton (Thayendanegea/Joseph's adopted nephew) in a failed attempt to purchase a land tract from the Six Nations on the Grand River suggests otherwise.[15] The brothers' business partnership continued until 1816, when Samuel moved to Lower Canada (now Quebec). Up until that time, Samuel remained a prominent presence in the Dundas area, both as a militia commander, political figure, and justice of the peace, until his service during the War of 1812 took him away for extended periods, while his family, and Sophia, remained in Dundas.

According to historical notes, during the War of 1812 Samuel "commanded the detachment of the Second York and Fifth Lincoln, which accompanied Sir Isaac Brock to Detroit" and "commanded the third militia division at Queenston from July 12 until the Battle of Queenston."[16] In 1813, a week after American forces took York, Samuel was in command at the King's Head Inn on Burlington Beach when it was "bombarded by hot shot" from enemy schooners. "The garrison were forced to retire, and reinforcements being brought from Burlington Heights, the enemy retreated to their boats."[17]

The victory at Detroit solidified a bond between the British army officer Brock and Tecumseh, the great Shawnee warrior and leader who rallied Indigenous nations to come together as allies with the British, believing (as Thayendanegea/Joseph had) that a confederacy fighting with the British was the best option in securing an independent future for Indigenous peoples. Like Thayendanegea/Joseph, Tecumseh was deceived by the British. He died at the Battle of the Thames in 1813, as the British fled the field along with his brother Tenskwatawa (known as "the Prophet"). This strained British-Indigenous relations, something acknowledged by Samuel in a letter he wrote from Burlington Heights on the eve of the 1814 American invasion and what became known as the Battle of Chippawa:

Burlington
4th July

My Dear Sir,

    I have this moment received information that the enemy has reached the Niagara River with 3000 men also some ordinance. I have received orders instantly to assemble the Militia at this Post in this I trust you will use every person. I have ordered Howitzer Guns as the finest here but fear I shall not be able to send a Gun for that purpose to Ancaster as we may have armaments to move here to surround the beach as it is expected the enemy [we are expecting the enemy]. . . . General Riall is most anxious to have the Prophet with his People hasten to Chippawa with the utmost expedition it appears the Prophet has taken some offense and left town a few days ago. I have not one of the Indian Department at this Post at present. Perhaps you could send on to the Grand River some person who might be able to persuade the Indians to return.

In trust,
Yours most humbly,
S. Hatt[18]

The Battle of Chippawa did not go well for the British, and while the Battle of Lundy's Lane a few weeks later halted the American invasion, the fighting was brutal, and it would prove a painful draw for both sides (the combined numbers were 1,731 casualties, including 258 killed, at Lundy's Lane).[19] A year later, the war also ended in a draw, but for Tecumseh's Confederacy, it was a heavy loss. It was the last time that either colonial power "needed" Indigenous allies, and so their already manipulative tactics expanded. No longer respected by the British or United States as belonging to independent nations, Indigenous peoples became an inconvenient barrier to colonial expansion on both sides of the border.

    There are two other obscure documents of note carrying Samuel's signature. Dated 1803 and 1810, they bracket Sophia's transition from the Brant household at Burlington to the Hatt household in Ancaster Township. The first (March 3, 1803) is an "indenture between Lawrence Lawrason and Peter Gordon, Ancaster, town wardens, with the consent of Richard and Samuel Hatt, Justices of the Peace, binding Ann Thayer, a 9 year old orphan, as an apprentice to Andrew Templeton, a farmer, until she is 18 years of age." The second (January 25, 1810) is an "indenture between Jean Baptiste Rousseau and John Jackson, Ancaster, town wardens, with the consent of Samuel Hatt and Henry Hagle, Justices of the Peace, binding Eli Brackenridge, a 5 year old 'orphan Negro,' as an apprentice to Elijah Secord, until he comes of age at 21."[20] In her essential book *The Journey from Tollgate to Parkway* (2010), historian and curator Adrienne Shadd succinctly addresses the significance of the difference between these two documents. She first describes the indenture conditions for the child Eli Brackenridge:

> The child was required to, "faithfully serve in all such lawful business as the said Eli Brackenridge shall be put unto by the command of his master, ... and honestly and obediently in all things shall behave himself towards his said master and honestly and orderly towards the rest of the family..." For his part, Elijah Secord promised to "get and allow unto the said Apprentice meat, drink, washing, lodging and all other things needful... for the Apprentice during the term aforesaid..." When the term of apprenticeship expired, Secord was also bound to give the young man a complete new suit of clothing, including a "coat, waistsash (*sic*), overhauls, hat, shoes, stockings, with suitable linen..."[21]

Shadd goes on to note that while the indenture of the white orphan Ann Thayer shared the above wording, it also included the following obligations, not required of Brackenridge's master:

> In addition, the indenture required that Templeton instruct the child in, "the craft, mastery and occupation of cooking, sewing, spining (*sic*) and such other qualifications... the indenture also specified that Templeton "at some convenient time within the term aforesaid shall cause the said Ann Thayer to be taught to read and write." These indentures always mandated that the apprentices be taught to read and write, ... So why had Eli Brackenridge been denied this right? Was it because town officials felt that a Black child did not need to know

how to read and write?... The fact that five-year-old Eli Brackenridge was denied his right to a basic education illustrates in stark terms the fundamental inequality of opportunity for Black children right from birth. This is echoed later in the century with the exclusion of Black children from schools that white children attended.[22]

Shadd refers to Samuel Hatt's enslavement of Sophia, then states: "Obviously, the existence of slavery and the slave-owning class had a tremendous impact on the fate and circumstances of all Blacks, whether they were enslaved or not."[23]

It is not a stretch to suggest that as Sophia's story has begun to slowly seep into public consciousness in recent years, Samuel Hatt's presence has been almost extirpated. The focus has been almost exclusively on the Brants, tainted by race-based misrepresentations of slavery in Indigenous cultures. It is as if these local historians and their institutions have adopted the motto of the Worshipful Company of Feltmakers of London and see Richard Hatt as an "ornament" to be "safeguarded." The efforts to marginalize Samuel works to also remove Sophia's faint presence. Again, as Michel-Rolph Trouillot states, "The ultimate mark of power may be its invisibility; the ultimate challenge, the exposition of its roots."[24]

The redacted stories of settlers and United Empire Loyalists (UELs), produced by public entities (local media, museums, and historical societies) and families committed to maintaining their legacies through amateur genealogy, continue to accumulate. This material, so widely available online, buries truths and reinvigorates the power to shape history to advantage. In these tales, UELs simply came up from the United States, the majority of Indigenous people were new here (there were only a few "scattered tribes"), and "Africans" were included in the "long tradition of welcoming peoples of many nationalities" as just a part of "Our Multicultural Province."[25] In the details and language of what has been naively gathered, however, we can find much to unearth and expose.

I want to return to Thomas Ridout, the attorney for the Hatts who became receiver general of Upper Canada in 1810, in order to dig deeper and expose some roots. Like many descriptions of UELs, his backstory is selectively mapped. The description in the *Dictionary of Canadian Biography* online (which ends up spreading as a collection of facts, when it is quoted in other sources) is a prime example of evasiveness and erasure:

In 1774 Thomas Ridout emigrated to Maryland where an elder brother, already established as a government official at Annapolis, financed his entry into *the carrying trade with the West Indies* [emphasis added] and France.... At the end of the revolutionary war, during which he had continued his *Atlantic trading* [emphasis added] activities, he was viewed as a friend and supporter of the new American nation.[26]

These two phrases, "the carrying trade with the West Indies" and "Atlantic trading," are euphemisms for the slave trade and hide the truth of Ridout's business. In the eighteenth century, Maryland was a major site of plantation slavery (primarily tobacco) and the West Indies were basically a network of slave colonies. A history guide of Maryland states: "By 1755, about one third of Maryland's population — in some places as much as one half — was derived from Africa.... The colony became as much an extension of Africa as of Europe."[27] A website focused on Chesapeake Bay in Maryland notes: "Between 1700 and 1770, the region's slave population grew from 13,000 to 250,000. By the beginning of the Revolutionary War in 1775 Black people made up nearly one-third of the region's population."[28]

Thomas Ridout was one of two sons of George Ridout and his second wife Mary (née Gibbs) of Dorset, England. George already had eight children with his first wife, including John, who emigrated to Maryland in 1753. A close friend and personal secretary to Horatio Sharpe, the governor of Maryland when it was still a

Annapolis, Sept. 29, 1767.
JUST IMPORTED,
In the Ship LORD LIGONIER, *Capt.* DAVIES, *from the River* GAMBIA, *in* AFRICA, *and to be sold by the Subscribers, in* ANNAPOLIS, *for Cash, or good Bills of Exchange, on Wednesday the 7th of* October *next,*

A CARGO of CHOICE HEALTHY SLAVES. The said Ship will take TOBACCO to LONDON, on Liberty, at 6*l.* Sterling per Ton.
JOHN RIDOUT,
DANIEL OF ST. THO*.* JENIFER.

N. B. Any Person that will contract for a Quantity of Lumber, may meet with Encouragement, by applying to D. T. JENIFER.

British colony, John Ridout was a judge, a member of Maryland's governing body, and a naval officer. In 1773, when Sharpe returned to England, Ridout bought Sharpe's grand estate, named Whitehall. An advertisement placed in the *Maryland Gazette* reveals the nature of the "trade" the Ridouts were engaged in.[29]

It would be hard to find a more significant event to connect the Ridouts and the slave trade than the vessel *Lord Ligonier*. In 1977, over 130 million people in North America watched the ABC network television miniseries based on Alex Hailey's novel *Roots: The Saga of an American Family* (1976).[30] The central character Kunta Kinte, as a journalist covering the Kunta Kinte Heritage Festival in Annapolis, Maryland, explains, "was one of 96 Africans aboard the *Lord Ligonier*."[31] The *Roots* series was a truly transformative cultural moment, revealing to most Americans (and Canadians) the horrors of chattel slavery. While the authenticity of Haley's research and the value of his work as "proper" history have been debated (Henry Louis Gates Jr. called *Roots* "a work of the imagination"[32]), one cannot deny its impact. Haley pointed many to the types of documents, such as personal and business records of slave holders and traders, where descendants could find their ancestors.

The debate around Haley's work points to a consistent challenge for anyone trying to surface representations of people who are largely absent from the archives. One has to be creative and imaginative—something Haley himself acknowledged he was doing, and something that has become far more common as forms of historical memory and oral histories have become more accepted in academia.[33] Haley's *Roots* influenced many Black writers (including Toni Morrison, Alice Walker, and Octavia Butler) who looked to the archives to build complex historical fiction and creative non-fiction that have been essential to expanding an understanding of hidden Black lives and, by extension, to complicating and subverting polished histories of whiteness.

The denial of the tools of language and memory (the ability to read and write; the right to speak, be educated, and educate others; the right to have your histories and their forms valued) that Adrienne Shadd highlights in relation to Eli Brackenridge, has and continues to be one of the most powerful weapons of marginalization. It is repeatedly identified in the writings and speeches of the formerly enslaved, and is central to contemporary writings that address legacies of slavery and systemic racism—for example, Octavia Butler's novel *Kindred* (1979), in which the character Dana travels through time and realizes what the act of learning to read means as an enslaved person: "But there stood Tom Weylin staring at me. He lowered his gaze a little and frowned. I realized that I was still holding the old speller. I'd gotten up with it in my hand and I hadn't put it down. I even had one finger in it holding my place. I withdrew my finger and let the book close. I was in for beating now."[34]

Kindred was published two years after the broadcast of *Roots*. In a story Butler often described as "a grim fantasy,"[35] Dana, a contemporary Black writer, finds herself transported back to the Maryland plantation of her ancestors. She believes she has been called back by a white ancestor (Rufus, the son of plantation owner Tom Weylin). It is her willingness to teach various enslaved children to read that causes her to be brutally punished. Butler grounds the narrative in the power of knowledge and language, the complexities of gaining a voice, the role of the writer and teacher, and constantly reminds us that history is not linear but circular, the past, present, and future all interwoven, connected: a *kinship*. In slavery, whiteness consistently denied Black kinship. Part of its legacy is the use of language and history (the truths told in academia and popular culture) to deny Black presence.

> Dear Sophia,
>   This text is meant to both honour your presence and
> memory here, while shaping and troubling how you have
> been represented and positioned. This is an extended act of
> *rememorari* (Latin, meaning "calling to mind"), combining
> *re-* ("expressing intensive force") and *memor* ("to be mindful").
> Engaging with you is also meant to acknowledge you *in situ*
> ("still, in place, precisely here") and to try and see a wider
> landscape; to also evoke change and to problematize worldings.
> I want to write well and to honour you, to be present but
> not overshadow. I struggle with how realistic I am being. Is
> it even possible to find such a balance, with you, with my
> collaborators, and with my readers?

When I was finishing art school, and starting to work as an artist and curator, the historian James Clifford's *The Predicament of Culture* (1988) had just been published, and while his text was certainly impactful, it was the cover image that stayed with me: a doubled image of a man, his head wrapped in white fabric, concealing his face, as he balances the carved head of white man wearing a pith helmet on his own head.[36] The caption beneath the image reads: *"'White Man,' Onyeocha*, a performer at Igbo masquerades. Amagu Izzi, southeast Nigeria, 1982." The "White Man" evoked in the image is the one who usually holds a notebook and moves about on the periphery of a group of performers; he is the ever-present white anthropologist or ethnographer who is always watching and recording, studying and cataloguing. The Igbo have incorporated this interloper into their living, evolving traditions with the performance costume shown in the image.

Clifford employed the tools of ethnography to critically analyze Western representations of the "other" in anthropology, travel writing, the collecting and exhibiting practices of museums, and art history. In 1988, his book offered a radical perspective, but this moment of self-awareness in academia and other institutions was quickly reabsorbed. Whiteness did not give up its position; it simply acknowledged its disruptive presence, adapted, and carried on in its newly self-described *post-colonial* and *post-racial* world. Once again, whiteness was compensated for its false loss, this time when its own theorizing enabled it to recalibrate and maintain its privileged status, choreographing diversity, while still holding the centre, leaving so many colonized, racialized, and othered. As Clifford emphasizes in another book: "One cannot avoid the global reach of Western institutions allied with capitalist markets and the projects of national elites. And what could be a better symbol of this global hegemony than the proliferation of museums? What more bourgeois, conservative, and European institution? What more relentless collector and commodifier of 'culture'?"[37]

We are decades past these reflections by Clifford, and yet the Western museum model continues to spread globally, stark evidence of a fundamental lack of change. Many of these institutions expect the kind of gratitude James Baldwin wrote about, which Eddie S. Glaude Jr. summarizes:

> In his introduction to his 1985 collection of essays, *The Price of the Ticket*, Baldwin noted that America had become quick to congratu-late itself on the progress it made with regards to race, and that the country's self-congratulations came with the expectation of black gratitude.... As Baldwin wrote, "People who have opted to be white congratulate themselves on their generous ability to return to the slave that freedom which they never had any right to endanger, much less

take away. For this dubious effort...they congratulate themselves and expect to be congratulated." The expectation was that he should feel "gratitude that not only is my burden...being made lighter but my joy that white people are improving."[38]

Many cultural organizations have only done the bare minimum, or limited their supposedly progressive gestures by maintaining the organizational structures and values that are inherently colonial—like abolitionists who argued for integration rather than for the fundamental dismantling of systems that have historically marginalized and oppressed.

❧

Back at the Fenimore Art Museum, where I encountered *Unknown Child* (1815–25, originally titled *Black Child*) by Cole Tilyard, a carving titled *Cigar Store Figure* (1825–50), carved by "a slave named Job for a tobacconist in Freehold, New Jersey,"[39] is prominently displayed. When I visited the museum in 2019, the label for the work stated: "It may be surprising to realize that slavery was not abolished in New Jersey until 1846, and that loopholes in the law permitted slave holding until the passage of the 13th Amendment after the Civil War." The wording suggested that this was news to the museum, and basically acknowledged that they believed their primarily white audience was ignorant of the complex history of enslavement in northern states. While the museum has since removed "surprising" from the text, the problematic history of such racist representations of Indigenous people is left unengaged on the label, revealing an unwillingness to address the deeper content and significance of this object as well. "It may be surprising to realize" is too polite a phrase to truly acknowledge the intentional obscuring of histories.

In 2021, a case shouldn't have to be made for transparency and context. Saidiya Hartman calls to mind the image of the enslaved man, kneeling and in chains, pleading "Am I Not A Man And A Brother?" on Charles Darwin's grandfather Josiah Wedgwood's Antislavery Medallion (1787): "Needing to make the case that we have suffered and that slavery, segregation and racism have had a devastating effect on black life is the contemporary analogue to the defeated posture of Wedgwood's pet Negro. The apologetic density of the pleas for recognition is staggering. It assumes both the ignorance and the innocence of the white world.

If only they knew the truth, they would act otherwise."[40] Hartman also quotes Baldwin to drive the point home:

> I am reminded of the letter that James Baldwin wrote his nephew on the centennial anniversary of the Emancipation Proclamation. "The crime of which I accuse my country and my countrymen," he wrote, "and for which neither I nor time nor history will ever forgive them, that they have destroyed and are destroying hundreds of thousands of lives and do not know it and do not want to know it. . . . It is not permissible that the authors of devastation should also be innocent. It is the innocence which continues the crime."[41]

To be innocent implies a genuine condition of not knowing or being naive ("lacking knowledge, experience of life, or good judgment, and willing to believe that people always tell you the truth"); authentic innocence cannot be willed or performed — that is the tainted "innocence" (or wilful ignorance) Baldwin and Hartman label "the crime."

Whiteness is wired to absorb all that it marginalizes into its mission, reducing "others" to artefacts (both things and narratives) and labour. Herman Melville's Ishmael wonders about the opulent houses of New Bedford, Massachusetts: "Whence came they?" He then answered his own query: "One and all, they were harpooned and dragged up hither from the bottom of the sea."[42] Like Frederick Douglass, who understood the true foundation of the United States in the amoral brutality of chattel slavery and racism, Melville understood the true foundation of New Bedford in the amoral brutality of whaling and, by extension, the mechanisms of colonization and empire (including slavery) in the United States. "The history of capital," the scholar Christina Sharpe reminds us, "is inextricable from the history of Atlantic chattel slavery."[43]

The writings of Butler, as just one example, are reminders of the importance of taking hold of the tools to write, teach, and speak, to communicate and shape one's own experience. But who am I to take up Sophia's story? I am trying to imagine her moving back and forth in time, like Dana in Butler's novel, perhaps responding to my search for her. I've been trying to work towards some fragile kinship, yet it seems that I am taking her on another long journey. Would she see me as another Daniel Outwater II or Simon Knox, stealing her away for my own benefit, or is it Benjamin Drew (whose surname echoes my given name An*Drew*) whose spirit I embody, using Sophia's memories to build my own narrative, holding Sophia in my pages, inside this book, a vessel that she did not sign on to?

Dear Sophia,

I know I have been carrying you on this journey, waiting for and willing you to appear, hoping we can travel on together, to look together at other obscured lives here, and this compels me to look, in your place, at these fields (across New York and Southern Ontario), and to keep asking: What is my place, do I even belong here? In whiteness, I consistently find voids of ignorance, artefacts that whiteness fails to comprehend, but that carry damning scars. I am trying to work in these spaces, learning from the wisdom, insights, and labour of Black and Indigenous people (as well as so many who have been "othered" working out of colonized spaces), trying not to take what is not mine, but always knowing that I cannot find in my whiteness essential truths by going alone. I am asking for kinship; I know I am asking a lot.

I'm trying to write to and with you, echoing the kinds of conversations I have with my mentors, colleagues, and friends, making connections, sharing knowledge, always reminding myself to listen, sometimes travelling and observing together, or following my companions' leads and queries, to go where they point me. I've been repeating your words and written details to make them stick. I return to questions only partially answered that have sent me on many tangents, keeping only those that appear to loop back into this web, believing that I am sharing information that you'd want to know. I replay names to keep them present, and in these scattered recollections, hope to recall you, without causing you the harm and trauma Dana experienced in *Kindred*.

An*Drew* the Hunter. The meaning of Hunter is obvious, emphasized on my family crest featuring a hound and three horns, along with the motto *Cursum Perficio* ("I finish the course"),[44] from old French *cors* (the flow of a river), from Latin *cursus* (a journey; direction, track navigated by a ship; flow of a stream). I remain on the deck of a vessel that seems determined to stay on course, that continues to trail a heavy wake.

CHAPTER 19
WHAT'S IN A NAME? (AGAIN)

With finger pointed and eye levelled at the Pequod, *the beggar-like stranger stood a moment, as if in a troubled reverie; then starting a little, turned and said:— "Ye've shipped, have ye? Names down on the papers? Well, well, what's signed, is signed..."*
   —Elijah, the prophet, in *Moby-Dick*[1]

What's in a name? I began with this question, parsing *Sophia*, *Burthen,* and *Pooley*, and I return to it now concerning the indentured orphan Eli Brackenridge. Like my surname, Hunter, Brackenridge is of Scottish origin. Both are prominent in Glasgow where variations of Brackenridge date back to the 1400s, and where there have been many Hunters. *Eli* is short for *Elijah*, meaning "My God is Yahweh" to Christians and Jews and "beautiful, smart, and loving" (as does *Sophia*) to Muslims. While my surname denotes an occupation, Brackenridge refers to place; it combines the old northern English words *bracken* and *rigg* ("ridge") and has many spelling variants. The family crest features red and white roses (but, oddly, no bracken). Bracken is a fern, genus *Pteridium* (from *pteron*, meaning "feather wing"). It is thought to be carcinogenic and is considered a weed to be pulled up from areas of cultivation and piled up to define edges of fields. We are back to borders and margins formed of unwanted material. Eli, *beautiful, smart, and loving*, whose origin is the abandoned *margin* of a vast field that will continue to be fertilized and nurtured. The Scots brought their model of agriculture to young Canada.

Amongst the first United Empire Loyalists (UELs) of Upper Canada was Francis Brackenridge, who settled in the Niagara area in Lincoln County in 1783. In 1824, however, he was "suspended" by an "order in council" from the official list of recognized Loyalists, according to the United Empire Loyalist Association of Canada.[2] Where did the "orphan" Eli Brackenridge come from? Was he connected in some way to this family at Niagara, or members of their family who settled near Ancaster Township? Who was he orphaned from? To be indentured, Eli must have been "free," as the child of an enslaved woman would be enslaved until age 25 under the laws of Upper Canada. Brackenridge is a thread to keep pulling on, as is another name written on Eli's indenture: Jean-Baptiste Rousseau.

Rousseau was born in Montréal in 1758 to a family engaged in the fur trade. He would become involved in many ventures upon settling in Ancaster Township, as a merchant, miller, administrator, and translator. Rousseau had very close ties to Thayendanegea/Joseph Brant, both business and personal. He acquired (with Richard Beasley and James Wilson) significant Haudenosaunee acreage (around 4900 hectares), and married Thayendanegea/Joseph's adopted daughter Margaret Clyne (or Klein). Margaret (a white woman) was born in 1759 in the Mohawk Valley near Canajoharie, was captured, held captive, and brought to Upper Canada by Thayendanegea/Joseph, who then adopted her. She and Rousseau were married in Thayendanegea/Joseph's home, and Sophia would have been present that day in Brant's Town. Instead of being married off to a wealthy friend as Margaret was, Sophia was sold into the same circle of local elites.

Rousseau had a son with Margaret whom he named Joseph Brant, born in 1799, and also an older daughter, Marie Reine, born in 1793. Marie Reine married Ancaster-born Elijah Matthew Secord, son of UEL John Secord of Westchester County, New York, and Susannah (née Wartman) of Niagara, who was born to German parents who came from Pennsylvania. In 1810, Elijah and Marie Reine acquired the labour of Eli Brackenridge, through documents signed by Marie Reine's father, Jean-Baptiste Rousseau, along with Samuel Hatt, in which no obligations were stipulated to educate or train him for sixteen years. (Imagine looking upon a five-year-old child and seeing him only as labour!) While Eli vanished from documentation once in the Secord household, I can find traces of the couple just five minutes from my parents' home. In St. Peter's Cemetery, a tall white headstone stands against the side fence, its surface eroded. The name *Secord* can only be revealed by photographing, then heightening the contrast.

Outside the cemetery, Mohawk Road continues west to Ancaster. First it passes Meadowlands (a typical "big box" commercial development) and Highway 403 (heading south to Brantford, and north to Burlington and Toronto), then passes an affluent neighbourhood with streets named for the other five of the Six Nations (Cayuga, Seneca, Tuscarora, Onondaga, and Oneida) and ones named Hiawatha and Tomahawk—a strange reconstitution of the Longhouse, anchored by Rousseau Public School. Just past Lime Kiln Road, Mohawk Road becomes Rousseaux Street (the added "x" is common). If you turn down Lime Kiln to Legacy Lane, you'll pass the Cooley-Hatt burying ground, formerly hidden on private land. Richard Hatt and his wife Mary (called Polly, née Cooley) are buried here, where it was once their family's land. The location of their graves was lost for decades because, a century ago, the Dundas "town fathers" removed their headstone and relocated it north to Dundas. Keen on literally grounding Richard in the founding narrative of their town, they left the Hatts' bodies unmarked (the location was only recently marked). Such a strange act of redaction, in essence preparing the body of their text for public consumption.

> Dear Sophia,
>   How strange to find these names, *Polly* and *Cooley*, carried by the wife of Richard Hatt. *Polly*, your married name, as spelled in the 1851 census, and then *Cooley*, the surname of ill-fated Chloe. Preserved Cooley, father of Mary, is the only Cooley to appear on the list kept by the United Empire Loyalist Association of Canada. Born in New York City in 1750, Preserved was the son of David Cooley of Orange County, New York, and grandson of Daniel Cooley of Fairfield, Connecticut. Daniel Cooley had married twelve-year-old Jemima Griffen in 1718; she bore him five children before she died at age 23. She was thirteen when Preserved's brother (and Mary's uncle) Isaac was born in 1720. Preserved settled in Ancaster Township, while Isaac moved to Dutchess County, where he lived and died at Fishkill, in 1780. You could have crossed paths with him. As I've said before, here and there are not separate, they remain contiguous, at times continuous, flowing together, bleeding into each other, weaving such a tangled web.

On the illustration titled *Sketch of Burlington Bay, Hamilton, and the Vicinity* (1846), reproduced on the endpapers of *A Mountain and a City* (1966), a cluster of black squares marks the locations of various buildings, including the Hatts' mills on Spencer Creek.[3] These buildings are grouped around the intersection of Main Street and Governor's Road, just down the hill from my former home. In 1846, five roads converged here: the road down from the Binkley family's land (now Ogilvie Street), King Street heading "to Waterloo" (as stated on the map), York Road coming from Rock Chapel (where Robert Whale painted one of his views of Hamilton), and Dundas Street (that becomes Governor's Road). Today, a fragile stone building rests at 2 Hatt Street, perched precariously on the corner, its stone wall bowing out towards traffic on Governor's Road. Built in 1804, this is all that still stands from the Hatts' industrial empire, lingering where Hatt Street terminates at Dundas Town Hall, whose "handsome exterior remains largely unaltered" (as an Ontario Heritage plaque outside points out). The town hall and 2 Hatt Street stand as physical manifestations of Dundas history and, like its written version, "remains largely unaltered," seemingly set in stone, and minus Samuel Hatt.

Richard lies buried in Ancaster, long separated from his grave marker, in what is now a modest park labelled *United Empire Loyalist Burying Ground*. Richard was *not* a UEL. Samuel, on the other hand, is interred in a decaying but still-robust family mausoleum surrounded by a rusting iron fence on the grounds of St. Stephen's Anglican Church at Chambly, 23 kilometres southeast of Montréal. The impressive grey stone church, with its double-tiered steeple, was built in 1820 (Samuel Hatt contributed one hundred pounds, and laid the cornerstone). It stands facing Fort Chambly on the Richelieu River. The British fort of heavy stone is positioned on the site of the wooden stockade that French army captain Jacques de Chambly built in 1665. Destroyed by Thayendanegea/Joseph's ancestors in 1702, it was rebuilt, then surrendered to the British in 1760. During the War of 1812, Lieutenant Colonel Charles-Michel d'Irumberry de Salaberry was in command, and the celebrated war hero, credited with repelling the 1812 attack on Montréal, drew Samuel Hatt to settle in Chambly following the conflict.

The Richelieu River connects the St. Lawrence River to its north, to Lake Champlain to its south. The energy of the river has been captured since 1898 by a massive hydro dam at Chambly, powering much of the region and Montréal. Out of Lake Champlain flows the Hudson River, passing the outlet of the Mohawk

Grave of Samuel Hatt, at the Hatt Family Mausoleum at St. Stephen's Anglican Church, Chambly, Quebec, 2019, photographed by the author

River, then Albany and the Fishkill Mountains. Back on the western edge of Chambly, a new industrial park has been carved out of farmland, its main artery is named rue Samuel-Hatt. Take Highway 10 a short drive west from there, and you'll come to Highway 35, follow it south and you'll cross into Vermont onto the Interstate 89, then connect with Highway 7. You will pass through Pittsfield, Massachusetts, where Herman Melville wrote *Moby-Dick*. Cut over to Route 9, follow it down the Hudson shore, and you'll be back in Fishkill.

We have come full circle. Samuel Hatt exited the Dundas Valley owning 5931 hectares in the area known as Home District, 197 hectares in Niagara District, and 526 hectares in London District.[4] Sophia exited the valley town with nothing, her future resting place unknown. There are no streets, parks, or towns named for her, yet she remains powerfully present here, denying erasure. She deserves redaction, in its original sense: to be "put in writing, to prepare and release broadly."

CHAPTER 20

"TO PIERCE THE HEART OF THE RECIPIENT WITH LOVE"

When Richard Beasley . . . first sent his Indian guides with the pioneer Mennonites to view the land that is now Waterloo County, then thickly wooded and uninhabited by the white man, they were amazed with what they saw. There was rolling land, rich soil and many varieties of trees, some of the giant pines being five to six feet in diameter, and towering 175 to 185 feet or more above them. . . . The woods had an abundance of large and small game, and the streams a large variety of fish. . . . There is no doubt that tribes of Indians occupied the district.

—Clayton W. Wells, in a report to the Waterloo Historical Society.[1]

In the beginning, we established the meaning of *Pooley*—it is *riparian* ("living near the banks of a river"). We have followed a number of rivers and crossed numerous bodies of water, tracing ley lines, to reach here, to reach her. In many texts, she is only referred to as *Sophia Pooley*; *Burthen* is too often dropped. This is really an affront to her memory, as Robert Pooley abandoned her, and possibly after only a brief marriage. Her parents Dinah and Oliver, her lost sister, they were Burthens; let's stick with this compelling name—Sophia Burthen.

Then I lived in what is now Waterloo. Sophia is referring to Waterloo Township (not the present city of Waterloo), which had, according to a map showing early property owners, over "90,000 acres [36 420 hectares] of land granted (Block 2 [of the Haldimand Tract], Waterloo Township) to the Six Nations Indians by the British Crown in 1784 and sold in 1798 to Richard Beasley, James Wilson, and John Baptist Rousseaux [*sic*] who looked to resell the land in small parcels."[2] These transactions were messy and remain highly contested by the Six Nations of the Grand River. The price for Block No. 2 was £8,887 (provincial currency), secured by a mortgage executed by the purchasers to the trustees for the Six Nations on May 10, 1798. Richard Beasley made arrangements to buy out his partners, the land was surveyed, sections were laid out around the confluence of the Speed and Grand Rivers. These sections were later known as Old Beasley Tract and Beasley's Broken Front. They are now part of Kitchener (formerly Berlin) as well as Blair and Preston (now part of Cambridge). This is where Sophia would come to live, temporarily.

The first white settlers were from Pennsylvania, but their modest settlement was thrown into turmoil at the end of 1802 when, as I.C. Bricker notes in a 1934 report to the Waterloo Historical Society (WHS), "settlers learned of the mortgage that was registered against the [Beasley] Tract. Beasley had kept this information a secret...the Pennsylvanians...could not secure a clear title to their property."[3] Beasley managed to negotiate a sale of the land (for £10,000) to a new group of Pennsylvania settlers (the German Company, led by Daniel and Jacob Erb). This cleared Beasley of his mortgage debt and left him with over 4000 hectares that he continued to sell into the 1830s.[4] The German Company was generous with those who had settled previously, by recognizing their title to the lands purchased from Beasley. In the WHS report, Bricker imagines that "their joy must have been unbounded when they learned that, through the Christian charity of the members of the German Company...the titles which Beasley had given them were now clear of all encumbrance.... Their reward was a blessing bestowed upon their transactions...highly lucrative not only to themselves but, in most cases, to their children and their children's children."[5] So much good Christian generosity among these "God-fearing founders of the County of Waterloo," as Bricker calls them, "which the purposeful and unerring hand of Divine Providence dropped into this vast wilderness...like the Israelites of old...crying unto Him for some Promised Land where that freedom and peace which they had previously enjoyed under the British flag, could again be realized." Many who came north to reshape the area were affluent Pennsylvanians, a fact that D.N. Panabaker expands upon in the same 1934 report to the WHS:

> Another indication of affluent circumstances...is the common reference to slaves in the possession of the families.... In 1775 we find reference not only to the negro slaves themselves but negro beds which

gives us some reassurance that the slaves were in some cases at least treated like human beings. . . . In the will of Samuel Shuller dated 1774 . . . his negro man slave was placed in the list of his assets at a price of 60 pounds, say $250.00 or $300.00, the black girl was valued at about half this figure. . . . It seems that it was a common thing to will one's slaves to one's children. Jacob Levering in 1753 willed to his daughter a negress, a girl called Peg, to his son a negro boy called Kit.[6]

Panabaker is being disingenuous in stating that the presence of "negro beds" suggests that the enslaved were treated as "human beings." His reference to them as, "further evidence of refinement in the tastes of the people" perhaps give a clearer insight into his own views.[7] Pennsylvania passed An Act for the Gradual Abolition of Slavery in 1780. Similar to Upper Canada's 1793 Act Against Slavery, it ended the importing of enslaved people but did not change the status of those already enslaved or challenge the rights of slaveholders to consider people as "property." It claimed to make all children, of any race and born after 1780, free, but the offspring of an enslaved mother were classified as "indentured servants," required to work for their mother's master until they were 28 years old. In Philadelphia, the temporary capital, the Pennsylvania Act didn't apply to congressmen. The population of Lancaster County, Pennsylvania, where many Waterloo settlers came from (many also came from Montgomery County) was around 3,500 between 1780 and 1790; 25 to 30 percent of that population were enslaved.[8]

Beasley would continue wheeling and dealing (and accumulating debt) until his death in Hamilton in 1850. There is a Beasley Drive in Kitchener, close to the Old Beasley Tract where those misled settlers had started out, and the German Company was flourishing when Sophia arrived around 1816. How she reached there, and with whom, remains unclear. Did Sophia originally meet Robert Pooley in Hamilton, then travel to Waterloo? Or did she meet him there, having made the journey on her own or with others? The connections between Waterloo, Head-of-the-Lake, Ancaster Township, and Thayendanegea/Joseph Brant, are significant, and while the *white people* who *put her up to running away* may have pointed Sophia in the direction of Waterloo, it is hard to imagine her travelling alone. Was Pooley formerly enslaved, brought from New York by United Empire Loyalists or from Pennsylvania by those "God-fearing" people? Was he freeborn, did he buy his freedom, or (like Peter Martin) had he gained freedom by fighting with the

British in the Revolution, only to end up working for his former master? Perhaps he was a fugitive. All Sophia says is: *He ran away with a white woman: he is dead.* There is an ominous weight to these paired phrases.

The surname *Pooley* rarely appears in any records or triggers a hit in the archives of Sophia's extended landscape. Robert Pooley surfaces only fleetingly in the *Waterloo Township Census* 1825–28, managing a 25 acre (10 hectare) farm, lot 5, at the west end of Broken Front Concession.[9] This is a decade after Sophia left Hatt; however, she is not recorded living with Pooley. The census lists only three adult men and one young woman (under sixteen). This is not Pooley's land; it belongs to one of the Pennsylvanians. There are several lots numbered "5" on an 1805 map of Waterloo Township, two within Beasley's Broken Front.[10]

Broken front (or *water lots*) refer to concessions that run along or end at shorelines; their boundaries are uneven on at least one side. The lot of John Erb (a relative of Jacob Erb) was split by the Speed River. Its broken front is on the shore of the Grand River, a floodplain of rich soil facing a thin island. These days Preston High School and its large sports field occupy the high ground on the east side of the Speed. Until recently, this land was cultivated. Now it is built up by the Grand River Woods housing development. Broken Front Concession (now Fountain Street South) ran along the western bank of the Speed, then curved north. Several cemeteries mark the upper edge of Erb's land — the likely location of the lot managed by Pooley.

I wish Sophia said more about leaving Dundas and her time with Pooley (did Benjamin Drew even ask her for more details?). I wonder if she'd been in Waterloo previously? Sophia said Thayendanegea/Joseph *lived part of the time at Mohawk, part at Ancaster, part at Preston, then called Lower Block: the Upper Block was at Snyder's Mills.* Pooley farmed at Preston; Snyder's (or Snider's) Mills is a name that doesn't appear until after 1829, when: "Abraham Erb transferred 240 acres [97 hectares] of land including his saw-mill and flour-mill to Jacob C. Snider, who had moved from Pennsylvania."[11] I imagine Sophia witnessed these white men prospering.

Dear Sophia,

In 1928, Clayton W. Wells claimed the official flower of Waterloo was *Gladiolus*, a large plant introduced to the Americas. Of the 260 known species of *Gladiolus*, almost all are endemic to Africa. It is known as the African lily, or sword lily (the Latin word *gladius* means "sword"), and "the flower spire is said to pierce the heart of the recipient with love."[12] I'm afraid that your heart was broken in Waterloo by Robert Pooley.

I'm certain you travelled to Waterloo soon after Samuel Hatt left for Chambly, Quebec, around 1815 or 1816 and that you were not with Pooley in 1825 to 1828. This means you either married before 1825 (and your marriage lasted less than a decade) or you met and married him after the census. The second scenario leaves a void: where were you between leaving the Hatts and marrying Pooley after 1828? It is more likely the first scenario is correct, that you'd left Pooley by 1825, and began your journey towards the Queen's Bush. The further we go, the more I have to imagine and dream, there is so little to go on as we move outside of history and written records. We are moving in and with shadows, denied presence.

Then we came by land, Sophia states, at Albany. I hear that phrase differently now, spoken by settlers, the emphasis shifting to a different meaning of *came by*: meaning "to obtain by chance." While for Sophia this phrase defines a surface and space traversed in progression towards a transaction, for settlers it speaks of taking possession. The sons-in-law *came by* the sisters, *came by* land they were granted, *came by* privileges. Whiteness proceeds in feigned innocence of the truths underlying the supposed chance or *somehow* of its continuing substantial fortune.

Follow Fountain Street North out of Preston and it bends around Kitchener, reaching Breslau at Highway 7. If you go west and take an immediate right, you'll pass through Bloomingdale. The road curves and you'll eventually come to Conestogo, where the river of the same name flows into the Grand. This name comes from Lancaster, Pennsylvania, where the Conestoga River runs (there is no deep meaning to the change from "a" to "o" in Canada). Conestoga wagons were used extensively by settlers and they feature prominently in historic narratives and the film genre of westerns: long wagon trains moving west, pushing Indigenous peoples off their lands.

The Susquehannock (called Conestoga) are Iroquoian-speaking people whose territory was around Lancaster. Their first European contact was with Swedes, then with the Dutch. The Susquehannock greatly suffered from introduced smallpox, and their remaining survivors were absorbed into other Indigenous nations (including the Six Nations). In 1764, a year after George III's Royal Proclamation attempted to limit settler expansion, the so-called Paxton Boys — a group of 250 Scottish men — massacred over two dozen innocent Susquehannock people during Pontiac's War. The Paxton Boys' leader was the Edinburgh-born Scottish Presbyterian "Fighting Pastor," John Elder. Few of the murdered were warriors; they were mostly women, children, and Elders.

Ontario's Conestogo River flows southeast out of Conestogo Lake (formed when the river was dammed in 1958). It winds its way through well-established farms and small towns. Traditional Mennonite horse-pulled black buggies are a constant presence here. Yellow and black highway signs remind drivers to watch for them. As Kitchener-Waterloo area's urban sprawl encroached on their way of life, many moved. Drive along Highway 17 on the north shore of Lake Huron's Georgian Bay, and you'll see those same buggy signs. The north shore is Anishinaabe territory, part of the Robinson-Huron Treaty of 1850. When Mississaugas living along the Credit River were pushed from their territories around Toronto, some moved there.

The lands where Sophia lived in Upper Canada are traditional Mississauga/ Anishinaabe territory,[13] and her time here overlaps with a series of dispossessions by the Crown, beginning with the Haldimand Tract in 1784. This is how a brochure published by the Mississaugas of the Credit First Nation (MCFN) describe these treaties:

> The land grant to the Six Nations was part of a series of "land sur-renders" (as the British conceived the agreements) involving the Mississaugas first in 1784, and then later between 1787 and 1805. ...According to the English texts of agreements, the British colonial government "purchased" tracts of land along the Grand River and the entire Niagara Peninsula. In 1787 and 1788 two additional large tracts of lands were purchased. The "Toronto Purchase" covered much of

what is today central metropolitan Toronto. The "Gunshot Treaty" covered Mississauga lands north of Lake Ontario. Both of these land agreements remain controversial today. . . . The 1787 Toronto Purchase was not ratified by the British government until 1805, and the Gunshot Treaty was almost immediately considered invalid by colonial authorities.

The validity of these early "land surrenders" by the Mississaugas of the Credit is also questionable on other grounds. . . . The British saw land as a commodity. . . . The Mississaugas conceived of their relationship to the land in spiritual terms. They did not believe that land could be "sold," or that their rights to use land and access resources for food and living, could be absolutely and permanently signed away.[14]

Many Mississaugas remained in the area after the Toronto Purchase, but as the MCFN brochure states, "It was becoming increasingly clear that the community would have to relocate to an area less directly disturbed by Euro-Canadian settlement. After considering several options, in 1848 the Mississaugas accepted an offer from the Six Nations to establish a new settlement . . . in the southwest portion of the Six Nations Reserve,"[15] on land originally acquired from the Mississaugas. It took over two hundred years for the Mississaugas to receive payment for the Toronto Purchase, which they did on June 8, 2010. By then, the city that now bears their name had a population of over seven hundred thousand.

It is important to witness this history in relation to Sophia, as it is another layer of evidence of the way the Crown dealt with those who stood in their way. Such tactics of deception, applying different laws and rules along cultural or racial lines, was also applied to Black communities struggling to become established in a climate of systemic racism in Canada, communities that were thriving, only to shrink and disappear, too often blamed for failing by historians, the state, and white missionaries and churches. There is, however, no great mystery: the barriers to success, historically, are significant and deeply entrenched. My hometown is a prime example. As Benjamin Drew said concerning the situation in Hamilton: "It is much to be regretted that the colored people do not to a greater extent avail themselves of the advantages presented by the perfect equality of the English laws. Yet it is scarcely to be wondered at, when we consider that prejudice against them prevails to too great an extent in Hamilton."[16]

This is not the first time Drew sounds naive; there was never anything "perfect" about English laws for those pushed to its margins. It is common today for Canadians to demand "the rule of law" be applied to quell the legitimate grievances of those it was never intended to serve and protect—as if the law were some neutral tool for "equality," and not the weapon of oppression it has been wielded as. In Sophia's time, many of those enforcing laws were born in Scotland, from the generation raised after the Highland Clearances of 1750 to 1860, when tenants were evicted from the Scottish Highlands and islands.[17] The English had tested strategies of colonization there, then employed Scots as their enthusiastic vanguard of more distant occupations: the missionaries, administrators, soldiers, and entrepreneurs of empire. Canada West / Upper Canada was a very Scottish place.

CHAPTER 21
THE HUMBLE PETITIONS

The North American Convention of Colored Freemen was organized in response to the passing of the US Fugitive Slave Act of 1850. Staged over three days in September 1851 at Toronto's St. Lawrence Hall, it followed several well-attended speeches by abolitionists earlier in the year, including by British MP George Thompson, Frederick Douglass, and the editors of Canada's first Black newspaper, *Voice of the Fugitive*, Mary and Henry Bibb of Windsor.[1] Reverend Josiah Henson attended, and the agricultural settlements of Dawn and Elgin were promoted. Not everyone agreed with the settlement model—for example, Mary Ann Shadd Cary. The first Black woman journalist in the country, she is described on a Heritage Toronto plaque at 143 King Street East (near where she lived) as "support[ing] economic self-reliance and the full integration of Black people into Canadian society and opposed segregated agricultural communities." Shadd Cary published the *Provincial Freeman*, published from 1853 through 1857, first in Windsor then Toronto. It was the first newspaper published by a Black woman in North America. The plaque says that she "returned to the United States in 1863 to recruit African American soldiers for the Union army during the American Civil War. She later became one of the first American women of African descent to earn a law degree."

I wonder how much Sophia knew of the political machinations in Upper Canada / Canada West, or if she engaged with the anti-slavery work being done. Did she read the newspapers of the Bibbs or Shadd Cary? Did she hear speakers in her community? What did she know about the political struggles going on in Toronto that would directly impact the latter decades of her life? Much of the political turmoil focused on who deserved the right to own, develop, and settle, who should be in control and profit from the land. The Rebellion of 1837 saw progressives/republicans follow the lead of the newspaper publisher and politician William Lyon Mackenzie (born in Dundee, Scotland) and face off against the conservative/ Tory Family Compact that controlled Upper Canada like oligarchs, embodied by John Strachan, the Scottish-born bishop of the Anglican Church in Upper Canada.

Michael Gauvreau describes Strachan as, "the most eloquent and powerful Upper Canadian exponent of an anti-republican social order based upon the tory principles of hierarchy and subordination in both church and state."[2] G.M. Craig states that Strachan "believed in an ordered society, an established church, the prerogative of the crown, and prescriptive rights."[3] In the 1791 Constitutional Act, one seventh of all surveyed Crown land, known as the Clergy Reserves (2 395 687 acres, or 969 500 hectares), was set aside for Protestants. Bishop Strachan fiercely argued this meant Anglicans only. As chairman of the Clergy Corporation he managed these lands, until 1854 when the reserves came under the control of the legislative assembly of the Province of Canada (now Quebec and Ontario). Strachan did not go down without a fight, expressing values still promoted by many as "Canadian values":

> Are the Koran, the Vedas, the book of the Mormons, and the Holy Bible, to be held equally sacred.... And in a nation of Protestants, who have high and peculiar interests to preserve and transmit to posterity, are all places of power and trust, and even the Throne itself, to be open equally to the Atheist, the Infidel, the Pagan, the Mussulman, the Romanist, the Mormon and the Protestant? Is the kingdom of Satan... to enjoy the same public favor as the Kingdom of God? Is a Christian Church, a Pagan temple, and a mosque, to be equally held in honor?[4]

Sophia never mentioned anything of her spiritual or religious beliefs to Benjamin Drew, unlike many others he interviewed. "My mind has ever been to trust the Lord," declared Reverend Alexander Hemsley (St. Catharines), interviewed by Drew.[5] "I feel thankful that I can mention that I have given a part of my time to the spiritual interests of the people here without pay," revealed Benjamin Miller (London), also interviewed.[6] The people of Fishkill were Dutch Reformists and Thayendanegea/Joseph Brant was an Anglican (as were the Hatts). Did Sophia ever attend church with any of them? So many slaveholders thought of themselves as "good" Christians, and so I have to wonder if that impacted her views.

The census of 1851 identifies Sophia as "MDST," an abbreviation indicating Methodist; in the Queen's Bush this would indicate membership to an African Methodist Episcopal / British Methodist Episcopal (AME/BME) Church. This church was founded in 1816 in Philadelphia by the Right Reverend Richard Allen (also the first AME bishop), who was born enslaved and managed to buy his freedom.[7] AME churches in Canada, such as Salem Chapel in St. Catharines, Ontario (where Harriet Tubman was a member), Oro African Methodist Episcopal Church (a national historic site in the Township of Oro-Medonte, Ontario), Hamilton's St. Paul's African Methodist Episcopal Church (now Stewart Memorial Church), and Toronto's Christ Church St. James (honoured in the contemporary art of Anique Jordan; the congregation is now located in Etobicoke) all became BME churches following the passing of the Fugitive Slave Act. Church leaders in Canada feared travelling south of the border, and so the church agreed to split. As early as the 1840s, there was an AME congregation in the Queen's Bush settlement.

Drew criticized "separate" institutions: "If the [white] people can but 'conquer their prejudices' much of good may be done. On the other hand, it is a question whether the colored people would not do well to give up their separate religious organizations, and separate schools, wherever they exist in Canada."[8] Once again, an abolitionist puts the onus on Black people to resolve prejudice, just as settlers wanted Indigenous people to abandon their culture and be absorbed into the colonial system. Today, new Canadians continue to be pressured to "fit in" and conform.

As in other colonies, the British used their standard model of chartering private companies to lead resource development, land settlement, and governance duties in Canada (the Hudson's Bay Company is a prime example). The Canada Company received its royal charter as a "colonization company" in 1825 (such companies were established across the British Empire to facilitate settlement). Directed by Scottish-born John Galt, the company purchased over 2 million hectares of land from the government, including about half of the Huron Tract Purchase (over 890 300 hectares of Anishinaabe territory covered by Treaty 29 of 1827),[9] and set about attracting settlers: "No person, except United Englishmen, Loyalists... or those entitled by existing regulations to the Government free grants, can obtain any of the waste Crown lands otherwise than by purchase."[10]

In the above quotation from a book of British Empire statistics, *waste* is used in the original Latin sense of *vastus*, a term absorbed into Middle English through French *wast(e)*, meaning "unoccupied" or "uncultivated." This is how the Canada Company viewed Indigenous use of land, calling to mind the contemporary definition of *waste* as "*bad use*" (an unnecessary or wrong use of money, substances, time, energy, abilities, etc.).[11] This so-called waste land was, of course, very useful to Indigenous societies it was taken from, but settler society failed to see how profoundly engaged with the extended landscape those societies were. Settlers perceived no meaningful connection with the environment that conformed to European models of productivity and therefore viewed Indigenous societies as the inhabitants of "wasteland." Coming from a place that had been depleted of most wilderness and wildlife, Europeans failed to recognize that the territories they were moving through had long been significantly managed and cultivated.

Waste also means "unwanted matter" — material of any type, especially what is left after useful substances or parts have been removed. For the Canada Company, useful parts were what had been set aside for public buildings and infrastructure, and for Clergy Reserves. It is important to emphasize the source of the company's directives, a publication whose full title is worth reproducing here: *Statistics of the Colonies of the British Empire in the West Indies, South America, Asia, Austral-Asia, Africa, and Europe: Comprising the Area, Agriculture, Commerce, Manufactures, Shipping, Custom Duties, Population, Education, Religion, Crime, Government, Finances, Laws, Military Defence, Cultivated and Waste Lands, Emigration, Rates of Wages, Prices of Provisions, Banks, Coins, Staple Products, Stock, Moveable and Immoveable Property, Public Companies, &c. of Each Colony with the Charters and Engraved Seals: From the Official Records of the Colonial Office*. These were the categories through which the land and people were viewed across the British Empire.

Galt would not stay long in Canada. His tenure lasted from just 1826 to 1829. Consistently at odds with the company's governors, he was finally called home and dismissed. He did manage to found Guelph in 1827, and a town on the Grand was named after him — another example of a man of questionable accomplishment being prominently remembered. His colleague William "Tiger" Dunlop, also has a tarnished legacy (of shady land deals and selfishly using a public position for private gain).

Both Galt and Dunlop were published authors, but their writings are of minimal literary import beyond informing an understanding of their respective personalities and values.[12] While they go unnamed on the Monuments Board of Canada bronze plaque at the end of Toronto Street / Highway 8 in Goderich (a town on the shore of Lake Huron), the dated and overblown language nonetheless offers an appropriate legacy of these "pioneers of the Huron Tract":

PIONEERS OF THE HURON TRACT
1828–1928

Commemorating the lifework of the men who opened the roads, felled the forests, builded [sic] the farmsteads, tilled the fields, reaped the harvests—and of the women who made the homes, bore the children, nursed them, reared them, brightened and ennobled domestic life in the Huron Tract during a hundred years.

The Canada Company carried on for decades after Galt returned to the thriving port of Greenock, Scotland. Tobacco from Virginia plantations, forwarded up the River Clyde to the "Tobacco Lords" of Glasgow, no longer arrived as sugar had become the main commodity, and it continued to pour in from the West Indies. Raw cotton was arriving from plantations in the American South, to be processed in Glasgow's textile mills, then returned to American in bolts of cheap cloth called "slave cotton."

The primarily Scottish politicians in Upper Canada carried on, "like two rams knocking their heads together."[13] The election that followed the Upper Canada Rebellion brought reforms, and the influence of the Family Compact declined. The government would assume direct oversight of land settlement, but the core principles continued of prioritizing white Protestant, then "Aryan" Europeans,[14] and offering them the choicest land on the best terms. These principles were applied to surveying, distribution, and settlement regardless of who was already present on lands referred to as the Queen's Bush, the name Benjamin Drew explained as "originally given to a large, unsurveyed tract of land, now comprising the townships of Peel and Wellesley, and the country extending thence to Lake Huron." He goes on to say that "while it was yet a wilderness, it was settled mainly by colored people, about the year 1846."[15]

Drew's description of the Queen's Bush is fairly accurate; however, there were already Black settlers in the 1820s, and missionaries arrived in the 1830s. Drew appears to be drawing on the memory of William Jackson, whom he interviewed and who came late to the area:

> My father and myself went to the Queen's Bush in 1846.... For years scarcely any white people came in, but fugitive slaves came in, in great numbers, and cleared the land. Before it was surveyed, there were as many as fifty families.... The colored people might have held their lands still, but they were afraid they would not be able to pay.... Many of them sold out cheap.... The climate of Canada agrees with them.... I have heard white people who lived at Queen's Bush say, that they never lived amongst a set of people that they had rather live with as to their habits of industry and general good conduct.[16]

Despite what he says, over the coming generations, climate would be consistently cited as a rationale for barring immigration from the African diaspora to the "Great White North."[17]

Because of the geography, the townships of Waterloo, Wellington, Wilmot, Woolwich, and the Huron Tract are triangles and irregular wedges, not the squared blocks of the Toronto Purchase, Brant Tract Purchase, or the Rice Lake Purchase. We are back in the *gore* again; overlapping and aligned puzzle pieces pattern Southern Ontario, which is itself a triangle jutting down below the 49th parallel. The entire Queen's Bush lay within a wedge of Crown land that widens as it progresses into Bruce County.

Queen's Bush has come to mainly refer to the historic Black settlement between the Conestogo and Grand Rivers. Throughout the wider territory it once defined, the name has been subsumed by names of towns, districts, counties, and townships, but it still appeared in late nineteenth and early twentieth century settler narratives, such as *The Queen's Bush: A Tale of the Early Days of Bruce County* (1932):

> In that pleasant land...where now are smiling fields and cosy farm-houses, pleasant glades and purling spring brooks, where verdant and prolific fields lift smiling faces to an azure sky, there was in the year

> 1851 one vast and primeval forest, extending...to the sounding shores
> of the Huron Sea.
>
> To the southward, Fergus and Guelph, were on the fringes of
> civilization. From that fringe a finger-thrust of civilization — the
> Garafraxa Road — had been pierced northwestwards...to strike the
> shores of the Georgian Bay.[18]

I'm not sure what "smiling fields" are, but Brown obviously did, as he repeats the description. His writing is consistent with the many local histories published on the "early years" or "pioneer days" of Ontario: anecdotes written by descendants of settlers, with repeated tales of overcoming hardship through good British fortitude, wisdom, and skill, a foundation for many white Christians. Too many of these stories became *the* official histories, defended by descendants and promoted in civic marketing. Many employ violent and disturbingly invasive metaphors like "finger-thrust of civilization."

One of many colonization roads built in the 1830s to 1840s around the province, Garafraxa Road brought surveyors who considered all those they encountered already settled to be squatters and thought they'd "improved" land through cultivation and the addition of buildings (solid log cabins and barns). The origin of the name Garafraxa is uncertain, but among a myriad explanations is: "Old English word *gara* or *gar*...a small *triangular* piece of land or *cloth as in a sail*, and the Township is considered part *fracta* of the Gore or Gara [italics added]," as it cuts through the original Gore District.[19]

Freedom-seekers who came to Canada after Sophia, including Henry William-son whom Drew interviewed in Hamilton, acknowledged that many carried a deep distrust of whites that could be harmful but valid. Williamson explains:

> This is because they have been so much deceived and kept down by
> the white people. I have seen people who had run away, brought back
> tied, like sheep, in a wagon. Men have told me, that when making
> their escape, they have been accosted, invited into a house in a friend-
> ly way, and, next thing, some officer or their owner would be there.
> The lowest class of people do this to get money — men who might
> get an honest living — some having good education, and some good
> trades.[20]

Dear Sophia,

You had certainly spent enough time around white administrators and church people that I imagine you never completely trusted any of them. Why would you? There were clearly many whose actions and attitudes toward you were far less than sympathetic. You told Drew, *this long scar over my eye, is where she cut me with a knife. The skin dropped over my eye; a white woman bound it up.* That white woman is more the exception than the rule. How many simply ignored you? I think of the sons-in-law who *came into the garden* prefiguring the surveyors and land speculators who came into the Queen's Bush (the "gardens" of farmland in your community), along with the colonial leadership that will ignore, and impose silence on, the "Humble Petitions," like the one below.

Petition to Charles Metcalfe, Governor General, 1843
On April 24, 1843

To His Excellency The Right Honorable Sir Charles Theopolis Metcalfe, Knight Grand Cross of the Most Honorable Military Order of the Bath, one of her Majesty's Most Honorable Privy Council, Governor General of British North America, and Captain General, and Governor-in-Chief; on and over the Province of Canada, Nova Scotia, New Brunswick, and the Island of Prince Edward, and Vice-Admiral of the same, etc. etc. etc.

The Humble Petition
Showeth, that your petitioners the Inhabitants of the Queens Bush now labouring under many disadvantages on the account of the state of the Lands on which we have settled not being surveyed consequently, we have no regular Roads and being a distance of fifteen miles to the nearest mill, and your Petitioners being extremely poor having lately emigrated from England and from the Southern states where

we have suffered all the horrors of Slavery and having no means of purchasing land, your Petitioners humbly pray that your Lordship's humanity to make us a grant of Land it will be most thankfully received by Lordship's dutiful and Loyal Petitioners and your Petitioners as is duty bound will ever pray.[21]

This petition (the second of four) was signed by 124 male residents of the Queen's Bush, including 51 identified as Black. Simon Ganseville and John Patten, the men Sophia mentioned in relation to Thyandanegea/Joseph, don't appear. Petitioning to have one's rights, labours, and property acknowledged, promises fulfilled, and reparations made is a regular action taken throughout the history and the afterlife of slavery, yet it often failed. For many, including the black abolitionists Robert Wedderburn and Frederick Douglass, it represented a re-entrenchment of their degraded status, as Saidiya Hartman explains:

> In 1817, the black abolitionist Robert Wedderburn had warned of the dangers of appeal... 'But do not petition, for it is degrading to human nature to petition your oppressors.' In 1845, Frederick Douglass echoed this sentiment when he described the slave's appeal as 'a privilege so dangerous' that anyone exercising it 'runs a fearful hazard' of inviting even greater violence.[22]

Hartman links these sentiments to contemporary demands for reparations: "It seems to me that there is something innately servile about making an appeal to a deaf ear or praying for relief from an indifferent and hostile court or expecting remedy from a government unwilling even to acknowledge that slavery was a crime against humanity."[23] Who was the man the "Humble Petitioners" hoped would show "humanity"?

Sir Charles Metcalfe had served in various senior roles in India before being appointed governor general of Canada (from 1843 to 1845). His charge from the British government included suppressing representative government. He was governor of Jamaica from 1839 to 1842, where he worked to maintain the privileges of sugar planters, five years after the Emancipation Act. Like numerous New England Quakers decades earlier, who "freed themselves" of the burden of slavery by selling (rather than manumitting) the enslaved, the British carried on designing and implementing systems and laws maintaining racial hierarchies, while continuing to trap the newly freed in poverty and coerced labour. They used the Church as a tool of oppression, as this account makes clear:

> Britain...has not only broken the chains which bound the bodies of her African brethren, but she has laboured indefatigably, and with success, to enable them to cast off those weightier and more degrading fetters which enslaved their souls. She has not only given them temporal liberty, but she has instructed them to obtain freedom from vice, and superstition, and ignorance. She has delivered them from cruel and tyrannical task-masters, and has placed them under protection of Him, whose "service is perfect freedom."[24]

The suggestion that there were "weightier and more degrading fetters which enslaved their souls" reads like Drew's "the misfortune to be descended from slave mothers," the implication of innate "lesserness" revealing again that many abolitionists carried racist ideas they passed forward to eugenicists and social Darwinists. These ideas live on in schools, cultural organizations, and religious institutions that continue to shape the "free world." Whiteness persist in blaming Blackness under a mask of charity and liberal values. In the Queen's Bush, the manipulations that benefited whites at the expense of Black settlers were hardly masked. In her last home, Sophia again witnessed a landscape *filling up with white people.*

There is evidence to suggest a definitive date for Sophia's arrival in the Queen's Bush. In the 1851 Peel Township census, Sophia appears living in the home of "Joseph Malott Sr"[25] and in her book on the Black pioneers in the Queen's Bush settlement, Linda Brown-Kubisch states that "the Mallot family found a permanent home in March 1841 when they settled on the south half of Lot 18, Concession 1, Peel Township."[26] (In the earliest records that are most relevant to Sophia's time, *Malott* is the consistent spelling, but it is later spelled *Mallot* by descendants and by Brown-Kubisch.)[27] They were not new to Canada; they had been living in the region since the 1820s. I will come to them in a moment.

Brown-Kubisch's claim that "Very little is known about the everyday lives of these pioneers" (such as the Mallots) is unfortunate.[28] Much is known about white settlers here, and we can easily extrapolate from their experiences to imagine early

Black lives in similar circumstances, while always remembering the barriers they faced (racism, lack of resources or government support, the traumas they carried, and the challenge of adapting to a life of precarious freedom). In fact, many Black settlers had more experience in preparing land and farming than their new neighbours, having done manual labour and skilled work for whites. In Drew's interviews, it isn't hard to find details of the Black settler experience, such as this account by a woman known as Mrs. John Little:

> I got to be quite hardy—quite used to [the] water and [to] bush-whacking; so that by the time I got to Canada, I could handle an axe, or hoe, or any thing [sic]. I felt proud to be able to do it—to help get cleared up, so that we could have a home, and plenty to live on. I now enjoy my life very well—I have nothing to complain of. We have horses and a pleasure-wagon, and I can ride out when and where I please, without a pass. The best of the merchants and clerks pay me as much attention as though I were a white woman: I am as politely accosted as any woman would wish to be.
>
> I have lost two children by death; one little girl is all that is spared to me. She is but four years old. I intend to have her well educated, if the Lord lets us.[29]

The basic everyday lives and labours of "pioneers" have been extensively recorded and are endlessly re-enacted at living history sites. The voids in historical records perpetuate further erasures in such spaces. Biased accounts, like W.M. Brown's *The Queen's Bush: A Tale of the Early Days of Bruce County* (1832) and Susanna Moodie's *Roughing It in the Bush* (1852), remain privileged sources for the descendants of these storytellers, whose ideas continue to be carried forward by historical and heritage societies, museums, and interpreters unwilling to confront a more complex past, or are intent on perpetuating their myths and racist stereotypes.

As Black lives in Canada have been so minimally documented, with so many early communities forced to disband and disperse (many returning to the United States), little exists in archives because there was neither the material to collect that conformed to biased standards nor knowledgeable individuals gaining access to archives (as employees or supported researchers). So one has to read between the lines, triangulate fragments, and also value what has historically been undervalued and supressed. As art historian and curator Charmaine Nelson notes, "Canadian denial of its colonial past can be measured in part by the extent to which the historical presence of blacks has been rubbed out of national consciousness along with the ongoing internal marginalization of black populations."[30]

I asked Lisa Hunter (my spouse for many years, the mother of our children Max and Claire, and now my close colleague and friend) to explain the likely details of Sophia's work to me. A museum professional and public historian, she has long focused on the history of early settlement in Upper Canada / Canada West, the daily labours of working people, and the demands of sustaining a homestead (with a particular focus on the lives of women and children). Lisa imagined Sophia was the primary domestic labourer in the Brant and Hatt homesteads. Highly skilled, she could have easily thrived on her own had she been granted freedom and resources: "The day-to-day work in the late eighteenth and early nineteenth century home was fundamentally about keeping a family fed, clean, and sheltered. These jobs break down into some general categories that include food preparation; small animal care; kitchen gardening; production and care of clothing and household textiles; childcare; care of the home; and seasonal work."[31] Lisa confidently itemizes these tasks, many of which she herself can execute in the manner they would have been done, using tools and equipment from that period, or managing without them:

> Food preparation would likely have included cooking daily meals; butchering, smoking/drying domestic animals, game, and fish; dairy work such as cheese and butter making; animal care, which may or may not have been done by outside workers but was sometimes considered part of the "kitchen" work, including feeding and watering chickens, ducks, pigs, cows, as well as milking and cleaning pens; maintaining a kitchen garden, sometimes also medicinal gardens (planting, weeding, harvesting, and pest control); then there was the production and care of clothing and household textiles — sewing, knitting, weaving, and laundry (a full-day endeavour), plus mending, alterations, and repairs.

Lisa paused to consider the type of dwellings Sophia laboured in — not modest — and then described the care of such homes and environs: "Hearths had to be cleaned, fires tended, firewood brought in; washing floors, beating carpets, air-ing mattresses, etc.; cleaning and fuelling lamps; cleaning windows and stoops; hauling and boiling water. Then there was the seasonal work such as lye and soap making, the refilling of mattresses with straw ticks, and maple sugar production." I reminded Lisa that one of the primary reasons both the Brants and the Hatts would have "acquired" Sophia was for childcare. "For sure," she replied, "even as a child of seven or eight, she would have fed, bathed, possibly taught, supervised, and cared for children when ill."

In all, Sophia would have laboured hard, constantly, all for the ultimate benefit of others. Over the years of enslavement, she would develop a phenomenal range of highly valuable skills and knowledge. All those heroic tales of white settlers omit the fact that most had resources and the support of government, power, and privilege to prosper, as well as the support of the cheaply recompensed physical labour done by people like Sophia, and the names so often championed in Canada are often directly linked with the oppressions, dispossessions, and disenfranchisement of the communities Black settlers tried to establish. Granted the same freedoms, rights, and government support as white settlers, Sophia's expertise would have afforded her the opportunity to thrive, not just struggle to survive.

Since we only know Sophia was present in Queen's Bush based on Drew's interview (in which she says very little about the place) and her name in one census, it isn't surprising that she is a minimal presence in Brown-Kubisch's book, but the book still provides valuable fragments to expand upon. For example, since the census shows Sophia was living for a time in the Queen's Bush with the Mallot family, Brown-Kubisch's research on the Malotts (who I believe were the same family) is generative, including information about the Colbornesburg settlement, a short-lived all-Black community in Woolwich Township, Waterloo County, initiated in the late 1820s. Adrienne Shadd offers more substantive details about Colbornesburg, and I draw from her work in piecing together what follows.

Joseph Malott was born enslaved in 1799 in Alabama, and spent time working as a cook on a Mississippi riverboat, making enough money to buy his freedom. He settled in Ohio, where he married Lucinda Brown. Like Josiah and Charlotte Henson, Reighen Grineage's ancestors (who also came via Ohio), and a Henry Williamson of Hamilton, the Malotts travelled to Canada with a large group. They were "being pushed out," Shadd relates, "by punitive *Ohio Black Codes*. An 1804 law, for example, required that Blacks had to obtain a certificate of freedom to live and work in Ohio. Three years later, they were required to post a $500 bond, signed by two white men, guaranteeing good behavior."[32] After finding the cost of land prohibitive in the all-Black community of Wilberforce, the Malotts chose to settle in a nearby area of Woolwich County known as Crooks Tract. They obtained 60 hectares, and the family now included a newborn son Daniel (born in 1828 or 1829). Their daughter Margaret was born in 1831, and by then, "four individuals plus three families, totalling twenty-four people... had settled on 720 acres [290 hectares] of Crooks Tract."[33] The population was enough to be the foundation for schools and churches.

We have met Crooks previously (see chapter 17) — the brothers who posted an ad "to purchase, A NEGRO GIRL."[34] In 1821, William Crooks purchased 2 832 hectares in Waterloo Township, which eventually became known as *Crooks Tract*. He divided the land and offered lots for sale. By this time, William's brother James "had amassed more than over 400 hectares along the Trent River, where about 1828 he erected a grist-mill at... *Crooks' Rapids* [at Hastings where Daniel and Nelly Outwater settled; original italics]. By 1834 he had built mills on the Speed River.... His complex on Spencer Creek had...a tannery, distillery, potashery, agricultural implement factory, woollen-mill, and oil-mill."[35]

Colbornesburg didn't last long. While a number of people moved to Hamilton, the Malotts relocated to nearby Bloomingdale, where they lived from approximately 1835 to 1840, and had two more children, Catharine and Joseph Jr. (born in 1836 and 1837). In 1841, they moved to the Queen's Bush. "It is unclear why the Colbornesburg Settlement that started with such promise disbanded so quickly," states Shadd. "For one thing, no record of any land deals exist for Crooks Tract involving the families. Perhaps, as was the case with the Queen's Bush, the families squatted on land hoping to establish productive farms that would enable them to eventually purchase their lots."[36] It needs to be remembered that many white settlers were encouraged to squat on land they desired with the understanding they would receive grants when surveying was completed. Black settlers likely expected similar arrangements.

According to the Woolwich Township website, "settlers came from a variety of origins, in the early years the majority were of German-Mennonite heritage, most of whom came from Pennsylvania and Waterloo Township. In general, they tended to settle west of the Grand River, while English (many of them Methodists) and Scots-Presbyterians settled to the east."[37] The township website makes no mention of Black settlers or Colbornesburg. The growing presence of settlers from Pennsylvania was likely unnerving for many who shared experiences similar to Queen's Bush resident Thomas Knox:

> I was born free in the eastern part of Pennsylvania, but removed to Pittsburgh. I should not have left the States only that I was not treated with respect. I would go to market with provisions off a farm I rented in New Brighton. When I got into Pittsburgh, other farmers would drive in with their teams into the tavern yard, and get their breakfasts and go and sell out, before I could get any thing [sic] to eat: so that by the time I would get to market, the best of it would be over. The same thing would run through all the conduct of the whites.[38]

Based on the 1851 census, we know that Joseph Malott was a 52-year-old widowed "Negro" from Ohio living in a single-storey "Log Cabin" housing one family. Joseph was living with his seven unmarried children (all born in Canada to his first wife Lucinda, who died in 1850): Daniel (22), Margaret (20), Catharine (15), Joseph (13), John M. (11), James (8), and Hanna (6). Joseph married Mary Ann Lightfoot after the census was taken. Next to Sophia "Polly," the following information is recorded: Place of Birth = *United States*, Residence if out of limits = *Brantford*, Age = *75*, Married or Single = *W* (widow), Colored persons — *Negroes* = *1*. The number of "Resident-Members" of the Malott home are also totalled next to Sophia's entry: *M=5*, *F=4*, confirming nine residents (the eight Malotts plus Sophia). The listing of Brantford under "residence if out of limits," suggests that Sophia identified this as her home prior to coming to the Queen's Bush. If she had only been visiting, she would have been counted in the "Not Members" column.

> Dear Sophia,
>   When and where did you meet the Malotts? You could have encountered them as early as the 1820s. You say, *Then I lived in what is now Waterloo*, and you also mention that, *the Upper Block was at Snyder's Mills*. This was located where the village of St. Jacobs is now, in Waterloo. You appear to have known the area well. Bloomingdale (where the Malotts lived briefly) is not far from St. Jacobs, and a road heading

west from there is called Snider's Flats. After Robert left you, did you remain in Waterloo? Did you meet the Malotts at Colbornesburg or Bloomingdale? All that is certain is that in 1851 you were living with them.

In 1855, you tell Drew that *I find plenty of people in the bush to help me a good deal*. I imagine that such kindness and generosity was not new to you by then, that as a lone woman, over fifty by the 1830s, moving within a Black community coalescing in the Upper Block of the Haldimand Tract, that you would have been welcomed and supported. You were an Elder who had lived in Upper Canada / Canada West for decades and knew the Grand River country. You witnessed numerous communities being established, growing, and thriving. Others, confronted by power and privilege, would be destroyed.

Following in your footsteps, moving back and forth in time, I often think of Octavia Butler. I hear her words, particularly those voiced through her characters Lauren Oya Olamina (in *Parable of the Sower* and *Parable of the Talents*) and Dana (in *Kindred*): Lauren, working out of crisis and chaos (her world is eerily prescient of today's times) and trying to shape a new worlding through her faith/philosophy she calls "Earthseed," and Dana, troubling and troubled by the past, carrying a fragile white man (her husband) through time and memory. Like you, they are survivors. Lauren Oya Olamina said: "That's all anybody can do right now. Live. Hold out. Survive. I don't know whether good times are coming back again. But I know that won't matter if we don't survive these times."[39] For many who you came to live among in the Queen's Bush, there hadn't been "good times" to return to, but many spoke of their kin and the kinship they'd lost. I imagine this is what you were hoping would come back again.

Many freedom-seekers had, like Sophia, been long separated from their families. They'd lost their parents and grandparents, had children taken away from them, been separated from siblings and relatives. As their new community was forming, everyone was likely looking for familiar faces, hoping for restoration. Together, they brought a diversity of experience and wisdom. Sophia had come to know much about this land and how to live off it, and she had experience dealing with the particular ways of the whites under British rule. I imagine community members learned a great deal from her, adding to the significant knowledge and skill that many already carried. Once again, the potential for home may have presented itself to Sophia, much as Butler describes it for everyone:

> The child in each of us
> Knows paradise.
> Paradise is home.
> Home as it was
> Or home as it should have been.
>
> Paradise is one's own place,
> One's own people,
> One's own world,
> Knowing and known,
> Perhaps even
> Loving and loved.
>
> Yet every child
> Is cast from paradise —
> Into growth and new community,
> Into vast, ongoing
> Change.[40]

In the census, Sophia appears immediately above John Bulmer (Farmer, 42), his spouse Fanny (Francis Hardy, 40), and their children William (22), John (16), Fanny (5), and MaryAnn (1); all were born in England except the youngest. "The Bulmer family and the Owens family," according to the obituary in 1922 for William R. Bulmer, "were the only white families living in Peel township for some time."[41] They were the Malott's neighbours. Bulmer does not appear on the Humble Petitions; he arrived after the first two were submitted (in 1842 and 1843), and the 1847 and 1850 petitions were signed only by Black residents. Bulmer had clear title to his land. According to the obituary for the son William (who died in 1922), the family came from Yorkshire, via New York and York (Toronto), arriving in the Queen's Bush when the boy was 17 (in 1846 or 1847).

William had lived on the homestead until around 1912, and died ten years later, at age 92. His father and mother died in 1888 and 1896 respectively. Joseph Malott's sons worked as labourers in the region, often for the Bulmer family. In 1862, the Bulmers gave John Michael and James Wilson Malott, together, 10 hectares of land. This generosity was not matched by the government; by the time Drew visited, many Black settlers had moved away, unable to secure title to their properties. That Drew only interviewed a small group in the Queen's Bush is telling. William Jackson had already left the settlement for Galt, so after Sophia, he interviewed only four other Queen's Bush residents; Mr. and Mrs. John Little (fugitives from Virginia), Thomas L. Wood Knox (a freeman from Pennsylvania), and John Francis (who had bought his freedom in Virginia). Francis detailed the fate of Black settlers:

> I came in ten years ago. Then there were few families. More kept coming, — colored people, — there were not many white.... We settled down where we saw fit...After considerable many settlers had come in...we sent a man to get a grant of the land if he could.... The answer was no, that we were on clergy reserves.... We kept at work, clearing and planting. The land came into market about seven years ago, being surveyed and a price set on it.... Then came a land agent, to sell and take payments.... The agent himself told me he would sell my land unless the instalment was paid. I sacrificed my two cows and a steer, to make the payment that I might hold the land.... One man, fearing to lose all he had done, sold out for ten dollars.... That property is now estimated at $15,000.... That is what has scattered the colored people away from here. There are now about three hundred, — there were three times as many.[42]

Francis says nine hundred Black settlers, but there were likely more. What petitioners were asking for was not unprecedented; their requests were consistent with arrangements being made in Upper and Lower Canada, and other areas that would become the Dominion of Canada, where many of the "preferred" were granted lands or offered easy terms to encourage settlement. But with the exception of a few with the means, or the willingness to "sacrifice" like Francis, most Black people had to abandon their homes.

Those who stayed survived by labouring to improve and expand the properties of whites, while they struggled to keep their own. Such circumstances had parallels with experiences of free Blacks in the northern United States, and prefigured the lives of those who became "free" after the Civil War in the South. There, restrictive Jim Crow laws held people (and their descendants) under the violent control of the very planters who had enslaved them. Like the enslaved who became indentured servants in Canada, Southern Blacks in the United States became sharecroppers, remained in the same homes, and continued to work familiar fields. Obligated to share half their crop with landowners, and to borrow the essentials of farming (at high interest), sharecroppers inevitably became burdened by debt in a system that was basically "slavery by another name."[43] While Queen's Bush petitioners sought to remind those in power what had been promised, their texts of 1847 and 1850 reveal another reason for the lack of government sympathy. Unfortunately, they'd pledged allegiance to the conservative government during the Upper Canada Rebellion in 1837, which was no longer able to fulfil its promises — if it had ever intended to. A petition in 1850 by ten Black residents of Queen's Bush reminded the Governor General, Lord Elgin

> that there was a proclamation issued in the year 1840 to the effect that every man of colour assisting in putting down the Rebellion of the year 1837 & 1838 by going to the Queen's Bush was to get a deed of 50 acres of land with the privilege of purchasing 50 acres more of the Lot if able to do so.[44]

Then this line appears in the 1850 petition: " Your petitioners are now informed by Mr. Gayters, Crown Land Agent in Elora that their farms and improvements are in the Market." The Elora agent was actually Mr. Andrew *Geddes,* born in Banffshire, Scotland. He came to Canada in 1834, lived in Elora, then Hamilton, and returned to Elora in 1844. It must have been a shock to Queen's Bush residents to hear that their land was up for sale, that all their labour and investments were to be sold "in the market" (a disturbing phrase, given that the formerly enslaved would have used it to describe the loss of family members or their own experiences).[45]

"In the twenty-one years that he was a resident of Elora," claims John Robert Connon in *The Early History of Elora* (1930), Geddes "was well known and respected by all. In him every new resident found a ready and reliable adviser. No one could be more punctual and methodical in attending to business. His early training had given him such exacting business habits that they had become like second nature to him."[46] Geddes's habits of being methodical and exacting could be seen in a positive light by other Scottish immigrants who benefited from his approach. But they could be seen as less appealing—as cold and calculating—by Black residents. Geddes was willing to ignore the fate of those in the Queen's Bush in favour of "every new resident" and his own community's needs. He likely believed that the Scottish economist and philosopher Adam Smith's idea of the "invisible hand" would look after those who signed the Humble Petitions. "When Providence divided the earth among a few lordly masters," Smith states in *The Theory of Moral Sentiments* (1759), "it neither forgot nor abandoned those who seemed to have been left out in the partition."[47] Sophia's community experienced the fallacy of Smith's theory. The "hand" was clearly visible, painfully familiar, and would easily forget and abandon them.

> Dear Sophia,
>   I see you moving as a strong presence in the Queen's Bush, that you were likely seen as a grandmother or an aunt. I imagine you sharing your knowledge, and children being fascinated by your stories of survival, amazed by the many deer hunts at the outlet, excited when you tell them I *had a tomahawk, and would hit the deer on the head . . . take it by the horns and paddle ashore . . . .* And these children would have witnessed your scars, and understood them through seeing their parents' scars, and experiencing their own. "Thus, you saw the blood for the first time," Palestinian poet Mahmoud Darwish wrote in *The Presence of Absence* (2006). "Your blood, which taught you that a scar is a memory that never ceases working."[48]

CHAPTER 22
HOARDINGS OF AMNESIA

Dear Sophia,

I have found so many threads across time and place connecting Benjamin Drew to a wider world and colonial history. I could keep going outward or return to follow other threads, generate further links. There is so much material to curate from, to weave a complex narrative placing Drew at the centre of a web of privilege and entitlement, of power and empires, and of whiteness with its seemingly endless freedom to carry on holding the centre.

Drew remembered "boys running through the streets shouting, 'Peace, Peace,'"[1] at the end of the War of 1812, while you recalled that in 1813, during the height of the conflict, *the cannonade made everything shake well*. For all his moves and career changes, Drew appears to have lived a very stable life, as did his ancestors and progeny, landing on their feet, empowered to make choices, passing in *Peace*. For you, the journey would be perilous and shaky. I am looking to secure your presence here, by disrupting the peacefulness of too many deeply embedded narratives. I'm working to interrogate Drew's narrative and, through it, my own.

I made another trip to Boston to look again at Drew's diaries at the Massachusetts Historical Society, going back over a few years prior to 1855 to see if anything resonated, but I found only a void—long periods with no entries. I stopped by the Museum of Fine Arts, Boston, to view one of my favourite paintings; the Boston-born artist Winslow Homer's *The Fog Warning* (1885). This was meant to be a distraction from my disappointment with Drew's diary, but it only led me back into your story.

Homer envisioned a lone fisherman in an open dory. The man has paused from rowing as he crests a wave, the oars projecting perpendicular to the boat and parallel to the turbulent grey waters. A good day's catch of halibut lies at his feet. He looks over his shoulder towards a schooner on the distant horizon that will soon vanish into the fog… "The stealthy fog enwraps him in its folds, blinds his vision, cuts off all marks to guide his course, and leaves him afloat in a measureless void."[2]

There is an unintended lesson in this painting, embodied by the catch at the fisherman's feet. These halibut are much larger and older than halibut harvested today, evidence there has been a significant drop in the abundance of this species.

Winslow Homer, *The Fog Warning*, 1885, oil on canvas, 76.83 cm × 123.19 cm, Collection of the Museum of Fine Arts, Boston, anonymous gift with credit to the Otis Norcross Fund, 94.72. Photograph © 2022 Museum of Fine Arts, Boston

Those who believe the sea is a "measureless void" fail to observe this change, due to what's called "the shifting baseline syndrome," explained as "the situation in which over time knowledge is lost about the state of the natural world, because people don't perceive changes that are actually taking place" and whose effect is that "people's perceptions of change are out of kilter with the actual changes taking place in the environment."[3] The theory of shifting baselines was "first elucidated by scientists exploring urban children's perception of nature in 1995"; marine biologist Daniel Pauly coined the term that same year.[4] Research has revealed both generational and personal amnesia as critical factors in how we see our current environments and histories:

> Generational amnesia is when knowledge is not passed down from generation to generation. For example, people may think of as "pristine" wilderness the wild places that they experienced during their childhood, but with every generation this baseline becomes more and more degraded.
>
> Personal amnesia is when people forget how things used to be during the course of their own lives, for example they may not remember that things which are rarely sighted now were once common. In this case, the individual actually "updates" the change involved, so that the change (and the past) is forgotten and the new state becomes the baseline.[5]

I find myself looking at natural history and environmental science for models of memory and loss. The myths that continue to bolster Canadian identity appear as such updates to memory.

Homer's fisherman is working the waters just south of Nova Scotia, where Canada's iconic schooner *Bluenose* was built at Lunenburg, a half century later, at the end of the age of the dominance of commercial sailing vessels. While the *Bluenose* is remembered for its racing success, catching cod had long been its purpose. Cod kept Europeans coming to North America to fish for centuries, and their North American descendants working the Grand Banks until, in living memory, the stocks collapsed. That the *Bluenose* would end its days stripped of its masts, working the coastal trade as a diesel-powered freighter for the West Indies Trading Company seems fitting. The schooner was wrecked on a reef off the coast of Haiti in 1946, in the heart of the West Indies, where vast amounts of salt cod had been shipped to feed the enslaved on British plantations.

To me, the parallels in cultural and social history that extend into distorted nationalist narratives of citizenship and belonging are obvious in places like the Queen's Bush (and throughout Southern Ontario), where the historic *baseline* of a significant Black presence has been erased, *shifted* by whiteness carrying both *generational* and *personal amnesia*. The *evidence* lies in these vessels of extraction: in the dory carrying the burthen laid at the fisherman's feet, and in the affluent museum with its walls adorned by Homer's highly valued painting. The collections of North American cultural institutions are bodies of evidence, not only of the objects caught, but of their provenance. A critical forensic eye brings to the surface the legitimation of wealth and privilege embodied by this colonial infrastructure. The narrator in W.G. Sebald's *The Rings of Saturn* (1995) describes encountering someone with such an eye:

> It was Cornelius de Jong who drew my attention to the fact that many important museums...were originally endowed by the sugar dynasties or were in some other way connected with the sugar trade. The capital amassed in the eighteenth and nineteenth centuries through various forms of slave economy is still in circulation, said de Jong, still bearing interest, increasing many times over and continually burgeoning anew. One of the most tried and tested ways of legitimizing this kind of money has always been the patronage of the arts, the purchase and exhibiting of paintings and sculptures.... At times it seemed to me, said de Jong, as if all works of art were coated with sugar glaze or indeed made completely of sugar.[6]

Many Canadian institutions remain invested in the economy de Jong describes, cultivating public interest in the residue of economies of extraction and exploitation.

The Fog Warning is one of Homer's most successful paintings, so it is not surprising that he repeated the composition in a later scene. *The Gulf Stream* (1899) features the same basic elements: an imperilled seaman, a vulnerable boat, threatening weather, and the silhouette of a vanishing ship on the horizon. Painted after Homer returned from the Bahamas, *The Gulf Stream* presents a far more dramatic scenario than did the earlier painting. Here, a prone figure lies across the deck of a

Winslow Homer, *The Gulf Stream*,
1899, oil on canvas, 71.4 cm × 124.8 cm,
collection of the Metropolitan Museum of Art, New York

rudderless sloop encircled by sharks with a waterspout rapidly coming on. The far distant square rigger calls to mind Turner's floundering *Slave Ship* and is clearly unreachable. Even if it were, it is not clear this would represent salvation for this lone sailor, a Black man who is looking away from the ship, accompanied by only a few stocks of sugarcane for subsistence that reveal where he has escaped from. This painting is in the collection of New York's Metropolitan Museum of Art, and they offered this brief description in 2019: "Some art historians have read *The Gulf Stream* as symbolic, connecting it with the period's heightened racial tensions. The painting has also been interpreted as an expression of Homer's presumed sense of mortality and vulnerability following the death of his father."[7] This conditional interpretation (employing modifiers like "some" and "presumed") was an unsatisfyingly generic reading, the phrase "heightened racial tensions" was vague, and the text misidentifies the distant vessel as a "schooner" (it is clearly a square-rigged ship, a barque). The text has since been rewritten to include: "*The Gulf Stream* also references some of the complex social and political issues of the era—war, the legacy of slavery, and American imperialism—as well as more universal concerns with the fragility of human life and the dominance of nature."[8]

While slavery in the Bahamas had ended in 1834, the sugar cane industry carried on, with the working conditions of "free" Black labourers barely changed from their conditions during enslavement. This man has taken flight, weathered storms, and now drifts aboard a rudderless and broken jury-rigged craft:

> History and Etymology for *Jury*:
> . . .
> Adjective
> Middle English *jory* (in *jory saile improvised sail*)[9]
>
> injury (n.)
> late 14c., "harm, damage, loss; a specific injury," from Anglo-French *injurie* "wrongful action" (Old French *injure*, 13c.), from Latin *iniuria* "wrong, an injustice, insult, unlawful violence, assault, damage, harm," noun use of fem. of *iniurius* "wrongful, unjust, unlawful," from *in-* "not, opposite of" (see in- (1)) + *ius* (genitive *iuris*) "right, law."

The *jory saile* lies crumpled on the foredeck next to the stump of a broken mast. The sailor lies broken as well, carrying injuries that may never heal.

He is caught in the Gulf Stream, that warm current flowing north from the Gulf of Mexico, along the east coast of the United States, but too far offshore to get provisions. Should he survive this and other storms, his vessel might veer eastward at Nantucket (where Ishmael ventured out on the *Pequod* in Herman Melville's *Moby-Dick*), then face the slim miraculous possibility of being carried past Nova Scotia, Newfoundland, and across the Atlantic to Britain or northern Europe, retracing one leg of the Triangle Trade—from the landscapes of enslavement, to ports still thriving and growing on the wealth extracted from this sailor and his ancestors. (Ancestor: from Latin *antecedere*, *ante* "before" + *cedere* "go"). Will this sailor survive this particular passage, or will he drop into the sea to join those who have *gone before,* looking for the elusive possibility of *return*? I find echoes of this treacherous voyage in John Francis's, revealed in his interview with Drew: "My mother was sold away from me, when I was about eleven years old. In escaping, I sailed over two hundred miles on the sea in an open boat with my father, a day without eating, and ten days without drinking. One night we were near being lost in a storm. We put in to get water and were taken: but we made out to clear ourselves."[10]

The writer Dionne Brand's description of a trip, offered a century and a half later, reveal the precarity of return:

> I am on my way to Johannesburg. It is my first flight to the continent. I will fly over the Door of No Return. I will not go there, but I will feel it somehow. This plane leaves Frankfurt and I sit riveted to the TV screen, which shows a map of Europe and Africa. The symbol of a plane marks our location, as we make our way painstakingly south toward the continent. It is night by the time we take off. Outside the darkness encloses; darkness is the air through which we travel. Moving through dark air or dark water, is the same. I can't help thinking, I at least know where I am going. I am going willingly.[11]

When Homer painted *The Gulf Stream*, the future for the African diaspora did not look promising. Too many remained cast adrift, threatened on all sides, deprived of the tools to steer themselves clear. Even those who made significant progress in society did so with the odds stacked against them. Those tools continue to be denied to some and controlled by others, the odds altered, but rarely reversed, in the latest postcolonial or decolonial turbulence.

As I stated earlier, the poet and artist Chantal Gibson challenged me to understand my relationship to the "wake work" articulated by academic Christina Sharpe[12] — to understand my place of responsibility. Sharpe spoke of working "in the wake," but I know that is not where I am working from; I remain on board the vessel, the ship of state that continues to generate turbulence and an expanding wake. Too many in the cultural field I've worked in remain comfortable to remain passengers on this vessel, enjoying its privileges, while expecting to be praised when they acknowledge all those labouring in the wake of the continuing voyage of whiteness, expecting the kind of gratitude James Baldwin spoke of. I have certainly been deceived by the comfort of privileged positions I've held, led to believe I was being progressive and worthy of praise.

In her poem "Veronica?" Gibson speaks directly to the controlled presence of Blackness in white institutions in general, and specifically in the Art Gallery of

Ontario (AGO), where I once worked as a curator responsible for the Canadian collection. Gibson addresses the subject of a small portrait by Yvonne McKague Housser (born in Toronto in 1897), positioned at the heart of the Canadian galleries during the decade that bracketed my four-year tenure. "Veronica?" pushes for institutional accountability, demands more critical effort, and questions what "service" Blackness is being "drafted into" here, and by whom.

Yvonne McKague Housser, *Untitled*, ca. 1933, oil on canvas, 66 cm × 50.8 cm, collection of the Art Gallery of Ontario, gift of Elizabeth and Tony Comper, 2011, 2011/326. © Estate of Yvonne McKague Housser

Veronica?

What's it like at the centre of the AGO?
Hmm. Imagine being coloured, drawn, and placed

in a wooden frame, another hung woman, positioned
just so in the middle of a landscape surrounded by rocks,

lakes, mountains, and trees, MacDonald to your right,
Carmichael to your left. Imagine being forced to look,

to spend every unblinking moment of an 8-day week
staring at a Lawren Harris landscape, a frozen wall

of whiteness, when you know, outside, the glaciers
are melting, the trees are falling, one by one,

and the Beaufort scale has shrugged and turned its
back on September. Now, the winter legends are

sold in the gift shop—T-shirts, handbags, journals, calendars,
coffee cups, board games. Puzzling, isn't it? Makes you want

to laugh, a little, knowing you've been placed *here*
by kinder hands, to reconcile the past, to challenge

the climate of the centre. I'm a sign of the times,
still, no one knows my name. *What's it like?*

It's like I'm the number one answer to the question
you haven't considered, the one you never thought

to ask, the one staring you right in the face.[13]

With Gibson's question in mind, I enter the Royal Ontario Museum (ROM),
to see the rehanging of the Sigmund Samuel Gallery of Canada. I come across a
pair of paintings of Niagara Falls, donations of Toronto steel executive Sigmund
Samuel. The paintings were completed when tourism was already well established
at the falls.

Frenchman Hippolyte Victor Valentin Sebron depicted the three falls in *Table
Rock, Niagara*, a location that remains favoured by crowds of tourists today. The
central figure in the painting is a red-shirted guide, on whom many of the other
figures are focussed, who gestures toward the cataracts. He is Black, a rare presence
in paintings of Canada. Sebron painted this around 1850, a precarious time for a
Black person to be lingering near the border; the Fugitive Slave Act had just been
passed, and slave hunters, active on the Canadian side, were not above seizing
anyone.

Niagara, Brink of Horseshoe Falls (1872) by German American Hermann
Ottomar Herzog does not actually show the falls, just the river's edge and a fraction

Hermann Ottomar Herzog, *Niagara, Brink of Horseshoe Falls*, 1872,
oil on canvas, 81.5 cm × 116.9 cm, Royal Ontario Museum, 991.41.1. © ROM

of the lip of the cataract. A rainbow in the distance arches over a railway bridge and
hotels loom to the left above a thin curtain of small trees. Two elegantly dressed
women are accompanied by two young girls. The older girl stands conversing with
a well-dressed man sporting a top hat, long coat, and a prominent white cravat. A
blanket is draped over his arm and he wears gaiters to protect his shoes against the
mud. As in Sebron's painting, the man is Black. "Herzog's unusual perspective," the
label states, "shows spectators a safe distance from the natural wonder. The subject
is less the falls than the luminous light bathing the built environment. The black
man escorting the women is likely privately employed but may be part of the local
tourist industry."[14] As the falls don't appear in the painting, the subject is obviously
"less the falls," but I disagree that it is actually "the luminous light." I would argue
that the subject is the exchange between the girl and man.

If you look closely, you'll see the girl leans on a parasol and wears the latest fashion: a tailored overcoat, white pantaloons, dark leather boots, and a delicate navy blue hat (similar to a beret) topped with a white bow. One of the women looks back while pointing ahead, perhaps encouraging the girl to approach the falls. Is this her mother? The man looks down at her; I imagine he is saying it is safe to move further up the path. The "luminous light" is set dressing, the falls a lingering presence off-stage that hints at the girl's trepidation and frames the relationships of the principal figures. Why distance the man by focusing only on his presumed employment status (using wording that emphasizes control); why not focus on the principal interaction of the scene? The girl's left arm is raised, the man reaches out to her, assuring her, and the closeness of the two figures reveals trust.

Too often, art historians and curators reach for what isn't there, ignoring what is staring them in the face, in this case the real significance of these figures in an exhibition meant to update a story of Canada. If you can't see what's in front of you, how can you even come close to *conjuring* what has been redacted out or lies hidden? This painting speaks of the precarity of a specific relationship in an emblematic landscape. This may not have been the artist's intended meaning, but viewed in the context of Canada's then-recent sesquicentennial (in 2017), it is irresponsible to not break the conservative frame around art history and curation.

CHAPTER 23
IN THE CURRENT

The fundamental black/white binary endures, even though the category of whiteness—or we might say more precisely non-blackness—effectively expands. As before, the black poor remain outside the concept of the American as an "alien race" of "degenerate families"...poverty in a dark skin endures as the opposite of whiteness, driven by an age-old social yearning to characterize the poor as permanently other and inherently inferior.

—Nell Irvin Painter, *The History of White People*[1]

It is safe to say that the observations of Nell Irvin Painter about the black/white binary in the United States applies also to Canada. These circumstances are the living legacies of slavery, colonialism, and whiteness. That whiteness carries both ignorance and an insistence on defensive denial (especially in Canada) remains an appalling privilege. In the midst of a global pandemic and protests sparked by the police murder of George Floyd in Minnesota (where Benjamin Drew once oversaw a segregated school system), I hear a CBC Radio reporter ignorantly state that "racism has existed in Canada for *decades*." Whiteness in Canada can only acknowledge anti-Black racism as *recent*, not *always*, because it doesn't know its own history, its place within the expanded frame of centuries of chattel slavery, and what academic Saidiya Hartman terms "the afterlife of slavery" in her discussion of the past's influence on the present:

> I wanted to engage the past, knowing its perils and dangers still threatened and that even now lives hung in the balance. Slavery had established a measure of man and a ranking of life and worth that

has yet to be undone. If slavery persists...it is not because of an antiquarian obsession with bygone days or the burden of a too-long memory, but because black lives are still imperilled and devalued by a racial calculus and a political arithmetic that were entrenched centuries ago. This is the afterlife of slavery—skewed life chances, limited access to health and education, premature death, incarceration, and impoverishment. I, too, am the afterlife of slavery.[2]

The word *afterlife* suggests Heaven, but also being trapped (caught in some form of purgatory) or lingering (a ghost that cannot move on as its corporeal existence is unresolved). Organizations often linger on; they are good at moving slowly. I've lost count of the number of times I've heard "Change takes time, it is slow" or "We would, but we lack space or resources." The speed of the spread and adaptations of the COVID-19 virus, concurrent with videos of brutal murders and assaults going *viral* in a different sense, is a blunt contradiction of the belief that the pace of change is *glacial* (a term itself that clearly requires a rethink as our glaciers are melting more rapidly). For Sophia, when the *sons-in-law . . . came into the garden,* systemic and catastrophic change came quickly. Whiteness sees itself mastering the flow of systems and time, and anyone caught in the turbulence of this flow has learned, over generations, to be prepared to respond and adapt with urgency.

> Dear Sophia,
>   No matter how much time I spend, or the amount of research and travel I undertake in search of you, often in dialogue with others, I will never come to a point of truly knowing you, no matter how much I wish for that. I do not look to speak for you. The best I can do is only to speak toward you, to reach for understanding and possibly an ability to see more and be changed by this journey. I have clearly progressed without your permission, but I need to believe that your willingness to speak to Benjamin Drew and trust him with your story can serve as a tentative proxy permission for me to carry what I can at this moment. I believe you felt that your story would contribute to shaping necessary change. "None of us knows very much," confesses the character Lauren Oya

Olamina in Octavia Butler's *Parable of the Sower*, "but we can all learn more. Then we can teach one another. We can stop denying reality or hoping it will go away by magic."

I see you sharing realities that cannot be magically erased, but do require conjuring with, and some sleight of hand to be revealed. *Conjure* is linked to the etymology of *jury* and relates to truth telling, as it comes from the Latin *conjurare*: "to join in taking an oath." When I say that your realities require conjuring with, I mean in the British sense, of "to treat or regard as important." This is my commitment to you having chosen to proceed without your explicit permission.

↯

At the eastern end of Gore Park, Sir John A. Macdonald remained standing until the summer of 2021, his bronze figure recently cleaned and restored, the tall granite base still flanked by two cannons. The momentum to address his legacy and remove or modify this statue (initiated by Indigenous Peoples in 2015, and voiced loudly again in 2021) had ebbed and flowed, until Indigenous activists toppled it.[3] The sculpture posed Macdonald extending his empty right hand; his gesture prefiguring the "correct" way for a politician to make a point without aggressively pointing (a slightly open fist with the thumb up but gently pressing on the side of the index finger). It's as if there is some invisible offering here.

Macdonald faced east, looking back along the old King's Highway to Niagara where Sophia crossed over. I'm heading back in this direction, through New York and Massachusetts, and ultimately to Scotland. I'm not heading down the same paths; I'm continuing to trace ley lines Sophia has revealed. In traditional/folk music, a *burthen* is the "refrain or chorus from a song" or the line you repeat, but this doesn't imply that the words retain the same meaning. As the poet Ciaran Carson explains: "Each time the song is sung, our notions of it change, and we are changed by it. The words are old. They have been worn into shape by many ears and mouths and have been contemplated often. But every time is new, because the time is new, and there is no time like now."[4] While I'm reaching the end of this book, I'm also trying to return and "begin again," accepting James Baldwin's challenge, as explained by Eddie S. Glaude Jr.:

Begin Again is shorthand for something Baldwin commended to the country in the latter part of his career: that we reexamine the fundamental values and commitments that shape our self-understanding, and that we look back to those beginnings not to reaffirm...or to double down on myths that secure our innocence, but to see where we went wrong and how we might reimagine or recreate ourselves in light of who we initially set out to be. This requires an unflinching encounter with the lie at the heart of our history.[5]

&

I'm on a train heading for Glasgow, Scotland, with my daughter, Claire, the city of our ancestors, having been invited to speak at the University of Glasgow about misrepresentations of Canada and to lead a workshop at the Glasgow School of Art in search of traces of colonial Canada in this "second city of Empire," as it used to be known. Our train from London cuts across tilled fields of Lanarkshire, all edged with bracken. I see a hound skirt along the ridge of bracken (and remember five-year-old Eli Brackenridge). A hunter waits a short distance away. The dog flushes a pheasant. These fields are home to birds released for organized hunts. This is a lucky survivor. An introduced species, the pheasant's origin is in Slavic countries, where Greeks and Romans once acquired many slaves. The word *slave* comes from *slavonic* ("captive" in Latin).

We enter Glasgow, cross the River Clyde, then disembark at Glasgow Central Station. We visit Barrowfield, now levelled and awaiting development. We gaze through a tall chain-link fence at the remnants of Bonnar Street where my grandmother Marion Crawford Hunter's home once stood, one in a long line of rowhouses. Only her primary school and one cotton mill remain of her childhood landscape; the ground has been surveyed into a grid of new streets and lots. A new police station is already in place. Barrowfield (where Marion lived from 1899 to 1920) was notorious for its poverty, industrial pollution, tensions between Irish Catholics and Scottish Protestants, crime, and violent gangs. The neighbourhood has now been buried. The primary meaning of *barrow* is "an ancient burial mound."

Leaving Barrowfield, we follow a path along the river, then traverse Glasgow Green, approaching the People's Palace from the back, its elegant glass-and-iron Winter Gardens clouded in moisture from the humidity within. In front of the museum, the Doulton Fountain stands dry, its red terracotta surface looking parched as no water is pumping through it. A centrepiece of the Glasgow International Exhibition of 1888, it is the largest ceramic fountain ever made. "Queen Victoria forms the apex of the elaborate three-tiered structure. Below, four groups of figures represent the peoples of Britain's colonies in Canada, South Africa, Australia and India," states a Clyde Waterfront plaque. The allegorical figures representing Canada are white people, surrounded by produce and wildlife.

Inside the People's Palace, we head upstairs to the top floor to find *The Glassford Family Portrait* (1764–68), a massive oil painting that depicts John Glassford with his seven children, his third wife, the family dog, and a parrot, along with a faint figure barely visible on the left, just over the patriarch's shoulder and blocked by a blue velvet chair. The significance of the recent reappearance of this figure is discussed by Anthony Lewis, curator of Scottish History on a website about slavery in the collections of Scottish museums:

> When the portrait of the tobacco merchant John Glassford and his family was given to Glasgow Museums...a myth grew about a black slave boy who had been painted over to erase Glasgow's association with the slave trade.

In 2007 the painting was moved from the People's Palace to Kelvingrove Art Gallery and Museum where conservation treatment was carried out in front of visitors. The results were spectacular. The legend...could be dismissed, as gentle cleaning revealed that he had simply been obscured by centuries of dirt.[6]

There is nothing "simple" about the obscuring of this person, who was first brought to my attention by Marenka Thompson-Odlum. Born in St. Lucia, Thompson-Odlum moved to Glasgow to undertake graduate studies in history at the University of Glasgow. In an article in the *Scotsman*, journalist Dani Garavelli describes meeting her at the People's Palace to see the painting:

Archibald McLauchlan, *The Glassford Family Portrait* (with profile of enslaved person emphasized on top left by the author), 1764–68, oil on canvas, 198 cm × 221 cm, People's Palace, collection of Glasgow Museums, Glasgow, Scotland

Marenka Thompson-Odlum perched precariously on a ladder set up in front of one of the city's best known artworks.... It shows tobacco lord John Glassford sitting in his finery, his extensive family at his side and a basket of fruit at his feet. Thompson-Odlum, however, is pointing out the barely visible profile of an enslaved boy's head in the top left-hand corner.... What has been recovered is not so much an image, as the shadow of an image; a spectral presence hovering on the periphery of the painting like a guilty conscience.[7]

This is an astute observation by Garavelli, the thinness of the enslaved person's image, tucked away to the far left, was clearly never prominent, compared with the bold articulation of all the other figures in the painting. The artist was little-known Archibald McLauchlan, who (Lewis notes) "was associated with the Foulis Academy of Fine Art, established at Glasgow College in 1753 with the financial support of Glassford."[8] This institution was absorbed into the University of Glasgow. Lewis goes on to state that "recent research has also revealed that the inclusion of a black boy slave and the parrot perched on the window serve as a celebration of slavery and plantation possessions," but the spectral discreteness of his presence is hardly celebratory. Glassford's tobacco wealth came from Virginia, and it is quite possible that the enslaved figure in the painting was brought from one of his plantations there.

In recent years, there has been much done in Glasgow to address the essential role of slavery in the flourishing of the city, particularly by the University of Glasgow which is finally hearing the voices of local Black communities and Black scholars who have come to the city to reveal its histories. The serious work being done in developing programs of reparations that acknowledge the continuing presence of assets seeded by slavery, and programs of public engagement with collections (with attention to how and by whom they are presented and interpreted) are models for Canadian institutions — especially in Hamilton with its deep Glasgow connections. Not put off by the supposed lack of material culture that is obvious in its revelations of connections to slavery, the work being done troubles the backstories and seeks transparency in opening up opportunities for retellings and adaptations. That said, much work is still hampered by merely modifying historic models of the university, the museum, and public history, which then sustains the overarching control of whiteness. How much further can these models be simply revised?

In whiteness, we have a responsibility to work harder, look deeper, and listen to our language. Clinging to positions of overseeing and only going so far as to initiate (and manage) revisions is to ultimately invest in maintaining the status quo, unwilling to disrupt (or dismantle) institutions that have become overvalued colonial artefacts in themselves. We should be beyond just adding nuanced layers, subtle variations, and limited pilot projects. Institutions know the consequences of their colonial origins, and to continue to acquire and define the limits of the intellectual content and labour of those still held at their margins serves to insulate, rather than ultimately disrupt, the fundamental wiring of these colonial mechanisms. Scholars Rinaldo Walcott and Idil Abdillahi point to the writer and cultural theorist Sylvia Wynter's critical writing which calls out the entrenchment of such boundary keeping:

> Sylvia Wynter made a call in both a 1984 essay and then more than a decade later in "No Humans Involved: Open Letter to my Colleagues"; she wrote, "I propose[d] that the task of black studies, together with those of all the other new studies in the wake of the 1960s uprisings, should be that of rewriting knowledge" (p. 16). As Wynter laments in 1994, such a project has barely gotten off the ground, and in 2014 it remains the same for the foreseeable future. Instead, humanist and social sciences have found themselves mired in a repetitive cycle of disciplinary boundary keeping...too few of us are willing to articulate or imagine worlds other than those we have experienced..... In the face of mounting and ever-growing evidence of the now global Black archipelagos of poverty, the desire to dream and reflect new contexts for human possibilities has fallen entirely on the intellectual shoulders of artists, we would argue. Or at least the ethical pause to make us think differently about our present and future now lies with artists.[9]

Artists who "dream and reflect" include Chantal Gibson, Anique Jordan, Camal Pirbhai, and Camille Turner (all discussed in earlier chapters), as well as Morayo and Moyo Akandé, whose work we'll come to shortly.

Glasgow Museum wants us to dismiss the "legend" of the intentional erasure of the enslaved child, but "gentle cleaning" feels too convenient an explanation, focussed only on the material "surface" of the painting. What if, in fact, the legend rose out of a collective dream? Having been repeated for decades in Glasgow, did these retellings of the reasons the "boy" had disappeared from view cause this presence to re-manifest? What if, instead of believing that the child was painted by McLauchlan and only revealed thanks to institutional intervention, we believed that this person had slowly materialized over time, made his way through the varnish and centuries of dirt—tobacco smoke, dust, and the glaze of sugar particles carried in a draft or tea's sweetened steam? Why let the museum take credit for this reveal?

If you look closely, you can see the Black person's hand, held in the same closed fist gesture of the Gore Park statue of Macdonald (a man born in the Merchant City of Glasgow). He appears to be entering the room; what is he about to reveal by sleight of hand? Will he step into the centre of this family group, this room that is *filling up with white people*, to reveal to whiteness (in James Baldwin's words) "precisely and inexorably, what they do not know about themselves."[10] In whiteness, we need to do more than congratulate ourselves for gestures of "gentle cleaning."

In a case near the Glassford painting, there is a slave collar. Around five inches in diameter, this thick silver item was made by the Glasgow jeweller Robert Luke around 1732 to be worn by an individual enslaved in the home of "John Crawfurd of Miltoun Esq. Owner 1732"—the inscription is in elegant cursive on the collar. This is likely the "John Crawford of Milntown " (now Milton) who appears in records of the University of Glasgow (ca. 1727).[11] Milton (current population 98) lies just over 40 kilometres north of Glasgow on the River Forth; to reach there you pass through Milngavie where my grandfather Thomas Hunter was born. This expensive piece of "jewellery" marked the enslaved as valuable property; to be seen with an enslaved person was a way for Crawfurd/Crawford to advertise his status. The English term *jewel* ("a valued person or thing") has its roots in the Old French *joel*, from *jeu* ("game or play"), which itself comes from Latin *jocus* ("joke or jest"). And indeed this silver neck piece was a sick joke. To wear it was not a privilege; it was not an adornment expressing that one is personally valued, highly regarded, or thought of as worthy. Before encountering this item in the museum, I encountered a similar one in *1745*, a film written by Scottish Nigerian actor Morayo Akandé.[12] The film stars Morayo and her older sister Moyo Akandé. The sisters were inspired to make the film after encountering the story of Joseph Knight, who had won his freedom in the Scottish courts after being captured in West Africa, transported to Jamaica, and brought to Scotland enslaved.

Claire and I met the Akandé sisters at the University of Glasgow, thanks to Thompson-Odlum who invited them to my lecture. Soon after, I saw their film (directed by Gordon Napier), which has been screened at numerous festivals and has won critical praise internationally. "I came across a newspaper advert from 1745, which had been placed by the master of a runaway slave [Joseph Knight],"

Morayo Akandé and Moyo Akandé in a film still from *1745: An Untold Story of Slavery* (2017), reproduced with permission of the filmmakers (original in colour)

Morayo says in an article in *The Herald* (Scotland), "I was shocked that these ads were actually being run in 18th-century Scotland — the sort of ad people would run if their dog had run away."[13] The ads are just like those that artists Camal Pirbhai and Camille Turner referenced in their WANTED series. "It certainly wasn't something I was taught at school," Morayo states in the article, reflecting on her shock at encountering such advertisements.

The film's engagement with a specific moment in Scottish history brings to mind the contradictions inherent in nations' dominant narratives — within the United States, a country founded on freedom and independence, and within Canada, a country that prides itself on multicultural inclusion and in being the end-destination of the freedom implied by the Underground Railroad:

> "The reason we decided to call the film *1745* was because this was the most important year in Scottish history in regards to fighting for our freedom — the Jacobite rebellion," explains Moyo.... "But

what isn't mentioned in the history books or taught in the Scottish
school curriculum is that there were also other people—people of
colour—fighting for their freedom at the same time."[14]

The film is set in the remote highlands, a landscape that has long been iconic
in Scotland, just as many see the wilderness and the north as representative of
Canada. Witnessing the two sisters, fleeing across an isolated and rugged landscape
in long-skirted tartan gowns, disrupts such a confident national vision. Only one
of the characters wears a silver collar—the older sister, who is African born; the
younger, born in Scotland, sees the country as her home. This is at the heart of the
tension between them as the older is compelled to flee what she sees as a foreign
land, while the younger sees Scotland as where she belongs. That the elder clearly
made sacrifices to protect her sibling from the advances of their "master," also plays
into the drama.

I had just begun to seriously think about Sophia when I first saw *1745*; I credit
this film, and my conversations with Morayo and Moyo, for leading me toward
a deeper engagement with landscapes and environments. The fact that they are
sisters took me back to the conversations with Reighen Grineage about what family
would have meant to Sophia. Seeing the joy and intensity in the Akandé sisters'
collaboration has left me haunted by the lost potential of Sophia's relationship
with her sibling.

> Dear Sophia,
>   I must admit that my adult children Max and Claire are
> always front of mind on this journey. I know I couldn't have
> progressed without them, and certainly would not have read
> these landscapes (in Fishkill with Max, Glasgow with Claire,
> and around Hamilton and Niagara with them both, for
> example) the same way on my own. Just as Reighen reads your
> words through the filter of her family, I cannot help but work
> to know you through my relationship with Max and Claire,
> always aware of how painful it would have been to lose them
> as children, and struggling to imagine your parents' experience,
> held as property and denied their right to protect and nurture
> their children.

I recently found a photograph of Max and Claire on my father's sailboat, taken a decade ago on Hamilton Bay. In it, they are 13 and 8. Max smiles, Claire laughs, and they lean against each other, illuminated by bright sunshine, and exhibiting a bond stolen from you. *Carried us to the vessel, placed us in the hold,* you said, *it was dark there all the time.*

I think of my time working and sailing on this same bay that you regularly traversed with Thayendanegea/Joseph and his children. The sloops I sailed are counter-balanced against the wind either by a heavy fixed keel or a "daggerboard" that can be raised and lowered depending on the vessel's angle to the wind. The crew has to work against the strength of the breeze, to keep the boat from heeling over too far and potentially capsizing. One sits on the edge of the boat, or leans out over the water, to counter the force of wind on the sails. If you keep the balance, the vessel stays on course and continues forward, the energy of the wind in the sails transferred to the momentum of the hull. But if you lose balance — fail to compensate for the increasing wind pressure — the boat will fight back, will turn into the wind, stall, and potentially roll over. It is impossible for the vessel to work with or against the wind without its counter-balance beneath the hull. Absent this, you will simply drift. The experience of being on the water, knowing how to perceive the unstable patterns, textures, and shades on the surface, the continuous shifting of the wind's strength and direction, every action balanced by a reaction, still lingers.

Sir Isaac Newton's third law of motion states that, for every action there is an equal and opposite reaction. I see you positioned in contradiction to this law: the "action" of your life and afterlife too often confronts a reaction that is profoundly unequal and profoundly out of balance.

୧୬

Claire and I have returned to the People's Palace to look once more at the faint figure in the Glassford painting and to take a closer look at the fine detail of the silver collar. "*Crawford* was your great Gran's maiden name," I tell Claire. We leave the museum talking about the connections between Glasgow and Hamilton as we head for the Merchant City, taking a short diversion to St. Andrew's in the Square. According to the Gazetteer for Scotland, "St Andrew's Parish Church...projected the affluence of the Tobacco Lords who paid for it and became the official place of worship for the city fathers.... The raw material for the fine wood-panelling is said to have been brought on the Tobacco Lords' ships from the USA and the Caribbean."[15]

"When the Presbyterian church split in Scotland," I tell Claire, "the breakaway congregations, or Free Churches, raised thousands of dollars in support from Southern plantation owners in the United States, at the same time that they were investing in their presence in Hamilton." When Frederick Douglass toured Britain in 1846, he gave speeches in Glasgow, Edinburgh, Aberdeen, and Dundee, as well as smaller communities throughout Scotland, directly criticizing the Presbyterian "Free" Church for cultivating the donations of American slave holders. "Send back the money!" became the chant during his speeches.[16] The once-ornate homes that form the square around St. Andrew's marked the area as the centre of Glasgow's wealth and power. The last Presbyterian service held here took place in 1993, and the A-listed heritage building is now Glasgow's Centre for Traditional Scottish Music, Song, and Dance. As in so many places dedicated to celebrating traditional arts and culture, history is selectively edited and performed. These traditions have been brought to Canada, reimagined, and celebrated as "authentic" Celtic/Gaelic/Highland culture in the communities surrounding the former Queen's Bush settlement.

We pass the Gallery of Modern Art (housed in the former mansion of William Cunninghame, one of the richest Tobacco Lords whose wealth came from the Triangle Trade) and then Claire takes the lead. I follow her to the corner of Union and Jamaica Streets, where a Tim Hortons now operates, one of four locations of the Canadian fast-food chain that opened in Glasgow in 2017, Canada's sesquicentennial year. Having spent time with Camille Turner and having just met Marenka Thompson-Odlum, Claire gets the significance of a Tim Hortons opening on Jamaica Street. Historically, many Canadians have seen the restaurant as a symbol of traditional Canadian values (i.e., working-class, small-town, family-centred, hockey-loving, and white). The very first location is located in Hamilton, on the corner of Ottawa Street North and Dunsmure Road, next to Memorial School, and only a few blocks from where my father was raised. Troubling the carefully cultivated homey image of "Timmies" (as the corporation is affectionately called by many Canadians) is the reality that the company is now owned by Restaurant Brands International, majority-owned by Brazilian investment firm 3G Capital, known for their "lean and mean approach."[17] The 3G Capital founders are settlers, carrying on in the traditions of their ancestors. "Costs," one of them claims, "are like fingernails: they always have to be cut."[18]

All these facts came to mind when I stood on the corner of Jamaica Street, another street (like Virginia Place in Glasgow) whose name links the city to sugar plantations and the historic reach of slave labour and global capitalism. Tim Hortons now has over 4,500 locations — equal to the number of migrant or Temporary Foreign Workers it employed in Canada in 2012, when Karl Flecker, national director of anti-racism and human rights for the Canadian Labour Congress, stated: "Many of these migrant workers who are coming in for work ... are put in incredibly vulnerable situations where exploitation, abuse, dangerous, unsafe working conditions are actually too often the norm."[19] The slogan of Tim Hortons is "Always Fresh," but they now par-bake all of their products at a single plant before shipping them all across the country. The plant is in Brantford, not far from where Sophia lived with Thayendanegea/Joseph.

My grandparents came to Canada as immigrants. While they didn't have much, they had the opportunity to become citizens, work, and to buy a modest home and raise and educate children. For migrant and temporary workers, this is not the case. If you travel across the agricultural terrain that remains throughout Sophia's landscape, you will see people of colour labouring on farms. They live in workers' quarters and their families and homes are far distant (many workers around Hamilton and Niagara come from Jamaica). Their homelands cannot sustain them, but they cannot build a life in Canada either — they remain trapped in an extended Middle Passage. What we are witnessing are the combined legacies of transatlantic slavery, European empires, and global colonization of "business":

> Such movements that we now call migration are founded in anti-blackness, taking their logic from transatlantic slavery.... This can be noticed in the simple fact of moving "labour" to sites of production as transatlantic slavery so glaringly inaugurated on a mass scale. The movement of people that we might call slavery, Indigenous colonization and displacement, European resettlement, indentureship and so on in historical moments, goes by other names today.[20]

Many Canadians cling to a wholesome "Timmies" identity: the good guys with the right values, community focused, fair-playing, supporters of the troops (Tim Hortons has a long association with military and police), etc. The identity is maintained by ignoring the country's historical foundation (which was an extension of the brutalities of empire and resource extraction) and what transpires outside national borders today (based on what was learned first at home). Like the English who first developed colonial tools in Britain before applying them globally, Canadian companies employ elsewhere techniques perfected first on Canadian soil—such as practices prevalent in some mining companies, as can be seen in this headline: "Canada Mining Firm Accused of Slavery Abroad Can Be Sued at Home, Supreme Court Rules: Case Brought by Three Eritreans against Nevsun Resources Can Continue as Companies Operating Overseas Face New Legal Risk."[21] This is just one example of the business practices of Canadian resource companies that tethers the present to the past. Contemporary business models (such as the reliance on migrant workers denied citizenship) are extensions of the systems that held Sophia in bondage and denied her the means to sustain true freedom.

The violence and ignorance (feigned innocence) of whiteness is also directly linked to the imposed hierarchies and compartmentalizing of history and culture practiced in cultural institutions and academia, that continue to operate based on a resilient belief that they have the right to set the terms for "decolonizing." But a colonizer cannot be responsible for decolonizing. As political philosopher Frantz Fanon clearly articulates in *The Wretched of the Earth* (1963), "decolonization is quite simply the substitution of one 'species' of mankind by another. The substitution is absolute, total and seamless,"[22] so the colonizer must be removed and the those formerly colonized must lead to truly have decolonization.

It is absurd to believe that those holding power truly want to see such fundamental change. Too often, the talk of freedom and emancipation articulated in

Sophia's time masked anti-Black racism. Today, the talk of decolonization voiced by those content to ignore the dominance of whiteness and those who live content-edly in whiteness, simply masks the fear of losing power. Fanon describes colonial institutions (military, police, schools, churches, cultural organizations) as "agents" of oppression; these institutions cannot also be the agents of decolonization. "What is singularly important," he states, is that decolonization

> starts from the very first day with the basic claims of the colonized. In actual fact, proof of success lies in a social fabric that has been changed inside out. Decolonization, therefore, implies the urgent need to thoroughly challenge the colonial situation. Its definition can, if we want to describe it accurately, be summed up in the well-known words: "The last shall be first."... The determination to have the last move up to the front, to have them clamber up (too quickly, say some) the famous echelons of an organized society, can only succeed by resorting to every means, including, of course violence.[23]

Many will hear Fanon echoed in the often-quoted words of Malcolm X (el-Hajj Malik el-Shabazz): "by any means necessary." The violence they spoke of was complex, yet many recoiled, hearing only a call for the kind of violence that means "the infliction of injury or damage through physical force." The violence of col-onization is equally complex, incorporating the social, cultural, and psychological. For Fanon, Malcolm X, and many others, the emphasis was on violence as "call to action," to act "vehemently, forcibly" and at times "impetuously," to counter deep histories of violation. The reality is that whiteness will see any effort to dismantle its privilege as violence and will consistently seek refuge behind well-established barriers to change.

> Dear Sophia,
>   I have come to realize, after so many years trying to disrupt from within institutions Fanon labelled "agents," that I was merely sheltering within spaces that gave me refuge to perform allyship. I was wrong to believe I could be the instigator of a process that would see systems "changed inside out." I was not

just in the system; I was of the system. There was no refuge there for me, only a hiding place of ignorance and innocence.

Drew positioned you as a "refugee," but you never found refuge in Canada; you did not arrive here a refugee but enslaved. Drew's inability to acknowledge the truth of your status works to not only obscure you, but also his own complicity in systems of whiteness. I often see myself in Drew, in his incomplete actions, and the fact that he is remembered as one of the "band of fearless men and women in the city of Boston" William Wells Brown spoke of in 1851.[24] Some of my work has been praised, but I do not feel "fearless." Like Drew, most of the vessels I worked in continue on their mission guided by their founding principles.

CHAPTER 24
TEMPUS FUGIT

Refugee (noun, first known usage 1685): From French réfugié, *a specific reference to Protestants (Huguenots) who fled France for England... becomes in English forced to flee to a place of safety—a* refuge...*can mean both a literal shelter and a figurative sanctuary...* fugitive *(one who flees or escapes)—with time, becomes wandering or moving from place to place without the urgency or danger of escape... as* fugitive *softened,* refugee *hardened by adding a meaning synonymous with* fugitive, *one who flees from justice (late 1700s... then* fugue*—one melody chasing another... now holds a psychological meaning, a state of disturbance when a person might do things that they can subsequently not recall—a* fugue *state...* Tempus Fugit*—Time Flies...*[1]

The Queen's Bush was supposed to be a sanctuary and a new beginning, just as the Dawn and Elgin settlements were: a refuge for fugitives and refugees. It did not work out that way. After the interview with Benjamin Drew, I don't know how long Sophia lived. While it's possible she was forced to relocate like many others, her connection to the Malott family suggests she remained in the Queen's Bush, that she was most likely laid to rest in this community that had become her home. The community's cemetery was located alongside the British Methodist Episcopal (BME) Church built on the property of the Reverend Samuel H. Brown. Services were held there into the 1920s, but the church and cemetery were extirpated—ploughed under and forgotten. An article written in 1979 in the local Kitchener-Waterloo paper about how Black settlers were for the most part ignored by historians, wrongly states: "The seeming neglect of local historians in writing about blacks was a direct result of the slaves' own inabilities to read and write."[2] Many were not illiterate; once again whiteness blames Blackness for its own erasure. The article features an image of a middle-aged man standing over a jumble of stone fragments he has salvaged, with the caption: "Norman Hisson, 53, of Glen Allan, the last surviving descendant of black fugitive slaves still living in Peel Township, looks at crumbled gravestones at the site of the former African Methodist / British Methodist Episcopal church near Yatton, Ontario. The church building is no longer standing."[3]

Various missionary and abolitionist organizations were active in the Queen's Bush promoting competing religious and education initiatives, with the American Missionary Association (AMA) and British Abolition Society (BAS) most prominent. There were significant tensions between them, as well as between individual Black ministers and white missionaries. Linda Brown-Kubisch covers this in great detail, capturing the tension in her observation that, "missionaries and the AMA had failed to appreciate the Black community's desire to preserve their independence and self-determination."[4] Considering Sophia's age, I don't believe these political battles over education and competing religions would have been a priority for her. I read her statement, *I find plenty of people in the bush to help me a good deal*, as referring to fellow Black settlers, not the white missionaries who were competing to raise funds and operate schools. Two of the more controversial figures were Fidelia (née Coburn) Brooks and John Sawyer Brooks who, after several turbulent years, moved on to Sierra Leone with the AMA.

John Sawyer Brooks was "a typical rank-and-file member of the abolitionist movement."[5] He was born near Boston in 1823 and had no religious training or equation beyond basic schooling. In 1845, Brooks was present at a lecture given by John N. Mars, "an eminent black abolitionist who worked among self-emancipated slaves in Upper Canada." Brooks took up the abolitionist cause and moved to Canada, where he was involved in the establishment of the Mount Hope School. Concurrently, abolitionist Fidelia Coburn, who had come from Maine and was an experienced teacher in around Mount Hope. "I'm situated in the midst of nearly 200 coloured families," Coburn wrote in a letter in 1846. Single and living alone, she was the target of suggestive gossip, and this encouraged her to marry Brooks (who was eighteen years her junior). "The couple encountered local opposition, and lost their schoolhouse to suspected arson," soon after, "they transferred to the Mendi Mission (Mo Tappan)."

Mo Tappan was named for New York abolitionist Lewis Tappan, a founder of the AMA who was famously involved in the *Amistad* case. Tappan orchestrated legal defence for the Mendi captives who took over the *Amistad*, a slave ship illegally transporting them in 1839 (*Amistad*, ironically, is Spanish for "friendship"). The Mendi returned to Sierra Leone, and the AMA followed, including the Brookses.

There was much discussion and debate in Upper Canada among Black leaders, missionaries, and abolition societies about the best way forward in the 1840s, the decade of the Humble Petitions (see chapter 21). White missionaries brought paternalistic views about what was best for the various Black populations. These earnest whites were blinded by their faith and zeal for conversions, and burdened with conflicting visions of progress (integration versus segregation, settlement here versus colonization schemes to return Black people to West Africa).

Fidelia Brooks stated that the "200 coloured families" in the Queen's Bush were "all poor, and destitute of course."[6] Why "of course"? Her perspective differs from that of the Reverend William King from the Elgin Settlement who, after visiting in 1848, observes, "many of the settlers have made large improvements for the time. I visited several of them at houses, found them living comfortably, and well supplied with necessaries of life," and he complimented the level of knowledge achieved by young "scholars," in spite of the lack of resources.[7] In retrospect, supporting Black settlers with the means to secure their land would have been the most productive act, and making space for them to continue to lead independent lives, unfettered by white overseers, would have been the best way to support that.

The first time I visited the Queen' Bush cemetery was with Reighen Grineage. We were collaborating on a small project about Sophia for the Guelph Black Heritage Society (GBHS) with Kerry-Ann Conway (then a board member of the GBHS). The GBHS home is in a former BME Church at 83 Essex Street. Founded in 1869, the first church was replaced in 1880 by the stone structure that remains today. A number of Black settlers displaced from the Queen's Bush moved into Guelph. The census of 1881 records 107 Black individuals living in the city, with the majority residing near the church in a neighbourhood that was populated primarily by English Methodists.[8]

I had once thought that Sophia left the Queen's Bush to settle in Owen Sound, Hamilton, or Toronto. Then realizing that, since some of the Malotts ended up in Guelph, that might be a more likely destination for Sophia, Reighen and I spent time in the neighbourhood around the church with Kerry-Ann. While I soon came to believe Sophia never left the Queen's Bush, the names on street signs in the vicinity of the church proved revealing: all are named for cities in Britain

(Nottingham, Yorkshire, Surrey, Essex, Bristol, Birmingham, and Glasgow), and such names continue in the neighbourhood to the north. Like Hamilton, Guelph saw a lot of financial investment from Britain soon after its founding by John Galt in 1827, and the ultimate foundation of those resources was slavery.

The neighbourhood that is home to the BME Church / GBHS Heritage Hall is shaped like a triangle. Walking the neighbourhood, Kerry-Ann, Reighen, and I were struck by the weight of its cultural geography and geometry — the streets named for major British cities critical to the Triangle Trade and the very triangular boundaries of the area. Later, sitting inside the church, with its half-metre-thick stone walls creating a weight of silence and sanctuary, we wondered what it meant for such a modest Black community to move into such visible constraints of whiteness, in a neighbourhood delineated by the legacies of slavery. "This progressive community stands as a monument to his efforts and ingenuity," declares a plaque in downtown Guelph honouring John Galt, city founder, then proceeds to offer a highly selective and slanted version of his accomplishments aligned with the city's crafted self-image.

Guelph is known as "the Royal City," it was founded in 1827, when George IV was on the British throne.[9] The king was of the House of Hanover, a branch of the House of Welf (sometimes spelled *Guelf* or *Gwelf*; *Guelfo* in Italian; *Welf* in Bavarian-German). On St. George's Day, April 23, in 1827, Galt, along with his colleague and friend "Tiger" Dunlop, chopped down a tree in a symbolic gesture of clearing the land. Guelph was incorporated in 1855, the year Sophia met Drew, and became a city in 1879. In 1979, the "grateful citizenry" chose to honour Galt with a plaque marking the "bi-centennial of his birth and the 100th anniversary of Guelph." "History maker, novelist, poet," the text on the plaque begins. It proceeds to describe the Huron Tract, "as the most important single attempt at settlement in Canadian history," a debatable claim as it is certainly countered by the scope of the Canadian government's program to settle the Western provinces of Manitoba, Saskatchewan, and Alberta (for example). Not mentioned is the brevity of Galt's tenure, or that he was fired and called back home. Instead, he (and Guelph) receives high praise for being "progressive." Whiteness likes to control its branding, and has the power and privilege to define (and redefine) its public image, but in Guelph there are obvious contradictions for all its "green," progressive, and woke talk. The city's motto is *Faith, Fidelity, and Progress*, and many associated with the local university claim that "Guelph is one of the most environmentally sustainable cities in Canada."[10] Yet the city and surrounding communities sprawl, aggressively eating up farmland with massive housing, commercial, and industrial developments (including a substantial Nestlé water-bottling plant and numerous gravel and stone quarries). These actions are consistent with developer Jake Page's "Law of Severed Continuity": "You name a place for what is no longer there as a result of your actions. So one has Foxcrest Farms, for example, where no fox will ever again hunt, and no plow ever make a furrow worth the name."[11]

Back in the BME church, Kerry-Ann reflected on growing up in Guelph. She was born in Guelph yet, like Reighen, she's constantly asked, "Where are you from?" Kerry-Ann studied at the University of Guelph, she was President of the Black Students Association as the administration sought to address racism on campus, including the recurring appearance of blackface during Halloween (a disturbingly persistent phenomena on campuses across Canada). "Guelph likes to think of itself as very woke, but it is a typical liberal white Canadian place," she said. "I never felt part of this community, or that my teachers were particularly committed to my potential. I don't think things have changed."[12]

There are three official Ontario historical plaques that honour Guelph's founder. The two downtown are titled "John Galt 1779–1839" and "The Founding of Guelph," and the one in front of the Marden Library and Community Centre, "The La Guayra Settlers." The plaque for Galt lacks the enthusiasm of the one previously mentioned. "Galt was conscientious and hard working," it states, "and showed considerable humanity in his dealings with the company's pioneer settlers." The "Founding of Guelph" plaque describes Galt as the "celebrated Scottish novelist." The text on the "La Guayra Settlers" plaque is the most revealing in relation to the Queen's Bush: "In 1827 some 135 destitute Scottish settlers arrived at Guelph. They formed part of a group sent in 1825 to La Guayra [La Guaira], Venezuela, by a British land company. Unsuited to the tropical climate and unable to work their poor land, they abandoned the colony and requested assistance from the British government."

By the time the Scottish settlers arrived in Venezuela in the 1820s, the Spanish and Portuguese had been driven out by revolutions led primarily by Simón Bolívar (known as "El Libertador"). From 1819 to 1831, this territory that became Venezuela was part of the much larger Gran Colombia. With the departure of the former colonial powers and the need for capital and investment in the newly independent states, the British saw a lucrative opportunity and "formally recognized the secession of Spain's former colonies in 1825."[13] The nature and impact of Britain's aggressive move into South America is captured in Uruguayan writer Eduardo Galeano's three-volume epic history of the Americas *Memory of Fire:*

> The new countries, fearful of Spanish reconquest, need official recognition by England; but England recognizes no one without first signing a Treaty of Friendship and Commerce which assures freedom of invasion for its industrial merchandise.
>
> I abhor the debts more than the Spaniards, writes Bolivar to the Colombian general Santander, and tells him that to pay those debts, he has sold the Potosí mines to England.[14]

The 153 survivors who arrived in Guelph the year of its founding were well looked after by Galt who decided (independent of his board of directors) to allot a farm to each family, as a local newspaper noted, continuing: "Descendants of the La Guayra Settlers still occupy the area today."[15] At the 2010 plaque unveiling, Mayor White said: "We just thought it would be nice to recognize the heritage and the folks that are still there."[16] If only the Queen's Bush settlers had been met with the same sympathetic generosity offered by Galt to fellow Scots. As the granting of land to "preferred" settlers was standard practice in Upper Canada, it is unlikely that Galt's support of La Guayra "refugees" was the primary reason for his dismissal; clearly his overall failings as businessman and director resulted in his tenure being distinctly brief. Hiring the "celebrated novelist" wasn't the best idea to run the Canada Company.

"Who is John Galt?" That the "hero" of Ayn Rand's novel *Atlas Shrugged* (1957) is also named *John Galt* is just coincidence.[17] The character's best known quote — "I swear by my life and my love of it that I will never live for the sake of another man, nor ask another man to live for mine" — has certainly informed many social and fiscal conservatives convinced the only barriers to personal freedom and success lie within the individual, and with the individual's willingness to forge their own destiny through hard work and rational thought (protected by police and armies of a minimal state). For Rand's John Galt, "all human relations become transactional," states Jerome Copulsky, adding: "The myriad problems raised by such a conception of a state should be obvious."[18]

In a lot of ways, the many "founders" of Sophia's landscape (Harris, the sons-in-law, Hamilton, Beasley, Hatt, Jarvis, Crook, Galt, Dunlop, et al., and even Thayendanegea/Joseph, to a degree) who saw the best path forward as defined by the rational business of applying "creative genius," and seemed to have little issue with the idea that "all human relations become transactional," were practicing Rand's philosophy articulated through Galt. Yet, as has been demonstrated repeatedly, such self-interest will consistently extend support to the social and cultural communities one identifies with. Whiteness tends to preach self-reliance, to believe that it earned its power and privileges, seeing itself as the peak of human evolution. The conscience of whiteness remains clear when it decides who has rights, categorizes peoples in hierarchies of worth, and determines, ultimately, who is human. If you see a people as outside your clan, then they exist like all other species (without culture, history, land) and can be commodified, rusticated (as in banished),[19] and extirpated.

There is a clear distinction between the treatment of the La Guayra settlers and the Black community in the Queen's Bush and the descendants of both. Both communities were deceived, shipped across the Atlantic, suffered and laboured in horrendous conditions, and watched their community die around them, but the Scots in Venezuela had *chosen* to buy into their journey (that transpired over a few years). They were rescued, transported north, and given sanctuary, all while chattel slavery continued in the British Empire. When Black freedom-seekers laboured hard to improve the land and build a community, they were denied title to their properties, and empathy. Whiteness continues to choose to forget the details of its trajectory to this here and now. It chooses intentional amnesia and continues to ignore the present, and those still present. As Queen's Bush resident John Francis told Benjamin Drew, "the teachers generally have not the feelings in regard to slavery that we have." Francis knew not to rely on whiteness; "When my children get old enough to read, I intend to instruct them about slavery, and get books to show them what we have been through, and fit them for a good example."[20]

એન્

I am heading for the Queen's Bush once again. It is cold and grey this morning, with heavy rain and high winds. Just as the saying predicts: March came in like a lamb, so it's going out like a lion. The wind pushes the rain horizontal. I park on

Remains of the Queen's
Bush BME Cemetery, 2020,
photographed by the author

the shoulder of the road, step down onto the slope of a ditch, which runs fast with several inches of water, and then up onto the cropped lawn of the burying ground. The area is defined by the remains of an old rail fence and a few trees. Two ancient apple trees mark the back corners. The margin is a thick blanket of periwinkle, an invasive species also known as *Vinca*, from the Latin *vincire* which means, "to bind or fetter," and fetters calls to mind shackles, leg cuffs, collars. Pushing up through this expanding web of groundcover are new pale green shoots of lemon daylily (*Hemerocallis lilioasphodelus*). *Hemerocallis* combines the Greek terms for "day" and "beautiful." Now very common here, it is also an invasive species, widely cultivated as a colourful border, for defining the margins and edges.

Dear Sophia,
    I feel that you lie here, though I have no concrete evidence.
I leave you a modest bouquet of purple flowers at the base of
the large tree at the back of the cemetery, then begin a slow

progress around the perimeter, plodding through the heavy soil, looking for something, I'm not sure what, some sign of your presence. I find fieldstones heaped into piles, and beneath one of the apple trees, a triangle of blood-red granite from the Canadian Shield among grey stones and rotting apples. It is out of place, I wonder how it got here, And who brought this stone *gore*?

Earlier in the day, I passed a sign in front of a gas station: "WE MAY HAVE ALL COME ON DIFFERENT SHIPS BUT WE'RE IN THE SAME BOAT NOW." Hardly, then or now. The sign is a response to the global pandemic we have found ourselves facing, but the idea that it is a "great equalizer" is popular nonsense. There is nothing equal about access to healthcare and legacies of privilege and marginalization that have given some a safety net while leaving too many adrift.

Norman Hisson was the last Black descendant to leave the Queen's Bush, having relocated to Toronto, where he died in 2012, age 87. I am standing where he did in 1979, looking over the gravestones he salvaged. A Peel Historical Site sign states: "British Methodist Episcopal Church & Cemetery, The Negro Church c.1840, Mount Hope Mission, 1847–1850, American Abolition Society." On a white stone marker "Albert Douglass" is clearly inscribed. Albert's surname stands out as it shares the unusual double "s" adopted by Frederick Douglass. (Sophia also mentions a Douglass relative, comparing him in size and weight to Thayendenaghea/Joseph: *He was as big as Jim Douglass who lived here in the bush, and weighed two hundred pounds*). One generation separates these Maryland-born men. There are around a dozen headstones remaining here, placed in a line, disconnected from the remains they were meant to mark. Half are fully legible, the rest are an assortment of broken, weathered chunks. Only the harder stones can be read. On the mixed-up fragments, a few names, dates, and carved symbols survive, along with a couple of pointing hands, a bible, a few flowers.

As I methodically photograph the stones, I discover I've missed a name, on the side of Pollie Zetz's stone ("Died Dec. 28 1908, Aged 84 Years): "Annie Malott Died Aug. 12, 1903 Aged 19 Years." A number of Malott graves are marked here, along with around a hundred now unmarked beneath ploughed ground in the adjacent cultivated fields. At one end of the line of stones, the top of Samuel H. Brown's marker has been rotated, the pointing hand, meant to direct attention heavenward, lies sideways, revealing a ragged tablet pockmarked with lichen. Barely perceptible is the date: "Dec 18." My birthday. To the left, another piece of white marker remains, with the text still very clear: "Aged 86 YRs" — the age Sophia would have reached several years after Drew came calling. I look at a carving of an open book on a different stone, the pages blank and encased in lichen. I am reminded of the blank page on Herman Melville's grave and of histories unwritten (not erased and forgotten), to be reimagined from the present.

I circle the cemetery once more, stopping to dig up a few daylilies to take home, pot, and add to my collection of objects from this long journey. I dig with my fingers. Even though the ground is sodden, it is difficult to extract a handful of tubers from the mass of roots that bind and fetter. I wonder: Who cultivated the first flowers here, who planted the apple trees, gnarled but still bearing fruit? Did Sophia's hands work this soil, did she nurture black currant bushes on the Malotts' farm? Obvious traces have been completely erased by industrial farming, yet Sophia seems present.

History is a position of the present, to paraphrase Michel-Rolph Trouillot.[21] James Baldwin saw that "history is not the past. History is the present"[22] — thoughts later echoed by Christina Sharpe: "In the wake, the past that is not past, the past reappears, always, to rupture the present."[23] Whiteness works to disrupt, to position the past as "no longer," not a continuous *now* of longing:

> Just as wake work troubles mourning, so too do the wake and wake work trouble the ways most museums and memorials take up trauma and memory. That is, if museums and memorials materialize a kind of reparation (repair) and enact their own pedagogies as they position visitors to have a particular experience or set of experiences about an event that is seen to be past, how does one memorialize chattel slavery and its afterlives, which are unfolding still? How do we memorialize an event that is still ongoing?[24]

These are the voices of Black writers, nurturing and encouraging Black histories, stories, and memories. Yet they also caution whiteness not to invade and bind

Blackness. Sharpe reveals the essential work for Blackness "in the wake," as "wake work." Those complacent in whiteness need to recognize that we also "carry our history with us," we have a responsibility to trouble it and be accountable, to take a position on this vessel we have crafted, know the currents we have charted, as we continue trailing a destructive wake.

CHAPTER 25
"AND THE GARDENER FOREVER HELD THE PEACE"

dark (n.)
Early 13c., derk, "absence of light, night-time," from dark (adj.). Figurative in the dark "in a state of ignorance" is from 1670s; earlier it meant "in secrecy, in concealment" (late 14c.).

epitaph (n.)
Late Middle English: from Old French epitaphe, via Latin from Greek epitaphion "funeral oration," neuter of ephitaphios "over or at a tomb," from epi "upon" + taphos "tomb."

The names and words on public signs, plaques, and banners are extended epitaphs, texts written upon what lies beneath. They are redacted messages and calls to memory. Sophia has no epitaph, and while I am certain she was buried in the Queen's Bush, I don't truly know where; she has no marker. At the end of Herman Melville's *Moby-Dick*, after the leviathan has vanished and the *Pequod* has descended to a watery grave, Queequeg's coffin is all that remains afloat. The pine box has become Ishmael's vessel. Whiteness survives to tell the tale, riding a coffin carrying no name, or words, for an "other" body held within. I hope that Sophia is at rest, but I fear she remains in the hold, *I know not for how long*, where it is still *dark there all the time*. Her presence needs to be publicly revealed in this landscape, needs to be raised out of concealment and ignorance.

In the Hamilton Cemetery, I see numerous repeated phrases one could choose for a headstone: *The Bright Translation to the Home Above was Clouded with No Shadow of Farewell... God Called You Home, He Thought It Best... Until the Day*

Break and the Shadows Flee Away... Who Plucked This Flower? The Master. And the Gardener Forever Held the Peace. Sophia deserves more than repeated words and a standard design, more than a name on a street sign, or a brief statement on a plaque. She deserves to be *remembered* (from Latin *re* + *memor*, "to be mindful"). Mindfulness has become a popular form of self-care, emphasizing the individual in the practice of paying attention in the present moment. This is too limiting. We need to be mindful of our collective presence through and across time.

℘

It is early when I leave my home, heading down Tweedsmuir Avenue in the dark, thinking of Sophia's presence here, in this place of ignorance. Tweedsmuir is the name of a Scottish village; *Tweed* (or *Tweddel*) is a family name and *Muir* means "moorland," so *Tweed's Moorland*. That village is situated on the River Tweed about 80 kilometres south of Glasgow. In the early nineteenth century, the region became a favourite haunt of British elite who built estates and played at being Highland gentry with their invented tartans (made of *tweel*, a traditional woollen fabric, now called *tweed* thanks to one London merchant's error in labelling). These estates were the model for Sir Allan MacNab's Dundurn Castle and Peter Carroll's Rock Bay Castle. According to the website for a company selling clan tartans, tweed had "humble beginnings as a practical peasant fabric," became "a symbol of wealth by landowners and royalty," was popularized by designers in the twentieth century, and most recently has been adopted "by hipsters and millennials, which still harks back to tweed's heritage as a signifier of both wealth and vintage authenticity."[1] All of these inventions of heritage and adopted signifiers of labour live on in Hamilton, as does the continuing amnesia of the deeper hidden truths.

I turn left onto South Street and follow the sidewalk that ends where Old Ancaster Road meets Ogilvie Street (the newer route down the hill). It takes me about five minutes to reach this spot. I walk down what's left of Old Ancaster Road and soon come to a dead end. A paved walkway continues on to Spencer Creek, fast-running behind a Tim Hortons. At the main intersection, four streets meet, watched over by the old town hall. I proceed west, passing the fragile stone mill building that lingers at the end of Hatt Street. This was the centre of the Hatts' town. I've walked this route hundreds of times; I wonder how many times Sophia passed this way.

I cross the creek a second time proceeding west and stop at a plaque for Dundas Mills at the corner, which reads: "By 1799 the Morden family had a sawmill near this site on Spencer Creek.... They sold this property in 1800 to Edward Peer who built a grist-mill.... Peer sold the property in 1804 to Richard and Samuel Hatt and a partner, but by 1807 Richard had become sole owner." We could add: "...and then Samuel purchased Sophia Burthen for $100."

Dundas was first known as *Cootes Paradise*, became *Dundas Mills*, and was officially named *Dundas* in 1814. The town was named after Dundas Street (that still runs west from the heart of what was York, now Toronto), which was itself named in honour of a powerful friend of John Graves Simcoe: Henry Dundas (1st Viscount Melville), an Edinburgh lawyer and politician who never visited North America, and never would. Henry Dundas was many things: a leading Tory, secretary of state for war, and the last politician to be impeached in Britain. He was popularly known as *King Harry the Ninth*, *The Great Tyrant*, and *The Uncrowned King of Scotland*, due to his seemingly unbridled control of the country. Melville Street (named for peerage title of Henry Dundas) is lined with the grand Victorian mansions of Dundas's wealthiest citizens, which seems fitting as he was one of the wealthiest citizens in Edinburgh. Lisa Williams, director of the Edinburgh Caribbean Association, makes clear the derivation and effects of that fortune in her discussion of his hometown statue:

> In the heart of the New Town [Edinburgh]: The statue of Henry Dundas...towers over St. Andrew Square. As you gaze around this prestigious square, your eyes will fall on several buildings that would have been homes or business premises of Scots who made their fortunes in the transatlantic slave trade.... It is fitting, perhaps, that this is where we find Dundas. With the immense power he held...he was able to use his influence to delay the abolition of the slave trade a further 15 years to 1807 and the subsequent abolition of British slavery in 1834.... Who knows how much more suffering was inflicted on African people in the Middle Passage during those 15 years?[2]

In 1795 to 1797, Melville's nephew, John Hope (4th Earl of Hopetoun), was a general with the British Forces in the French and Spanish West Indies. He was second-in-command during the suppression of Fédon's Rebellion in Grenada (named for its leader, Julien Fédon), which had been inspired by the revolt of the enslaved in San Domingo (Haiti) that Simcoe fought to suppress, under Melville's ultimate leadership as secretary for war. Enslaved peoples were rising up throughout the region. There were revolts in Jamaica, Dominica, St. Lucia, St. Vincent, Curaçao, Venezuela, Barbados, Guyana, the British Virgin Islands, Puerto Rico, and Brazil. In North America, there were over 250 uprisings during the seventeenth to nineteenth centuries.

If I had turned left back at the Old Ancaster Road and followed it south, I would have come to Old Dundas Road, passing the site of the Hatts' first mill, eventually reaching Ancaster, where another plaque promotes the usual suspects (local founders Wilson, Beasley, Rousseau, the Hatts). The observation made by Janaya Khan (of Black Lives Matter, Toronto) concerning William and Samuel Jarvis comes to mind: "We hear these neat stories of heroic initiatives of white men, but we don't get to hear the whole story."[3] Sophia's story publicly troubles the local founders legacies here.

Sadly, some of the few notable changes in the names on public facades around Hamilton have done more to erase then enhance. George R. Allen School (no relation to my grandfather Herbert Allen) is now called Cootes Paradise Elementary School. While people may associate this name with natural areas nearby, they have actually enhanced the name of a colonial British officer who took great pleasure in gunning for game in "his" paradise. Sophia hunted here many times; a better name would have been *Sophia Burthen Elementary School*. The school sits in the centre of Westdale, a 1920s neighbourhood whose original developers explicitly limited homeownership to white Protestants.

Thanks to the real estate boom in Hamilton, obscure names of old neighbourhoods are being resuscitated as marketing brands, particularly in areas that were historically home to working people (including the working poor), new Canadians, and marginalized communities at risk. These names erase histories, like the gentrification of tweel/tweed that shifts a commoner's durable garment into a fashion signifier of authenticity for the landed gentry (*gentry* is at the root of *gentrification*). One of the most egregious branding exercises has been the promotion of the Beasley name, all too prominent on neighbourhood signage, a city park, and community centre. On Ferguson Avenue, a series of brightly coloured banners carry the embellished words "BeLong," "BeKind," and "BeFair," with the slogan "Welcome to the Beasley Neighbourhood: A place where you

Not part of the Beasley neighbourhood branding: The KKK (Ku Klux Klan) Riding Up
James Street North, Hamilton, Ontario, 1930, photographer unknown (although likely a
staff photographer for the *Hamilton Spectator*), Hamilton Public Library Special Collections

can *be your best*!" I often encounter designers digging in the local archives for
inspiration to support their heritage branding schemes. Unfortunately, a complete
picture has not been archived. A figure like Richard Beasley will be remembered
as a hard-working first settler, confirming nostalgic ideas of early Canada (such
as fur trading, clearing land, and living rough and rugged). Until recently, the
Beasley neighbourhood was one of the poorest in Canada. It is now marketed as
"hip, trendy, and very desirable," an area of "vintage authenticity."[4]

Beasley is buried behind the Anglican cathedral on James Street North. The
statement on his tombstone claims he was "The First Settler at the Head of the
Lake," which is repeated in many publications, as well as on a newer Beasley
family marker in Woodland Cemetery: "Col. Richard Beasley, U.E.L. 1761–1842

First Settler in 1777 at Dundurn Park." Beasley likely didn't arrive at the Head-of-the-Lake until later (he first moved to Quebec from Albany in 1777), and he was long associated with shady land deals, and the holding of enslaved or indentured people. "Beasley's dealings have been well documented in the annals of Hamilton's history," states Adrienne Shadd, "However, the fact that he and his family of nine children owned slaves is not usually mentioned."[5] Shadd refers to stories published in Hamilton newspapers concerning two enslaved men (Jackson and Wilson, who were owned by the Beasley family): "According to [Beasley] family lore, when Britain abolished slavery, the Beasley slaves were generously provided for and given a start in life."[6] Free in 1834, both men chose to remain in the service of the Beasleys, leaving one to wonder what real opportunities there truly were for two Black men here.

Stewart Memorial Church (formerly St. Paul's African Methodist Episcopal Church, founded in 1835), continues to welcome parishioners just a short distance from Beasley's grave. According to a plaque at the church site, it is "the longest surviving predominantly Black congregation in the city of Hamilton." A number of the original parishioners at Stewart Memorial first settled on the mountain in the 1840s (where another AME church was located). That successful Black community on Concession Street lasted only a few decades. A City of Hamilton heritage plaque (2014) explains that "the vast majority of inhabitants sold their property and purchased homes below the Mountain or moved to other Ontario locales"[7] and to the United States. For an established and vibrant community of educated and skilled people to disperse is distinctly unusual. Their history was long buried beneath the patronizing racism of historian Mabel Burkholder, from one of Hamilton's founding families, who dismissed these successful citizens as "illiterate, childish and rather dependant in their attitude toward life, as was only natural to a people reared in servitude." Burkholder—who called the community "Little Africa"—would go on to claim these "children of the south" could not survive in a northern climate.[8]

"This narrative of 'Little Africa' came to be repeated by writers, historians and the public without question," states Shadd, while dismissing Burkholder's disparaging fiction by pointing out that those "who had the wherewithal to buy the plots of land in the first place...subdivided them and sold the subdivisions to other Blacks."[9] A City of Hamilton heritage plaque mounted to the facade of Hamilton Public Library, Concession Branch, offers an accurate condensed narrative (thanks to research done by Shadd), but what is left unaddressed are the reasons the community dispersed. Back downtown, *Stewart Memorial* would be a more appropriate name than *Beasley* for the neighbourhood the church sits in the heart of.

Another Hamilton family whose name continues to define an affluent neighbourhood in the city are the Durands. Coming from Abergavenny, Wales, they acquired 40 hectares at the Head-of-the-Lake in 1804, and also held enslaved people, as revealed in the following quote:

> Charles Durand, the son of James Durand, told the story that one day his father, and his father's wife, and their baby, were descending the Mountain when tragedy struck. The baby...was in the care of an enslaved woman on horseback....There was an accident and Mrs. Durand was thrown out of the vehicle and onto the rocks, dying not long thereafter. The enslaved woman, whose name has been lost to history, became nurse to the children of James Durand's second marriage.[10]

Durand built mills and invested in local industry and infrastructure, and served in the parliament of Upper Canada; his name has not been "lost to history."[11]

Honouring the Durand name is specific to Hamilton, while Tweedsmuir can be found on signage across the country. While the name does point back to a Scottish village, it actually refers to John Buchan (1st Baron Tweedsmuir) and Susan Charlotte Buchan (Baroness Tweedsmuir), who were, respectively, the Governor General and viceregal consort of Canada from 1935 to 1940. Before becoming Governor General, John Buchan was a Free Church minister and a Member of Parliament. Both were writers, Susan of children's books, John of fiction for adults (including *The Thirty-Nine Steps*, published in 1915). Immediately after graduating from Oxford in 1901, he became private secretary to Alfred Milner, the high commissioner for Southern Africa, governor of Cape Colony, and colonial administrator of Transvaal and the Orange Free State. Like Canada, South Africa began to thrive in the latter part of the nineteenth century, at the same time that race-based policies became more rigid in both countries. "Cape legislation that discriminated specifically against black Africans"—and which would inform the apartheid system in place from 1949 to 1993—"began appearing shortly before

1900,"[12] building on white supremacist policies initiated by the Dutch East India Company in the 1600s.

To seriously address the legacy of apartheid, South Africa initiated a Truth and Reconciliation Commission in 1995, which has been described as "the gold standard for how a divided society with a violent past might work through that past and move forward."[13] The lesson from South Africa is that "working through a complicated past takes time, and is still taking time."[14] Decades later, Canada launched its own Truth and Reconciliation Commission, focused on the legacies of residential schools and anti-Indigenous racism. Many Indigenous peoples voiced their disappointment that Canadians were rushing to *reconciliation,* while avoiding the *truth.* Canadians, as the cliché goes, like to say "sorry." But as an automatic response an apology can lack sincerity and is more to the benefit of the apologizer, not those harmed by their actions — leading to the kinds of "expectations of gratitude" that James Baldwin observes.[15] Whiteness wants to keep moving forward, to stay in command, and to set the terms and timeline of reconciliation, while using time to delay and avoid real reparations.

☙

I head out again. At the end of Tweedsmuir Avenue, I follow the same route along South Street, but this time I turn sooner, going down an abandoned lane that connects to Osler Drive. Cutting between two palatial homes, it is primarily used by deer avoiding traffic and channels a river of storm runoff. Back at the bridge over Spencer Creek, I descend metal steps to a footpath that runs east along the north bank. I cannot keep pace with the speed of the current, the liquid energy that once powered the Hatts' mills. The large brick housing complex of Cotton Mill Estates looms over me. The path goes behind more housing, then curves out to Dundas Street. At the northeast corner where Dundas meets Cootes Drive, a stone and iron gateway welcomes me to Desjardins Centennial Park. There are more plaques here, for the canal and "the Founding of Dundas" — the repetition of the narrative is everywhere. This park was laid out in 1967 on earth dumped into the former turning basin of the Desjardins Canal. A narrow ditch, between the park and Cootes Drive, carries the diverted creek towards the outlet, passing a small wooded area; a distinct grove of tall trees is clearly visible.

The Old English *græf* (meaning "ditch") and *grafan* (meaning "to dig") have given us the word *grave*. *Grove* shares etymological roots with *grave*; this Middle Dutch word comes from Proto-Indo-European and later Proto-Germanic terms meaning "to dig, to engrave, or to scratch." *Grove* in Old English was *graf* (a "copse or small wood"), akin to *græf* ("thicket"). That *groves* and *graves* are etymologically linked should not be surprising. Both are sacred spaces holding and protecting bodies and souls, and they often exist together or in close proximity. The cemetery in Dundas, where Richard Hatt's headstone lies detached from his body, is called Grove Cemetery.

I leap across the ditch and land on a narrow path leading into the woods. There I enter a grove that is composed of black walnut. I am surrounded by twenty mature trees; two straight rows form a corridor. The ground hosts a scattering of squirrel-gnawed nuts, grooved skulls I've found at other locations. Split in half, they resemble hearts. It is spring, the trees are still bare. Grey clouds scud past as the last snow flurries of the season dust the ground, joining clusters of deer droppings amongst the dead leaves. Several thin paths have been inscribed into the earth by the passing of white-tailed deer stalked by coyotes and coywolves. At each end of this corridor, a large tree closes off the meadow. The two rows of perfectly aligned trunks are regularly spaced. One side faces the water, and the whole effect is architectural, like a *loggia* (a covered porch or balcony open to the elements or a garden along one side), a transitional space between private ritual and public ceremony, between interior (self) and exterior (kinship). Once I measure and map out the arrangement of trees on paper, its shape is revealed to be pointed at one end, making the grove the form of a ship's hull. Roughly 35 metres long, it is equal to the length of the Spanish schooner *Amistad* and the standard dimension

Max Hunter, *Black Walnut (*Juglans nigra*)
"Skulls" with Ship/Grove Pattern
(at Dundas at the outlet)*, 2021, tattoo
illustration by Max Hunter (for the author)

for ships that plied the Middle Passage (including the Quebec-built slave ship *Diamond*). I imagine this vessel being launched sideways into the canal.

Sophia is very much present for me in various places. First, with her family at Fishkill— *in the garden where my sister and I were playing among the currant bushes*; second, where I am now standing— *at Dundas at the outlet . . . let the hounds loose . . . run for the canoe . . . I had a tomahawk . . . we would not give it up*; third, in the Queen's Bush— *plenty of people in the bush to help me a good deal.* First, as a child; second, as an adult; third, as an Elder. Two of these places now feel depleted and deserted. At Fishkill, her family was forced out, memories of them have been erased, and the KEEP AMERICA AMERICAN signs of the Patriot Front make it clear a person of colour is unwelcome. In the Queen's Bush, where I believe Sophia's body lies in an unmarked, vaguely located grave, I sense only loneliness, an empty place her community was long ago dispossessed of. But here, *at Dundas at the outlet,* her ley lines all cross over a ghost ship of allelopathic timber, a place where *Juglans nigra* roots and bleeds out its essence into the soil and nearby waters, feeding a process of redaction that will alter the stories we tell, erasing some while nurturing others, once the vessel of whiteness is revealed. Sophia belongs here, not in the sense of belonging to (as the property of) another as before, but in the sense of being a person of essential presence, a member of this community, its history and memory, its present and future. She deserves to *be,* and to *long,* here.

Back at the beginning of this journey, in chapter 2, "On Whiteness," I shared Charmaine Nelson's declaration: "The history of slavery is all of our history. This isn't just Black history; we all have responsibility to do this hard work." My decision to write this story, while academic, was also emotional and moral. It felt necessary to make a commitment to engage and be present with Sophia's *afterlife*, and to *render* (in both senses of the word, to *depict* and to *extract from*) whiteness. Eddie S. Glaude Jr. writes that Baldwin "wanted us to see that whiteness as an identity was a moral choice, an attitude towards the world based on ugly things."[16] Those *of whiteness* have a choice to make that involves more than a shift in attitude and language. A real change requires a rupture of the systems and institutions that centre and sustain us. We all must recognize that the continuation of systems based on colonial models of leadership in which people who have traditionally held positions of power continue to do so will not lead to the kinds of inclusive societies and communities necessary. I see too many of my former colleagues maintaining their positions by simply modifying words and methodologies, while remaining committed to enabling institutions and systems they have been embedded in for too long, hoping to absorb their "others" into whiteness and call it change. It looks no different than the transition from slavery to indenture to sharecropping or simply modifying the curriculum (but continuing the basic premise of what is valued and what is not) in the residential schools system. This amounts to the defensive mindset of an abuser: still sustaining their position by continuing to manipulate victims.

I am *dead reckoning* (trying to determine my position in relation to unstable elements) contemplating the weight carried, appalled by the *burthen* that continues to be transported in the hold. Slavery is not a limited and past event with specific start and end points, it is a manifestation of a virulent racist system that persists, effectively shape-shifting as it progresses and spreads. The *darkness* Sophia described as engulfing herself and her sister was more than a temporary *absence of light* that dissipated when they stepped out onto the landing at Albany. The *darkness* serves to emphasize the oppressive whiteness that held them. *I know not for how long,* she said, wondering how long that darkness would last within the vessel of whiteness. Those of us on board this ship are obligated to become far more accountable. Significant reparations must be made. There is a profound need to witness and act—not just course correct—and run this vessel aground. "Racism," Christina Sharpe quotes Elizabeth M. DeLoughrey as asserting, "cuts through all of our lives inside and outside the nation, in the wake of its purposeful flow."[17] "To think otherwise," as James Baldwin declared, "is criminal."[18]

ACKNOWLEDGEMENT

Dear Sophia,

I wrote this book to honour you and to trouble whiteness, to map out the geographies and unnatural histories you've traversed, and to acknowledge your continuing presence here and now, as well as my presence now and then. You are not just of the past; we are moving together in an unequal space that is definitely not post-racial or post-colonial. I have much more work to do, but I don't intend to take the next steps alone, nor have I been working in isolation.

This narrative developed in dialogue and collaboration with a number of mentors, colleagues, and friends, and it is with them that this work for and with you will be collaboratively developed. I see my role as a caretaker and witness, not the lead, in what will be public work (school workshops, screenings, roundtable discussions, public information campaigns, and an exhibition of art and artefacts) created with the Workers Arts and Heritage Centre (WAHC). Situated in the old Custom House in Hamilton's north end, overlooking the railyards and the harbour, WAHC is a cultural organization that values labour and honours the lives of working people and their representative organizations by focusing on education, community, and creative research. It seems fitting to transition this work with you into a space that was once the site of the processing of goods and chattel, and has now shifted to valuing people, their lives, and their labours. Your experience as an enslaved person moving into a freedom that was still highly constrained needed to be positioned within the ongoing history of work here (in Hamilton and in Canada, connected to global networks) and understood within continuing systems of coerced migration and the exploitation of labour that is too often still racialized and controlled by whiteness.

Many of the individuals who have guided, advised, and supported me on this journey will be part of the WAHC program, including Chantal Gibson, Anique Jordan, Charmaine Nelson, Shelley Niro, Adrienne Shadd, Raven Spiratos, Jeff Thomas, Syrus Marcus Ware, Tim Whiten, Camille Turner, and of course Reighen Grineage, who offers the following closing invocation.

Sincerely,
Andrew Hunter
(2021)

CLOSING INVOCATION

To Sophia,

 My grandmother, mother, sister, and friend. You have cleared a path for me to live in a land I claim as my home. You and I are no different but for the time and space in which we walked. I thank you for the strength you had in your struggle toward a freedom you had to create for yourself; that strength has made my struggle a much lighter load. I adopt you now as forever a part of my family and ancestry, a family that is bound not by ownership but by honour and love.

 The darkness has lifted; your family is free; your story has been brought into the light.

 Rest well,
Reighen
(2021)

APPENDIX

The original published text of Benjamin Drew's 1855 interview with Sophia Burthen (Pooley) at Queen's Bush was published a year later (with his editorial insertions as below) in: Benjamin Drew, *A North-Side View of Slavery. The Refugee: or the Narratives of Fugitive Slaves in Canada. Related by Themselves, with an Account of the History and Condition of the Colored Population of Upper Canada* (Boston: John P. Jewett and Company / Cleveland, OH: Jewett, Proctor and Worthington / New York: Sheldon, Lamport and Blakeman; London: Trübner, 1856), 192–95.

The electronic version is a part of the University of North Carolina at Chapel Hill digitization project *Documenting the American South*, and can be found at https:// docsouth.unc.edu/neh/drew/drew.html.

Sophia Pooley

I was born in Fishkill, New York State, twelve miles from North River. My father's name was Oliver Burthen, my mother's Dinah. I am now more than ninety years old. I was stolen from my parents when I was seven years old, and brought to Canada; that was long before the American Revolution. There were hardly any white people in Canada then — nothing here but Indians and wild beasts. Many a deer I have helped catch on the lakes in a canoe: one year we took ninety. I was a woman grown when the first governor of Canada came from England: that was Gov. Simcoe.

My parents were slaves in New York State. My master's sons-in-law, Daniel Outwaters and Simon Knox, came into the garden where my sister and I were playing among the currant bushes, tied their handkerchiefs over our mouths, carried us to a vessel, put us in the hold, and sailed up the river. I know not how far nor how long — it was dark there all the time. Then we came by land. I remember when we came to Genesee, — there were Indian settlements there, — Onondagas, Senecas, and Oneidas. I guess I was the first colored girl brought into Canada. The white men sold us at Niagara to old Indian Brant, the king. I lived with old Brant about twelve or thirteen years as nigh as I can tell. Brant lived part of the time at Mohawk, part at Ancaster, part at Preston, then called Lower Block: the Upper Block was at Snyder's Mills. While I lived with old Brant we caught the deer. It was at Dundas at the outlet. We would let the hounds loose, and when we heard them bark we would run for the canoe — Peggy, and Mary, and Katy, Brant's daughters and I. Brant's sons, Joseph and Jacob, would wait on the shore to kill the deer when we fetched him in. I had a tomahawk, and would hit the deer on the head — then the squaws would take it by the horns and paddle ashore. The boys would bleed and skin the deer and take the meat to the house. Sometimes white people in the neighborhood, John Chisholm and Bill Chisholm, would come and say 't was their hounds, and they must have the meat. But we would not give it up.

Canada was then filling up with white people. And after Brant went to England, and kissed the queen's hand, he was made a colonel. Then there began to be laws in Canada. Brant was only half Indian: his mother was a squaw — I saw her when I came to this country. She was an old body; her hair was quite white. Brant was a good looking man — quite portly. He was as big as Jim Douglass who lived here in the bush, and weighed two hundred pounds. He lived in an Indian village — white men came among them and they intermarried. They had an English schoolmaster, an English preacher, and an English blacksmith. When Brant went among the English, he wore the English dress — when he was among the Indians, he wore the Indian dress, — broadcloth leggings, blanket, moccasins, fur cap. He had his ears slit with a long loop at the edge, and in these he hung long silver ornaments. He wore a silver half-moon on his breast with the king's name on it, and broad silver bracelets on his arms. He never would paint, but his people painted a great deal. Brant was always for making peace among his people; that was the reason of his going about so much. I used to talk Indian better than I could English. I have forgotten some of it—there are none to talk it with now.

Brant's third wife, my mistress, was a barbarous creature. She could talk English, but she would not. She would tell me in Indian to do things, and then hit me with any thing that came to hand, because I did not understand her. I have a scar on my head from a wound she gave me with a hatchet; and this long scar over my eye, is where she cut me with a knife. The skin dropped over my eye; a white woman bound it up. [The scars spoken of were quite perceptible, but the writer saw many worse looking cicatrices of wounds not inflicted by Indian savages, but by civilized (?) men.] Brant was very angry, when he came home, at what she had done, and punished her as if she had been a child. Said he, "you know I adopted her as one of the family, and now you are trying to put all the work on her."

I liked the Indians pretty well in their place; some of them were very savage,—some friendly. I have seen them have the war-dance—in a ring with only a cloth about them, and painted up. They did not look ridiculous—they looked savage,—enough to frighten anybody. One would take a bowl and rub the edge with a knotted stick: then they would raise their tomahawks and whoop. Brant had two colored men for slaves: one of them was the father of John Patten, who lives over yonder, the other called himself Simon Ganseville. There was but one other Indian that I knew, who owned a slave. I had no care to get my freedom.

At twelve years old, I was sold by Brant to an Englishman in Ancaster, for one hundred dollars,—his name was Samuel Hatt, and I lived with him seven years: then the white people said I was free, and put me up to running away. He did not stop me—he said he could not take the law into his own hands. Then I lived in what is now Waterloo. I married Robert Pooley, a black man. He ran away with a white woman: he is dead.

Brant died two years before the second war with the United States. His wife survived him until the year the stars fell. She was a pretty squaw: her father was an English colonel. She hid a crock of gold before she died, and I never heard of its being found. Brant was a freemason.

I was seven miles from Stoney Creek at the time of the battle—the cannonade made everything shake well.

I am now unable to work, and am entirely dependent on others for subsistence: but I find plenty of people in the bush to help me a good deal.

NOTES

FRONT MATTER

1 James Baldwin, "Unnameable Objects, Unspeakable Crimes," *The White Problem in America, By the Editors of Ebony* (Chicago: Johnson, 1966), 174.

2 Charmaine Nelson, *Slavery, Geography and Empire in Nineteenth-Century Marine Landscapes of Montreal and Jamaica* (London: Routledge, 2019), 7–8.

3 Octavia Butler, *Parable of the Sower* (New York: Four Walls Eight Windows, 1993), 33–34.

4 James Baldwin, from a letter written to Jay Acton (Spartan Literary Agency), June 30, 1979, quoted in the documentary film *I Am Not Your Negro* (2016), directed by Raoul Peck, written by (writings) James Baldwin and (scenario) Raoul Peck.

CHAPTER 1
WHAT'S IN A NAME?

1 All definitions and etymologies of words and phrases in this book, whether directly quoted or summarized and unless otherwise noted, are from the *Oxford English Dictionary* or the Online Etymology Dictionary website, https://www.etymonline.com.

2 *Tons* (also *tuns* or *tonnage*) *burthen* is the volume or cargo carrying capacity of a ship. The weight of the vessel is *displacement*.

3 *New-York Gazette*, January 30, 1732.

4 The Slave Trade (or Triangular Trade) had three stages, of which the Middle Passage refers to the second. In the first stage, ships carried currency and trade goods from European ports to be exchanged for captured and stolen bodies on the coast of West Africa. The Middle Passage refers to the transportation of enslaved people across the Atlantic to South America, the Caribbean, and British North America (which would become the United States and Canada). The third stage was the transportation of slave-grown produce back to Europe.

5 Slave Voyages online database, www.slavevoyages.org/voyage/database (voyage ID numbers 80989, 80990) and Lloyd's Register Foundation, Heritage & Education Centre website, hec.lrfoundation.org.uk/archive-library/lloyds-register-of-ships-online.

6 Slave Voyages database online, voyage ID numbers 80991, 80992, 80993.

7 Drew, *The Refugee*, 199.

8 "Death," Harriet Tubman Historical Society website, http://www.harriet-tubman.org/death/.

9 Charmaine Nelson, in conversation with author, January 2019.

10 *1851 Census, Canada West, Districts and Sub-districts: District 39 — Wellington (county), Peel Township*, Sub-district number *373*, Sub-district name *Peel*, microfilm C-11756, the website for Library and Archives of Canada, https://www.bac-lac.gc.ca/eng/census/1851/Pages/canada-west.aspx#w.

11 The area known as Southern Ontario since 1867 was known as Upper Canada from 1791-1841 and Canada West from 1841-1867.

12 Throughout this book and wherever possible, Indigenous-language self-names have been given first, with the larger group or nation, where needed, preceding the smaller group or tribe. "Known-as" or Anglicized names are given in parentheses.

13 Saidiya Hartman, *Lose Your Mother: A Journey*

along the Atlantic Slave Route (New York: Farrar, Straus and Giroux, 2007), 17.

14 The practice of forms of slavery within Indigenous cultures is often misrepresented and overemphasized as a way to downplay the fact that chattel slavery of one specific racialized group was a uniquely European invention. For example, the English historian Edward Mair misleadingly states in the subhead line of his 2020 essay "Slaves and Indians" that "Europeans did not introduce slavery to North America," and goes so far as to criticize Frederick Douglass's view that the enslaved found refuge with Indigenous peoples—see *History Today* 70: 2 (February 2020), https://www.historytoday.com/archive/feature/slaves-and-indians. The adoption of chattel slavery of the African diaspora by Indigenous peoples is evidence of European colonization, not Indigenous traditions. I address this in detail in relation to Thayendanegea/Joseph Brant in chapter 16.

15 Charmaine Nelson has consistently addressed these absences in Canadian schools, stating, "in my fifteen years as a university professor, I have yet to come across one student who has entered my classroom already knowing that slavery existed here. What they have all been schooled in, without fail, is that white Canadians were valiant abolitionists, who freed the northward-bound African American enslaved people through the nineteenth-century networks known as the Underground Railroad." From Nelson, "The Canadian Narrative about Slavery Is Wrong," *The Walrus* online, https://thewalrus.ca/the-canadian-narrative-about-slavery-is-wrong/, July 21, 2017 (updated June 12, 2020). A.J. Williams-Myers addresses erasures in the historiography of the region where Sophia was born: "The frustration arises because prior to the mid-twentieth century writers simply refused to acknowledge the significant role of the African in the economic development of the region." From Williams-Myers, *Long Hammering: Essays on the Forging of an African American Presence in the Hudson River Valley to the Early Twentieth Century* (Trenton, NJ: Africa World Press, 1994), 2.

16 Margaret Washington, *Sojourner Truth's*

America (Urbana: University of Illinois Press, 2011), 23.

17 Maureen G. Elgersman Lee, *Unyielding Spirits: Black Women and Slavery in Early Canada and Jamaica* (New York: Garland Publishing, 1999), 31.

18 There were numerous Black settlements across what is now Southern Ontario. Most were situated around Windsor, Chatham, London, and Hamilton, with smaller settlements near Barrie, Owen Sound, and Guelph, as well as neighbourhoods in Toronto. Prominent settlements include Dawn (site of present-day Dresden), Queen's Bush (where the present-day counties of Wellesley and Wellington meet), Wilberforce (near Lucan), Elgin Settlement (at Buxton), and Oro Township. Benjamin Drew interviewed many residents of these communities.

19 William Henry Bradley, interviewed by Benjamin Drew in 1855 at the Dawn settlement, in Drew, *The Refugee*, 313.

20 Michael E. Groth, *Slavery and Freedom in the Mid-Hudson Valley* (Albany: State University of New York Press, 2017), 30.

21 Washington, *Sojourner Truth's America*, 30.

22 Drew, *The Refugee*, 193

23 All quotations in this paragraph from Drew, *The Refugee*, 15.

24 It is critical to remember that while the patrilineal order of descent was maintained in British North America and the United States, and for economic reasons which privileged men, an enslaved person's status was strategically determined by matrilineal descent.

25 Ngũgĩ wa Thiong'o, *Something Torn and New: An African Renaissance* (New York: Basic Civitas Books, 2009), 5.

26 Yves Engler, *Canada in Africa: 300 Years of Aid and Exploitation* (Halifax: RED Publishing and Fernwood Publishing, 2015), 7.

27 Natasha L. Henry, *Emancipation Day: Celebrating Freedom in Canada* (Toronto: Natural Heritage Books, 2010), 41.

28 wa Thiong'o, "Dismembering Practices: Planting European Memory in Africa," *Something Torn and New*, 1–30.

29 Engler, *Canada in Africa*, 17–18.

30 "CIBC celebrates 185 Years in Downtown Halifax Today" (news release), http://cibc

.mediaroom.com/2010-09-01-CIBC
-celebrates-185-years-in-downtown-Halifax
-today,1.

31 Bradley interviewed in Drew, *The Refugee*, 133.

32 Sidney Katz, "Jim Crow Lives in Dresden," *Maclean's*, November 1, 1949, 9.

33 Katz, "Jim Crow Lives," 9.

34 The legacy of Harriet Beecher Stowe's *Uncle Tom's Cabin* is complicated. While the Reverend Josiah Henson used the novel to promote abolition (and republished his memoir directly referencing the book to promote sales), the story was adapted for the stage in the form of "minstrel shows" (known as "Tom shows") performed by white men in blackface. In these versions, Tom was a caricature, happy to sell out his own people, and always looking to please his master. It's important to remember that, while the book itself became a bestseller, the racist shows had even wider audiences, and are the reason for the perversion, that still remains, of the term "Uncle Tom." See: https://www.smithsonianmag.com/history/story-josiah-henson-real-inspiration-uncle-toms-cabin-180969094/.

35 Officially titled An Act to Prevent the Further Introduction of Slaves and to Limit the Term of Contracts for Servitude within this Province, the act was commonly referred to as An Act Against Slavery.

CHAPTER 2
ON WHITENESS

1 Herman Melville, *Moby-Dick; or, The Whale* (New York: Modern Library, 1926 [1851]), 194–95. This quote is from chapter 42, "The Whiteness of the Whale."

2 James Baldwin, "Down at the Cross: Letter from a Region in My Mind," published in *The Fire Next Time* (New York: Vintage International, 1962), 89–90.

3 Nell Irvin Painter, *The History of White People* (New York: W.W. Norton, 2010), ix.

4 Ibram X. Kendi, *How to Be an Anti-Racist* (New York: One World, 2019), 38.

5 Kendi, *How to Be an Anti-Racist*, 38.

6 Kendi, *How to Be an Anti-Racist*, 39.

7 *Worlding* is a concept introduced by Gayatri Chakravorty Spivak in in her essay "The Rani of Simur: An Essay in Reading the Archive," *History and Theory* 24, no. 3 (October 1985): 247–72. It encapsulates all of the distinct elements and forces (social and physical) that shape an individual's, community's, or culture's experience of being in the world. Spivak argued that colonial power redefines the worlding of the colonized.

8 Kendi, *How to Be an Anti-Racist*, 38.

9 Robyn Maynard, *Policing Black Lives: State Violence in Canada from Slavery to the Present* (Halifax: Fernwood, 2017), 3.

10 See chapter 3, "White Slavery," in Painter, *The History of White People*, 34–58.

11 Painter, *The History of White People*, 396.

12 Dr. Collins, *Practical Rules for the Management and Medical Treatment of Negro Slaves in the Sugar Colonies by a Professional Planter* (1803), quoted in Rana A. Hogarth, *Medicalizing Blackness: Making Radical Difference in the Atlantic World, 1780–1840* (Chapel Hill: University of North Carolina Press, 2017), xi.

13 From Ulric Barthe, comp., *Wilfrid Laurier on the Platform: Collection of the Principal Speeches Made in Parliament Or Before the People, by the Honorable Wilfrid Laurier… Member for Quebec-East in the Commons, Since His Entry Into Active Politics in 1871* (Quebec, 1890), 598.

14 Order-in-Council P.C. 1324 banned Black persons from entering Canada. It was approved on August 12, 1911, by the cabinet of Prime Minister Sir Wilfrid Laurier.

15 Such rational (based on discredited race-based theories) continues to inform racism in Canada, a reality clearly documented in Nan DasGupta, Vinay Shandal, Daniel Shadd, and Andrew Segal, in conjunction with CivicAction, "The Pervasive Reality of Anti-Black Racism in Canada: The Current State, and What to Do about It," BCG website, December 14, 2020, https://www.bcg.com/en-ca/publications/2020/reality-of-anti-black-racism-in-canada.

16 Stephen Azzi and Norman Hillmer, "Ranking Canada's Best and Worst Prime Ministers: A Survey of Scholars across the Country

Weigh In on Canada's Best and Worst Prime Ministers, Ranked in Duration of Their Terms," *MacLean's* online, October 7, 2016, https://www.macleans.ca/politics/ottawa/ranking-canadas-best-and-worst-prime-ministers/.

17 Neil Reynolds, "By Restoring Laurier's Lost Tenets, This Century Could Be Ours," *Globe and Mail*, May 24, 2010, https://www.theglobeandmail.com/opinion/by-restoring-lauriers-lost-tenets-this-century-could-be-ours/article4320093/.

18 Maynard, *Policing Black Lives*, 3.

19 Charles Officer, "Don't Believe the Hype: Canada Is Not a Nation of Cultural Tolerance," *Behind the Lens* blog, CBC online, n.d., https://www.cbc.ca/firsthand/m_blog/dont-believe-the-hype-canada-is-not-a-nation-of-cultural-tolerance. Officer's television documentary *The Skin We're In* (2017) was produced by 90th Parallel Film and Television Productions and distributed by the Canadian Broadcasting Corporation.

20 Officer, "Don't Believe the Hype."

21 Charmaine Nelson, in conversation with author, McGill University, Montréal, January 2019.

22 Chantal Gibson, in conversation with author, Simon Fraser University, Surrey, BC, August 2019.

23 Christina Sharpe, *In the Wake: On Blackness and Being* (Durham, NC: Duke University Press, 2016), 13. I also found this conversation helpful: Patricia J. Saunders, "Defending the Dead, Confronting the Archive: A Conversation with M. NourbeSe Philip," *Small Axe* 12, no. 2 (June 2008): 63–79.

24 Melville, *Moby-Dick*, 187.

25 Eddie S. Glaude Jr., *Begin Again: James Baldwin's America and Its Urgent Lessons for Our Own* (New York: Crown, 2020), 193–94.

26 From Sojourner Truth's speech, "Ain't I a Woman?" 1851, quoted in Margaret Washington, *Sojourner Truth's America* (Urbana: University of Illinois Press, 2011), 33–34.

27 Syrus Marcus Ware in conversation with Nathaniel Basen, "Rallying Against Racism: A BLM Toronto Member on Building a Better Society," *Society*, TVO online, June 10, 2020, https://www.tvo.org/article/rallying-against-racism-a-blm-toronto-member-on-building-a-better-society.

28 Simukai Chigudu, "'Colonialism Had Never Really Ended': My Life in The Shadow of Cecil Rhodes," The Long Read, *The Guardian* online, January 14, 2021, https://www.theguardian.com/news/2021/jan/14/rhodes-must-fall-oxford-colonialism-zimbabwe-simukai-chigudu.

29 Malcolm X (el-Hajj Malik el-Shabazz), a line from his speech "The Ballot or the Bullet," first given in 1964, published in 1965. Variations of this speech were given on multiple occasions. It can be accessed online at http://www.digitalhistory.uh.edu/disp_textbook.cfm?smtid=3&psid=3624.

30 See https://sojournertruthmemorial.org/sojourner-truth/her-words/.

31 *Uncle Tom's Cabin* first appeared serialized in the *National Era*, an abolitionist newspaper published in Washington, DC, June 5, 1851.

32 Justice Lemuel Shaw's ruling in favor of the constitutionality of school segregation in *Roberts v. City of Boston* (1849) established "separate but equal" as a legal doctrine in the state.

CHAPTER 3
ALLELOPATHY—OF BLACK WALNUT

1 Josiah Henson, *Uncle Tom's Story of His Life: An Autobiography of the Rev. Josiah Henson (Mrs. Harriet Beecher Stowe's "Uncle Tom"). 1789–1876. With a Preface by Mrs. Harriet Beecher Stowe, and an Introductory Note by George Sturge, and S. Morley, Esq., M.P.,* edited by John Lobb (London, 1876), 139.

2 From the description of the Eugene-Louis Lami's painting *The Opening of the Great Exhibition 1851*, Royal Collection Trust website, https://www.rct.uk/collection/452380/the-opening-of-the-great-exhibition-1851.

3 Henson, *Uncle Tom's Story of His Life*, 139.

4 Josiah Henson, *The Life of Josiah Henson, Formerly a Slave, Now an Inhabitant of Canada, as Narrated by Himself* (Boston, 1849).

5 William Farmer, from a letter published in the *Boston Liberator*, July 18, 1851. The letter

appeared in the paper almost one month after the demonstration took place on June 21, 1851.

6 From "Speech by William Wells Brown, Delivered at the Hall of Commerce, London, England, 1 August 1851," quoted from C. Peter Ripley, et al., eds., *The Black Abolitionist Papers, Vol. I: The British Isles, 1830–1865* (Chapel Hill: University of North Carolina, 1985), originally published in *The Liberator*, September 5, 1851, https://docsouth.unc.edu /fpn/brownw/support4.html.

7 William Wells Brown, *Three Years in Europe: Or, Places I Have Seen and People I Have Met* (London, 1852), 237.

8 From "Speech by William Wells Brown."

9 From "Speech by William Wells Brown."

10 The text of Tubman's interview is extremely brief, a paragraph, compared to others in Drew's volume, suggesting that her words may have been taken from a previously printed source.

11 Nehemiah Adams, D.D. [Doctor of Divinity], *A South-side View of Slavery; or, Three Months at the South in 1854* (Boston, 1855).

12 Solomon Northup, as told to David Wilson in David Wilson, ed., *Twelve Years a Slave* (Auburn, NY, 1853).

13 From W.S. Merwin, "Elegy for a Walnut Tree," a poem from Merwin's collection *The Moon Before Morning* (Port Townsend, WA: Copper Canyon Press, 2014).

CHAPTER 4
"A GOODLY PORTION OF THE LIFE OF BENJAMIN DREW" (AND MINE)

1 The obituary of Benjamin Drew, *Old Colony Memorial*, July 25, 1903.

2 Benjamin Drew, *Pens and Types: Or, Hints and Helps for Those Who Write, Print, or Read* (Boston, 1872); Benjamin Drew, *Burial Hill, Plymouth, Massachusetts: Its Monuments and Gravestones Numbered and Briefly Described, and the Inscriptions and Epitaphs Thereon Carefully Copied* (Boston, 1894).

3 Under "curate" in *Cambridge Dictionary* online, dictionary.cambridge.org/dictionary /english/curate.

4 Under "caretaker" in *Merriam-Webster* online, https://www.merriam-webster.com/dictionary /caretaker.

5 Lord Rosebery, as quoted in "Touring People's Palace and Winter Garden," Scotland.com website, https://www.scotland.com/blog /touring-peoples-palace-winter-gardens/.

6 Multiple sources, including https:// en.wikipedia.org/wiki/Andrew.

7 Nell Irvin Painter, *The History of White People* (New York: W.W. Norton, 2010), 41.

8 Nathaniel Philbrick, *Mayflower: A Story of Courage, Community and War* (New York: Penguin, 2006), 90–91.

9 That Herman Melville chose to name the whaling ship *Pequod* in *Moby-Dick* is significant; a doomed vessel, symbolic of the American state and captained by a white patriarch, is named for a people exploited and extirpated.

10 Douglas Harper, "Slavery in Massachusetts," Slavery in the North website, 2003, slavenorth .com/massachusetts.htm.

11 Katy Werlin, "Ruffs," *The Fashion Historian* blog, n.d., www.thefashionhistorian.com/2011 /11/ruffs.html.

12 Frederick Douglass, *My Bondage and My Freedom* (New York, 1855), 34

13 Stephen Kendrick and Paul Kendrick, *Sarah's Long Walk: The Free Blacks of Boston and How Their Struggle for Equality Changes America* (Boston: Beacon Hill Press, 2004), 268.

14 Kendrick and Kendrick, *Sarah's Long Walk*, 143.

15 William D. Green, as quoted in Kendrick and Kendrick, *Sarah's Long Walk*, 148.

16 William D. Green, "Race and Segregation in St. Paul's Public Schools 1846–69," *Minnesota History* (Winter 1996–97): 138–49, http:// collections.mnhs.org/MNHistoryMagazine /articles/55/v55i04p138-149.pdf.

17 Jane McClure, "Benjamin Drew Elementary," Saint Paul Historical website, https:// saintpaulhistorical.com/items/show/67.

18 Jamie Bradburn, "The Story of Ontario's Last Segregated Black School," TVO online, February 26, 2018, tvo.org/article/the-story -of-ontarios-last-segregated-black-school.

19 Christina Sharpe, *In the Wake: On Blackness and Being* (Durham, NC: Duke University Press, 2016), 3.

20 "Speech by William Wells Brown, Delivered

at the Hall of Commerce, London, England, 1 August 1851," quoted from C. Peter Ripley, et al., eds., *The Black Abolitionist Papers, Vol. I: The British Isles, 1830–1865* (Chapel

Hill: University of North Carolina), originally published in the *Liberator*, September 5, 1851, https://docsouth.unc.edu/fpn/brownw /support4.html.

CHAPTER 5
LEY LINES: AT FISHKILL

1   Michael E. Groth, *Slavery and Freedom in the Mid-Hudson Valley* (Albany, NY: SUNY Press, 2017), 1, 9.

2   "Report of the Lords of Trade on the Petition of the Wappinger Indians," in John Romeyn Brodhead, Esq., *London Documents: 1756–1767,* vol. 7 of *Documents Relative to the Colonial History of the State of New-York; Procured in Holland, England and France*, ed. E.B. O'Callaghan (Albany, NY, 1856), 870.

3   "Report of the Lords of Trade," 870.

4   Margaret Washington, *Sojourner Truth's America* (Urbana: University of Illinois Press, 2011), 10.

5   Groth, *Slavery and Freedom*, 11.

6   Henry Louis Gates, Jr., "What Was the Second Middle Passage?" *The African Americans: Many Rivers to Cross* website, https://www.pbs.org/wnet/african-americans -many-rivers-to-cross/history/what-was-the -2nd-middle-passage/.

7   Christy Clark-Pujara, interviewed (with Joanne Melish) by Daniel Denvir, "Capitalism and Slavery, Part 1," May 15, 2019, in *The Dig: Discussing the Politics of Class Warfare* with Daniel Denvir, podcast, 52:45 to 53:15. https:// www.thedigradio.com/podcast/capitalism-and -slavery-part-1/.

8   Helen Wilkinson Reynolds, *Dutch Houses in the Hudson Valley Before 1776* (New York: Payson and Clarke, 1929), 13–14.

9   Washington, *Sojourner Truth's America*, 23.

10 Drew, *The Refugee*, 194.

11 I would like to acknowledge the historians Ira Berlin, Michael E. Groth, Margaret Washington, and A.J. Williams-Myers, whose publications pointed me to various invaluable sources.

12 Throughout *Slavery and Freedom in the Mid-Hudson Valley* (2017), Groth draws a number of statistics from Evarts B. Greene

and Virginia D. Harrington, *American Population Before the Federal Census of 1790* (New York: Columbia University Press, 1932), specifically from pages 6, 50, 158, and 185.

13 Groth, *Slavery and Freedom*, xviii.

14 William E. Farrell, "Office of Fishkill Mayor and Police Chief Is Her Purse," *New York Times*, July 26, 1970, 42.

15 Hermann Hesse, *Siddhartha*, trans. Hilda Rosner (New York: New Directions, 1951), 87.

16 Groth, *Slavery and Freedom*, xvii.

17 Groth's book *Slavery and Freedom* (2017) is one of the essential general histories on slavery in this region, as are: A.J. Williams-Myers, *Long Hammering: Essays on the Forging of an African American Presence in the Hudson River Valley to the Early Twentieth Century* (Trenton, NJ: Africa World Press, 1994); Ira Berlin, *Slavery in New York* (New York: NY Historical Society, 2005), a catalogue to the exhibition by the same name; and Washington, *Sojourner Truth's America* (2011).

18 Ira Berlin, *Many Thousands Gone: The First Two Centuries of Slavery in North America* (Cambridge, MA: Belknap Press of Harvard University Press, 1998), 10. Berlin's conception of distinct forms of slavery is expressed in his contrasting of "societies with slaves" with "slave societies," the latter being a society (British North America and the United States, for example) where slavery forms the economic foundation.

19 Clark-Pujara, in Denvir, "Capitalism and Slavery," 48:50–49:00.

20 Melish, in Denvir, "Capitalism and Slavery," 51:35–51:40.

21 Clark-Pujara, in Denvir, "Capitalism and Slavery," 49:00–49:20

22 Williams-Myers, *Long Hammering*, 23.

23 Williams-Myers, *Long Hammering*, 26.

24 Washington, *Sojourner Truth's America,* 11.

CHAPTER 6
"SO THAT HIS MASTER MIGHT HAVE HIM AGAIN"

1 Raven Spiratos, "Defying Systems of Surveillance: Redefining Nationhood in Camille Turner and Camal Pirbhai's WANTED Series" (conference paper presented at "Black Portraiture[s] V: Memory and the Archive Past. Present. Future.", New York University, October 17–19, 2019).

2 In the original printed advertisements, the "s" in names like *Poughkeepsie, Joseph,* and *Janse* appears as the archaic long "s" (that looks, to the modern eye, like an elongated "f").

3 *New-York Gazette,* April 14, 1755, 3.

4 *New-York Gazette,* January 20, 1755, 3. Montgomerie (Montgomery) Ward was in lower Manhattan, at Beekman Swamp and Frankfort Street, now the location of New York City Hall at Broadway and the Woolworth Building. The Minisink Patent (a huge piece of land granted in 1704) is now the tristate region of Pennsylvania, New Jersey, and New York (Orange County), on the Delaware River.

5 It is not unusual to find the same enslaved person appearing in both types of advertisements over time, and in fact an enslaved person's tendency to flee often led to the owner's decision to sell.

6 *New-York Gazette,* January 27, 1755, 3.

7 *New-York Gazette,* February 25, 1755, 3.

8 *New-York Gazette,* September through October, 1756, 3.

9 *New-York Gazette,* September through October, 1756, 3.

10 *New-York Gazette,* March 31, 1755, 3.

11 *New-York Gazette,* March 31, 1755, 3.

12 *New-York Gazette,* July 30, 1755, 3. Rockaway is now part of Brooklyn.

13 From an ad for "Goldsmith, a Negro Fellow Named Duke," *New-York Gazette,* August 30, 1756, 3.

14 *New-York Gazette,* June 23, 1755, 3.

15 *New-York Gazette,* June 23, 1755, 3.

16 *New-York Gazette,* July through August 1755, 3–4.

17 *New-York Gazette,* December 13, 1756

18 Helen Wilkinson Reynolds, *Dutch Houses in the Hudson Valley Before 1776* (New York: Payson and Clarke, 1929), 13–14.

19 *New York in the Revolution as Colony and State, Vol. I.: A Compilation of Documents and Records from the Office of the State Comptroller* (Albany, NY: J.B. Lyon Company, 1904), 240.

20 *1790 Census Index—Dutchess County NY,* https://dutchess.nygenweb.net/1790/1790index.htm.

CHAPTER 7
ON THE "NORTH" RIVER

1 A.J. Williams-Myers, *Long Hammering: Essays on the Forging of an African American Presence in the Hudson River Valley to the Early Twentieth Century* (Trenton, NJ: Africa World Press, 1994), 26.

2 Lena Williams, "For Ossining, A Sing Sing Prison by Any Other Name Didn't Smell as Sweet," *New York Times,* November 19, 1983, section 1, 27

3 The Great Tree of Peace (Skaęhetsiʔkona) was planted over one thousand years ago by the Five Nations who created the Haudenosaunee Confederacy and who, in peace, were brought together at Onondaga Lake by the Peacemaker and Hayenhwátha' (Hiawatha). It is, according to the Indigenous Values

Initiative website, "a metaphor for how peace can grow if it is nurtured." See: "The Great Tree of Peace (Skaęhetsiʔkona)," https://indigenousvalues.org/haudenosaunee-values/great-tree-peace-skaehetsi%CB%80kona/.

4 The Great Peace was signed at Montréal in the summer of 1701 between the French and thirty-nine Indigenous nations from across eastern North America, including the Five Nations of the Haudenosaunee. The Haudenosaunee concept of the *Tree of Peace or Great Law of Peace* that had ended hostilities among many nations significantly shaped the 1701 treaty. See: https://www.thecanadianencyclopedia.ca/en/article/peace-of-montreal-1701.

5   John R. Stigloe, "How to Read the Land: A Lexicon of Landscape as Word, Concept, and Path to Discoveries," The MIT Press Reader website, December 30, 2019, https://thereader.mitpress.mit.edu/reading-landscape/.

6   A landscape (the depiction of natural scenery) of course is not unique to European cultures. The genre can be traced back to fourth-century China, for example (see: https://www.britannica.com/art/landscape-painting), and many cultures developed formats for picturing land or scenery. It is the European way of describing and framing the land, reflecting a colonial perspective and ownership, that has primarily informed settler understandings of place.

7   Robert E. Duncanson would at times be criticized (even by his own son) for not using his art to explicitly speak out against slavery and the anti-Black racism that plagued the United States, but he appears to have chosen to speak through his success and his abilities rather than through representation and explicit subject matter. Frederick Douglass praised the artist's accomplishments and status in a newspaper article, "Daguerrean Gallery of the West," *Frederick Douglass' Paper*, May 5, 1854, 1.

8   C.S. Giscombe, *Here* (Champaign, IL: Dalkey Archive Press, 1994), 30.

9   Pictorial performance spectacles were plentiful in the late-eighteenth and the nine-teenth century, and included John Banvard's *Panorama of the Mississippi*, which he—the best known of these artists in the nineteenth century—premiered in Boston in 1846.

10 James Presley Ball, "Preface," *Ball's Splendid Mammoth Pictorial Tour of the United States* (Cincinnati, 1855).

11 Ball, "Preface," *Ball's Splendid Mammoth Pictorial Tour.*

12 Cornelius Mathews, *Behemoth: A Legend; Or, the Mound-Builders* (Boston, 1839).

13 Perry Miller, *The Raven and the Whale: The War of Words and Wits in the Era of Poe and Melville* (New York: Harvest Books, 1956), 170.

14 Curtis Dahl, "Moby Dick's Cousin Behemoth," *American Literature* 31, no. 1 (1959): 21–29.

15 Thomas Campbell's 1809 poem "Gertrude of Wyoming; A Pennsylvanian Tale," as quoted in A. Ellston Cooper, "That Chivalrous Savage…Joseph Brant," *Maclean's*, January 15, 1954, 48.

16 All Ball's quotations from Ball, "Wyoming Valley" section of *Ball's Splendid Mammoth Pictorial Tour.*

17 Barbara Graymont, *The Iroquois and the American Revolution* (Syracuse, NY: Syracuse University Press, 1972), 172–73.

18 Ball, "Natchez" section of *Ball's Splendid Mammoth Pictorial Tour.*

19 Charmaine Nelson, *Slavery, Geography and Empire in Nineteenth-Century Marine Landscapes of Montreal and Jamaica* (London: Routledge, 2019), 7–8.

20 Nelson, *Slavery, Geography and Empire*, 7.

21 Katherine Tweedie and Peggy Cousineau, "Photography," *The Canadian Encyclopedia* online, April 20, 2006 (last edited March 4, 2015), https://www.thecanadianencyclopedia.ca/en/article/photography.

CHAPTER 8
THE WHITE CITY

1   "About AIHA," Albany Institute of History & Art website, https://www.albanyinstitute.org/about-the-albany-institute.html.

2   Maryland Historical Society, "Path Toward Preeminence" (pdf), https://21346h1fi8e438kioxb61pns-wpengine.netdna-ssl.com/wp-content/uploads/2020/07/MdHS-Strategic-Plan.pdf.

3   While I prefer *free persons, freemen* is the common historical term with specific meaning.

4   See Peter Wagner and Daniel Kopf, "The Racial Geography of Mass Incarceration," the Prison Policy Initiative website, https://www.prisonpolicy.org/racialgeography/report.html, July, 2015; E. Ann Carson, "Prisoners in 2018," U.S. Bureau of Justice Statistics website, https://www.bjs.gov/index.cfm?ty=pbdetail&iid=6846), April 29, 2020.

5   "Race, Crime and Justice in Canada," the John Howard Society of Canada website,

October 19, 2017, https://johnhoward.ca/blog/race-crime-justice-canada.

6   Christina Sharpe, *In the Wake: On Blackness and Being* (Durham, NC: Duke University Press, 2016), 19.

7   Emily Owens, exploring the question of what slavery and freedom mean for women for whom sex was work, as interviewed on "Discussing the Politics of American Class Warfare, Capitalism and Slavery Part 1," May 19, 2019, *The Dig: Discussing the Politics of Class Warfare* with Daniel Denvir, podcast, 1:58:30–1:59:00.

CHAPTER 9
ON THE MOHAWK TRAIL

1   A first-person narrator, possibly the author, reflecting on viewing the still extant *Waterloo Panorama*, painted in 1912 by Louis Dumontin, in W.G. Sebald, *The Rings of Saturn* (London: New Directions Books, 1988), 125.

2   James Presley Ball, "Preface," *Ball's Splendid Mammoth Pictorial Tour of the United States* (Cincinnati, 1855).

3   Benjamin Drew, *The Refugee*, vi.

4   As its official website explains: "Called the Iroquois Confederacy by the French, and the League of Five Nations by the English, the confederacy is properly called the Haudenosaunee Confederacy meaning People of the long house." See: https://www.haudenosauneeconfederacy.com/who-we-are/.

5   Francis Whiting Halsey, part 1, chapter 2, "Indian Villages in the Upper Valley," *The Old New York Frontier: Its Wars with Indians and Tories, Its Missionary Schools, Pioneers and Land Titles 1614–1800* (New York: Charles Scribner's Sons, 1901), n.p.

CHAPTER 10
"AND THEN WE CAME BY LAND"

1   Mark Catesby, *The Natural History of Carolina, Florida and the Bahama Islands: Containing the Figures of Birds, Beasts, Fishes, Serpents, Insects, and Plants* (London, 1754), vol 1.

2   For a discussion of the Haudenosaunee Longhouse, see chapter 9.

3   The Haudenosaunee are composed of the original five nations represented from east to west in the sequence of two squares, a white pine (the Tree of Peace), and two more squares in the white and purple shells of the Hiawatha Wampum. After the Skarù·rę̓ (Tuscarora) came north and were welcomed in 1722, the confederacy became known to the English as the Six Nations and was recognized as such at Albany. The French knew them as the *Iroquois* and the *Confederate Indians*.

4   Robert S. Allen and Heather Conn, "Joseph Brant (Thayendanegea)," *The Canadian Encyclopedia* online, July 8, 2008 (last edited September 4, 2019), https://www.thecanadianencyclopedia.ca/en/article/joseph-brant.

5   Allen and Conn, "Joseph Brant (Thayendanegea)."

6   These four paintings, now in the collection of Library and Archives Canada, depict *Sa Ga Yeath Qua Pieth Tow "King of the Maquas," Ho Nee Yeath Taw No Row "King of Generethgarich," Etow Oh Koam "King of the River Nation,"* and *Tee Yee Neen Ho Ga Row "Emperor of the Six Nations."* See: http://www.virtualmuseum.ca/edu/ViewLoitLo.do;jsessionid=7EA2015C097F0AACD229AE0FDA47E729?method=preview&id=399&lessonId=128&lang=EN.

7   *The Canadian Encyclopedia* online states that Thayendanegea/Joseph's "first wife Margaret ('Peggie')," was "an assimilated slave and the daughter of unknown Virginia planters." Unfortunately, the source of this information is not cited. If this is true, her father would have been white, and her mother could have been Black, Indigenous, or of mixed race. That Thayendanegea/Joseph's first wife (and their two children) may have been of African descent adds another troubling layer to his slave owning. See: https://www.thecanadianencyclopedia.ca/en/article/joseph-brant.

8   See my discussion of *landscape* in chapter 7.

9 "The Battle of Cherry Valley (Massacre): November 10, 1778 at Cherry Valley, New York" (brackets in the original), American Revolutionary War 1775 to 1783 website, n.d., revolutionarywar.us/year-1778/battle-cherry -valley-massacre/.

10 "Fenimore Art Museum" (video), C-SPAN website, April 5, 2002, https://www.c-span .org/video/?163810-2/fenimore-art-museum.

11 Drawn from the 1810 United States census, compiled by Professor Terry Bouton, table from "Slave, Free Black, and White Populations, 1780–1830," University of Maryland, Baltimore County, https:// userpages.umbc.edu/~bouton/History407 /SlaveStats.htm.

12 The paintings of George Catlin did much to perpetuate this myth in the nineteenth century. The specific term was used by photographer Edward S. Curtis for his image *The Vanishing Race, Navajo* (1904), first published in *The North American Indian*, vol. 1 (Cambridge, MA, 1907).

13 James Fenimore Cooper, *The Last of the Mohicans: A Narrative of 1757* (New York: H.C. Carey and I. Lea, 1926), 27.

14 Cooper, *Last of the Mohicans*, 192–93.

15 Cora would likely have been referred to by more derogatory terms than *Negro* (that did not have the heightened negative meaning it does today).

16 Albert Perry Brigham and Charles T. McFarlane, *Essentials of Geography, First Book* (New York: American Book Company, 1916), 87.

17 Brigham and McFarlane, *Essentials of Geography*, 88–89.

18 Clyde B. Moore, Fred B. Painter, Helen M. Carpenter, and Gertrude M. Lewis, *Building Our America* (New York: Charles Scribner's Sons, 1955), 364.

19 For the continuing erasure of Black history, consider the slogan "Make America Great Again" and the resurgence of White Supremacist organizations inspired by post–Civil War Reconstruction era myths of a kind and gentle "Old South," first popularized in D.W. Griffith's 1915 film *Birth of A Nation*, based on *The Clansmen: A Historical Romance of the Ku Klux Klan* (1905) by Thomas Dixon Jr., and later in Victor Fleming's 1939 film *Gone With the Wind*, based on Margaret Mitchell's 1936 novel of the same title.

20 Some examples include George W. Brown's *Building A Canadian Nation* (Toronto: J.M. Dent, 1942) and Aileen Garland's *Canada: Then and Now* (Toronto: Macmillan, 1954). John Murray Gibbon's *Canadian Mosaic: The Making of a Northern Nation* (Toronto: J.M. Dent, 1938), while establishing a multicultural idea of Canada, perpetuated a very British definition of the nation. Gibbon excludes BIPOC peoples from his vision of Canada.

21 The publisher's foreword to the 1977 edition of *The Indians of Canada* (Toronto: University of Toronto Press, Scholarly Publishing Division) by anthropologist Diamond Jennes says it "remains the most comprehensive work available on Canada's Indians." First published in 1932, it was the standard textbook in schools across Canada for decades.

22 "Hiawatha Belt," Onondaga Nation website, https://www.onondaganation.org/culture /wampum/hiawatha-belt/.

23 The Five Nations became the Six Nations in the 1720s when the Skarù·ręʼ (Tuscarora) relocated from North Carolina where the British had forced them off their lands and sold many into slavery. Lenape (Delaware) peoples, and people of other Indigenous nations, were also absorbed into the confederacy.

24 Walter Hood, "Introduction," *Black Landscapes Matter*, Walter Hood, and Grace Mitchell Tada, eds. (Charlottesville: University of Virginia Press, 2020), 1–2.

CHAPTER 11
IN THE LONGHOUSE

1 The Covenant Chain is a series of agreements between the Haudenosaunee and Anglo-American settlers, initiated in the 1600s. See chapter 13 for a detailed discussion.

2 A.J. Williams-Myers, *Long Hammering: Essays on the Forging of an African American Presence in the Hudson River Valley to the*

Early Twentieth Century (Trenton, NJ: Africa World Press, 1994), 24, 29–30.

3 Ghana did not become independent of Great Britain until 1957. Slave raiding and trading continued locally until the Abolition of Slavery Ordinance (1928).

4 Saidiya Hartman, *Lose Your Mother: A Journey Along the Atlantic Slave Route* (New York: Farrar, Straus and Giroux, 2007), 222–27.

5 Margaret Clyne (or Klein), for example, was born near Canajoharie in 1759. She was captured, held captive, and brought to Upper Canada by Thayendanegea/Joseph Brant. He adopted her and she eventually married

his friend Jean Baptiste Rousseau (see chapter 19).

6 Original copies of the petitions for army pensions for patriot veterans of the American Revolutionary War, and for veterans' widows, are held in the Library of Congress.

7 The shift from the "k" to the "h" in the spelling of Skenandoah/Shenandoah is common.

8 W.H. McIntosh, *History of Ontario Co., New York: With Illustrations Descriptive of Its Scenery, Palatial Residences, Public Buildings, Fine Blocks, and Important Manufactories from Original Sketches by Artists of the Highest Ability* (Philadelphia, 1878), 103.

CHAPTER 12
A NOW AS WELL AS A THEN

1 From Peter Martin's original testimony, quoted in William Riddell, "The Slave in Upper Canada," *Journal of Negro History* 4 (1919), 377.

2 From the "Petition of Adam Vrooman to the [Upper Canada] Court of Quarter Sessions, Newark [now Niagara-on-the-Lake, Ontario]," April 18, 1873. Library and Archives Canada, Upper Canada Land Petitions (1763–1865), 205131.

3 "Last Name: Cooley," Surname DB: The Internet Surname Database website, https://www.surnamedb.com/Surname/Cooley.

4 Shelley Niro in conversation with the author, March 2019.

5 Patrick Campbell's encounters in Niagara, Hamilton, and Brant's Town/Ford will be discussed in more detail in chapter 15.

6 Patrick Campbell, *Travels in the Interior Inhabited Parts of North America: In the Years 1791 and 1792; in Which Is Given an Account of the Manners and Customs of the Indians, and the Present War between Them and the Federal States, the Mode of Life and System of Farming among the New Settlers of both Canadas, New York, New England, New Brunswick, and Nova Scotia; Interspersed with Anecdotes of People, Observations on the Soil, Natural Productions, and Political Situation of these Countries; Illustrated with Copper-Plates* (Edinburgh, 1793), 164.

7 In a 1792 diary entry, Mrs. John Graves

Simcoe described his dress (and facial expression) in detail: "Capt. Brant (Thayendanegea), Chief of the Six Nations Indians, dined here. He has a countenance expressive of art or cunning. He wore an English coat, with a handsome crimson silk blanket, lined with black and trimmed with gold fringe, and wore a fur cap; round his neck he had a string of plaited sweet hay." Elizabeth Simcoe and J. Ross Robertson, entry marked "Sunday [month not written] 9th, 1792," *The Diary of Mrs. John Graves Simcoe: Wife of the First Lieutenant-Governor of the Province of Upper Canada, 1792–6; with Notes and a Biography* (Toronto: W. Briggs, 1911), 142.

8 For information about smudging and sacred medicines, see "The Four Sacred Medicines," Northern College website, http://www.northernc.on.ca/indigenous/four-sacred-medicines/.

9 The area now known as Hamilton (particularly the western end linked with Ancaster and Dundas) was known as the Head-of-the-Lake to the British and early settlers. This area is distinct from that covered in the Head of the Lake Purchase, Treaty No. 14 (1806) that covered land between Toronto and Burlington. Hamilton falls under the Between the Lakes Purchase, Treaty No. 3 (1792).

10   James Baldwin, *Just Above My Head* (New York, Random House, 1979), 1.

11   Just two such examples are the entry for "Ohtowaʔkéhson (Ahdohwahgeseon, Adonwentishon, Catharine, Catharine Brant)" in the *Dictionary of Canadian Biography* online, http://www.biographi.ca/en/bio /ohtowakehson_7E.html, and a newspaper article by John Goddard that includes many unsupported facts provided by the Joseph Brant Museum in Burlington, "Exhibit Tells Story of Mohawk Chief's Slave," *Toronto Star*, May 2, 2009, https://www.thestar.com /news/gta/2009/02/02/exhibit_tells_story_of _mohawk_chiefs_slave.html.

12   "Racial Wage Gap: Provincial and Territorial Ranking," Conference Board of Canada website, 2021 (first published in 2010 and regularly updated), https://www .conferenceboard.ca/hcp/provincial/society /racial-gap.aspx.

13   "American Community Survey: Data Profiles," United States Census Bureau website, 2018, https://www.census.gov /acs/www/data/data-tables-and-tools /data-profiles/2018/.

14   Sarah McCammon, "The Story Behind 'Forty Acres and a Mule,'" *Code Switch: Race in Your Face* podcast, NPR website, January 12, 2015, www.npr.org/sections /codeswitch/2015/01/12/376781165/the-story -behind-40-acres-and-a-mule.

15   Tracy Matsue Loeffelholz and Jeff Neumann, "40 Acres and a Mule Would Be at Least $6.4 Trillion Today—What the U.S. Really Owes Black America" (infographic), *YES! Magazine* online, May 14, 2015, https://www .yesmagazine.org/issue/make-right/2015/05/14 /infographic-40-acres-and-a-mule-would-be -at-least-64-trillion-today.

16   Loeffelholz and Neumann, "40 Acres and a Mule."

CHAPTER 13
"THE PEN-AND-INK WORK"

1   Canasatego was a chief of the Onoñda'gega' (Onondaga) Nation and a diplomat for the Haudenosaunee (Iroquois) Confederacy. Quoted in Susan M. Hill, *The Clay We Are Made Of: Haudenosaunee Land Tenure on the Grand River* (Winnipeg: University of Manitoba Press, 2017), 109.

2   The complex system of alliances that were formed beginning in the early seventeenth century between the Haudenosaunee (Iroquois) and Anglo-American colonies are known as the Covenant Chain, which figuratively evokes how the multiple allied parties are bound together. The Covenant Chain is often invoked in discussion of contemporary affairs, as a representation of the long tradition of diplomatic relations in North America between the state and Indigenous peoples. See: https://www .thecanadianencyclopedia.ca/en/article /covenant-chain.

3   Quoted in Hill, *The Clay We Are Made Of*, 130–31.

4   From a speech made by Thayendanegea/

Joseph Brant at Quebec on May 27, 1783, transcribed by Haldimand, at Library and Archives Canada, MG 21, Vol. 21, C-11893, 235.

5   Pokquan, as quoted in Hill, *The Clay We Are Made Of*, 144.

6   All quotations in this paragraph are of Jeff Thomas, in conversation with the author, March 2021.

7   Thomas, in conversation with the author, March 2021.

8   Natasha L. Henry, "Black Enslavement in Canada," *The Canadian Encyclopedia* online, June 16, 2016 (last updated by Celine Cooper, June 9, 2020), https://www .thecanadianencyclopedia.ca/en/article /black-enslavement#.

9   Henry, "Black Enslavement in Canada."

10   Tracy K. Smith, "Declaration," published in her collection *Wade in the Water* (Minneapolis, MN: Graywolf Press, 2018), 75.

11   Smith, "Declaration." Reproduced by permission of author and publisher.

CHAPTER 14
OF BLACK CURRANT

1 Asa Grey, MD, *Botany for Young People and Common Schools: How Plants Grow, a Simple Introduction to Structural Botany with a Popular Flora or an Arrangement and Description of Common Plants Both Wild and Cultivated Illustrated By 500 Wood Engravings* (New York, 1858), 155.

2 Lisa Hunter, in conversation with the author, October 2019.

3 While this specific quote comes from a recorded conversation (September 2020), this is a story my mother repeats often.

4 "The Brant Tract Treaty, No. 8 (1797)," Mississaugas of the Credit First Nation website, http://mncfn.ca/treaty8/.

5 Barbara Graymont, "Thayendanegea," the *Dictionary of Canadian Biography* online (last

updated 2019), http://www.biographi.ca/en/bio/thayendanegea_5E.html.

6 See: Thomas Melville Bailey, ed., *Dictionary of Hamilton Biography*, vol. 1 (Hamilton: W.L. Griffin, 1981), 42.

7 Thomas McIlwraith recorded over two hundred distinct species in his *List of Birds observed in the Vicinity of Hamilton, C.W. arranged after the System of Audubon* (Toronto[?], 1860).

8 Sophia's use of the term *squaw* was likely not derogatory, while it was certainly intended to be by many white speakers. As always, it needs to be remembered that Sophia's words were transcribed and likely edited by Drew. Until his original notes are found (if they still exist) the extent of his editing of the interviews remains unknown.

CHAPTER 15
"THE INTERIOR INHABITED PARTS"

1 Patrick Campbell, *Travels in the Interior Inhabited Parts of North America. In the Years 1791 and 1792* (Edinburgh, 1793), iii–iv.

2 Campbell, *Travels in the Interior Inhabited Parts*, iii–iv.

3 Campbell, *Travels in the Interior Inhabited Parts*, vi.

4 Campbell, *Travels in the Interior Inhabited Parts*, 180.

5 Campbell, *Travels in the Interior Inhabited Parts*, vi.

6 Quotations from this and next paragraph are from Campbell, *Travels in the Interior Inhabited Parts*, 180–84.

7 Madge Dresser (with contributions from the Bristol Museums Black History Steering Group), "Bristol and the Transatlantic Slave Trade," Bristol Museums website, https://www.bristolmuseums.org.uk/stories/bristol-transatlantic-slave-trade/.

8 Marenka Thompson-Odlum is a research associate at the Pitt Rivers Museum whose doctoral research at the University of Glasgow explores Glasgow's role in the transatlantic slave trade through the material culture housed at Glasgow Museums; see: https://www.prm.ox.ac.uk/people/marenka

-thompson-odlum. Tom M. Devine, ed., *Recovering Scotland's Slavery Past: The Caribbean Connection* (Edinburgh: Edinburgh University Press, 2015).

9 Dani Garavelli, paraphrasing the scholar Marenka Thompson-Odlum, "Facing Up to Slavery in the Second City of Empire," *The Scotsman* online, September 24, 2017, https://www.scotsman.com/news/dani-garavelli-facing-slavery-second-city-empire-1439061.

10 Campbell, *Travels in the Interior Inhabited Parts*, 184.

11 See: Barbara Graymont, "Thayandanegea," *Dictionary of Canadian Biography* online, http://www.biographi.ca/en/bio/thayendanegea_5E.html.

12 The narrative of the death of Karaguantier/ Isaac Brant is told in many sources. Ontario educator William Raymond Frank Wilson provided a succinct encapsulation of the most consistent details in his curriculum guide; see "Tragedy in Upper Canada," Historical Narratives of Upper Canada website, http://www.uppercanadahistory.ca/lteuc/lteuc5.html.

CHAPTER 16
NUMBERS

1   Maureen G. Elgersman Lee, *Unyielding Spirits: Black Women and Slavery in Early Canada and Jamaica* (New York: Garland Publishing, 1999), 30–31.

2   Elgersman Lee, *Unyielding Spirits*, 31.

3   An article in *The Canadian Encyclopedia* online points out that even though the myth persists of better treatment for people enslaved in Canada as compared to those enslaved in the United States or the Caribbean, "it stands to reason that the treatment of enslaved Black people in Canada was comparable" since "the belief that Black persons were less than human was used to justify enslavement in all three places." See: https://www.thecanadianencyclopedia.ca/en/article/black-enslavement.

4   Robert S. Allen and Heather Conn, "Joseph Brant (Thayendanegea)," *The Canadian Encyclopedia* online, July 8, 2008 (last edited September 4, 2019), https://www.thecanadianencyclopedia.ca/en/article/joseph-brant.

5   Isaac Weld Jr., *Travels through the States of North America and the Provinces of Upper and Lower Canada During the years 1795, 1796, and 1797* (London, 1799), 487.

6   Weld, *Travels through the States*, 115.

7   Weld, *Travels through the States*, 483.

8   Weld, *Travels through the States*, 484.

9   Campbell, *Travels in the Interior Inhabited Parts*, 164.

10   Isabel Thompson Kelsay, *Joseph Brant, 1743–1807: Man of Two Worlds* (Syracuse, NY: Syracuse University Press, 1984), 279.

11   Kelsay, *Joseph Brant*, 279.

12   A.J. Williams-Myers, *Long Hammering: Essays on the Forging of an African Presence in the Hudson River Valley to the Early Twentieth Century* (Trenton, NJ: Africa World Press, 1994), 107. Williams-Myers cites Vernon Leslie, *The Battle of Minisink: A Revolutionary War Engagement in the Upper Delaware Valley* (Middletown, NY: T. Emmett Henderson, 1976), and cf. R. Emmet Deyo, "Colonel Lewis DuBois and the 5th N.Y. Continental Regiment in the Revolution," *Newburgh Bay Historical Society History Papers* no. 13 (1906): 191–98.

13   Thayendanegea/Joseph initially was to be offered the rank of colonel, but it was determined that such a high rank would exacerbate tensions and jealousies with other Haudenosaunee.

14   Barbara Graymont, "Thayendanegea," *Dictionary of Canadian Biography* online, http://www.biographi.ca/en/bio/thayendanegea_5E.html.

15   Linda Brown-Kubisch, *The Queen's Bush Settlement: Black Pioneers, 1839–1865* (Toronto: Natural Heritage/Natural History, 2004), 49.

16   Brown-Kubisch, *The Queen's Bush Settlement*, 49.

17   Jeff Thomas in conversation with author, April 2021.

CHAPTER 17
"BEATEN OR SHAPED BY HAMMERING"

1   T.M. Bailey and C. Carter, *Up and Down in Hamilton, 1770's to 1970's: A History in Pictures* (Hamilton: W.L. Griffin Printing, 1971).

2   Bailey and Carter, "Foreword," *Up and Down in Hamilton*, ii.

3   "Iroquois Bar" is the name used by geologists and geographers for the landform that was once a sand/gravel bar beneath a much larger lake (called "Lake Iroquois") that covered the region following the last ice age. The term has come into more common usage to refer to the Burlington Heights.

4   On July 8, 2021, Hamilton city council voted 12-3 not to remove this statue. On August 18, 2021, the statue was pulled down by activists following an Indigenous Unity Rally at city hall.

5   Adrienne Shadd, *The Journey from Tollgate to Parkway: African Canadians in Hamilton* (Toronto: Dundurn, 2010), 44.

6   Bruce G. Wilson, "Robert Hamilton," *Dictionary of Canadian Biography* online, www.biographi.ca/en/bio/hamilton_robert_5E.html.

7   See Charmaine Nelson, quoted in Amir Hotter Yishay, "10 out of 1726: Confronting McGill's Colonial Past and Racist Present," McGill, News, *The McGill Tribune* online, September 29, 2020, http://www .mcgilltribune.com/news/10-out-of-1726 -confronting-mcgills-colonial-past-and-racist -present/. Nelson also addresses links between McGill and other Montréal elites to the slave trade in *Slavery, Geography and Empire in Nineteenth-Century Marine Landscapes of Montreal and Jamaica* (Oxfordshire, UK: Routledge, 2016).

8   Under "gore" in *Cambridge Dictionary* online, https://dictionary.cambridge.org/dictionary /english/gore.

9   Mary Prince, *The History of Mary Prince, a West Indian Slave / Related by Herself; with a Supplement by the Editor. To Which Is Added, The Narrative of Asa-Asa, a Captured African* (London, 1831), 9.

10 While this phrase has become a marketing message for the city, it is based on fact, as a travel magazine confirms: "Though the numbers are slightly disputed—*Smithsonian* reports 156 waterfalls, the most in any city in the world, while the latest tally from non-profit City of Waterfalls put the number closer to 130—one thing is certain: Hamilton has a lot of waterfalls." Cassie Shortsleeve, "Why Hamilton Canada is the Waterfall Capital of the World," *Condé Nast Traveler* online, July 24,1017, https://www.cntraveler.com /story/why-hamilton-canada-is-the-waterfall -capital-of-the-world.

11 *Upper Canada Gazette*, weekly throughout October, 1792.

12 Edith G. Firth, "Russell, Peter," in the *Dictionary of Canadian Biography online*, 2021, http://www.biographi.ca/en/bio/russell _peter_5E.html.

13 Quoted by Senator Anne C. Cools in "Simcoe and the True Builders of Canada," on the Senate of Canada website, August 7, 2017, https://sencanada.ca/en/sencaplus/opinion /simcoe-and-the-true-builders-of-canada -sen-cools/.

14 "John Graves Simcoe," Wikipedia, https:// en.wikipedia.org/wiki/John_Graves_Simcoe.

15 C.L.R. James, *The Black Jacobins: Toussaint L'Ouverture and the San Domingo Revolution* (New York: Vintage Books, 2nd ed., 1963), ix.

16 James, *The Black Jacobins*, 136.

17 Michel-Rolph Trouillot, *Silencing the Past: Power and the Production of History* (Boston: Beacon Press, 1997), xxiii.

18 Anique Jordan, "Tangential Tableau: Reworking Canadian Content," *Every. Now. Then.: Reframing Nationhood* (Toronto: Art Gallery of Ontario; Fredericton: Goose Lane Editions, 2017), 131.

19 Jordan, "Tangential Tableau," 131.

20 Thomas Dorland in documentation for *Upper Canada Land Petitions (1763–1865)*, Outwater, Daniel, Adolphustown, 1810, vol. 392A, bundle 10, petition 9, Library and Archives Canada, RG 1, L3, microform c-2485, page 36.

21 Thomas Ridout in documentation for *Upper Canada Land Petitions*, page 33.

22 "Macdonald, Sir John A. National Historic Person," Parks Canada website, www.pc.gc.ca /apps/dfhd/page_nhs_eng.aspx?id=1663&i =59863.

23 Transcribed from Camille Turner's audio/ walking art project *BlackGrange*, Toronto, 2018. Stills of the project can be seen at Camille Turner's website, www.camilleturner .com/project/blackgrange/.

24 Turner, in a phone conversation with author, February 2021.

25 "WANTED," Camille Turner website, http:// camilleturner.com/project/wanted/.

26 Raven Spiratos, "Defying Systems of Surveillance: Redefining Nationhood in Camille Turner and Camal Pirbhai's WANTED Series" (conference paper presented at "Black Portraiture[s] V: Memory and the Archive Past. Present. Future.", New York University, October 17–19, 2019).

27 Charmaine A. Nelson, "Re-Imaging the Enslaved: Eighteenth-Century Freedom-Seekers as Twentieth-Century Sitters," *WANTED: Camille Turner and Camal Pirbhai* (Toronto: Art Gallery of Ontario, 2017), 1–7.

28 Spiratos, "Defying Systems of Surveillance," 2019.

CHAPTER 18
"DECUS ET TUTAMEN (AN ORNAMENT AND A SAFEGUARD)"

1   These are the official slogans printed or embossed on Ontario license plates, in chronological order: 1981, 1982–2019, and 2020 to the present.

2   Patrick Campbell, *Travels in the Interior Inhabited Parts of North America. In the Years 1791 and 1792* (Edinburgh, 1793), 164.

3   Campbell, *Travels in the Interior Inhabited Parts*, 164.

4   Campbell, *Travels in the Interior Inhabited Parts*, 187.

5   William Renwick Riddell, "Upper Canada–Early Period: The Slave in Canada," *The Journal of Negro History* 5, no. 3 (July 1920): 321.

6   "Livery Companies" (alphabetical list), City of London website, accessed May 31, 2019, http://www.cityoflondon.gov.uk/Corporation /LGNL_Services/Leisure_and_culture/Local _history_and_heritage/Livery/linklist.html (page discontinued).

7   "Worshipful Company of Feltmakers," https:// www.heraldry-wiki.com/heraldrywiki/wiki /Worshipful_Company_of_Feltmakers.

8   D.V. Glass, "Introduction," *London Inhabitants Within the Walls 1695* (London: London Record Society, 1966), vol. 2.

9   James Walvin, "Slavery and the Building of Britain: Banks and Banking," BBC online, *History* (last updated February 17, 2011), www .bbc.co.uk/history/british/abolition/building _britain_gallery_02.shtml.

10 "Heritage," St. Peter-upon-Cornhill website, https://www.stpeteruponcornhill.org.uk/.

11 *Letter from Richard Hatt Sr. to his son, Richard Hatt, December 26, 1794, in Upper Canada Land Petitions (1763–1865)*, Library and Archives Canada, "H" bundle 1, petition number 66b. There are numerous documents recording the extensive land dealings of the Hatts accessible through Library and Archives Canada.

12 T. Roy Woodhouse, *The History of the Town of Dundas, Part One of a Series* (Dundas, ON: Dundas Historical Society, 1965), 8.

13 Kerry McNamara, *Historical Dundas* (Burlington, ON: North Shore Publishing, 2016) and *More Historical Dundas* (Burlington,

ON: North Shore Publishing, 2019). Published by the Dundas Museum and Archives.

14 Petitions made in 1801 for land in Clarke Township (now Durham Region), Glanford (now part of Hamilton), and Cootes Paradise are all signed on the Hatts' behalf by "T. Ridout," usually with the phrase quoted. There are numerous documents recording the extensive land dealings of the Hatts, digitized and accessible at Library and Archives of Canada, https: //www.bac-lac .gc.ca/eng/discover/land/land-petitions -upper-canada-1763-1865/Pages/land-petitions -upper-canada.aspx.

15 In collaboration with Bruce A. Parker, "Hatt, Richard," in *Dictionary of Canadian Biography* online, http://www.biographi.ca/en/bio /hatt_richard_5E.html.

16 H.H. Robertson, "Some Historical and Biographical Notes on the Militia within the Limits Now Constituting the County of Wentworth, in the Years 1804, 1821, 1824, 1830, 1838, 1839, with the Lists of Officers, Part 1" in *The Gore District Militia and the Militia of West York and West Lincoln within the Territory Now Wentworth* (Hamilton: Griffin and Kinder Co, 1904), 18.

17 Robertson, "Some Historical and Biographical Notes," 20.

18 Letter from Samuel Hatt to Colonel Hercules Scott concerning the Indian leader "the Prophet," 1814, Library and Archives of Canada, Samuel Hatt fonds, 1814, Item ID 104511.

19 See: https://www.battlefields.org/learn/war -1812/battles/lundys-lane.

20 From the "Scope and Content File Descriptions," Archives of Ontario, F 493-1: Jean Baptiste Rousseau family personal and business correspondence.

21 Adrienne Shadd, *The Journey from Tollgate to Parkway: African Canadians in Hamilton* (Toronto: Dundurn Press, 2010), 50–51.

22 Shadd, *Journey from Tollgate to Parkway*, 52.

23 Shadd, *Journey from Tollgate to Parkway*, 52.

24 Michel-Rolph Trouillot, *Silencing the Past: Power and the Production of History* (Boston: Beacon Press Books, 1995), xxiii.

25 The Niagara Settlers website ("dedicated to the history and genealogy of the early families in the Niagara Region of Ontario") is a particularly egregious example of such work. In December 2020, Richard Beasley was added to the site, repeating material accessible elsewhere and ignoring evidence of his family's slave owning and the questionable legality of many of his land dealings. The site appears to be based primarily on the genealogical research and publishing work of Robert Mutries. See: https://sites.google.com/site/niagarasettlers/home?authuser=0.

26 Robert J. Burns, "Ridout, Thomas," *Dictionary of Canadian Biography*, www.biographi.ca/en/bio/ridout_thomas_6E.html.

27 The Maryland State Archives and the University of Maryland College Park, *A Guide to the History of Slavery in Maryland* (Annapolis, Maryland, 2008), 4.

28 "African Americans in the Chesapeake," Chesapeake Bay Program website, www.chesapeakebay.net/discover/history/african_americans_in_the_chesapeake_region.

29 *Maryland Gazette*, Annapolis, September 29, 1767.

30 Bethanie Bethune, "Everyone Was Talking about 'Roots' in 1977—including Ronald Reagan," *The Washington Post*, May 30, 2016, https://www.washingtonpost.com/news/arts-and-entertainment/wp/2016/05/30/everyone-was-talking-about-roots-in-1977-including-ronald-reagan/.

31 Janice Hayes Williams, "Our Legacy: Coming Home to the Kunta Kinte Heritage Festival," *Capital Gazette* online, September 29, 2012, www.capitalgazette.com/cg2-arc-2b316868-aa8e-5a60-9fe8-e3fd6cbe91cd-20120929-story.html.

32 Henry Louis Gates Jr., as quoted in John Dugdale, "Roots of the Problem: The Controversial History of Alex Haley's Book," *The Guardian* online, *Books Blog*, February 9, 2017, www.theguardian.com/books/booksblog/2017/feb/09/alex-haley-roots-reputation-authenticity

33 Dugdale, "Roots of the Problem."

34 Octavia Butler, *Kindred* (Boston: Beacon Press, 1979), 106.

35 Lisa Yaszek, "'A Grim Fantasy': Remaking American History in Octavia Butler's *Kindred*," *Signs*, 28, no. 4 (Summer 2003): 1053–66.

36 James Clifford, *The Predicament of Culture: Twentieth-Century Ethnography, Literature, and Art* (Cambridge, MA: Harvard University Press, 1988).

37 James Clifford, *Routes: Travel and Translation in the Late Twentieth Century Culture* (Cambridge, MA: Harvard University Press, 1997), 9.

38 Eddie S. Glaude Jr., *Begin Again: James Baldwin's America and Its Urgent Lessons for Our Own* (New York: Crown, 2020), 195.

39 From the label accompanying *Cigar Store Figure* in the Fenimore Art Museum, 2019.

40 Saidiya Hartman, *Lose Your Mother: A Journey Along the Atlantic Slave Route* (New York: Farrar, Straus and Giroux, 2007), 169.

41 Hartman, *Lose Your Mother*, 169.

42 Herman Melville, *Moby-Dick; or, The Whale* (New York: Modern Library, 1926 [1851]), 36.

43 Christina Sharpe, *In the Wake: On Blackness and Being* (Durham, NC: Duke University Press, 2016), 5.

44 There are many variations of the translation of *Cursum Perficio* related to the Hunter clan crest, including "I will complete the course" (or "finish the race") and "I accomplish the hunt." See, for example: https://www.clanhunterscotland.com/arms-of-the-clan-chief/ and http://www.rampantscotland.com/clans/blclanhunter.htm.

CHAPTER 19
WHAT'S IN A NAME? (AGAIN)

1 Herman Melville, *Moby-Dick; or, The Whale* (New York: Modern Library, 1926 [1851]), 93.

2 Under "Francis Brackenridge," in "Loyalist Directory," United Empire Loyalists' Association of Canada website, http://www.uelac.org/Loyalist-Info/detail.php?letter=b&line=512.

3 Marjorie Freeman Campbell, *A Mountain and a City: The Story of Hamilton* (Toronto: McClelland and Stewart, 1966).

4   "1816 Assessment Rolls for Upper Canada,"
    in *Ontario (1719 to 1907)*, under years 1803 to
    1850: "census and assessment rolls, names of
    heads of household," Library and Archives
    Canada (MG 9 D 9), https://www.bac-lac
    .gc.ca/eng/census/Pages/Finding-Aid-300
    .aspx#k.

CHAPTER 20
"TO PIERCE THE HEART OF THE RECIPIENT WITH LOVE"

1   Clayton W. Wells, *A Historical Sketch of the
    Town of Waterloo, Ontario,* sixteenth annual
    report of the Waterloo Historical Society
    (Waterloo, ON: Chronicle Press, 1928), 26.
2   Ellis Little, *Waterloo Township Map with
    Names of Early Property Owners,* from the Ellis
    Little Papers, Waterloo Public Library, images
    .ourontario.ca/waterloo/2488549/data.
3   I.C. Bricker, "The History of Waterloo
    Township Up to 1825," *Twenty-Second
    Annual Report of the Waterloo Historical
    Society 1934* (Kitchener, ON: WHS, 1935), 93.
4   "The History of Waterloo Township," Ken
    Seiling Waterloo Region Museum website,
    https://www.waterlooregionmuseum.ca/en
    /collections-and-research/waterloo-township
    .aspx#.
5   Bricker, "The History of Waterloo Township,"
    93.
6   D.N. Panabaker, "President's Address to the
    Waterloo Historical Society," *Twenty-Second
    Annual Report* (1934), 79–80.
7   Panabaker, "President's Address," 80.
8   Martha Bladen Clark, "Lancaster County's
    Relation to Slavery," *Journal of the Lancaster
    County Historical Society* 15, no. 2 (1911): 43–61,
    quoted from an article in the *New Holland
    Clarion* posted at https://www.lancasterhistory
    .org/images/stories/JournalArticles
    /vol15no2pp43_61_481369.pdf.
9   *1825–1828 Canadian Census, Gore District,
    Waterloo Township;* original is held by the
    Archives of Ontario, www.archives.gov.on.ca
    /en/tracing/the_records.aspx; Linda Brown-
    Kubisch was the first to identify these records
    in her book, *The Queen's Bush Settlement:*
    Black Pioneers, 1839–1865 (Toronto: Natural
    Heritage/National History Books, 2004), 257.
10 See: *Map of Block Number 2, German
    Company Tract, Waterloo Township, Ontario,
    1805.* Available at Waterloo Public Library.
11 Wells, *A Historical Sketch,* 26.
12 Definitions according to numerous
    sources, including under "Gladiolus" at
    flowermeaning.com.
13 Other First Nations also have traditional
    rights in these areas as they historically lived
    and hunted on these lands, including the
    Haudenosaunee (Iroquois), Wendat (Huron),
    and Attawandaron (Neutral).
14 Praxis Research Associates, "The History
    of the Mississaugas of the New Credit First
    Nation" pdf brochure, Mississaugas of the
    Credit First Nation website, 13, mncfn.ca
    /wp-content/uploads/2018/04/The-History
    -of-MNCFN-FINAL.pdf.
15 Praxis Research Associate, "The History of
    the Mississaugas," 14.
16 Benjamin Drew, introduction to "Hamilton"
    section, *The Refugee,* 133.
17 The forced eviction of people who lived in
    the Highlands and western islands of Scotland
    began around the middle of the eighteenth
    century and continued, intermittently, for
    about a century. The primary goal of these
    "Highland Clearances" of people from the
    land was to allow for the introduction of
    sheep pastoralism. At the same time, they
    began a pattern or depopulation from the
    countryside, emigration from Scotland, and
    the destruction of the traditional clan society.
    See: https://www.britannica.com/event
    /Highland-Clearances.

CHAPTER 21
THE HUMBLE PETITIONS

1   *Voice of the Fugitive* was founded in Sandwich,
    Canada West (now part of Windsor, Ontario),
    in 1851. On October 9, 1853, the newspaper's
    office in Windsor burned down, an event
    still considered suspicious. See: Daniel G.
    Hill, *The Freedom-Seekers: Blacks in Early*

Canada (Toronto: Book Society of Canada, 1981) 201–202.

2   Michael Gauvreau, "Strachan, John (1778–1867)," *Oxford Dictionary of National Biography* online, https://doi.org/10.1093/ref:odnb/26619.

3   G.M. Craig, "Strachan, John," *Dictionary of Canadian Biography* online, http://www.biographi.ca/en/bio/strachan_john_9E.html.

4   John Strachan, *The Clergy Reserves: A Letter from the Lord Bishop of Toronto to the Duke of Newcastle, Her Majesty's Secretary to the Colonies* (Toronto, 1853), 26–27.

5   Drew, *The Refugee*, 34.

6   Drew, *The Refugee*, 188.

7   Richard Allen, *The Life, Experience, and Gospel Labours of the Rt. Rev. Richard Allen. To Which Is Annexed the Rise and Progress of the African Methodist Episcopal Church in the United States of America. Containing a Narrative of the Yellow Fever in the Year of Our Lord 1793: With an Address to the People of Colour in the United States* (Philadelphia, 1833).

8   Drew, *The Refugee*, 118–19.

9   Records of all Ontario treaties/purchases of Indigenous territory can be accessed from the Government of Ontario website, www.ontario.ca/page/map-ontario-treaties-and-reserves.

10 Robert Montgomery Martin, *Statistics of the Colonies of the British Empire in the West Indies, South America, North America, Asia, Austral-Asia, Africa, and Europe* (London, 1839), 209.

11 Under "waste (bad use)" in *Cambridge Dictionary* online, https://dictionary.cambridge.org/dictionary/english/waste.

12 William "Tiger" Dunlop published as both "Dr. Dunlop" and "a backwoodsman," writing exaggerated tales of his life as a soldier, politician, and settler in Upper Canada.

13 From Octavia Butler's *The Parable of the Sower* (discussed later in this chapter): "All struggles are essentially power struggles, and most are no more intellectual than two rams knocking their heads together" (New York City: Four Walls Eight Windows, 1993), 33–34.

14 *Aryan* was widely used as an ethno-cultural term for white Europeans in Canada, and throughout the British Empire and the United States, during the nineteenth and into the twentieth centuries. *Race Life of the Aryan Peoples*, written by Joseph Pomeroy Widney (New York: Funk & Wagnalls, 1907), became the primary defining text on this hypothesis.

15 Drew, *The Refugee*, 189.

16 William Jackson, as interviewed by Benjamin Drew in Drew, *The Refugee*, 189–90.

17 The Government of Canada Order-in-Council P.C. 1324, August 12, 1911, passed by the Cabinet of Prime Minister Sir Wilfrid Laurier, banned Black persons from entering Canada because "the Negro race...is deemed unsuitable to the climate and requirements of Canada." Library and Archives Canada, Privy Council Office Fonds, RG2-A-1-a vol. 1021, PC-1911-1324.

18 W.M. Brown, *The Queen's Bush: A Tale of the Early Days of Bruce County* (London: John Bale, Sons & Danielsson, 1932), 1.

19 "About East Garafraxa," Township of East Garafraxa website, https://www.eastgarafraxa.ca/en/resident-services/About-East-Garafraxa.aspx.

20 Henry Williamson, as interviewed by Benjamin Drew in Drew, *The Refugee*, 134.

21 An original copy of this petition is held by the Archives of Ontario.

22 Saidiya Hartman, *Lose Your Mother: A Journey Along the Atlantic Slave Route* (New York: Farrar, Straus and Giroux, 2007), 166–67.

23 Hartman, *Lose Your Mother*, 166.

24 *A Dreadful Account of a Negro who, for Killing the Overseer of a Plantation in Jamaica, Was Placed in an Iron Cage Where He Was Left to Expire* (London, 1834), pdf at *National Library of Jamaica Digital Collection* website, https://nljdigital.nlj.gov.jm/items/show/2569, page 5.

25 "Districts and Sub-districts: Census of 1851, Canada West (Ontario)," under Wellington (county), Peel, at Library and Archives Canada, https://www.bac-lac.gc.ca/eng/census/1851/Pages/canada-west.aspx.

26 Linda Brown-Kubisch, *The Queen's Bush Settlement: Black Pioneers 1839–1865* (Toronto: Natural Heritage/National History Books, 2004), 218.

27 The original spelling appears on the grave of

Annie Malott ("Died Aug. 12, 1903 Aged 19 Years") in the Queen's Bush BME Cemetery.

28 Brown-Kubisch, *The Queen's Bush Settlement*, xi.

29 Mrs. John Little, as interviewed by Benjamin Drew in the Queen's Bush, in Drew, *The Refugee*, 233.

30 Charmaine Nelson, *Slavery, Geography and Empire in Nineteenth-Century Marine Landscapes of Montreal and Jamaica* (London: Routledge, 2016), 6.

31 These and all quotes from Lisa Hunter from conversations with the author, September 2019.

32 Adrienne Shadd, *The Journey from Tollgate to Parkway: African Canadians in Hamilton* (Toronto: Dundurn Press, 2010), 65.

33 Shadd, *Journey from Tollgate to Parkway*, 66.

34 *Upper Canada Gazette*, October 1792.

35 David Ouellette, "James Crooks," *Dictionary of Canadian Biography* online, biographi.ca/en /bio/crooks_james_8E.html.

36 Shadd, *Journey from Tollgate to Parkway*, 70–71.

37 "History of Woolwich Township," Woolwich Township website, https://www.woolwich.ca /en/doing-business/History.aspx.

38 Thomas L. Wood Knox, as interviewed by Benjamin Drew at Queen's Bush, Drew, *The Refugee*, 191.

39 Octavia Butler, *Kindred* (New York: Doubleday, 1979), 76. Butler's other books mentioned here are *Parable of the Sower* (New York: Four Walls Eight Windows, 1993)

and *Parable of the Talents* (New York: Seven Stories, 1998).

40 Butler, *Parable of the Talents*, 108.

41 From the obituary of William Bulmer: "Pioneer of Town Gone: Late William R. Bulmer Recalled Elmira with Three Log Huts; Early Settler of Peel; He Came into Elmira Walking Blazed Trail with Father," *Elmira Signet*, October 5, 1922, 4.

42 John Francis, as interviewed by Benjamin Drew in Drew, *The Refugee*, 196–97.

43 The documentary *Slavery by Another Name* (2012), directed Sam Pollard, which delves into the history of sharecropping, can be viewed at the PBS website: https://www.pbs .org/tpt/slavery-by-another-name/home/.

44 Petition to Lord Elgin, submitted by ten Black residents of the Queen's Bush, 1850. Archives of Ontario, R.G. 1, C1-1, Volume 42, Petitions 1827–1856 (*Queen's Bush*).

45 As one man who was enslaved wrote, "A slave may be bought and sold *in the market* like an ox [emphasis added]." From Henry Bibb, *Narrative of the Life and Adventures of Henry Bibb: An American Slave, Written by Himself* (New York, 1849), 18.

46 John Robert Connon, *The Early History of Elora, Ontario and Vicinity* (Waterloo: Wilfrid Laurier University Press, 1975 [1930]), 122–23.

47 Adam Smith, *The Theory of Moral Sentiments* (London, 1759), 5.

48 Mahmoud Darwish, *In the Presence of Absence*, trans. from Arabic by Sinan Antoon (San Francisco: Archipelago Books, 2006) part 2, page 10.

CHAPTER 22
HOARDINGS OF AMNESIA

1 Quoted in the obituary of Benjamin Drew published in the *Old Colony Memorial* newspaper July 25, 1903, 4.

2 Anonymous, *The Fisheries of Gloucester from the First Catch by the English in 1623, to the Centennial Year, 1876* (Gloucester, MA, 1876), 58.

3 E.J. Milner-Gulland quoted in Jeremy Hance, "Proving the 'Shifting Baselines' Theory: How Humans Consistently Misperceive Nature," Mongabay website, June 24, 2009, news.mongabay.com/2009/06/proving-the

-shifting-baselines-theory-how-humans -consistently-misperceive-nature/.

4 Hance, "Proving the 'Shifting Baselines' Theory."

5 Milner-Gulland quoted in Hance, "Proving the 'Shifting Baselines' Theory."

6 W.G. Sebald, *The Rings of Saturn* (New York: New Directions Publishing, 1995), 194.

7 Text accompanying an image of *The Gulf Stream* on the Met website, www .metmuseum.org/art/collection/search/11122 (in September 2019; since removed).

8   Text for *The Gulf Stream*, the Met website (accessed May, 2021).

9   Under "jury" in *Merriam-Webster Dictionary* online, https://www.merriam-webster.com /dictionary/jury.

10 John Francis, interviewed at the Queen's Bush settlement by Benjamin Drew, in Drew, *The Refugee*, 197.

11 Dionne Brand, *A Map to the Door of No Return: Notes to Belonging* (Toronto: Penguin Random House Canada, 2002), 88.

12 Christina Sharpe, *In the Wake: On Blackness and Being* (Durham, NC: Duke University Press, 2016), 13.

13 Chantal Gibson, "Veronica?" from the collection *How She Read* (Halfmoon Bay, BC: Caitlin Press, 2019), 78.

14 From the gallery wall label for *Niagara, Brink of Horseshoe Falls* at the Royal Ontario Museum, viewed in person, October 2019.

CHAPTER 23
IN THE CURRENT

1   Nell Irvin Painter, *The History of White People* (New York: W.W. Norton, 2010), 396.

2   Saidiya Hartman, *Lose Your Mother: A Journey Along the Atlantic Slave Route* (New York: Farrar, Straus and Giroux, 2007), 6.

3   See Joey Coleman's article "City Staff 'Seriously' Considering Removal of Macdonald Statue from Downtown Hamilton," *The Public Record* online, December 4, 2020, https://www .thepublicrecord.ca/2020/12/city-staff -seriously-considering-removal-of-macdonald -statue-from-downtown-hamilton/, and reporting by Muriel Draaisma and Jessica Ng, "Sir John A. Macdonald statue toppled in Hamilton park after hundreds attend rally, march," CBC News, August 14, 2021, https: //www.cbc.ca/news/canada/hamilton/rally -macdonald-statue-gore-park-hamilton -1.6141279. At the time of writing it is uncertain if the city intends to return the statue to its pedestal.

4   Ciaran Carson, *Last Night's Fun: In and Out of Time with Irish Music* (New York: North Point Press, 1996), 116.

5   Eddie S. Glaude Jr., *Begin Again: James Baldwin's America and Its Urgent Lessons for Our Own* (New York: Crown, 2020), 193–94.

6   Anthony Lewis, "John Glassford's Family Portrait," Legacies of Slavery in Glasgow Museum Collections website, August 14, 2008, https://glasgowmuseumsslavery.co.uk /2018/08/14/john-glassfords-family-portrait/.

7   Dani Garavelli, "Facing up to Slavery in the Second City of Empire," *The Scotsman* online, September 24, 2017, https://www.scotsman .com/news/dani-garavelli-facing-slavery -second-city-empire-1439061.

8   Lewis, "John Glassford's Family Portrait."

9   Rinaldo Walcott and Idil Abdillahi, *BlackLife: Post-BLM and the Struggle for Freedom* (Winnipeg: ARP Books, 2019), 29. Sylvia Wynter's "No Humans Involved: An Open Letter to My Colleagues" appeared in *Forum F.H.I.: Knowledge for the 21st Century* 1, no. 1 (Fall), 42–73.

10 James Baldwin, "Letter from a Region in My Mind," published in *The Fire Next Time* (New York: Vintage International, 1962), 44.

11 "Crawford, John," *Munimenta Alme Universitatis Glasguensis: Records of the University of Glasgow from its Foundation until 1727, Vol. 1. — Privileges and Property* (Glasgow, 1854), xvii.

12 *1745: An Untold Story of Slavery* (2017), directed by Gordon Napier, written by Morayo Akandé, starring Morayo Akandé and Moyo Akandé, running time 18 minutes.

13 Brian Beacom, "The Forgotten Runaways: Actors Moyo and Morayo Akandé on Illuminating a Dark Chapter of Scotland's History," *The Herald* (Scotland), May 20, 2017. www.heraldscotland.com/arts_ents /15299308.the-forgotten-runaways-actors-moyo -and-morayo-akande-on-illuminating-a-dark -chapter-of-scotlands-history/.

14 Beacom, "The Forgotten Runaways."

15 "St Andrew's in the Square (St. Andrew's Parish Church)," the Gazetteer for Scotland website, www.scottish-places.info/features /featurefirst1469.html.

16 Frederick Douglass, "The Free Church of Scotland and American Slavery: An Address

Delivered in Dundee, Scotland, on January 30, 1846," *Dundee Courier*, February 3, 1846, reproduced in John Blassingame et al., eds., *The Frederick Douglass Papers: Series One–Speeches, Debates, and Interviews* (New Haven: Yale University Press, 1979), vol. 1, 144.

17 Scheherazade Daneshkhu, Lindsay Whipp, and James Fontanella-Khan, "The Lean and Mean Approach of 3G Capital," *The Financial Times*, May 7, 2017, www.ft.com/content /268f73e6-31a3-11e7-9555-23ef563ecf9a.

18 Carlos Sicupira, as quoted in Richard Ingram, "Case Study: How 3G Capital Squeezed More out of Heinz," RI CEO website, September 4, 2017, www.riceoweek.com/entertainment /case-study-how-3g-capital-squeezed-more -out-of-heinz.html.

19 Fabiola Carletti and Janet Davison, "Who's Looking Out for Tim Hortons Temporary Foreign Workers?," CBC News online, December 12, 2012. www.cbc.ca/news/canada /hamilton/headlines/who-s-looking-out-for -tim-hortons-temporary-foreign-workers -1.1282019.

20 Walcott and Abdillahi, *BlackLife*, 22.

21 Associated Free Press in Ottawa, *The Guardian*, February 28, 2020.

22 Frantz Fanon, *The Wretched of the Earth* (New York: Grove Press, 1994 [1963, in French]), 1.

23 Fanon, *The Wretched of the Earth*, 2–3.

24 "Speech by William Wells Brown, Delivered at the Hall of Commerce, London, England 1 August 1851," from C. Peter Ripley et al., eds. *The Black Abolitionist Papers, Vol. I: The British Isles, 1830–1865* (Chapel Hill: University of North Carolina Press, 1985). Originally published in *The Liberator*, September 5, 1851.

CHAPTER 24
TEMPUS FUGIT

1 Under "refugee," *Merriam-Webster.com Dictionary*, https://www.merriam-webster .com/dictionary/refugee.

2 Gerald Wright, "Ex-Slaves Farmed in Peel and Wellesley: Black Settlers Largely Ignored by Historians," *Kitchener-Waterloo Record*, July 20, 1979, 31.

3 Norman Hisson died in Toronto aged 87, on May 24, 2012.

4 Linda Brown-Kubisch, *The Queen's Bush Settlement: Black Pioneers 1839–1865* (Toronto: Natural Heritage/National History Books, 2004), 107.

5 All quotations in this paragraph from Joseph Yannielli, "Mo Tappan: Transnational Abolitionism and the Making of a Mende-American Town," *Journal of the Civil War Era* 8, no. 2, 193–94.

6 Fidelia Coburn Brooks in a letter to Ruben Whitcomb, February 25, 1846, as quoted in Yannielli, "Mo Tappan," 193–94.

7 Reverend William King, "To the Editor of the Missionary Record. Toronto 15th Nov., 1848," published in *The Ecclesiastical and Missionary Record for the Presbyterian Church of Canada* 5, no. 2 (December 1848): 26–27.

8 The Guelph BME church survived up until 2009, and soon after the GBHS raised the funds to acquire and restore the building. While many AME churches continue to operate in the United States, few BME churches remain in Canada.

9 From "About Guelph: History," City of Guelph website, guelph.ca/living/about -guelph/.

10 Danielle Subject, "Sustainability around the City," *The Ontarion: Independent News for the University of Guelph Community* online, September 3, 2015, https://theontarion.com /2015/09/03/sustainability-around-the-city/.

11 "Jake Page's Law of Severed Continuity," quoted in Joel Garreau, *Edge City: Life on the New Frontier* (New York: Anchor Books, 1991), 471.

12 Kerry-Ann Conway, in conversation with author, March 2021.

13 Robert Kuttner, *Debtor's Prison: The Politics of Austerity vs. Possibility* (New York: Alfred K. Knopf, 2013), 241.

14 Eduardo Galeano, *Memory of Fires: II. Face & Masks (Part Two of a Trilogy)*, trans. Cedric Belfrage (New York: Pantheon Books, 1987), 129.

15 "Early Settlers Honoured with Historical Plaques at Marden Library," *Wellington Advertiser*, June 26, 2010, https://www .wellingtonadvertiser.com/early-settlers

-honoured-with-historical-plaques-at-marden
-library/.

16 "Early Settlers Honoured."

17 The question "Who is John Galt?" is repeated throughout Ayn Rand's novel *Atlas Shrugged* (New York: Random House, 1957).

18 Jerome Copulsky, "The Impotent Irrationality of John Galt," *The Atlantic* online, March 22, 2013, www.theatlantic.com/politics/archive /2013/03/atlas-shrugged-book-club-entry-7 -the-impotent-irrationality-of-john-galt /274273/.

19 In British academic institutions (particularly Oxford and Cambridge), this term originally referred to the expulsion of a student (in essence, being sent out of culture and banished into unsophisticated, rustic nature).

20 John Francis, as interviewed by Benjamin Drew in Drew, *The Refugee*, 195–96.

21 Michel-Rolph Trouillot, *Silencing the Past: Power and the Production of History* (Boston: Beacon Press Books, 1995), 15.

22 James Brown, quoted in *I Am Not Your Negro* (2016), documentary directed by Raoul Peck, written by (writings) James Baldwin and (scenario) Raoul Peck, 95 min.

23 Christina Sharpe, *In the Wake: On Blackness and Being* (Durham, NC: Duke University Press, 2016), 9.

24 Sharpe, *In the Wake*, 19–20.

CHAPTER 25
"AND THE GARDENER FOREVER HELD THE PEACE"

1 Nick Fiddes, "Guides and Insights: The History of Tweed," on Clan by Scotweb website, clan.com/blog/history-of-tweed.

2 Lisa Williams, "Edinburgh's Part in the Slave Trade," Historic Environment Scotland website, November 15, 2018, https://blog .historicenvironment.scot/2018/11/edinburghs -part-slave-trade/.

3 Janaya Khan, as quoted in Joshua Errett, "Was Jarvis Street Named after a City-Builder, or a Slave-Owner? Prepare for a Debate," CBC online, May 7, 2016.

4 Mark Brown and Romana King, "Hamilton's Top Neighbourhoods: The Increasingly Young and Hip City Has Affordable Homes on Offer," *Maclean's* magazine online, April 11, 2017, https://www.macleans.ca/economy /realestateeconomy/hamiltons-top -neighbourhoods/, and "Hamilton's Top 5 Up-and-Coming Neighbourhoods (2021)," Woolcott Real Estate website, https:// woolcott.ca/hamiltons-top-5-up-and-coming -neighbourhoods/.

5 Adrienne Shadd, *The Journey from Tollgate to Parkway: African Canadians in Hamilton* (Toronto: Dundurn, 2010), 36–37.

6 Shadd, *Journey from Tollgate to Parkway*, 36–37.

7 The text of this plaque is based on research by Adrienne Shadd in 2012.

8 Mabel Burkholder, as quoted in Shadd, *Journey from Tollgate to Parkway*, 37–38.

9 Shadd, *Journey from Tollgate to Parkway*, 147–48

10 Shadd, *Journey from Tollgate to Parkway*, 37–38.

11 John C. Weaver, "James Durand," *Dictionary of Canadian Biography* online, as of 2021, http://www.biographi.ca/en/bio/durand _james_6E.html.

12 Vivian Bickford-Smith, *Ethnic Pride and Racial Prejudice in Victorian Cape Town: Group Identity and Social Practice, 1875–1902* (Cambridge: Cambridge University Press, 1995), 190–92.

13 Mary Kay Magistad, "Truth and Reconciliation in South Africa Revisited" on the *Whose Century Is It?* podcast series, https://whosecenturyisit.com/truth -reconciliation-in-south-africa-revisited.

14 Magistad, "Truth and Reconciliation."

15 Eddie S. Glaude Jr., *Begin Again: James Baldwin's America and Its Urgent Lessons for Our Own* (New York: Crown, 2020), 195.

16 Glaude, *Begin Again*, 209.

17 Elizabeth M. DeLoughrey, as quoted in Christina Sharpe, *In the Wake: On Blackness and Being* (Durham, NC: Duke University Press, 2016), 3.

18 James Baldwin, "Unnameable Objects, Unspeakable Crimes," in *The White Problem in America, By the Editors of Ebony* (Chicago: Johnson, 1966), 174.

Andrew Hunter is a Hamilton-born writer, artist, curator, and educator and a member of the advisory board for the Institute for the Study of Canadian Slavery at NSCAD University. His work is multi-disciplinary and exploratory, incorporating visual art, writing, performance, archival research, and story-telling. *It Was Dark There All the Time* is his fifteenth book.

Hunter has held senior curatorial positions at galleries and museums throughout Canada, including the Vancouver Art Gallery and the Art Gallery of Ontario. He has organized exhibitions and written or edited publications for institutions such as the Art Gallery of Ontario, the National Gallery of Canada, and the Museum of Fine Arts in Boston. His publications include *Every. Now. Then.: Reframing Nationhood*, a rewriting of official Canadian history; *In the Ward: Lawren Harris, Toronto & the Idea of North*; *Colville*; and *The Polar World: Shuvinai Ashoona*. Hunter regularly writes and speaks about cultural and historical erasure, marginalization by colonial institutions, and the responsibilities and accountabilities of settler communities.

Photo: Claire Hunter